Germany's future electors

Nora E. Sánchez Gassen

Germany's future electors

Developments of the German electorate in times of demographic change

Springer VS

Nora E. Sánchez Gassen
Munich, Germany

Dissertation at Universität der Bundeswehr, Munich

ISBN 978-3-658-06941-4 ISBN 978-3-658-06942-1 (eBook)
DOI 10.1007/978-3-658-06942-1

The Deutsche Nationalbibliothek lists this publication in the Deutsche Nationalbibliografie; detailed bibliographic data are available in the Internet at http://dnb.d-nb.de.

Library of Congress Control Number: 2014946726

Springer VS

Printed on acid-free paper

Springer VS is a brand of Springer DE.
Springer DE is part of Springer Science+Business Media.
www.springer-vs.de

Foreword

Many scientific publications at least claim to be interdisciplinary; the work of Nora Sánchez Gassen truly meets this challenge: By combining political with demographic analysis her thesis enriches not only both disciplines but is also of importance for all legislators dealing with electoral law.

The composition of the electorate is fundamental to democracy for different reasons: First, voters decide through their electoral behaviour about the political orientation of a country. Second, the (quantitative) relation between the electorate and the population of a country becomes increasingly important for the democratic legitimacy of political decisions.
Who may and who may not vote in public elections is defined by electoral law, as is the size and composition of the electorate. But demographic developments too, determine what the electoral clientele eligible to elect the government will look like. The development of every electorate is mainly due to changes in the fertility behaviour and the development of life expectancy. The book analyses not only the influence of fertility and mortality trends on population and electorate with regard to Germany but also the changes due to migration and the fertility behaviour of immigrants. Based on a clear analytical perspective Nora Sánchez Gassen identifies in a very inspiring and readable way the different dependencies between demographic facts and political/judicial interventions.

In the second part of her thesis the author examines the extent to which demographic developments will change the size and age structure of the electorate up to 2030. Her projections based on the cohort component method combine not only different population scenarios but also different policy scenarios. With the German fertility and mortality trends in mind her very accurate and complex calculations show that the electorate will age in the future and that the proportion of the population not eligible to vote – this will include in the main people living in Germany without having German citizenship and children – will increase. It is symptomatic for this outstanding interdisciplinary approach that Nora Sánchez Gassen does not limit her work to this analysis but that she combines her demographic work with the question about the appropriate political reaction to these challenges. The elaboration shows that both developments could be influenced, at least attenuated, by amendments to electoral laws and citizenship laws.

In the future the German population and the German electorate may become increasingly less congruent. This development has to be part of the political agenda. Besides this relevance for political consulting the work of Nora Sánchez Gassen delivers important impulses for both disciplines: Due to her profound expertise in both fields not only demographers interested in the political and sociological significance of their own research will benefit; but also political scientists with an orientation to demographic questions. And those who do not belong to one of these groups should read the book in order to learn more about one of the most important questions of democratic theory for the next generations.

Prof. Dr. Ursula Münch

Universität der Bundeswehr München/Akademie für Politische Bildung Tutzing

Acknowledgements

This book is the outcome of several years of research, carried out at the Max Planck Institute for Demographic Research (MPIDR) and funded by the Max Planck Society. I thank both institutions for giving me the opportunity to realize my thesis project in an excellent and truly stimulating working environment.

This thesis deals with very current topics: It analyses the influence of ongoing demographic trends and possible legal reforms on the development of the German electorate. The calculations for this work were finished in 2012; it was submitted and defended in 2013. Demographic trends and legal developments that took place during the last two years could not be taken into account anymore. Nonetheless, it may be of interest for some readers that the German government is currently discussing the abolishment of the obligation of young dual citizens to choose between their citizenships (*Optionspflicht*). I discuss this legal provision in detail in several chapters of this work and one of the policy scenarios presented in Chapter 7 partly corresponds to the reform that is discussed now. The results of the scenario may be of interest for readers who are following the current debate and reform suggestions.

This work is of an interdisciplinary nature, located at the boundary of political science and demography. It could not have been written without the support of many colleagues and friends from both academic fields.
First and foremost, I would like to thank my doctoral advisor Prof. Dr. Ursula Münch for her guidance, intellectual input and continuous support throughout the research process. Writing a PhD is a challenging endeavor, and I have greatly appreciated the time she took to discuss my work and to give valuable advice, but also her trust in my ability to complete this dissertation project. I am also grateful to Prof. Dr. Wolfgang Bonß for providing inspiring suggestions in his evaluation of my thesis as well as to Dr. Gerda Neyer, Prof. Dr. Dirk

Lüddecke and Prof. Dr. Franz Kohout for their stimulating discussion of my work during the final dissertation colloquium.

I am indebted to my fellow political science PhD students at the University of the Federal Armed Forces (*Universität der Bundeswehr)* who provided helpful suggestions and encouragement during our biannual meetings. In particular, I thank Birgit Bujard, who read and discussed this entire work in great detail with me in person, on skype and via e-mail.

For their support and invaluable input on demographic concepts and approaches, I am grateful to my colleagues from the Max Planck Institute for Demographic Research, among them Domantas Jasilionis, Brienna Perelli-Harris, Gerda Neyer, Hal Caswell, Saskia Hin, Christa Mattys, Christina Westphal, Juliane Steinberg, Anne Fink, Alice Cheng, Annett Döpke, and the members of the Population and Policy Laboratory.

From the first day of writing this dissertation to the last, my colleague and friend Marie Carnein has encouraged and motivated me to proceed with this project, has constructively critizised my work when she felt I was going in the wrong direction, and has been the most supportive office mate I could have wished for. I am thankful for having had the opportunity to work with her for so many years and to become her friend.

Finally, my biggest thanks go to my family and in particular to my parents Martina Gassen and Dr. José Sánchez Otero who have unconditionally supported and encouraged me during the last years and who are reading this dissertation with a dictionary lying next to them. Vielen Dank für alles – Gracias por todo.

Southampton, 14.05.2014 Nora Sánchez Gassen

Table of Contents

Foreword V
Acknowledgements VII
Table of Contents IX
List of Tables XIV
List of Figures XV
List of Abbreviations XXI

Chapter 1. Introduction 1

1.1. Electoral law, demography and membership in democratic electorates 1
1.2. Aim of the study 4
1.3. Spatial and thematic scope 11
1.4. Methods and data 15
1.5. Structure of the study 18

Part 1: Conceptual Framework 21

Chapter 2. The influence of legal changes on the development of the electorate 23

2.1. Restrictions to the right to vote across space and time 23
2.1.1. Electoral law 23
2.1.2. Democratic theory 32
2.1.3. International law 36
2.2. Influence of changing restrictions on electorates across space and time 39
2.3. Restrictions to the right to vote in Germany, 1949-2010 42
2.3.1. The Basic Law 42
2.3.2. The Federal Election Acts 47

2.3.3. The Citizenship Act 58
2.4. Influence of changing restrictions on the German electorate, 1949-2010 67

Chapter 3. The influence of demographic changes on the development of the electorate 79

3.1. Demographic trends across space and time 79
3.2. Influence of demographic trends on electorates across space and time 82
3.3. Demographic trends in Germany, 1949-2010 94
3.3.1. Fertility developments 96
3.3.1.1. German citizens 96
3.3.1.2. Foreign residents 101
3.3.2. Mortality developments 105
3.3.2.1. German citizens 105
3.3.2.2. Foreign residents 108
3.3.3. Migration developments 111
3.3.3.1. German citizens 111
3.3.3.2. Foreign residents 115
3.3.4. Citizenship acquisition at birth 120
3.3.4.1. Children born to German citizens 120
3.3.4.2. Children born to foreign residents....................120
3.3.5. Changes of citizenship during the life course 122
3.3.5.1. German citizens (majority population) 122
3.3.5.2. Ius soli-citizens 123
3.3.5.3. Foreign residents 124
3.4. Influence of demographic trends on the German electorate, 1949-2010 129

Part 2: Estimating the German electorate, 2010-2030 137

Chapter 4. Methods, data and software 139

4.1. Demographic projections 139
4.1.1. Method 139
4.1.2. Uncertainty 144
4.1.3. Data 149
4.1.3.1. Data for the base-year 2010 149
4.1.3.2. Assumptions for the years 2011-2030 159

4.2. Policy scenarios 161
4.2.1. Method 161
4.2.2. Uncertainty 164
4.2.3. Data 165
4.3. Software and indicators 166

Chapter 5. Base-year data projection 169

5.1. Base-year demographic data 169
5.2. Base-year projection results 175

Chapter 6. Demographic projections: The influence of demographic trends on the development of the electorate 181

6.1. Demographic assumptions 181
6.1.1. Fertility assumptions 182
6.1.1.1. German citizens 182
6.1.1.2. Foreign residents 189
6.1.2. Mortality assumptions 191
6.1.2.1. German citizens 191
6.1.2.2. Foreign residents 196

6.1.3. Migration assumptions 199
6.1.3.1. German citizens 199
6.1.3.2. Foreign residents 206
6.1.4. Assumptions on citizenship acquisition at birth 218
6.1.4.1. Children born to German citizens (majority population) 218
6.1.4.2. Children born to ius soli-citizens 218
6.1.4.3. Children born to foreign residents...................218
6.1.5. Assumptions on citizenship changes during the life course 221
6.1.5.1. German citizens (majority population) 221
6.1.5.2. Ius soli-citizens 222
6.1.5.3. Foreign residents..226
6.2. Overview of scenarios 231
6.3. Projection results...235
6.3.1. The total resident population of Germany 235
6.3.2. The population of underage German citizens 239
6.3.3. The foreign population 242
6.3.4. The electorate 244
6.3.5. Summary of main findings 248

Chapter 7. Policy scenarios: The influence of legal changes on the development of the electorate 251

7.1. Policy assumptions 252
7.1.1. The age criterion..252
7.1.1.1. Academic debates 252
7.1.1.2. Political debates 262
7.1.2. The citizenship criterion 268
7.1.2.1. Academic debates 269
7.1.2.2. Political debates 282

7.2. Overview of scenarios 298
7.3. Projection results...300
7.3.1. Single assumption scenarios 300
7.3.2. Mixed assumption scenarios...317
7.3.3. Summary of main findings 321

Chapter 8. The development of the German electorate: Trends and consequences 325

8.1. Studying developments of the German electorate from an interdisciplinary perspective 325
8.2. The influence of demographic trends on the development of the electorate 327
8.3. The influence of legal changes on the development of the electorate.....330
8.4. Future changes in the size and age structure of the electorate and their consequences 336

Annex 1: Constitutions and electoral laws which regulate the right to vote in European countries (for Table 1)...................................341
Annex 2: The Federal Election Acts and legal reforms that have regulated the right to vote in Germany, 1949–2010 (for Table 2)...345
Annex 3: International treaties, legal acts and parliamentary documents referred to in the dissertation 347
Bibliography 361

List of Tables

Table 1: Current restrictions of the franchise based on membership and competence in Western European countries in 2011 28

Table 2: Restrictions of the franchise based on membership and competence in Germany in years of Bundestag elections (1949-2010) 51

Table 3: Effects of changes in the size of different population groups on the proportion of eligible voters and the median age of the electorate 91

Table 4: Data requirements for population projections by age, sex and citizenship 150

Table 5: Data sources used for demographic assumptions, 2011-2030 160

Table 6: Projected number of German children, eligible voters and foreign residents living in Germany each year, 2010-2030 (in 1,000) 178

Table 7: Overview of demographic assumptions, 2011-2030 232

Table 8: Overview: Combining demographic assumptions into scenarios 234

Table 9: Bills, resolution proposals and motions to change or abolish the minimum voting age, tabled during electoral terms 15 to 17 264

Table 10: Bills and motions to change the citizenship criterion of the franchise or to change access to German citizenship, tabled during electoral terms 15 to 17 290

Table 11: Overview of policy assumptions 299

Table 12: Overview: Combining policy assumptions into scenarios 299

Table 13: Overview of results, policy scenarios 1 to 6 316

Table 14: Overview of results, policy scenarios 7 to 10 322

List of Figures

Figure 1: The interplay between demography, law and the electorate 18

Figure 2: Resident population and demos 40

Figure 3: Acquisition of German citizenship at birth 61

Figure 4: Size of the foreign population in Germany (all ages) in absolute numbers and as a proportion of the total population, 1970-2010 68

Figure 5: Naturalization rate of foreign residents (all ages), 1974-2010 69

Figure 6: Number of ius soli-children born between 1990 and 2010 70

Figure 7: Size of the population of underage German citizens (ages 0-17) in absolute numbers and as proportion of the total population, 1970-2010 73

Figure 8: Size of the electorate in absolute numbers and as a proportion of the total population, 1949-2010 76

Figure 9: Median age of electorate, 1953-2009 77

Figure 10: Demographic factors which change the size of a population over time 79

Figure 11: Demographic factors which change the size and age structure of a population over time 80

Figure 12: Demographic factors which change the size and age structure of population subgroups over time 81

Figure 13: Demographic factors which change the size and age structure of citizenship groups 82

Figure 14: Hypothetical stable population 86

Figure 15: Effects of an increase of the child population over time 88

Figure 16: Effects of an increase of the population of younger electors over time 89

Figure 17: Effects of an increase of the population of older electors over time 89

Figure 18: Effects of an increase of the foreign population 90

Figure 19: Demographic factors which change the size and age structure of citizenship groups in Germany over time 95

Figure 20: Total fertility rate of German women, 1972-2010 97

Figure 21: Age-specific fertility rates of German women, selected years 98

Figure 22: Total fertility rate of German women and foreign women, 1972-2010 101

Figure 23: Age-specific fertility rates of foreign women, selected years 102

Figure 24: Life expectancy at birth of German men and women, 1980-2010 105

Figure 25: Age-specific mortality rates of German men, selected years 107

Figure 26: Migration trends of German citizens, 1954-2010 112

Figure 27: Age-specific migration numbers of German citizens, 2010 115

Figure 28: Migration trends of foreign residents, 1954-2010 116

Figure 29: Age-specific migration numbers of foreign residents, 2010 119

Figure 30: Citizenship acquired by children born to foreign women in Germany, 1972-2010 121

Figure 31: Number of ius soli-children born between 1990 and 2010 123

Figure 32: Naturalization rate of foreign residents, 1974-2010 125

Figure 33: Age-specific naturalization rate of foreign residents, 2010 129

Figure 34: Demographic factors which have changed the size and age structure of citizenship groups in Germany, 1974-2010 131

Figure 35: Structure of the population in Germany by age, sex and citizenship in 1974, 1986, 1998 and 2010 133

Figure 36: Projection of age groups 1 to 94 141

Figure 37: Projection of age group 0 142

Figure 38: Projection of age group 95 and older 143

Figure 39: Population of Germany by age, sex and citizenship, 2009/2010 170

Figure 40: Age-specific fertility rates of German and foreign women, 2010 ... 170

Figure 41: Age-specific mortality rates of German men and women, 2010 ... 171

Figure 42: Age-specific mortality rates of foreign men and women, 2010 ... 172

Figure 43: Age-specific migration numbers of German citizens, 2010 ... 173

Figure 44: Age-specific migration numbers of foreign residents, 2010 ... 173

Figure 45: Citizenship acquired by children born to foreign women (in %), 2010 ... 174

Figure 46: Age-specific naturalization rates of foreign men and women, 2010 ... 175

Figure 47: Projected population of Germany by age, sex and citizenship, 2010 and 2030 ... 176

Figure 48: Projected relative size of different population groups in Germany, 2010-2030 (in %) ... 177

Figure 49: Projected development of the median age of the electorate, 2010-2030 ... 179

Figure 50: Fertility assumptions for German women (FG1 and FG2), 2011-2030 ... 188

Figure 51: Fertility assumptions for foreign women (FF), 2011-2030 ... 191

Figure 52: Mortality assumptions for German men and women (MG1 and MG2), 2011-2030 ... 195

Figure 53: Mortality assumptions for foreign men (MF), 2011-2030 ... 198

Figure 54: Different groups of German immigrants, 1954-2010 ... 200

Figure 55: Migration trends of German citizens (immigration numbers excluding ethnic Germans and GDR citizens), 1954-2010 ... 202

Figure 56: Migration assumptions for German citizens (MiG), 2011-2030 ... 204

Figure 57: Migration assumptions for foreign residents (MiF1 and MiF2), 2011-2030 ... 215

Figure 58: Assumptions about citizenship acquired at birth by children born to foreign mothers (CAF), 2011-2030 ... 221

Figure 59: Assumptions about changes in citizenship among foreign residents (CCF1 and CCF2), 2011-2030 ... 230

Figure 60: Projected size of the population living in Germany, 2010-2030 ... 236

Figure 61: Projected population of Germany by age, sex and citizenship, 2010 and 2030 (scenarios 4 and 8) ... 237

Figure 62: Projected population of Germany by age, sex and citizenship, 2010 and 2030 (scenarios 9 and 13) ... 238

Figure 63: Projected median age of the total population of Germany, 2010-2030 ... 239

Figure 64: Projected number of underage German citizens, 2010-2030 ... 240

Figure 65: Projected proportion of underage German citizens among the total population, 2010-2030 ... 241

Figure 66: Projected number of foreign residents (all age groups) in Germany, 2010-2030 ... 243

Figure 67: Projected proportion of foreign residents among the total population, 2010-2030 ... 244

Figure 68: Projected number of eligible voters, 2010-2030 ... 245

Figure 69: Projected proportion of eligible voters among the total population, 2010-2030 ... 247

Figure 70: Projected median age of the electorate, 2010-2030 ... 248

Figure 71: Proportion of foreign residents (all ages) by residence duration in Germany, 2000-2010 ... 296

Figure 72: Projected number of German citizens aged 16 and 17, 2010-2030 ... 300

Figure 73: Projected proportion of eligible voters among the resident population of Germany, 2010-2030. No legal changes (left) versus policy scenario 1 (right) ... 301

Figure 74: Projected median age of the electorate, 2010-2030. No legal changes (left) versus policy scenario 1 (right) ... 302

Figure 75: Projected number of underage German citizens, 2010-2030 ... 303

Figure 76: Projected proportion of eligible voters among the resident population of Germany, 2010-2030. No legal changes (left) versus policy scenario 2 (right) 304

Figure 77: Projected median age of the electorate, 2010-2030. No legal changes (left) versus policy scenario 2 (right)....................304

Figure 78: Projected number of adult foreign residents in Germany, 2010-2030....................305

Figure 79: Projected proportion of eligible voters among the resident population of Germany, 2010-2030. No legal changes (left) versus policy scenario 3 (right) 306

Figure 80: Populations of German citizens and of foreign residents by age and sex, 2010 307

Figure 81: Projected number of naturalization cases in Germany, 2010-2030....................308

Figure 82: Projected proportion of eligible voters among the resident population of Germany, 2010-2030. No legal changes (left) versus policy scenario 4 (right) 309

Figure 83: Projected median age of the electorate, 2010-2030. No legal changes (left) versus policy scenario 4 (right)....................310

Figure 84: Projected additional number of children who would acquire German citizenship qua ius soli, 2010-2030....................311

Figure 85: Projected proportion of eligible voters among the resident population of Germany, 2010-2030. No legal changes (left) versus policy scenario 5 (right) 312

Figure 86: Projected median age of the electorate, 2010-2030. No legal changes (left) versus policy scenario 5 (right)....................312

Figure 87: Projected number of additional ius soli-citizens who would keep their German citizenship, 2010-2030....................313

Figure 88: Projected proportion of eligible voters among the resident population of Germany, 2010-2030. No legal changes (left) versus policy scenario 6 (right) 314

Figure 89: Projected median age of the electorate, 2010-2030. No legal changes (left) versus policy scenario 6 (right)....................314

Figure 90: Projected proportion of eligible voters among the resident population of Germany, 2010-2030. No legal changes (left) versus policy scenario 7 (right) 317

Figure 91: Projected proportion of eligible voters among the resident population of Germany, 2010-2030. No legal changes (left) versus policy scenario 8 (right) 318

Figure 92: Projected proportion of eligible voters among the resident population of Germany, 2010-2030. No legal changes (left) versus policy scenario 9 (right) 319

Figure 93: Projected median age of the electorate, 2010-2030. No legal changes (left) versus policy scenario 9 (right)..............................319

Figure 94: Projected proportion of eligible voters among the resident population of Germany, 2010-2030. No legal changes (left) versus policy scenario 10 (right) 320

Figure 95: Projected median age of electorate, 2010-2030. No legal changes (left) versus policy scenario 10 (right)............................321

List of Abbreviations

1. BWahlG...................	Erstes Bundeswahlgesetz (*First Federal Election Act*)
2. BWahlG...................	Zweites Bundeswahlgesetz (*Second Federal Election Act)*
ALLBUS.....................	Allgemeine Bevölkerungsumfrage für die Sozialwissenschaft *(German General Social Survey)*
AZR..........................	Ausländerzentralregister (*Central Register of Foreigners*)
BC	Before Christ
BGBl.........................	Bundesgesetzblatt (*Federal Law Gazette*)
BR-Drs.	Bundesratsdrucksache (*Bundesrat document*)
BT-Drs.	Bundestagsdrucksache (*Bundestag document*)
BVFG........................	Bundesvertriebenengesetz (*Act on the matters of expellees and refugees*)
BWahlG.......................	Bundeswahlgesetz (*Federal Election Act*)
CAF..........................	Assumption on citizenship acquisition of children born by foreign women
CAG.........................	Assumption on citizenship acquisition of children born by German women
CAI...........................	Assumption on citizenship acquisition of children born to ius soli-Germans
CCF (1 and 2)...............	Assumption on changes of citizenship among foreign residents
CCG.........................	Assumption on changes of citizenship among Germans
CCI...........................	Assumption on changes of citizenship among ius soli-citizens
CDU.........................	Christlich Demokratische Union Deutschlands (*Christian Democratic Union of Germany*)
CRPD........................	Convention on the Rights of Persons with Disabilities
CSU..........................	Christlich-Soziale Union (*Christian-Social Union*)

DIP	Dokumentations- und Informationssystem für Parlamentarische Vorgänge (*Parliamentary Material Information System*)
DM	Deutsche Mark
ECHR	European Convention for the Protection of Human Rights and Fundamental Freedoms
EU	European Union
FDP	Freie Demokratische Partei (*Free Democratic Party*)
FF	Assumption on fertility of foreign residents
FG (1 and 2)	Assumption on fertility of Germans
FRG	Federal Republic of Germany (*Bundesrepublik Deutschland*)
GDR	German Democratic Republic (*Deutsche Demokratische Republik*)
GG	Grundgesetz (*Basic Law*)
GMBl	Gemeinsames Ministerialblatt (*Joint Ministerial Gazette*)
ICCPR	International Covenant on Civil and Political Rights
IIASA	International Institute for Applied Systems Analysis
MF	Assumption on mortality of foreign residents
MG (1 and 2)	Assumption on mortality of Germans
MiF (1 and 2)	Assumption on migration of foreign residents
MiG	Assumption on migration of Germans
N (1 to 3)	Naturalization model
OECD	Organisation for Economic Co-operation and Development
OPEC	Organization of the Petroleum Exporting Countries
PDE	Population – Development – Environment population projection software
PDS	Partei des Demokratischen Sozialismus (*Party of Democratic Socialism*)
PV	Proxy vote model
RGBl	Reichsgesetzblatt (*Law Gazette of the* Reich)
RuStAG	Reichs- und Staatsangehörigkeitsgesetz (*Nationality Act of the German Empire and States*)

SPD...........................	Sozialdemokratische Partei Deutschlands (*Social Democratic Party of Germany*)
StAG..........................	Staatsangehörigkeitsgesetz (*Citizenship Act*)
TFR...........................	Total fertility rate
UDHR........................	Universal Declaration of Human Rights
UK............................	United Kingdom
UN............................	United Nations
USA..........................	United States of America
VA............................	Voting age model
VR............................	Voting rights model

"The health of democracies,
of whatever type and range,
depends on a wretched technical
detail - electoral procedure."

José Ortega y Gasset

"Rules and conventions […] are not enough to maintain political institutions. […] In a sense, indeed, demography is destiny. To understand the future as well as the past of the present political institutions, one must consider the demographic context of the development, maintenance, and demise of these political institutions."

Rey Koslowski

Chapter 1. Introduction

1.1. Electoral law, demography and membership in democratic electorates

One of the most fundamental rights that representative democracies bestow on their members is the active right to vote. This right is also referred to as the suffrage or franchise. It entitles its bearers to shape political decision making and to influence the development of the polity according to their interests and preferences. Their influence may be direct, if members of the polity participate in referenda to decide on questions of common concern. Most frequently, however, citizens influence political developments indirectly by casting votes in competitive elections. They choose the parties or individual political representatives who compose the parliament or government for the next electoral term, who will adopt public policies and decide how public resources will be spent. By exercising their right to vote, the members of a polity thus influence and ultimately legitimize all political acts that are made on behalf of the community.[1] This makes the franchise one of the hallmarks of democratic systems. It constitutes part of the electoral procedure of a country, which Ortega y Gasset describes as a "technical detail".[2] Nonetheless, as he stresses, it is an indispensable detail on which the thriving and survival of all democratic practice depends.

The idea that the franchise is an essential ingredient of democratic polities implies that it should be granted to as many members of the polity as possible.[3] Historic examples show that democratic societies may become unstable if large parts of the population are excluded from equal political participation. The legitimacy of public policies and the state apparatus may also suffer. The Suffragette movement in the United Kingdom (UK) during the early 20th century, the African-American civil rights campaigns in the United States of

---

1 See *Schreiber, W.*, Handbuch, 2002, p. 29 f.; *Thaa, W.*, Einleitung, 2007, p. 9; *Nohlen, D.*, Wahlrecht, 2007, p. 27.

2 *Ortega y Gasset, J.*, Revolt, 1932, p. 158.

3 For a thorough discussion of this see *Beckman, L.*, Frontiers, 2009, especially pp. 1-22.

America (USA) in the 1960s or the anti-apartheid movement in South Africa in the 1980s are cases in point.[4] In order to ensure that political and social conflicts may be identified, addressed, and peacefully resolved by all members of society, democracies today follow the ideal that the franchise should be 'universal' and 'equal'.[5] In other words, access to the franchise should be inclusive and every vote should count the same.

It is often stated that most democracies in Western Europe had fully implemented the ideal of universal and equal suffrage for men and women by the end of the Second World War.[6] In a presidential address at the American Political Science Association in 1996, Arend Lijphart for instance implied that universal access to the right to vote has been reached: "after universal suffrage, the next aim for democracy must be universal […] *use* of the right to vote".[7] Strictly speaking, however, no election in history has been truly universal, since no democracy has ever entitled all members of the population to vote. Until the early 20th century, women and illiterate persons were not granted the right to vote in many democratic states. Racial and religious groups were also often barred from voting. These restrictions have been abolished across Europe during the last century, but some population groups remain disenfranchised. Most notably, children and foreigners may generally not vote in democracies and also prison inmates or cognitively impaired persons often remain excluded.[8]

Rules about who may and who may not vote in public elections are usually defined in constitutions or in electoral laws. These legal documents form the "core of representative democracy".[9] As individuals, the persons who are enfranchised on the basis of electoral law are referred to as electors or eligible voters. As a collective entity, they are referred to as the electorate, the demos or

---

4 For an overview of the development of the franchise in different countries see *Bader-Zaar, B.*, Überblick, 2004.

5 In addition, elections are considered to be democratic if the exercise of the franchise is secret, free, and – although this principle is not followed in all democracies – direct in character (See *Schreiber, W.*, Handbuch, 2002, pp. 84-146).

6 For a discussion of examples taken from encyclopaedias and political science literature see *Beckman, L.*, Who should vote?, 2008, p. 29; *Beckman, L.*, Frontiers, 2009, p. 2.

7 *Lijphart, A.*, Unequal participation, 1997, p. 11. Italics are used in the original.

8 For extensive discussions, see *Massicotte, L./Blais, A./Yoshinaka, A.*, Rules of the game, 2004; *Beckman, L.*, Frontiers, 2009.

9 *Schreiber, W.*, Handbuch, 2002, p. 30.

simply 'the people'.[10] By changing electoral laws, policy makers can influence the size and composition of the electorate; they can make it more or less exclusive.[11]

The size and composition of electorates however does not depend on electoral law alone. Demographic developments also matter. The degree to which members of a polity bear children or migrate to other countries as well as their longevity influence the size and composition of the electorate. The degree to which immigrants join the population and are integrated into the electorate also matters.[12] In other words, even if the legal criteria that define membership in a demos remain stable over long periods of time, its size and composition may change due to demographic trends. Koslowski refers to this influence of population change as the "demographic context of [...] political institutions".[13] He urges that population changes must be taken into consideration when studying the development of political practices and institutions over time.

Overall, then, electorates of democratic states are subject to two main types of influence: demographic trends and changes in electoral law. In order to understand how demoi develop in past, present and future, both factors have to be considered.[14] Knowledge about the development of the electorate, in turn, may be important to understand how and why democratic practices and institutions change over time. Koslowski has suggested that political dynamics within a polity may change if its electorate grows or declines in size or if its composition changes.[15] The topics which are discussed most prominently in the polity, the values, visions and preferences which receive the strongest support as well as the style of political debates may alter if membership structures of electorates change. Understanding how demographic trends or changes in

---

10 See *Dahl, R. A.*, Democracy, 1989, p. 98; *Sartori, G.*, Democracy, 1987, p. 21 f.; *Earnest, D. C.*, Voting rights, 2003, p. 3. In this study, the term 'the people' will only be used if it appears in quotes of other academic texts. Otherwise it will be avoided, as it is too easily understood as referring to human beings in general.

11 See *Hattenhauer, H.*, Minderjährigenwahlrecht, 1998, p. 239.

12 See *Koslowski, R.*, Migrants, 2000, p. 24.

13 *Koslowski, R.*, Migrants, 2000, p. 186.

14 Apart from demographic changes and legal reforms, changes of borders may alter the size and composition of electorates. After the reunification of Germany in 1990, for instance, all citizens of the former German Democratic Republic obtained the right to vote in the reunified Germany.

15 See *Koslowski, R.*, Migrants, 2000, pp. 19 f. and 94.

electoral law influence current and future developments of European demoi is therefore of fundamental importance to comprehend the development of democracies as such.

1.2. Aim of the study

In recent years, the interdependency of demography, electoral law and membership in democratic electorates has gained new interest among academic observers and policy makers in Europe, since the populations of many states are undergoing profound changes. Fertility rates have declined and then remained at low levels across European countries during the last decades. At the same time, life expectancy has increased. Both trends have led to a rise in the average age of populations and in some countries to population decline. Many European countries have also experienced substantial immigration during past decades, which increased the heterogeneity of populations.[16] These demographic developments have affected the size and age structure of European electorates: Increasing numbers of foreigners live in European countries and are not included in their demoi due to lack of citizenship. In addition, the rise in the average age has been accompanied by an increase in the number of older electors. Many observers expect that these trends are likely to continue in the future. It has been suggested that reforms may be required to adapt electoral law to changing demographic contexts.[17]

It is the aim of this study to gain new insights into the interplay between demographic trends and electoral law on the one hand and the size and age structure of democratic electorates on the other hand. In particular, this study will investigate to which extent demographic changes will indeed change the size and composition of democratic electorates in the near future, as has been suggested in the literature. In addition, it will analyse to which extent potential

---

[16] For an overview of past demographic trends in Europe, see *European Commission*, Demographic future, 2007.

[17] See *Enquete-Kommission 'Demographischer Wandel'*, Zwischenbericht, 1998, p. 48; *Münz, R./Ulrich, R.*, Wachstum, 1997; *Krieger, T.*, Generationengerechtigkeit, 2008, p. 10.

reforms of the electoral law may be used to influence the development of the electorate. The following central questions will guide the research project:

1. Who will be able to vote in the near future? Will the electorate age in the coming decades and will the proportion of the population who is entitled to vote decline?
2. Which effect would legal reforms have on the size and age structure of the electorate, if they were enacted?

These questions will be analysed by focusing on Germany. Demographic changes are especially pronounced in this country. Understanding the interplay between demographic trends, electoral law and the composition of the demos is thus of specific relevance here: (West) Germany was the first country worldwide in which the number of deaths surpassed the number of births. For the first time, this happened in 1972. High levels of immigration could offset the birth gap until 2003, but during later years the population has decreased in size. The population of Germany is also ageing. Today it ranges among the oldest worldwide. In 2010 only Japan had a higher proportion of individuals aged 65 or older. Finally, after several decades of immigration the number of foreign residents, i.e. persons who live in Germany but do not have German citizenship, is the highest in the European Union (EU). These trends of population decline, ageing and increasing heterogeneity are collectively referred to as 'demographic change' (*demographischer Wandel*).[18]

The influence of demographic developments on the electorate are well recognized and widely debated in the academic and political sphere. Debates have revolved especially around two demographic trends: First, the ageing process and second, the increasing number of disenfranchised foreign residents in Germany. The state of research in these two types of debates shall briefly be summarized in the following.

Researchers as well as policy makers who are interested in the *ageing process* of the German population expect that the number of older electors in Germany will

[18] See *Dorbritz, J.*, Germany, 2008, p. 558 f.; *Population Reference Bureau*, World population, 2010; *European Commission*, Demography report, 2011, p. 49; *Enquete-Kommission 'Demographischer Wandel'*, Zwischenbericht, 1998, p. 47.

increase in the future and that they will on average use their right to vote more frequently than younger eligible voters.[19] Based on these expectations, researchers have controversially discussed whether older electors will become an important, possibly pivotal, electoral group in the future and to what extent they will influence election results and policy outcomes: On the one side, some academics assert that elderly electors share similar political values and age-related interests, for instance in the fields of pension and health, which might lead them to vote for the same parties. Analyses by Wagner and colleagues as well as by Rattinger for instance suggest that the Christian Democratic and the Christian Social parties CDU/CSU are likely to profit from the demographic changes, while the Social Democratic party SPD and the green party Bündnis 90/Die Grünen may be disadvantaged.[20] It has also been discussed whether older persons might found new age-based parties. Peschel-Gutzeit and others hypothesize that the interests of younger voters might not be adequately represented any more if parties start to compete for the votes of the elderly. They suspect that age-based conflicts about policy reforms and public spending might arise.[21]

On the other side, some researchers are sceptical about these expectations. Wilson as well as Walker and Maltby have cautioned that older electors are not a homogeneous group, but that they have different socioeconomic backgrounds, interests and party affiliations.[22] Thus, they question whether a growing number of elderly electors will invariably translate into electoral gains or losses for specific parties. Goerres adds that the voting behaviour of elderly electors cannot be straightforwardly predicted due to processes of de-alignment and

---

19 Regarding demographic expectations, see *Sanderson, W. C./Scherbov, S.*, Electoral majority, 2007, p. 546; *Enquete-Kommission 'Demographischer Wandel'*, Zwischenbericht, 1998, p. 48; *Naegele, G.*, Politics, 1999, p. 93; *Hinrichs, K.*, Enfranchising children, 2002, p. 44 f. Regarding differences in turnout across age groups, see *Menning, S.*, Wahlverhalten, 2009; *Nie, N. H./Verba, S./Kim, J.-o.*, Political participation, 1974.

20 *Wagner, C./Konzelmann, L./Rattinger, H.*, Germany, 2010, pp. 18-20; *Rattinger, H.*, Demography, 1992.

21 *Peterson, P. G.*, Gray dawn, 1999, p. 52; *Peschel-Gutzeit, L. M.*, Wahlrecht, 2004. See also *van Parijs, P.*, Disenfranchisement, 1999; *Priddat, B. P.*, Demokratie, 2008, p. 204 f.

22 *Wilson, G.*, Ageing electorate, 1993, p. 97; *Walker, A.*, Aging, 2006, p. 350; *Walker, A./Maltby, T.*, Ageing Europe, 1997, p. 110.

increasing electoral volatility.[23] Walker and Maltby also question whether new age-based parties will indeed be successful in Germany and other European countries. The results of a Eurobarometer study revealed that, at least in the late 1990s, only a minority of elderly respondents in Germany considered joining such a party (13%). The lack of electoral success of parties such as the 'Grey Panthers' confirms this point so far.[24] In a similarly controversial tone, Hinrichs and others have debated whether older electors necessarily have cohesive interests in terms of policy outcomes. Even if older voters would unite around individual policy issues in the future, their influence on policy outcomes will not only depend on their quantitative group strength, but also on their degree of mobilization and the perceived legitimacy of their claims. These authors therefore argue that ageing populations do not necessarily lose their ability to adopt important policy reforms, even if these are against the interests of older electors.[25] Overall, the debate about potential future effects of population ageing on election outcomes or policy reforms remains very controversial.

In order to account for the ageing of the electorate and to find solutions for the potential consequences, social scientists have debated whether adolescents and/or children should be granted the right to vote. The reform proposals range from lowering the voting age to 16 years to abolishing age restrictions to the franchise altogether.[26] During the last twenty years, these reform proposals have been taken up by political parties. Several bills to lower the voting age were tabled in the *Bundestag* (the national Parliament of Germany) and two proposals to dare "more democracy by granting the right to vote from birth" were discussed in 2003 and 2008.[27] After sometimes very controversial debates, all bills and proposals were rejected. The frequency with which they have been

---

23 *Goerres, A.*, Grey vote, 2008.

24 *Walker, A./Maltby, T.*, Ageing Europe, 1997, p. 112; see also *Naegele, G.*, Politics, 1999, p. 98.

25 *Hinrichs, K.*, Enfranchising children, 2002, p. 38; see also *Streeck, W.*, Rentnerdemokratie, 2009; *Walker, A.*, Aging, 2006, p. 347 f.; *Wilson, G.*, Ageing electorate, 1993, p. 98.

26 For a comprehensive discussion see *Palentien, C./Hurrelmann, K.*, Jugend, 1998 and *Stiftung für die Rechte zukünftiger Generationen*, Wahlrecht, 2008.

27 See for example Bundestag document (*Bundestagsdrucksache*, hereafter abbreviated BT-Drs.) 16/3543 of 22.11.2006; BT-Drs. 15/1544 of 11.09.2003. For an overview of these and other bills and motions, see Chapter 7.1.1.2.

tabled and the support which they received across party lines suggest, however, that similar proposals might resurface in the future.

Debates on the second core demographic trend, the *increasing number of foreign residents in Germany* have also been controversial. Academics have pointed out that after decades of high immigration and low naturalization rates, 7.2 million foreign residents live in Germany today (around 8.8 % of the total resident population). While especially long-term foreign residents enjoy a range of social, economic and civic rights, they are not granted full political rights and, most importantly, they do not enjoy the right to vote. Citizens from member states of the EU are a partial exception, since they may vote in municipal elections and in elections to the European parliament. Nonetheless, even EU citizens may not vote in elections to the German Bundestag and in elections to the parliaments of the German states (*Landesparlamente*).[28] Most commentators expect that the number of foreign residents will continue to increase in the near future, making the electorate less inclusive.[29]

In the academic context, Tomas Hammar was among the first to address the exclusion of foreign residents from full political participation in Western democracies such as Germany. In articles and a monograph published in the 1980s, he argued that as long as foreign residents do not have the right to vote even after many years of residence, they cannot properly protect their interests and influence political outcomes that may have an impact on their lives. In the long term, the exclusion of foreign residents from the political arena would therefore lead to a loss of representativeness and legitimacy of the democratic system.[30] Most other political and legal researchers have since agreed with Hammar's argument that long-term foreign residents need to be integrated into the political community to increase the inclusiveness of the demos, or, in

28 See *Bundesamt für Migration und Flüchtlinge*, Migrationsbericht 2008, 2010, pp. 219-244; *Davy, U.*, Rechtliche Instrumente, 1999; *Rubio-Marín, R.*, Immigration, 2000.

29 See *Bryde, B.-O.*, Ausländerwahlrecht, 1989, p. 257; *Coleman, D.*, Immigration, 2006, pp. 403 and 430 ff.; *Münz, R./Seifert, W./Ulrich, R.*, Zuwanderung, 1999, p. 196; *Schuck, P.*, Plural citizenships, 2002, p. 76.

30 See *Hammar, T.*, Dual citizenship, 1985; *Hammar, T.*, State, 1989.

Tienda's terms, to "realign [...] democratic ideals with demographic realities".[31] Two approaches have been discussed to achieve this goal: Some academics have argued in favour of granting long-term foreign residents the right to vote irrespective of whether they acquire German citizenship. Other scholars have suggested that the inclusiveness of the demos should be increased by encouraging foreign residents to naturalize and by granting German citizenship to children of foreign parents who are born and raised in Germany.[32]

These suggestions have been taken up by parties in the Bundestag and by state delegations in the *Bundesrat* (the Federal Council representing the federal states of Germany). During the last decades, they tabled bills to introduce the franchise for long-term foreign residents, to grant German citizenship to their children or to facilitate naturalization processes. A major reform of the citizenship law was in fact successfully adopted in 1999. It changed naturalization procedures and under certain conditions entitles children of foreign residents to acquire German citizenship at birth. Other proposals and bills, by contrast, were defeated after often heated debates.[33]

Overall, academic and political debates about the development of the demos have been very controversial. This is not surprising, given that they deal with questions of political power. In particular, the debates revolve around the question how demographic trends *will* change the allocation of political influence within society in the future and whether political influence *should* be re-allocated through legal reforms. This study aims at contributing to these debates by focusing on three issues that warrant further clarification and insights from research:

First, most existing studies do not analyse the effect of demographic changes and legal reforms on the electorate comprehensively. Instead, they focus on

[31] *Tienda, M.*, Demography, 2002, p. 588 (with a focus on the USA); see also *Masing, J.*, Wandel, 2001, p. 24; *Monz, L.*, Reform, 1999, p. 43; *Davy, U.*, Integration, 1999; *Beckman, L.*, Citizenship, 2006, p. 153.

[32] See *Thränhardt, D.*, Allgemeines Wahlrecht, 1999, p. 23; *Bauböck, R.*, Demokratische Beteiligung, 2003; *Hammar, T.*, Democracy, 1990, p. 206.

[33] See Act to Reform the Citizenship Law (in German: *Gesetz zur Reform des Staatsangehörigkeitsrechts – Staatsangehörigkeitsgesetz; StAG*) of 15.07.1999. For an overview of other bills and motions, see Chapter 7.1.2.2.

some demographic factors while ignoring others. Academics interested in the future size of the foreign population in Germany for instance tend to focus on migration and naturalization trends. They only briefly discuss that fertility and mortality trends among foreign residents as well as demographic trends among the German native population may also play a role.[34] Similarly, researchers who discuss the future proportion of elderly voters among the electorate focus on fertility trends and ageing processes in Germany, but rarely consider the effect which a stronger political integration of the foreign population might have.[35] A more comprehensive discussion could provide more reliable insights into how the German demos might develop in the future. This study will take such a wider perspective by analysing all demographic components that may be relevant for the development of the German electorate.

Second, despite the attention that the topic has received in the academic literature, few quantitative estimations of the future development of the German electorate exist. Population projections that have been published by statistical offices such as the Federal Statistical Office of Germany (Destatis) or the European Statistical Office (Eurostat) as well as by scientific institutions generally focus on the future age- and sex-structure of the population and do not include information on citizenship, which is necessary to estimate the development of the electorate.[36] Other projections that were published in recent years and available at the point of writing distinguish between the German and the foreign population, but define foreigners in terms of migration background or place of birth, and not in terms of citizenship.[37] Only a few exceptions exist: Münz and colleagues as well as Ulrich have estimated the future development of the population in Germany by age, sex, and citizenship. These studies, however, fall short of aggregating the projection results in a way that would allow measuring the future size and age structure of the demos. In addition, these

---

34 See for instance chapters in *Davy, U.*, Integration, 1999; *Münz, R./Ulrich, R.*, Wachstum, 1997; *Bundesministerium des Innern*, Modellrechnungen, 2000.

35 See, for example, *Hinrichs, K.*, Enfranchising children, 2002; *Sanderson, W. C./Scherbov, S.*, Electoral majority, 2007.

36 *Statistisches Bundesamt*, Bevölkerung Deutschlands, 2009; *Eurostat*, Online database, 2012.

37 See *Birg, H./Flöthmann, E.-J.*, Projektionsrechnungen, 2001; *Lanzieri, G.*, Projections, 2011.

projections were published more than ten years ago.[38] Therefore, some of them do not reflect important reforms of the citizenship law that have been enacted since then. At the time of writing, more timely projections were not available. Given the fact that data and software are available to calculate such projections and the keen interest that has been expressed in the topic in recent years, this lack of quantitative projection data is somewhat surprising. This thesis contributes to fill this research gap by estimating how the size and composition of the electorate in Germany will develop in the future. In particular, it will estimate whether the electorate is indeed likely to age and whether an increasing number of foreign residents may be excluded from full political participation, as has been suggested in the academic and political debate.

Third, since little information is available on the future development of enfranchised and disenfranchised population groups in Germany, it is also not clear which impact reforms of the electoral law would have. Would the expected pace of ageing of the electorate slow down if the voting age was lowered? How many foreigners would profit from the different legal reforms aiming at including them into the German demos? Some researchers have sought to estimate the effect of electoral reforms by considering the current composition of the electorate. They however did not analyse the future effect of legal reforms.[39] In order to estimate whether the proposed electoral reforms would have long-term effects on the development of the electorate or if their effect would be temporary or marginal only, a detailed population projection is needed as a basis. The projections offered in this study will be used to analyse the effects of potential changes in law.

1.3. Spatial and thematic scope

Before analysing the effect of legal reforms on the development of the electorate, it is important to stress that Germany does not have one cohesive set

38 *Münz, R./Seifert, W./Ulrich, R.*, Zuwanderung, 1999; *Münz, R./Ulrich, R.*, Wachstum, 1997; *Ulrich, R.*, Bevölkerungsstruktur, 2001.

39 See *Krieger, T.*, Generationengerechtigkeit, 2008, p. 312; *Hattenhauer, H.*, Minderjährigen-wahlrecht, 1998, p. 240. For a notable exception see *Sanderson, W. C./Scherbov, S.*, Electoral majority, 2007.

of legal rules to determine membership in the demos, but several. Elections in Germany are held at federal (*Bund*), state (*Länder*) and municipal levels (*Kommunen*) and every five years, elections to the European parliament take place. These elections are governed by different legal frameworks: Elections on state and municipal levels are regulated by state law, while federal level elections are determined by the Federal Election Act. Directives of the EU have to be taken into consideration for elections to the European parliament.[40] The electorate is defined somewhat differently across these legal acts. Some states such as Baden-Württemberg and Hesse for instance allow only citizens aged 18 or older to participate in municipal level elections, while other states such as Lower Saxony have set the minimum voting age at 16 years. As stated before, foreign citizens from EU member states who live in Germany are entitled to vote in municipal elections and elections to the European Parliament, but may not participate in state and federal level elections.[41] Due to differences such as these, individual residents of Germany may be entitled to vote in some elections, but might be excluded from others.

This study will exclusively focus on the demos in federal level elections, i.e. the group of persons that are given the active right to vote in elections to the German Bundestag. The Bundestag is considered to be the most important constitutional body and national elections a "fundamental process of constitutional life".[42] The research results that are obtained about the future development of the demos in Bundestag elections are not necessarily transferable to state or municipal levels. Depending on the size and age distribution of the population in different states and municipalities as well as on their electoral law, demographic changes of their respective demoi might occur at a faster or slower pace than at the federal level. Nonetheless, since many regions in Germany experience trends of population ageing and increasing

40 See *Schreiber, W.*, Handbuch, 2002, pp. 29 and 54; *Oeter, S.*, Allgemeines Wahlrecht, 1999, p. 43; *Maurer, A.*, Europawahlen, 2009, p. 232.

41 See *Schmilowski, F.*, Demokratisierung, 2008, pp. 88-90; *van der Eijk, C./van Egmond, M.*, Political effects, 2007, p. 562 f.

42 *Schreiber, W.*, Handbuch, 2002, p. 32.

diversity, the results obtained for the federal level should be representative for at least some subnational regions as well.

In recent years the role of nation states as loci of democratic decision making has become a topic of content in the literature. Researchers have discussed whether democratic practices and policy making will increasingly take place at the supranational level within the EU and other international organisations and whether democratic practices on the nation state level will be eroded.[43] Researchers who are interested in these developments may argue that a study on future democratic rights and practices should not focus on the national but at the supranational level and analyse to what extent demoi are forming there.

It is acknowledged here that democratic processes on supranational levels may become more important in the near future. More and more decisions are made within the EU and other international bodies which have deep financial, economic and social repercussions in nation states. Nonetheless, as Bauböck has pointed out, elections held within nation states currently remain an important source of democratic legitimacy for policy makers. With the exception of members of the European parliament, office holders who act on the national and supranational level so far receive their democratic legitimacy from elections held in nation states. As long as this remains the case, the demoi in nation states remain important sources of democratic legitimacy. Studying their demographic development remains important to understand democratic processes and outcomes.[44]

In addition to the spatial scope of this study, a few words are in order to justify its thematic focus. As has been stated, this study deals with the future entitlement of population members to vote in Bundestag elections. It will not deal with two other related topics, even though they may be relevant to understand future developments of the German democracy:

First, the question whether and how the right to vote will be exercised by electors in the future will not be discussed here. Admittedly, an analysis of voter turnout and electoral choices may help to anticipate future political dynamics,

---

43 See *Bauböck, R.*, Public culture, 2001, p. 1 f.; *Brodie, J.*, Introduction, 2004; *Held, D.*, Globalization, 1997; *Cohen, J. L.*, Changing paradigms, 1999.

44 See *Bauböck, R.*, Public culture, 2001, p. 2.

election results and policy outcomes. Therefore, it may be considered an important aspect to understand future developments of democracy.[45] Nonetheless, in terms of sequence, debates about the exercise of the franchise are logically secondary to discussions about the access to it. In other words, present and future turnout and voting behaviour can only be discussed once it is clear which parts of the population in fact enjoy the right to vote.[46] By dealing with the latter question, this study may be considered a basis and precursor for studies on the future exercise of the franchise.

Second, the access and use of other political rights, such as the right to join demonstrations, to petition the government, to join associations or unions or to influence public opinion and decision making thorough new social media is not discussed in this study.[47] This does not mean that these rights and forms of participation are not relevant to understand future political dynamics and processes. Quite the contrary is the case. Especially the spread of the Internet and social media such as Twitter and Facebook may lead to a closer exchange between policy makers and the population. New social media may strengthen the opportunities of enfranchised and disenfranchised population members alike to insert their interests and views into the political discourse.[48] Nonetheless, the right to vote was chosen as a subject for this study since it is likely to remain a crucial political right in the near future. It is the only political right that entitles its bearers to choose political representatives and to vote them out of office. It is often stated that policy makers, in the interest of being re-elected, are more prone to listen and respond to the needs and concerns of eligible voters than to disenfranchised population members.[49] As long as this remains the case, the right to vote will remain a crucial right irrespective of the spread and use of

45 See *Walker, A.*, Political participation, 1999. For a brief discussion with a view to the United States of America, see *Binstock, R. H.*, Older people, 2000, pp. 25-27; *Bauböck, R.*, Demokratische Beteiligung, 2003, p. 20 f.; *Diehl, C./Blohm, M.*, Entscheidung, 2008, p. 437; *Linden, M.*, Interessensymmetrie, 2007, p. 79.

46 This argument is taken from *Beckman, L.*, Frontiers, 2009, p. 21.

47 In addition, only the active the right to vote, but not the passive right to vote (the right to run for office) will be considered in this study. For more information on the passive right to vote, see *Schreiber, W.*, Handbuch, 2002, especially the section on '*Wählbarkeit*'.

48 For a discussion on this see *Beckman, L.*, Frontiers, 2009, p. 21 f.

49 See for example *Thränhardt, D.*, Allgemeines Wahlrecht, 1999, p. 21.

other forms of political participation. Changes in the size and structure of the electorate will remain important to understand changes in political dynamics over time.

1.4. Methods and data

This study is of an interdisciplinary nature, located at the boundary between political sciences and demography. Methods and approaches of both scientific fields will therefore be combined to answer the above-mentioned research questions.

In order to test whether the electorate will indeed age and become less inclusive in the near future due to demographic trends, so-called 'multistate' population projections are calculated. Population projections are mathematical operations that calculate how expected future trends in mortality, fertility and migration would change the size, the age- and sex-structure of a population. Multistate projections do not only estimate the future age- and sex-composition of a population, but also take additional characteristics into account.[50] For the purposes of this study, the population of Germany is projected by age, sex and citizenship. The projections are based on a range of assumptions about future trends in fertility, mortality, migration and changes of citizenship. These assumptions will be combined to 16 demographic scenarios. Each scenario shows how combinations of different demographic trends would influence the future development of the electorate as well as the main disenfranchised population groups: children and foreign residents.

It is important to stress that population projections cannot deliver irrefutable results about the future demographic development of the population of Germany and its electorate. Projections are based on expectations of human behaviour. Since human behaviour is complex and driven by a multitude of factors, it can never be predicted with complete certainty.[51] It is especially difficult to make assumptions about demographic behaviour beyond a time horizon of two or

---

50 See *Preston, S. H./Heuveline, P./Guillot, M.*, Demography, 2001, pp. 117 and 127 f.

51 See *Booth, H.*, Demographic forecasting, 2006, p. 571; *Wilson, T./Rees, P.*, Recent developments, 2005.

three decades, since the likelihood that unexpected factors will influence demographic trends increases. Therefore the projections in this study will focus on the more immediate future and cover the years 2010 to 2030. While being inherently uncertain, projections do provide valuable information. Most importantly, they can show how the size and composition of the demos and of disenfranchised population groups are likely to develop, given that underlying demographic assumptions are accepted as plausible. They can also reveal which demographic factors will have the strongest influence on the future structure of the population.

The influence of legal changes on the electorate will be analysed with the help of policy scenarios. Policy scenarios show the future impact of current policy choices. As other types of scenarios, they "generate a body of orientational knowledge which can serve as a compass for lines of action in the present".[52] In this study, different legal reforms which have been debated in academia and among policy makers in recent years are introduced into the population projections. Ten different policy scenarios are calculated. Each of these scenarios provides insights into whether the different proposed reforms would mitigate demographically-induced changes of the demos, provided that they would be enacted in 2010 and remain in force throughout the projection period.

Together, the multistate population projections and policy scenarios show how different enfranchised and disenfranchised population groups are likely to develop in the near future. For the purposes of this study, three different population groups are of interest: First, German citizens aged 18 years or older who – with few exceptions – enjoy the right to vote in Bundestag elections. German citizens are defined here as all individuals who are in possession of German citizenship, irrespective of whether they also hold the citizenship of one or more foreign countries. Second, German citizens aged 0 to 17, who may not (yet) vote due to their young age. Finally, the population of foreign residents in Germany is considered here, who may not vote in Bundestag elections due to

52 *Kosow, H./Gaßner, R.*, Scenario analysis, 2008, p. 13; see also *Wilson, T./Rees, P.*, Recent developments, 2005, p. 353.

lack of citizenship. Foreign residents are defined as all residents of Germany who do not have German citizenship.[53]

In order to quantify the influence of demographic changes and policy reforms on the electorate in the near future, this study relies on two principal indicators: First, the median age of the electorate is used to measure whether the electorate will age in the future. The median age is defined as "the age that divides a population into two numerically equal groups; that is, half the people are younger than this age and half are older".[54] The median age of the electorate is thus the age that divides the electorate into two groups of equal size. Second, the proportion of eligible voters among the total population of Germany is used to measure its inclusiveness. This indicator measures in a relative number how many members of the population are enfranchised and thus form part of the electorate. Since the indicator controls for population size, it makes the effects of demographic changes and legal reforms comparable over time. The proportion of eligible voters and the median age of the electorate are calculated for each population projection and each policy scenario to trace shifts in the inclusiveness and age structure of the electorate over time. Other indicators, such as the relative size of different electoral groups (e.g. the proportion of foreign residents among the population), are used as need be to complement and illustrate research findings.

Figure 1 summarizes the link between demographic trends, legal reforms and membership in the German demos that will be analysed in this study, the methods that will be used as well as the manner in which data will be aggregated.

---

[53] This definition of foreign residents should not be confused with alternative definitions that are often used in the literature. Many studies are interested in 'immigrants' or 'migrants', i.e. individuals who have migrated to Germany. Other studies look at persons with 'migration background', i.e. immigrants as well as their descendants who may or may not have acquired the German citizenship (see, for example, *Bundesamt für Migration und Flüchtlinge*, Migrationsbericht 2008, 2010, p. 235). These definitions are not used in this study unless explicitly stated.

[54] *Haupt, A./Kane, T. T.*, Handbook, 2004, p. 59.

Figure 1: The interplay between demography, law and the electorate

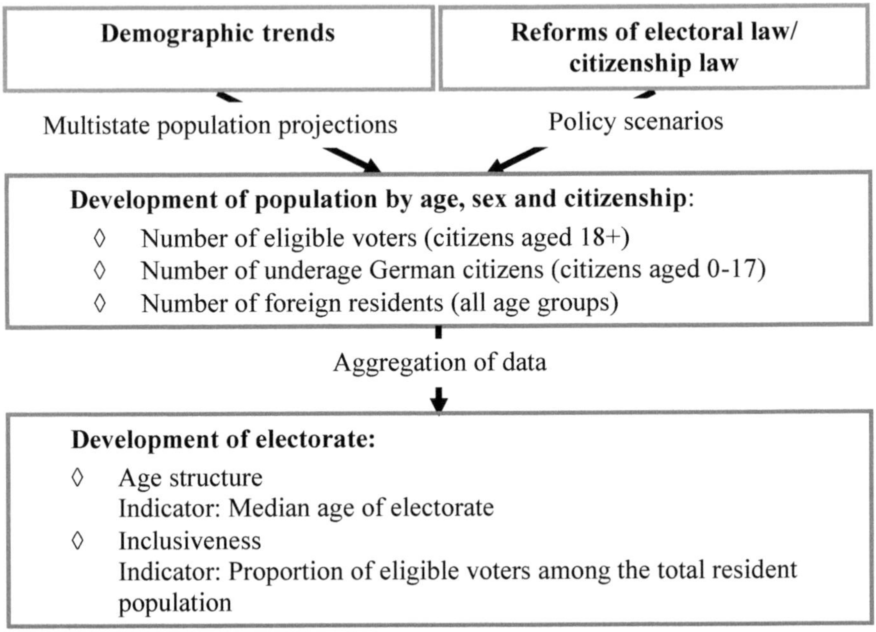

Source: Own illustration

1.5. Structure of the study

The study is structured as follows: Part 1 'Conceptual framework' starts with a basic discussion of the influence of legal changes and demographic trends on the size and composition of electorates in democratic states. First, the impact of legal changes will be discussed (Chapter 2). Electoral law of democratic states, developments in democratic theory and international law will be compared exemplarily. This comparison will show that the definition of membership in democratic demoi has changed across time and space and that these changes have shaped membership structures of demoi in democratic states (Chapters 2.1. and 2.2.). The discussion will then move to the study country Germany (Chapters 2.3. and 2.4.). It will trace how membership in the German electorate has been defined since 1949, the year in which the first Bundestag election was held. The Basic Law, the Federal Election Acts and the Citizenship Act will be consulted for this purpose. As far as data permit, the influence of legal changes on the size and age structure of the German electorate between 1949 and 2010 shall be quantified. The second section of Part 1 (Chapter 3) will shift the focus to demography. The key demographic factors which shape democratic electorates over time will be identified (Chapter 3.1.). Then, it will be described how demographic trends can be measured and how changes in trends can influence the size and age structure of an electorate in often contradictory ways (Chapter 3.2.). After this general discussion, the focus will again move to the study country Germany. Chapter 3.3. will trace how different demographic trends – fertility, mortality, migration as well as citizenship acquisition at birth and during the lifecourse – have changed since 1949. Chapter 3 will conclude by describing how these changes in demographic trends have shaped the German population and its electorate during the past decades (Chapter 3.4.).

Part 2 of the study will turn from the past and present to estimate how changes in demography and electoral law may shape the German demos in the future. It will start by describing the methods as well as by commenting on the data and software used for the population projection and the policy scenarios (Chapter 4). In Chapters 5 to 7, the population projections and policy scenarios will then be carried out. A base year projection will be calculated first (Chapter 5). This projection illustrates how different enfranchised and disenfranchised population groups in Germany would develop in the near future if current demographic trends were to remain stable and if current legal definitions of the demos were retained throughout the projection period. It thus shows the long-term effects of current demographic and legal conditions on the electorate. Nonetheless, it is unlikely that demographic trends and electoral law will remain unchanged for the next twenty years. Especially demographic trends do not tend to remain stable over the course of several decades, but also future changes in law may not be ruled out. Chapters 6 and 7 will therefore proceed to discuss how demographic trends and electoral law may change in the future and they will calculate how such changes would influence the development of the German electorate and of disenfranchised population groups: In Chapter 6, a set of 16 multistate population projections will be presented. These projections are based on sets of assumptions about future developments in demographic trends. These demographic assumptions will be discussed first (Chapters 6.1. and 6.2.). Next, the results of the multistate projections will be presented (Chapter 6.3.). They illustrate how different combinations of alternative demographic trends would influence the size and age structure of the population in Germany and its electorate in the future. Chapter 7 will move on to investigate the influence of possible legal reforms on the development of the electorate. Academic and parliamentary discussions of potential electoral law and citizenship law reforms will be reviewed first (Chapters 7.1. and 7.2.). The proposed reforms will be incorporated as policy scenarios into the previously calculated 16 population projections. The results of the scenarios will be presented in Chapter 7.3. Each of the policy scenarios shows the extent to which the different proposed changes in law would mitigate the demographic changes of the electorate, provided that these reforms would be enacted in the starting year of the projection, 2010, and remain in force throughout the projection period.

The last chapter of this study (Chapter 8) will summarize the research findings and discuss their quality and implications. It will first stress the importance of studying the future development of the German electorate from an interdisciplinary perspective (Chapter 8.1.). The following subchapters will summarize the main insights gained from the demographic projections and policy scenarios and comment on their reliability and implications (Chapters 8.2. and 8.3.). The study will close by critically reflecting whether changes in the size and composition of the electorate may influence political processes and outcomes in the future as well as by pointing out directions for future research (Chapter 8.4.).

Part 1: Conceptual Framework

The electorate of a state is shaped by electoral law and demography. Changing the legal criteria that define access to the franchise and changing demographic trends can both alter the size and age structure of an electorate in important ways. Part 1 of this study discusses this interplay between law, demography and membership structures of demoi. The influence of legal and demographic factors will be discussed successively in Chapter 2 and Chapter 3. Both chapters will start with a general discussion before turning to the study country Germany and tracing as far as data permit how changes in electoral law and demographic trends have shaped the German demos during the past sixty years.

Chapter 2. The influence of legal changes on the development of the electorate

2.1. Restrictions to the right to vote across space and time

Democracy is the 'government of the people, by the people and for the people'. According to this definition, attributed to Abraham Lincoln, the people are a fundamental element of all democratic systems. Democracy is the rule *of* the people, since governments are composed by individuals who belong to the people. It is a rule *by* the people, since its members participate in decision-making processes. Finally, democracy is a rule *for* the people, since governments are expected to rule in accordance with the people's best interests.[55] While there is a wide agreement that the rule of, by and for the people is a hallmark of democratic systems, much less agreement exists on how membership of 'the people', or electorate, should be defined.[56] In the following sections, examples from electoral law[57], democratic theory and international law will be contrasted to show that conceptions about who should be a member of a demos have changed over time. Even today a consensus on who should be able to vote does not exist. After the comparison of these examples, it will briefly be discussed in Chapter 2.2. how changing conceptions about who should be entitled to vote have shaped the size and structure of electorates in European countries over time.

2.1.1. Electoral law

In the ancient Greek polis of Athens (around 5th/4th century before Christ; BC) membership in the demos was restricted to free adult male citizens. Citizenship was defined by descent: only individuals whose parents or even ancestors of

---

55 See *Breit, G.*, Lincoln, 2003, p. 166.

56 See *Rubio-Marín, R.*, Immigration, 2000, p. 25 f.; *López-Guerra, C.*, Expatriates, 2005, p. 218.

57 Access to the franchise has not always been regulated by law, but was regulated by customs and unwritten rules during long parts of history (see for instance *Wölk, M.*, Wahlbewußtsein, 1984, p. 316 and *Payling, S. Y.*, Elections, 1999, p. 237). While this chapter is especially interested in definitions of the demos which are incorporated in written law, it will also refer to polities in which such unwritten rules existed.

higher order had already been citizens of Athens were also considered citizens. The members of the demos, thus defined, regularly met in public assemblies, debated and decided political questions, legislated and distributed public offices by lot or by vote and controlled the magistrates. Slaves, women, children and resident aliens were excluded from these processes of public decision making. Members of the demos who were convicted of a crime could also be deprived of their right to participate. In addition, since physical presence in the assembly was required, membership in the demos was de facto limited to men living in or close to Athens.[58] Membership in the demos of Athens was thus, as Koslowski stresses, of a "highly exclusionary nature".[59]

During the times of the Roman Republic (from 5th century BC), political power lay with the magistrates, the senate and – to a lesser extent – with different types of public assemblies. The most important of these assemblies were the *comitia centuriata* which was composed of Roman men of military age and the *concilium plebis tributa* which was open to all male citizens with the exception of patricians. In contrast to Athens, membership in the assemblies was also open to non-natives and to free inhabitants of conquered cities and regions who had obtained citizenship rights. The latter group of persons however could generally not exercise their political rights, since it required physical presence in the assemblies held in Rome.[60] The functions of the different assemblies were more limited than in Athens. Instead of arguing about political questions that could be put on the agenda by all, the members of the Roman assemblies decided by means of yes/no-answers about questions that were put to their notice by the Senate or the consuls of Rome. The members of the assemblies also elected magistrates and tribunes. During elections votes were not counted individually but by units. These units could be rural or city tribes or military units, and they were designed to give higher influence to wealthier groups of the population.[61]

---

58 See *Saage, R.*, Demokratietheorien, 2005, pp. 50-55; *Koslowski, R.*, Migrants, 2000, p. 73; *Pammett, J. H.*, Elections, 1988, pp. 137-139; *Lippke, R. L.*, Disenfranchisement, 2001, p. 559.

59 *Koslowski, R.*, Migrants, 2000, p. 82.

60 See *Pammett, J. H.*, Elections, 1988, p. 131 f.; *Saage, R.*, Demokratietheorien, 2005, p. 64.

61 See *Roth, K.*, Cicero, 2003, p. 48 f.; *Saage, R.*, Demokratietheorien, 2005, p. 64 f.; *Pammett, J. H.*, Elections, 1988, p. 131 f.

During the Medieval ages and early modern period, public assemblies as they had existed in Athens or during the Roman Republic were held mainly in villages, for instance in 14th and 15th century Switzerland, San Marino or in medieval Scandinavia. Membership in these assemblies was generally open to adult free men, but in some cases additional criteria to limit membership were used. In San Marino, for instance, only male heads of households could participate. Public assemblies in Scandinavia, so-called 'things', were only open to free adult men who could fulfil property requirements.[62] Apart from local assemblies, the Medieval period witnessed the development of city councils, for instance in Flanders, German cities or Italy. Again, the right to elect or become member of these bodies was the prerogative of small groups of the population. In Italian city states of the 11th to 13th century, for instance, peasants, workers, the poor, women and children did not enjoy political rights and could not become members of councils. In contrast to the practice in ancient Rome, inhabitants of conquered towns were also excluded from participation.[63]

In addition to assemblies and city councils, early forms of regional and national parliaments developed in medieval times, for instance in France, Spain or England. In these bodies, members of noble families or the clergy were generally most influential, but towns were sometimes represented as well.[64] England is often considered a forerunner of representative parliamentary practice, since elections to the House of Commons were held from a very early period. The first documents dealing with electoral regulations date back as far as the early 15th century. Throughout the medieval and early modern period, the right to vote in these elections remained similarly restrictive as in village assemblies or city councils. Only adult males with property could vote, while women, children and less wealthy men were not enfranchised.[65]

---

62 On Switzerland, see *Im Hof, U.*, Schweiz, 2007, pp. 35-37 and *Hansen, M. H.*, Athenian democracy, 1992, p. 21 f. On San Marino, see *Sundhaussen, U.*, Peasants, 2003, p. 217. On Scandinavia, see *Wildte, F.*, Thing-steads, 1928, p. 329 and *Myrberg, N.*, Room for all, 2008, pp. 135 and 143-145.

63 On Italy, see *Jones, P. J.*, Communes, 1964, p. 74 f. For a general overview of developments in Europe, see *Blockmans, W. P.*, Typology, 1978.

64 See *Blockmans, W. P.*, Typology, 1978, p. 204 ff.

65 See *Payling, S. Y.*, Elections, 1999; *Phillips, J. A./Wetherell, C.*, Reform act, 1995, p. 413.

The criteria used to limit membership in the demos were also set high when the first large-scale representative democratic systems developed after the French and American Revolutions. The first written constitution of France, enacted in 1791, contained an extensive list of criteria to define membership in the demos. While some of the criteria had been used in previous times already, other restrictions appear to not have been used before. The constitution stipulated that only French men, aged 25 or older, who lived in France and paid direct taxes in the amount of at least three days' work, who were registered in the municipal list of the national guard and had taken a civic oath, were 'active citizens', i.e. members of the electorate. Servants were excluded, as were citizens who were indicted or bankrupt, who had been deprived of their civil rights by court ruling, who had been sentenced *in absentia* or who had joined foreign orders of knights or similar corporations. Male foreign residents in France could become French citizens and join the electorate after five years of residence, if they fulfilled all other electoral requirements and if they had married a French woman, bought property or had founded a farm or an enterprise in France.[66] Active citizens, thus defined, were entitled to participate in biennial elections, in which the members of an electoral college were chosen. The college members then elected the members of parliament.

In contrast to the first French constitution, the constitution of the USA, adopted in 1787, did not contain any regulation on who should be entitled to vote. Instead, the states of the Union were given the right to define which members of their population should form part of the demos.[67] Due to this lack of definition at the national level, access to the franchise developed differently across states during the following century. Most states restricted the franchise to adult, property-owning white men, but they varied with regard to exact property or income requirements as well as with regard to the rights granted to women, foreign residents, prison inmates, native Americans and other population

66 See *Saage, R.*, Demokratietheorien, 2005, p. 119, see also French Constitution of 03.09.1791, Second title, Second article and Third title, First chapter, Second section.

67 See *Keyssar, A.*, Right to vote, 2009, p. 18.

groups.[68] A stronger approximation of franchise regulations across states was only reached when successive constitutional amendments during the 19th and 20th century declared illegal all suffrage restrictions based on "race, colour or previous condition of servitude"[69], established the suffrage for women and set the minimum voting age at 18 years.[70]

In Germany, the right to vote was introduced during the 19th century. Different German states which formed the German Confederation (*Deutscher Bund*) in 1815 established bi-cameral parliaments and entitled male adult citizens of Christian faith to elect the members of the second chambers. Electors generally had to fulfil property or income requirements. A homogeneous set of electoral rules was only introduced after the foundation of the North-German Confederation (*Norddeutscher Bund*) in 1866. The constitution of the Confederation stipulated that the members of parliament (*Reichstag*) should be elected by resident male citizens aged 25 and older. Electors could be excluded from elections if they were receiving poor support, were bankrupt, were placed under guardianship or had lost their civil rights through court ruling. Soldiers also had to abstain from voting.[71]

The above examples show that criteria to restrict membership in assemblies or electorates have differed across time and space. Some groups such as children, women or foreign residents were excluded in many or all examples mentioned above. Other population groups such as the poor, racial or religious minorities formed part of the demos in some polities, but not in others. In addition, some polities varied the degree to which individual electors could influence election results, e.g. by means of a census suffrage. Especially since the late 19th century, many franchise restrictions have been abolished in Western democracies.

68 See *Neale, T. H.*, Eighteen year old vote, 1983, p. 2; *Aylsworth, L. E.*, Alien suffrage, 1931; *Keyssar, A.*, Right to vote, 2009, pp. 305-368.

69 15th constitutional amendment of 1869, quoted in *Neale, T. H.*, Eighteen year old vote, 1983, p. 3. This regulation was initially circumvented by many Southern states. The disenfranchisement of African-American citizens was only completely abolished in the 1960s.

70 See *Neale, T. H.*, Eighteen year old vote, 1983, p. 2 f.

71 For a detailed description of the historic development of the franchise in Germany, see *Schreiber, W.*, Handbuch, 2002, pp. 60-66; *Schmilowski, F.*, Demokratisierung, 2008, pp. 79-90.

Table 1: Current restrictions of the franchise based on membership and competence in Western European countries in 2011

Countries	Elections to	Community Membership			Competence	
		Citizenship: Only citizens allowed to vote?	**Residence**: Disenfranchisement of expatriates possible?	**Law abidingness**: Disenfranchisement of prison inmates possible?	**Age**: Which minimum voting age?	**Mental health**: Disenfranchisement of people with mental disabilities possible?
Austria	Nationalrat	Yes	No	Yes	16	No
Belgium	Congrès national	Yes	No	Yes	18	Yes
Denmark	Folketing	Yes	Yes	No	18	Yes
Finland	Eduskunta	Yes	No	No	18	No
France	Assemblée Nationale	Yes	No	Yes	18	Yes
Germany	Bundestag	Yes	No	Yes	18	Yes
Greece	Vouli Ton Ellinon	Yes	No	Yes	18	Yes
Iceland	Althingi	Yes	Yes	No	18	No
Ireland	Dáil	Yes, or British citizenship	Yes	No	18	No
Italy	Camera dei Diputati	Yes	No	Yes	18	Yes

Continuation of Table 1

Countries	Elections to	Community Membership			Competence	
		Citizenship: Only citizens allowed to vote?	**Residence**: Disenfranchisement of expatriates possible?	**Law abidingness**: Disenfranchisement of prison inmates possible?	**Age**: Which minimum voting age?	**Mental health**: Disenfranchisement of people with mental disabilities possible?
Luxem-bourg	Chamber of Deputies	Yes	No	Yes	18	Yes
Nether-lands	Tweede Kamer	Yes	Yes	Yes	18	No
Norway	Storting	Yes	No	Yes	18	No
Portugal	Assembleia da República	Yes or Brazilian citizenship with equal rights status	No	Yes	18	Yes
Spain	Cortes Generales	Yes	No	Yes	18	Yes
Sweden	Riksdag	Yes	No	No	18	No
Switzer-land	Nationalrat	Yes	No	No	18	Yes
United Kingdom	House of Commons	Yes or qualifying citizen of Commonwealth countries or Ireland	Yes	Yes	18	No

Source: *Blais, A./Massicotte, L./Yoshinaka, A.*, Right to vote, 2001, pp. 44-50. Information was adjusted, updated and complemented by own research (see Annex 1).

Poor persons, women or workers, for instance, are today entitled to vote. In addition, the votes cast in elections count equal, since systems of census suffrage have been abolished. Definitions of the electorate have thereby become somewhat more similar across countries. Nonetheless, in a comparative study of 63 democracies, Blais and colleagues show that membership in electorates continues to differ across countries today.[72] Table 1 shows the findings on current voting restrictions in national parliamentary elections of Western European states.[73] As can be seen, these countries use citizenship, residence and law abidingness as well as age and mental health to restrict access to the franchise. Blais and colleagues subsume these restrictions into two subgroups: community membership restrictions and competence restrictions.

Citizenship, residence and law abidingness are defined as membership restrictions. States use them to ensure that only fully integrated members of the political community are enfranchised. Foreign residents are not considered to be full members of the community in most states and are therefore not entitled to vote. Only Ireland, Portugal and the United Kingdom are exceptions. The UK entitles citizens of Commonwealth countries and Ireland who are resident in the UK to participate in elections to the House of Commons. Ireland reciprocates this entitlement by granting the suffrage in *Dáil* elections to British citizens living in Ireland. Portugal entitles resident Brazilian citizens who enjoy an equal political rights status to vote in elections to the *Assembleia da Republica*.[74]

Citizens who live abroad – so-called expatriates – today retain the right to vote in many Western European countries. Only Denmark, Iceland, Ireland, the Netherlands and the United Kingdom have enacted provisions that allow for their disenfranchisement. These countries thus do not consider all expatriates as

72 *Blais, A./Massicotte, L./Yoshinaka, A.*, Right to vote, 2001.

73 The content of the table is based on *Blais, A./Massicotte, L./Yoshinaka, A.*, Right to vote, 2001, pp. 44-50. It was adjusted, completed and updated by own research. Constitutions, electoral laws and webpages of parliaments and governments were consulted to verify whether electoral criteria have changed since the publication of Blais' and colleagues' book. The legal sources that were consulted in the updating process are included in Annex 1 at the end of this study.

74 See *Blais, A./Massicotte, L./Yoshinaka, A.*, Right to vote, 2001, p. 54. Regarding the UK and Ireland, also see *Miller, M. J.*, Participation, 1989, p. 129. States differ with regard to how citizenship can be acquired: See *Bauböck, R., et al.*, Acquisition and Loss, 2006.

full members of the polity. The exact conditions under which disenfranchisement is possible however differ.[75]

Finally, Blais and colleagues classify law abidingness as a membership restriction. They argue that the disenfranchisement of prison inmates can be interpreted as their (temporary) exclusion from membership in the political community. In Western Europe, countries appear to be divided on this issue.

The last two criteria that Western European countries employ to restrict access to the franchise – age and mental health – are classified as competence restrictions by Blais and colleagues. Western European states use these criteria to restrict the franchise to persons who are judged competent enough to make autonomous and informed decisions about political questions.[76] Children are generally not considered mature enough for these tasks. States therefore define a minimum voting age. With the exception of Austria, which entitles 16- and 17-year-olds to vote, all countries currently define 18 years as the minimum voting age for parliamentary elections at the national level.

Similarly, where persons with mental disabilities are excluded from voting, this reflects the view that these persons cannot make an independent and informed choice at the ballot box. Belgium, Italy and Spain belong to the group of countries which disenfranchise persons with mental impairments. This might include persons who are placed under guardianship or are in psychiatric hospitals. Other countries like Norway or Sweden allow all mentally impaired persons to vote and hence consider them competent to participate in elections.[77]

The membership and competence restrictions which individual countries currently define are used cumulatively: Persons are excluded from the franchise if any of the restrictions applies to them. Conversely, individuals who are granted the right to vote have to fulfil all requirements. Table 1 reveals that countries in Western Europe have enacted at least one restriction based on community membership and competence each. They however differ with regard

---

[75] For an extensive description and discussion of expatriates' voting rights in different countries see *Ellis, A., et al.*, Voting, 2007 and *Bauböck, R.*, Stakeholder citizenship, 2007.

[76] *Blais, A./Massicotte, L./Yoshinaka, A.*, Right to vote, 2001, p. 42.

[77] See *Blais, A./Massicotte, L./Yoshinaka, A.*, Right to vote, 2001, p. 51 f. See also *Nash, M.*, Voting, 2002.

to the number and type of restrictions which are used. Only for two criteria we find a stronger degree of concurrence: The right to vote remains a prerogative of citizens in most countries and the minimum voting age is nearly always set at 18 years. Apart from this, many differences in the definition of the demos remain.

2.1.2. Democratic theory

Just as electoral criteria which polities have used differ across time and space, opinions about how membership in a demos *should* be defined have changed over the course of history.

Until the early modern period, political thinkers discussed democratic participation with reference to the ancient polis of Athens. Democratic participation in this context meant direct participation in a city state or village assembly. This form of rule did not receive much support from political thinkers.[78] Already ancient philosophers like Aristotle (384-322 BC) and Plato (427-347 BC) were critical of the direct democratic practices that existed in Athens. They considered democracy to be the rule of the poor, or the mob, that uses political power to further their own personal interest rather than the common good. The 'poor mob' in their understanding included adult male citizens. The exclusion of women, resident aliens, children, slaves or convicted criminals from political participation, as it was practiced in the polis of Athens, was not put into question by them.[79] Aristotle and Plato acknowledged that direct democratic practices would promote personal freedom better than other political systems, but also criticised that it would lack discipline and stability. Thus, they considered democracy to be inferior to other types of government. Aristotle for instance favoured 'mixed' political systems in which democratic participation would be just one element.[80]

Between the rediscovery of Aristotle's oeuvre in the 13th century and the beginning of the modern period, political theorists such as Jean Bodin (~1529-

---

78 See *Hansen, M. H.*, Athenian democracy, 1992, p. 23; *Schmidt, M. G.*, Demokratietheorien, 2006, p. 59 f.

79 See *Schmidt, M. G.*, Demokratietheorien, 2006, p. 34 f.; *Salkever, S. G.*, Women, 1986, p. 242.

80 See *Hansen, M. H.*, Athenian democracy, 1992, p. 16; *Saage, R.*, Demokratietheorien, 2005, p. 58 f.; *Schmidt, M. G.*, Demokratietheorien, 2006, pp. 38-55.

1596), Thomas Hobbes (1588-1679) and Niccolò Machiavelli (1469-1527) largely remained in the tradition of ancient thinkers. They considered direct democratic practice to be an unstable form of rule that would be applicable to small polities, if at all. Some of these political thinkers also promoted systems of mixed political rule in which democratic processes would co-exist with aristocratic and monarchical elements.[81] Since democracy was not considered a viable form of rule, the question of how the demos should be composed was not of primary concern.[82]

The idea of democratic participation was only slowly reappraised during the period of Enlightenment. Political theorists such as John Locke (1632-1704), Charles de Montesquieu (1689-1755), Baruch de Spinoza (1632-1677), Jean-Jacques Rousseau (1712-1778) and the authors of the Federalist papers (written in 1787/88) advocated that 'the people' should participate in governing their polities either through direct democratic practices or through representative parliaments, within constitutional monarchies or based on republican constitutions.[83] While these authors contributed to revalue the idea of democratic participation, they did not question or advance traditional views about who should be a member of the demos. Instead, they remained in the tradition of Aristotle in implicitly taking for granted the exclusion of women, children, foreigners and other population groups. Some thinkers even explicitly defended the exclusion of certain population groups. Locke and Montesquieu for instance argued that only free adult men with property would be capable to participate in political life. The authors of the Federalist papers James Madison, Alexander Hamilton and John Jay held similar views. Spinoza stated in his 'Political

81 See *Saage, R.*, Demokratietheorien, 2005, pp. 70, 74 f. and 90 f.; *Schmidt, M. G.*, Demokratietheorien, 2006, pp. 60-66. Only few political thinkers expressly promoted the idea that the population living in a polity should be entitled to participate in its ruling. Marisilius of Padua (1275-1342) was probably the most influential proponent of the time. He remained in the tradition of Aristotle in considering that slaves, aliens, children and women should have no say in political decision making (see *Roth, K.*, Marsilius, 2003, p. 80 f.).

82 See *Schmidt, M. G.*, Demokratietheorien, 2006, p. 59 f.

83 For a detailed discussion on these authors, see especially *Saage, R.*, Demokratietheorien, 2005; *Schmidt, M. G.*, Demokratietheorien, 2006 and *Massing, P./Breit, G.*, Demokratie-Theorien, 2003.

Treatise' that foreign residents, women, slaves, children, persons under guardianship and criminals should not participate in political rule.[84]

The idea that political participation in general and the suffrage in particular are individual rights which should be open to broader groups of the population only became a subject of debate in the context of the French revolution. Political thinkers in England, France and the German states of the Holy Roman Empire started to discuss the legitimacy of different electoral restrictions. Especially income and property requirements as well as the exclusion of servants and other professions were subject to debate. Some democratic theorists such as Thomas Paine (1737-1809) and James Mill (1773-1836) argued that the suffrage should not depend on these criteria, while others such as Immanuel Kant (1724-1804) defended them. John Stuart Mill (1806-1873) and August Ludwig von Schlözer (1735-1809) proposed to make the franchise dependent on education rather than on property. J.S. Mill and Schlözer were also among the first to question the exclusion of women from political participation. Kant and Johann Gottlieb Fichte (1762-1814) by contrast defended the exclusion of women and stressed that their only means of political involvement should be the interaction and deliberation with their husbands.[85]

Electoral criteria such as income, property and sex have been abolished in the 19th or 20th century. Nonetheless, debates about which criteria states may legitimately use to limit access to the franchise are ongoing today. Democratic theorists especially debate whether children and adolescents as well as foreign residents should be given the right to vote. These debates will be commented on in detail in later chapters of this study.[86]

---

84 On Locke see *Schmidt, M. G.*, Demokratietheorien, 2006, p. 72 and *Dahl, R. A.*, Democracy, 1989, p. 124. On Montesquieu and the Federalist papers, see *Schmidt, M. G.*, Demokratietheorien, 2006, pp. 78 and 126. As regards Spinoza, see *Saage, R.*, Demokratietheorien, 2005, p. 86.

85 On Paine, James Mill and Kant see *Saage, R.*, Demokratietheorien, 2005, pp. 151 and 162. While arguing that the right to vote should not depend on property, Mill agreed with previous thinkers that only tax-payers should be entitled to vote. On John Stuart Mill and Schlözer, see *Schmidt, M. G.*, Demokratietheorien, 2006, p. 154 f.; *Pesch, V.*, Mill, 2003, pp. 161 and 163 and *Saage, R.*, Demokratietheorien, 2005, p. 166 f. On Kant and Fichte, see *Saage, R.*, Demokratietheorien, 2005, p. 169 f.

86 See Chapter 7. For a discussion of current exclusions from the franchise see *Beckman, L.*, Frontiers, 2009.

While being less prominently discussed, theorists such as Michael Nash or Richard Lippke also critically reflect other remaining types of disenfranchisement. Nash for example argues that mentally ill persons should not be barred from voting, because mental illness is not to be equated with incompetence. He stresses that voting may be a means to promote the social inclusion of mentally impaired persons. Similarly, Lippke has argued that felons may be at the margins of society already and that this status is reinforced if they are excluded from voting.[87] Finally, the political rights of expatriates have been critically discussed in political science and legal literature, with many authors arguing that they should not be given the right to vote.[88]

In addition to debating *individual* restrictions to the franchise, democratic theorists have sought to define *general* principles according to which membership in democratic demoi may be restricted. Some theorists argue that all individuals who are affected by the political decisions of a government should participate in elections. The term 'affected' has been interpreted in several different ways. Beckman, for example, suggests that it may refer to all persons who have a financial or economic stake in a polity or to all persons who are subject to the legal authority of a government. Which of these or other interpretations is most convincing and how they may be applied in practice remains subject to debate.[89]

Other theorists propose to use the principle of inescapability (*Unentrinnbarkeit*) to define membership in the demos. According to this principle, the demos should be composed of all individuals who are inextricably linked to the fate and development of a polity. Some proponents of this view conclude that foreign residents should not be members of the demos, since they have the right to move back to their country of origin and thus to escape from undesired developments of the polity in which they currently live.[90]

---

87 *Nash, M.*, Voting, 2002; *Lippke, R. L.*, Disenfranchisement, 2001, p. 577. Also see *Schriner, K./Ochs, L. A./Shields, T. G.*, Suffrage, 1997 and *Beckman, L.*, Frontiers, 2009, p. 144 f.

88 See *Beckman, L.*, Citizenship, 2006, p. 161; *Bauböck, R.*, Stakeholder citizenship, 2007, p. 2447; *López-Guerra, C.*, Expatriates, 2005.

89 *Beckman, L.*, Citizenship, 2006, pp. 158-612. See also *Bernhardt, B.*, Self-determination, 2010; *Gusy, C./Ziegler, K.*, Volksbegriff, 1999, p. 226 f.

90 See *Gusy, C./Ziegler, K.*, Volksbegriff, 1999, p. 229 f.

Finally, Brennan has argued in a recent article that membership in the demos should be based on political competence. He stresses that if members of the demos base their electoral choice on irrational grounds, they may negatively influence the future development of the entire polity. Therefore, he insists that eligible voters should prove a minimum level of political competence. Brennan suggests that this proof might be provided in the form of a 'voter qualification exam', "which tests generally relevant basic social science and basic knowledge about the candidates"[91] who are running for election.

Given the long history of debates about how membership in democratic demoi should be defined, Schumpeter has suggested that a general definition may never be found: "Must we leave it to every *populus* to define himself?"[92] Most other democratic theorists object and insist that democratic states have to follow certain core principles when defining membership of their demoi.[93] Nonetheless, a consensus on which core principles should be respected has not yet emerged.

2.1.3. International law

These differences in opinion about who should be entitled to vote are also reflected in international law: So far, democratic states have not agreed on a conclusive set of common standards to define membership in democratic demoi. Several international and European conventions and treaties mention criteria according to which access to the franchise may or may not be limited. The list of criteria is however not comprehensive. Consequently, while international law places some restrictions on countries' competence to define membership in their demoi, they retain a substantial degree of discretion in this matter.[94]

The Universal Declaration of Human Rights, adopted by the United Nations (UN) General Assembly in 1948, for instance states that "everyone has the right to take part in the government of his country, directly or through freely chosen

91 *Brennan, J.*, Competent electorate, 2011, p. 714.

92 *Schumpeter, J. A.*, Capitalism, 1976, p. 245. Italics are used in the original.

93 Critical for instance *Dahl, R. A.*, Democracy, 1989, p. 121; *Rubio-Marín, R.*, Immigration, 2000, p. 25.

94 For an overview of franchise regulations in international law see *Fox, G. H.*, Political participation, 2000 and *Kirshner, A.*, International status, 2003.

representatives".[95] The Declaration however does not define the term 'everyone' nor does it state whether specific groups of persons may legitimately be excluded from the franchise.[96]

The International Covenant on Civil and Political Rights, adopted by the UN General Assembly in 1966, provides more detailed regulations. It is legally binding for the signatory states, among them all European countries.[97] Article 25 of the Covenant states that every citizen should have the right to vote "without unreasonable restrictions".[98] The Covenant clarifies this point by stating that any discrimination based on "race, colour, sex, language, religion, political or other opinion, national or social origin, property, birth or other status"[99] shall be forbidden. These criteria are thus considered 'unreasonable'. The formulation of Article 25 however implies that at least some types of criteria may be 'reasonable' and thus be legitimately used by the signatory states. Citizenship is the only criterion that is explicitly mentioned. Other types of restriction, such as age or law abidingness, are neither explicitly accepted nor prohibited. They can therefore at least potentially be considered as 'reasonable' criteria that are permitted under the Covenant.[100]

Other UN Conventions add only few other criteria that signatory states may not use to restrict membership of their demoi. The Convention on the Rights of Persons with Disabilities stipulates that physically, mentally, intellectually or sensorily disabled persons have a right to participate in elections. The International Convention on the Protection of the Rights of All Migrant Workers and Members of their Families adds that migrants should be entitled to vote in their countries of origin and that states of employment may allow them to participate in local communities. While most Western European countries have

---

95 Universal Declaration of Human Rights (UDHR) of 10.12.1948, Article 21(1).

96 See *Earnest, D. C.*, Voting rights, 2003, p. 17; *Kirshner, A.*, International status, 2003, p. 3.

97 Only Kosovo and Vatican City are exceptions. See the following webpage for the status quo on signature, accession and ratification of different countries (accessed 14.04.2014): http://treaties.un.org/Pages/ViewDetails.aspx?src=TREATY&mtdsg_no=IV-4&chapter=4n&lang=en.

98 International Covenant on Civil and Political Rights (ICCPR) of 16.12.1966, Article 25.

99 ICCPR, Article 2.

100 See *Fox, G. H.*, Political participation, 2000, p. 53 f.; *Hammar, T.*, Democracy, 1990, p. 130.

signed and/or ratified the first Convention, the latter one has not been ratified by any Western European country and is thus not legally binding for them.[101]

In the European context, legal documents add few other regulations. The European Convention for the Protection of Human Rights and Fundamental Freedoms of 1950, adopted within the framework of the Council of Europe, requires that member states regularly hold free elections, but does not restrict states in their choice of electoral criteria. Article 16 of the Convention even expressly entitles the signatory states to restrict political activities of foreign residents.[102] The European Convention on the Participation of Foreigners in Public Life at Local Level of 1992 qualifies this regulation. It stipulates that the municipal right to vote should be granted to foreigners who have been lawfully resident in the signatory states for at least five years. The Convention, however, has as yet been signed and ratified by few Western European countries only and therefore does not have a far-reaching impact.[103]

Within the European Union, the only legally binding rule regarding the franchise concerns EU citizens. The Treaty of Maastricht of 1993 granted citizens of one EU member state who live in another member state the active right to vote in elections to the European Parliament and in municipal elections in their country of residence. While not prohibiting that this right be extended, the European Treaties do not require that third country nationals share these rights and do not extend EU citizens' right to vote to any elections beyond the municipal and European level.[104]

---

[101] Convention on the Rights of Persons with Disabilities (CRPD) of 13.12.2006, Article 29; International Convention on the Protection of the Rights of All Migrant Workers and Members of their Families of 18.12.1990, Articles 41 and 42; *Bauböck, R.*, Stakeholder citizenship, 2007, p. 2410.

[102] European Convention for the Protection of Human Rights and Fundamental Freedoms (ECHR) of 04.11.1950, Protocol no. 1, Article 3. See also *Beckman, L.*, Citizenship, 2006, p. 154.

[103] European Convention on the Participation of Foreigners in Public Life at Local Level of 05.02.1992, Article 6. The Convention has entered into force in Albania, Denmark, Finland, Iceland, Italy, the Netherlands, Norway and Sweden. Information available at: http://conventions.coe.int/Treaty/Commun/ChercheSig.asp?NT=144&CM=8&DF=27/08/2010&CL=ENG (accessed 14.04.2014). See also *Waldrauch, H.*, Wahlrechte, 2003, p. 56.

[104] See *Day, S./Shaw, J.*, European Union, 2002, p. 185; *Waldrauch, H.*, Wahlrechte, 2003, pp. 53-59.

Overall, international law limits the freedom of Western European countries to define their electorates in certain respects, but does not provide a comprehensive set of rules as to how membership in their demoi may be restricted. Democracies in Europe thus retain, as Earnest puts it, "considerable sovereignty over the constitution of their political communities".[105]

2.2. Influence of changing restrictions on electorates across space and time

The previous chapters have revealed that the restrictions which polities *have* used to limit membership in their demoi have changed across space and time, as have opinions about which restrictions they *should* use and international legal rules about which restrictions democratic states *may* use. Despite these changes and evolutions, the examples of the previous chapters allow two general insights about the influence of electoral law on electorates.

First, irrespective of which polity is considered across space and time, there has never been a complete congruence between resident population and demos. Such congruence would only exist if all persons living within the territory of a polity would be entitled to vote and if all members of the demos would live within the borders of the polity (See Figure 2, left side). If these conditions were fulfilled, the principle of universal suffrage would be achieved in its literal sense, there would be a "perfect *symmetry* between rulers and ruled".[106]

In practice, however, these conditions have never been fulfilled by any polity (see Figure 2, right side). On the one hand, membership in demoi has always been exclusive. As has been described above, polities across space and time have never entitled all members of the resident population to vote, but have always excluded certain groups such as the poor, the young or foreign residents. With a special view on foreigners, Bryde refers to these groups of disenfranchised residents as 'subjects'.[107] The fact that all democracies across space and time have excluded some subjects from full political participation has

[105] *Earnest, D. C.*, Resident aliens, 2003, p. 27; see also *Guiraudon, V.*, Citizenship rights, 1998, p. 282.

[106] *Beckman, L.*, Who should vote?, 2008, p. 43; Italics are used in the original.

[107] Bryde uses the term ‚Untertanen' in the German text. Bryde, B.-O., Ausländerwahlrecht, 1989, p. 257.

led Cohen to ask whether exclusiveness is in fact a necessary element of democratic rule: "The question that must be faced [...] is whether or not exclusion is constitutive of the very ideal of democratic citizenship."[108]

Figure 2: Resident population and demos

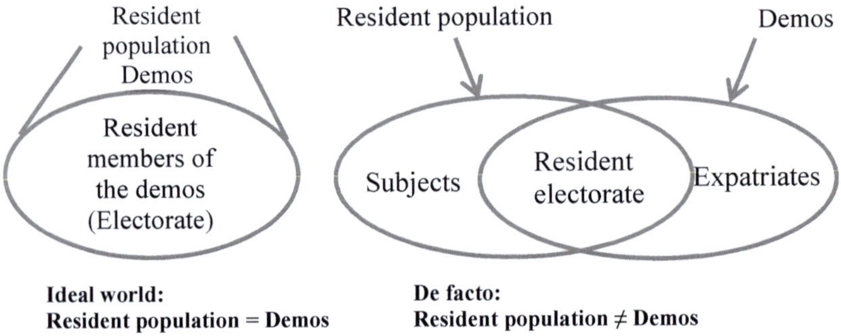

Source: Own illustration based on *Hagedorn H*, Einbürgerung, 2001, p. 25.

On the other hand, some members of the demos have always more or less permanently lived abroad. In the past, these expatriates were seldom entitled to participate in elections in their home countries.[109] This practice only became more common in recent decades, when communication and transportation technologies improved. Today, many countries allow expatriates to vote, either in embassies or polling stations abroad, by mail or by proxy. Some states also require that expatriates return home and vote in country if they want to participate in elections.[110]

The second insight that can be gained on the basis of the previous chapters is that while a complete congruence between resident population and demos has never been reached in any polity, the degree of congruence has increased over time. Restrictions to the franchise based on race, religion, income, property or sex have been abolished. Other restrictions such as the minimum voting age were lowered and thus apply to fewer persons. These changes or abolishment of restrictions have led to the enfranchisement of large groups of individuals. They

---

108 *Cohen, J. L.*, Changing paradigms, 1999, p. 249; slso *Benhabib, S.*, Political theory, 2002, p. 419.

109 See *Ellis, A.*, History, 2007, p. 41.

110 For a discussion of external voting practices, see *Bauböck, R.*, Stakeholder citizenship, 2007.

have reduced the gap between resident population and demos in democracies across Western Europe. The extension of the franchise also affected the age structure of the demoi in many cases. If the newly enfranchised members of demoi were on average younger than previous electors, the median age of the demoi declined. Conversely, if new members of the demos were on average older than the previous members, the median age rose.

While the dominant trend over time has been towards extending the right to vote, exceptions exist. Historical studies show that the right to vote, once granted to previously disenfranchised population groups, was sometimes restricted again. Foreign residents for instance enjoyed the right to vote in many states of the USA during the 19th century. One state after another however withdrew this right until by 1926 foreign residents were no longer allowed to vote in state or national level elections anywhere in the USA.[111] Women, African Americans and Native Americans are other population groups that enjoyed the right to vote in the USA for certain periods of time, but were later disenfranchised.[112] In Germany, the adoption of new constitutions or electoral laws led to several re-definitions of the minimum voting age during the 20th century, resulting both in increases and decreases of the age limit. While citizens aged 20 years or older could for instance participate in elections during the Weimar Republic, the Basic Law of 1949 set the minimum voting age one year higher to 21 years.[113] While most reforms of electoral laws thus extended the franchise and increased the congruence of resident population and demos over time, this was not always the case.

Overall, by (re-)defining eligibility criteria for the franchise, policy makers have strongly influenced membership structures in demoi over time. The following chapter shows that such re-definitions of the boundaries of the demos also occurred during the last sixty years of German history.

---

[111] See *Aylsworth, L. E.*, Alien suffrage, 1931.
[112] See *Keyssar, A.*, Right to vote, 2009, p. 43 f.
[113] See *Schmilowski, F.*, Demokratisierung, 2008, p. 89 f.

2.3. Restrictions to the right to vote in Germany, 1949-2010

Since 1949, Bundestag elections have been regulated by the Basic Law and by Federal Election Acts. The former determines general principles according to which elections in Germany are held, while the latter set out in detail restrictions to the franchise and electoral procedures.[114] Three Federal Election Acts have been enacted to date: The first Federal Election Act of 1949 regulated the first Bundestag election held in that same year; the second Federal Election Act of 1953 regulated the second Bundestag election. The third Federal Election Act of 1956 has regulated all Bundestag elections since then. It remains in force today, but has been subject to many reforms.[115] In the following sections, the core principles which are defined in these legal documents to determine membership in the demos will be described. First the focus will be on the Basic Law. After that, the successive Federal Election Acts will be compared. The analysis will show that legal reforms of the past six decades have made the German electorate more inclusive. Chapter 2.4. will discuss to what extent these changes in law have quantitatively affected the size and age structure of the demos in Germany.

2.3.1. The Basic Law

In the Basic Law, the political participation of the German demos is first mentioned in Article 20(2). It stipulates that

> "All state authority is derived from the people. It shall be exercised by the people through elections and other votes and through specific legislative, executive and judicial bodies."[116]

---

[114] See *Schreiber, W.*, Handbuch, 2002, pp. 33-35.

[115] Election Act for the first Bundestag and the first Federal Convention of the Federal Republic of Germany (in German: *Wahlgesetz zum ersten Bundestag und zur ersten Bundesversammlung der Bundesrepublik Deutschland – Erstes Bundeswahlgesetz; 1. BWahlG)* of 15.06.1949; Election Act for the second Bundestag and the Federal Convention (in German: *Wahlgesetz zum zweiten Bundestag und zur Bundesversammlung – Zweites Bundeswahlgesetz; 2. BWahlG*) of 08.07.1953; Federal Election Act (in German: *Bundeswahlgesetz; (3.) BWahlG*) of 07.05.1956.

[116] Basic Law for the Federal Republic of Germany (in German: *Grundgesetz für die Bundesrepublik Deutschland – Grundgesetz*; GG) of 23.05.1949, Article 20(2). In German, the text reads: "Alle Staatsgewalt geht vom Volke aus. Sie wird vom Volke in Wahlen und

While the article identifies 'the people' as the source of state power, it does not define its membership. To interpret the term, legal experts therefore consult the preamble as well as Articles 33, 56, 64(2) and 146 of the Basic Law, which also elaborate on the exercise of state power.[117] These articles explicitly refer to 'each German' or 'the German people'. Constitutional commentators such as Schreiber deduce by analogy that the authors of the Basic Law also intended 'the people' in Article 20(2) to refer to Germans only.[118]
If this interpretation is followed, the boundaries of the electorate depend on who is considered to be 'German'. This definition is provided in Article 116(1) of the Basic Law. According to this article,

> "unless otherwise provided by law, a German within the meaning of this Basic Law is a person who possesses German citizenship or who has been admitted to the territory of the German Reich within the boundaries of 31 December 1937 as a refugee or expellee of German ethnic origin or as the spouse or descendant of such person."[119]

This article determines membership in the German people not only on the basis of citizenship, but also in terms of ethnicity. In addition, it goes beyond both principles in declaring that persons who are not citizens or of German origin themselves, but who are married to (or descending from) a German refugee or expellee shall be considered German as well.[120] According to Hagedorn, such a wider conceptualization of the term 'German' was necessary when Basic Law was adopted in 1949 due to the societal and political situation in the immediate after war period. Large numbers of persons of German origin fled or were

---

Abstimmungen und durch besondere Organe der Gesetzgebung, der vollziehenden Gewalt und der Rechtsprechung ausgeübt."

117 See *Gusy, C./Ziegler, K.*, Volksbegriff, 1999, p. 241 and *Hanschmann, F.*, Stellungnahme, 2008, p. 3.

118 *Schreiber, W.*, Handbuch, 2002, p. 41; see also *Rennert, K.*, Stellungnahme, 2008, p. 2.

119 Art. 116(1) GG. In German, the text reads: "Deutscher im Sinne dieses Grundgesetzes ist vorbehaltlich anderweitiger gesetzlicher Regelung, wer die deutsche Staatsangehörigkeit besitzt oder als Flüchtling oder Vertriebener deutscher Volkszugehörigkeit oder als dessen Ehegatte oder Abkömmling in dem Gebiete des Deutschen Reiches nach dem Stande vom 31. Dezember 1937 Aufnahme gefunden hat."

120 See also *Hobe, S.*, Staatsvolk, 1994, p. 192.

expulsed from Eastern European regions and moved to the newly founded Federal Republic of Germany. Article 116(1) of the Basic Law was devised to allow for their speedy integration into German society.[121] It entitled ethnic German resettlers to acquire German citizenship and, as a consequence, the right to vote.

While determining that ethnic Germans belong to the German people, Article 116(1) of the Basic Law does not specify how the ethnic German origin of a person can be proven. This information is provided by the Federal Expellees Act of 1953. Art. 6 of this Act determines that persons are German, if they

> „have committed themselves in their homelands to Germanness, in as far as this commitment is confirmed by certain facts such as descent, language, upbringing, or culture."[122]

The status and rights of ethnic Germans were maintained after the first waves of post-war migration ended. Only small numbers of resettlers could migrate to Germany from Eastern Europe and make use of these rights during the post-war decades due to travel and migration restrictions in the countries belonging to the Soviet Union. The regulation however became relevant again when the borders to Eastern European countries were opened after the end of the Cold War. Large numbers of persons of German origin then moved to Germany, acquired German citizenship and became members of the electorate.[123] As a reaction to the large influx of German migrants, the Federal Expellees Act was amended several times during the 1990s, making it more difficult for individuals to prove their 'Germanness' and to migrate to Germany. The annual number of persons who

---

121 *Hagedorn, H.*, Einbürgerung, 2001, p. 37.

122 Act on the Matters of Expellees and Refugees (in German: *Gesetz über die Angelegenheiten der Vertriebenen und Flüchtlinge – Bundesvertriebenengesetz; BVFG*) of 22.05.1953, Article 6. The English translation of the German legal text is taken from: *Anil, M.*, Citizenship law, 2006, p. 448 f. In German, the text reads: "Deutscher Volkszugehöriger im Sinne dieses Gesetzes ist, wer sich in seiner Heimat zum deutschen Volkstum bekannt hat, sofern dieses Bekenntnis durch bestimmte Merkmale wie Abstammung, Sprache, Erziehung, Kultur bestätigt wird."

123 See Chapter 6.1.3.1. for data on immigration of ethnic Germans.

are recognized as ethnic German resettlers has substantially declined since then.[124]

Apart from ethnic German refugees and resettlers, citizens of the German Democratic Republic (GDR) were considered to be citizens of the Federal Republic of Germany (FRG) until reunification in 1990. If they managed to cross the German-German border and fulfilled all electoral criteria, they could obtain a passport in West Germany and participate in elections.[125] After reunification, all citizens of the former GDR became citizens of the FRG and eligible to vote in the now all-German Bundestag elections.

To summarize the preceding points, if the German demos in Article 20(2) of the Basic Law is understood as comprising all Germans as defined in Article 116(1), it encompasses all German citizens, all persons without German citizenship who are recognised as ethnic Germans on the basis of language, upbringing, descent and culture, as well as their spouses and descendants. Based on this interpretation, commentators have argued that membership in the German demos has traditionally been ethno-cultural in character.[126]

Not all legal scholars however share the view that 'the people' in Article 20(2) of the Basic Law necessarily refers to Germans only. Bryde for instance argues:

> "The formulation of Art. 20 II 1 [...] is first of all a traditional affirmation of the democratic principle and a differentiation from undemocratic forms of governance [...]. If 'the people' is understood here as a non-formalized constituent power, this pouvoir constituant may not be forced into the straightjacket of a technical-legal institution such as the citizenship law."[127]

---

[124] See *Münz, R./Seifert, W./Ulrich, R.*, Zuwanderung, 1999, p. 30 ff. Also see Chapter 3.3.3.1. for a brief overview of other factors which led to the decline in immigration numbers.

[125] See *Hailbronner, K.*, Germany, 2006, p. 218; *Schreiber, W.*, Handbuch, 2002, p. 262.

[126] See *Earnest, D. C.*, Voting rights, 2003, p. 21.

[127] *Bryde, B.-O.*, Ausländerwahlrecht, 1989, p. 259. In German, the text reads: „Die Formel des Art. 20 II 1 [...] ist zunächst einmal eine traditionelle Bekräftigung des demokratischen Prinzips und Abgrenzung gegen undemokratische Herrschaftsformen [...]. Versteht man das ‚Volk' hier als unverfassten Träger der verfassungsgebenden Gewalt, läßt sich dieser pouvoir constituant [...] nicht in das Korsett eines technischen Rechtsinstituts wie des Staatsangehörigkeitsrechts zwängen."

Other legal and political scholars agree with Bryde in pointing out that Article 20(2) of the Basic Law does not explicitly restrict membership in the demos to German citizens or ethnic Germans. They stress that the term 'the people' as it is used in this article is in fact open to interpretation and might be read as including non-citizens as well. Some legal experts even argue that the extension of the franchise to foreign residents is required by the principles enshrined in the Basic Law, such as the principle that elections be 'universal' in character.[128]

The Federal Constitutional Court of Germany has so far sided with the interpretation of Article 20(2) of the Basic Law as referring to Germans only. The court judged in two rulings on the municipal franchise for foreigners in 1990 that the right to vote is a prerogative of Germans as defined in Article 116(1) of the Basic Law and may not be extended to long-term foreign residents. The court stressed that foreign residents in Germany should be included in the demos, but advised that this incorporation has to be achieved through naturalization.[129] It only made an exception for EU citizens: The court declared that the extension of the right to vote in municipal elections to EU citizens might be permissible under the Basic Law.[130]

Only three years later, the municipal franchise for EU citizens was in fact introduced by the Treaty of Maastricht in 1993. This extension of the franchise has led some commentators to discuss whether the traditional link between citizenship, ethnicity and the franchise has been broken. Hobe for instance has urged that a debate about the meaning and the boundaries of the demos in Germany is required. He argues that the traditional assertion according to which the franchise is the prerogative of Germans no longer holds.[131] Other legal experts however see little room for debate and maintain that any further

---

128 See *Oeter, S.*, Allgemeines Wahlrecht, 1999, p. 37 f.; *Gusy, C./Ziegler, K.*, Volksbegriff, 1999, p. 241 f.; *Rubio-Marín, R.*, Immigration, 2000; *Hanschmann, F.*, Stellungnahme, 2008, p. 5.

129 See *Oeter, S.*, Allgemeines Wahlrecht, 1999, pp. 32-37; *Rubio-Marín, R.*, Immigration, 2000, pp. 203-206; *Pechstein, M.*, Stellungnahme, 2008, pp. 3-6.

130 See *Hobe, S.*, Staatsvolk, 1994, p. 193.

131 *Hobe, S.*, Staatsvolk, 1994, pp. 193-195; also *Hanschmann, F.*, Stellungnahme, 2008, pp. 11-16 and 26.

extension of the franchise to non-citizens would be unconstitutional.[132] Overall, Article 20(2) of the Basic Law thus provides ample room for debate on whether citizenship is to be used as a restriction to the franchise.

In later articles of the Basic Law, only one restriction to the franchise is explicitly mentioned. Article 38(2) defines a minimum voting age. When the Basic Law was enacted in 1949 it defined 21 years as the minimum voting age. In 1970, this age limit was lowered to 18 years.[133] Apart from the minimum voting age, all other membership and competence restrictions that have been used to define membership of the German demos are not included in the Basic Law, but in the Federal Election Acts. As we shall see in the following, these restrictions have been repeatedly amended. The understanding of who should be a member of the demos in Bundestag elections has thus changed in the past sixty years.

2.3.2. The Federal Election Acts

Table 2 provides an overview of the most important types of restrictions which have regulated membership in the German demos in each federal level election between 1949 and today.[134] These restrictions are based on citizenship/ethnicity, residence, law abidingness as well as on age and mental health. Following the classification proposed by Blais and colleagues (see Chapter 2.1.1.), the first three count as membership restrictions, while the latter two are competence criteria.[135]

Between the first Bundestag election in 1949 and the last election in 2009, most criteria have been subject to at least one reform. Some restrictions have even changed repeatedly, suggesting that views on whether and how they should be applied have changed most strongly. Table 2 shows which changes have been

---

132 See *Pechstein, M.*, Stellungnahme, 2008, p. 1 f.; *Rennert, K.*, Stellungnahme, 2008, p. 9. See also Chapter 7.1.2.

133 Art. 38(2) GG; see also *Schreiber, W.*, Handbuch, 2002, p. 263.

134 For this table and the following analysis, only restrictions that were considered to apply to the largest numbers of persons were considered. Regulations applying to smaller groups of persons, e.g. to homeless persons or persons living on ships, were not taken into account. For a discussion of these regulations, see *Schreiber, W.*, Handbuch, 2002, especially pp. 255-306.

135 *Blais, A./Massicotte, L./Yoshinaka, A.*, Right to vote, 2001, p. 42. See Chapter 2.1.1.

enacted over time. The first section of the table shows changes in membership criteria, while the second section displays reforms of the competence criteria. The rows of the tables visualize the restrictions that were in force during each Bundestag election since 1949. Changes that were enacted over time are highlighted in italics. Ellipses show where regulations were abolished. In the following, the most important legal developments will be commented on in turn.

Of the five electoral restrictions to the franchise, the citizenship/ethnicity restriction has remained most stable over time (see column 'citizenship/ ethnicity' in first section of Table 2). Since the first election in 1949, the Federal Election Acts have restricted the franchise to German citizens and ethnic Germans. Since 1952, the Federal Election Acts have explicitly referred to Article 116(1) of the Basic Law to define who is considered to be German.

The second membership restriction, residence, has been subject to more frequent changes (column 'residence' in Table 2). During the first Bundestag election in 1949 expatriates were not entitled to vote. This option was first introduced by the Second Federal Election Act in 1953. Civil servants, employees and workers employed in public service who were sent abroad on duty but lived close to the German borders as well as the members of their household became entitled to vote. From the third Bundestag election, this regulation was successively widened to include other groups of expatriates. First, the requirement that expatriates employed in public service live close to the German borders was dropped and the suffrage was extended to soldiers staying abroad in 1956. Thirty years later, in 1985, all German citizens living abroad became entitled to participate in Bundestag elections, provided that they had ever lived in Germany for at least three consecutive months after May 1949 and fulfilled all other electoral criteria.[136] The requirement of previous residence was introduced to ensure that electors had at least a minimum connection to Germany and basic knowledge of political processes and parties.[137] In addition, the law of 1985 distinguished between German citizens living in member states of the Council of

[136] Before German reunification, only residence in the old Länder of the Federal Republic of Germany was relevant. Since reunification, previous residence in the German Democratic Republic is also taken into account (See *Schreiber, W.*, Handbuch, 2002, p. 285).

[137] See *Schreiber, W.*, Handbuch, 2002, p. 286.

Europe[138] and German citizens in other countries. Germans living in Council of Europe member states were entitled to vote in Bundestag elections without any time restriction, while Germans in third countries were granted the right to vote during the first ten years of their stay abroad. In 1998, this period was extended to 25 years. According to Schreiber, the privileged position of Germans in member states of the Council of Europe was intended to reflect the close political, social and economic ties and geographic proximity between these countries and Germany. It was assumed that expatriates in these countries would remain better informed about political developments than German expatriates in third countries.[139] During the most recent reform in 2008, the distinction between expatriates in Council of Europe countries and expatriates in third countries was abolished. All German citizens who live abroad are today entitled to vote in Bundestag elections, provided that they have ever lived in Germany for at least three months and fulfil all other electoral criteria. If they move back to Germany, they continue to enjoy the franchise without any interruptions. By contrast, Germans who have never lived in Germany, for instance because they were born and raised abroad, only acquire the right to vote after having lived in Germany for at least three months.[140]

The third membership restriction which has limited access to the franchise in all Bundestag elections is law abidingness (column 'law abidingness', first section of Table 2). This restriction also has been changed frequently, indicating that the status of prison inmates and convicted criminals has been a contentious issue. The first Election Act of 1949 excluded all prison inmates and persons who have been deprived of the right to vote through court ruling from participating in elections. In addition, persons who had been disenfranchised in the process of denazification on the basis of state regulations could not participate in the Bundestag election of 1949. Persons who were not yet classified in the denazification process, but had already been convicted or dismissed from their

---

[138] In 1985, Austria, Belgium, Cyprus, Denmark, France, Germany, Greece, Iceland, Ireland, Italy, Liechtenstein, Luxembourg, Malta, Netherlands, Norway, Portugal, Spain, Sweden, Switzerland, Turkey and the United Kingdom were members of the Council of Europe. Since then, other European countries have joined.

[139] *Schreiber, W.*, Handbuch, 2002, p. 283 ff.

[140] See *Schreiber, W.*, Handbuch, 2002, p. 267 f.

jobs or positions due to a connection with the Nazi regime were also disenfranchised. In the later Federal Election Acts, the latter two reasons for disenfranchisement were not included anymore. The process of denazification thus only played a role during the first Bundestag election.

In addition to prison inmates and persons who had lost the right to vote through court ruling, the second Federal Election Act of 1953 mandated the disenfranchisement of persons for whom custodial measures of rehabilitation or incapacitation (*mit Freiheitsentziehung verbundene Maßregel der Sicherung und Besserung)* had been ordered by court judgment. These measures include preventive detention, placement in detoxification clinics or psychiatric hospitals.[141] These regulations did not remain unchanged for long. Already for the next Bundestag elections of 1957, the general disenfranchisement of prisoners was abolished. The general disenfranchisement of persons under custodial measures of rehabilitation or incapacitation ended in 1974. After the latter reform, only convicted criminals who were placed in a psychiatric hospital because they committed a crime in a state of insanity or diminished responsibility (*Schuldunfähigkeit oder verminderte Schuldfähigkeit*) and were considered a threat to society remained excluded from the franchise. Persons who were undergoing custodial addiction treatment or who were placed in preventive detention, by contrast, became eligible to vote. In 1985, finally, criminals who had committed a crime in a state of diminished responsibility acquired the right to vote. Under current law convicted criminals thus remain excluded from the franchise in two cases only: First, if they are placed in a psychiatric hospital by court ruling because they committed a criminal deed in a state of insanity and are judged to be a menace to society. Second, judges can disenfranchise criminals for two to five years. This is however possible only if convicts have committed certain political crimes such as high treason, manipulation of elections or espionage activities. Other types of crime such as murder or theft do not lead to disenfranchisement.[142]

---

[141] See *Schreiber, W.*, Handbuch, 2002, p. 299.

[142] See *Schreiber, W.*, Handbuch, 2002, p. 300 for a complete list of cases in which a court can order disenfranchisement.

Table 2: Restrictions of the franchise based on membership and competence in Germany in years of Bundestag elections (1949-2010)

Year of Bundestag election	Membership		
	Citizenship/Ethnicity: Which citizenship groups are entitled to vote?	**Residence:** Which groups of expatriates are entitled to vote?	**Law abidingness:** Which groups of convicted criminals are disenfranchised?
1949	German citizens and ethnic German refugees and resettlers (since 1952 explicit reference to Art. 116(1) GG)	---	Persons who ◦ have lost their civil rights due to judicial sentence ◦ are serving a sentence in prison ◦ have lost their right to vote due to state regulations on political cleansing ◦ are not yet classified in the process of denazification, but who have been convicted or dismissed, suspended or excluded from their job or influential position in public or private life by the military government owing to connections to the Nazi regime
1953		*Civil servants, employees and workers in public service who are living abroad close to the German border by orders of their employer as well as members of their household*	Persons ◦ who have lost their civil rights *or right to vote* due to a judicial sentence ◦ who are serving a sentence in prison ◦ *[...]* ◦ *[...]* ◦ *for whom custodial measures of rehabilitation or incapacitation (mit Freiheitsentziehung verbundene Maßregel der Sicherung und Besserung) have been ordered by court ruling*
1957 1961 1965 1969		Civil servants, *soldiers,* employees and workers in public service who are living abroad *[...]* by orders of their employer as well as members of their household	Persons ◦ who have lost their civil rights or right to vote due to a judicial sentence ◦ *[...]* ◦ for whom custodial measures of rehabilitation or incapacitation have been ordered by court ruling

Continuation of Table 2

<table>
<tr><th rowspan="2">Year of Bundestag election</th><th colspan="3">Membership</th></tr>
<tr><th>Citizenship/Ethnicity:
Which citizenship groups are entitled to vote?</th><th>Residence:
Which groups of expatriates are entitled to vote?</th><th>Law abidingness:
Which groups of convicted criminals are disenfranchised?</th></tr>
<tr><td>1972</td><td rowspan="7">German citizens and ethnic German refugees and resettlers (since 1952 explicit reference to Art. 116(1) GG)</td><td rowspan="4">Civil servants, soldiers, employees and workers in public service who are living abroad by orders of their employer as well as members of their household</td><td>Persons
◦ who have lost their [...] right to vote due to judicial sentence
◦ for whom custodial measures of rehabilitation or incapacitation have been ordered by court ruling</td></tr>
<tr><td>1976</td><td rowspan="3">Persons who
◦ have lost their right to vote due to judicial sentence
◦ [...]
◦ are accommodated in a psychiatric hospital because they committed a crime in a state of insanity or diminished responsibility (Schuldunfähigkeit oder verminderte Schuldfähigkeit)</td></tr>
<tr><td>1980</td></tr>
<tr><td>1983</td></tr>
<tr><td>1987</td><td rowspan="3">◦ Civil servants, soldiers, employees and workers in public service who are living abroad by orders of their employer as well as members of their household
◦ Germans living in member states of the Council of Europe, provided that they have lived in Germany for at least three months since 23. May 1949
◦ Germans living in other foreign countries if they have lived in Germany for at least three months and if they did not move from there more than ten years ago.</td><td rowspan="3">Persons who
◦ have lost their right to vote due to a judicial sentence
◦ are accommodated in a psychiatric hospital because they committed a crime in a state of insanity [...]</td></tr>
<tr><td>1990</td></tr>
<tr><td>1994</td></tr>
</table>

Continuation of Table 2

Year of Bundestag election	Membership		
	Citizenship/Ethnicity: Which citizenship groups are entitled to vote?	**Residence:** Which groups of expatriates are entitled to vote?	**Law abidingness:** Which groups of convicted criminals are disenfranchised?
1998	German citizens and ethnic German refugees and resettlers (since 1952 explicit reference to Art. 116(1) GG)	◦ Civil servants, soldiers, employees and workers in public service who are living abroad by orders of their employer as well as members of their household ◦ Germans living in member states of the Council of Europe, provided that they have lived in Germany for at least three months since 23. May 1949 ◦ Germans living in other foreign countries if they have lived in Germany for at least three months and if they did not move from there more than *25* years ago.	Persons who ◦ have lost their right to vote due to a judicial sentence ◦ are accommodated in a psychiatric hospital because they committed a crime in a state of insanity
2002			
2005			
2009		*All Germans living abroad provided that they have lived in Germany for at least three months since 23. May 1949*	

Continuation of Table 2

Year of Bundestag election	Competence	
	Age: Which minimum voting age applies?	**Mental health:** Which groups of mentally impaired persons are disenfranchised?
1949	21	Persons who are ◦ under disability (entmündigt) ◦ put under temporary tutelage (vorläufige Vormundschaft) ◦ put under guardianship owing to mental infirmity (wegen geistigen Gebrechens unter Pflegschaft) ◦ placed in a psychiatric hospital due to mental illness or infirmity (Geisteskrankheit oder Geistesschwäche)
1953		
1957		
1961		
1965		
1969		
1972	*18*	
1976		Persons who are ◦ under disability ◦ *[...]* ◦ put under guardianship owing to mental infirmity ◦ *permanently* placed in a psychiatric hospital due to mental illness or infirmity *owing to a judicial decision based on Länder law*
1980		Persons who are ◦ under disability ◦ put under guardianship owing to mental infirmity, *unless they can prove by means of an attestation of the guardianship court that the guardianship was ordered on the basis of their agreement* ◦ permanently placed in a psychiatric hospital due to mental illness owing to a judicial decision based on Länder law
1983		
1987		Persons who are ◦ under disability ◦ put under guardianship owing to mental infirmity, unless they can prove by means of an attestation of the guardianship court that the guardianship was ordered on the basis of their agreement ◦ *[...]*
1990		

Continuation of Table 2

Year of Bundestag election	Competence	
	Age: Which minimum voting age applies?	**Mental health:** Which groups of mentally impaired persons are disenfranchised?
1994	18	*Persons for whom a custodian (Betreuer) has been appointed not only by means of a temporary order to attend to all their affairs*
1998		
2002		
2005		
2009		

All parts of the table:
Source: Own analyses based on original legal documents which are available at the online platform of the Federal Legal Gazette (*Bundesgesetzblatt*): www.bundesgesetzblatt.de. The legal sources that were consulted to create this table are shown in Annex 2 at the end of this study. The author of this study is responsible for the English translation.

In addition to membership criteria, the electoral law has included two competence restrictions since 1949. The first of these restrictions is age (column 'age' in second section of Table 2). The Federal Election Act of 1949 stated that only Germans aged 21 years or older enjoy the active right to vote. This age limit was maintained until 1970/72. In these years, the Basic Law and the Federal Election Act were amended, respectively, and the minimum voting age reduced to 18 years. According to Jesse, the reform was mainly motivated by a previous reform of the Compulsory Military Service Act which had reduced the age at which young men could be drafted to military service from 20 to 18 years. Parliamentarians across party lines agreed that if 18- to 20- year-old citizens could be forced to fight in case of war, they should have the right to participate in elections and influence political developments. Many proponents of the voting age reform also suggested that most 18- to 20-year old citizens were responsible and well-informed about political developments and could therefore be trusted to make reasoned choices at the ballot box. Finally, the voting age reform was used as a means to show willingness to compromise towards students who were protesting at the time.[143] Overall, the proposal to lower the voting age met with little resistance in parliament. The reform was adopted without a dissenting vote and only few abstentions.[144] Since the reform of the early 1970s, the minimum voting age for Bundestag elections has remained at 18 years.

The second competence restriction that has been used throughout the last sixty years is mental health (column 'mental health' in second section of Table 2). The first Federal Election Act of 1949 provided for the disenfranchisement of persons who were under disability *(entmündigt)*, placed under temporary tutelage (*vorläufige Vormundschaft)*, under guardianship (*Pflegschaft*) or in a psychiatric hospital owing to mental illness or infirmity (*Geisteskrankheit oder Geistesschwäche)*. Most of these legal provisions were changed at least once or abolished. The first reform in 1975 abolished the disenfranchisement of persons

[143] See *Jesse, E.*, Wahlrecht, 1985, pp. 325-340, for a detailed description of these and other arguments that were exchanged during the debate.

[144] See *Jesse, E.*, Wahlrecht, 1985, p. 330.

under temporary tutelage and persons in psychiatric hospitals were henceforth only excluded from voting if they had been permanently placed there through judicial decision based on state law. Persons who sought treatment in a psychiatric hospital by their own wish thus gained the franchise. The next legal reform in 1979 concerned persons under guardianship. They regained the right to vote from the Bundestag election in 1980 if the guardianship had been ordered by court on the basis of their consent. Persons who were under guardianship against their will or who were unable to express their opinion on the matter remained excluded from voting. In 1985, the franchise was further extended to persons who were in psychiatric hospitals due to a court judgement based on state law. According to Schreiber, this reform was motivated by considerations of equity. Before the reform, the enfranchisement or disenfranchisement of mentally ill persons depended essentially on whether they were taken care of by their families or whether they were placed in a psychiatric institution either on the basis on their own will or by court judgement. Only the last group of individuals had been excluded from the franchise. This constituted an inequality in treatment which eventually triggered the reform.[145] The latest legal reform was enacted in 1992. It abolished the previous regulations and provided that mentally impaired persons may only be disenfranchised if a custodian *(Betreuer)* has been appointed by a guardianship court to permanently take care of all of their affairs. In other words, where a custodian has been appointed to administer only some aspects of the live of a mentally impaired person, such as finances, this person retains the right to vote.[146] It is currently discussed whether the remaining restriction based on mental health stands in contradiction to the UN Convention on the Rights of Persons with Disabilities.[147] This Convention, which has been signed and ratified by Germany, demands the political inclusion of disabled persons (see chapter 2.1.3.).

[145] *Schreiber, W.*, Handbuch, 2002, p. 306.
[146] See *Schreiber, W.*, Handbuch, 2002, p. 302 f.
[147] See *Author not named*, Wahlrecht, 2011.

Apart from changes in terms of content, the electoral law has also changed in terms of its territorial application. Upon German reunification in 1990 the electoral principles guiding Bundestag elections became applicable in the new Länder.[148] German citizens living in West Berlin also became eligible to vote in 1990. Before then, the Berlin City Parliament (*Abgeordnetenhaus*) used to elect 22 parliamentarians who represented citizens living in West Berlin in the Bundestag. This practice only changed upon reunification.[149]

Overall, the membership and competency criteria defined in the Federal Election Acts have been frequently changed during the last decades, although not all criteria have been subject to the same number of reforms. Current disputes about whether access to the franchise should be reformed due to demographic changes are not a historical anomaly, but stand in a long tradition of negotiation and reform.

The citizenship/ethnicity restriction is one of the most important restrictions to the franchise which remains in force today. The acquisition of German citizenship remains a necessary requirement to be included in the electorate and conversely, loss of German citizenship entails disenfranchisement. Due to the importance of this electoral criterion, it will briefly be illustrated in the next chapter how German citizenship can be acquired and lost.

2.3.3. The Citizenship Act

Citizenship is defined as "membership in a state".[150] It entails a number of rights, but also obligations. According to a classical definition by T. H. Marshall, the rights of citizenship encompass civil rights, social rights and political rights, among them the right to vote. The obligations of citizens include the duty to pay taxes, to obey the laws and to fight for the country in case of

---

148 See *Schreiber, W.*, Handbuch, 2002, p. 71.

149 For more information on this point see *Schreiber, W.*, Handbuch, 2002, p. 275. Exceptionally, citizens living in Berlin could vote in Bundestag elections if they had a second residence in one of the other German Länder. In this case, they could vote in the respective electoral district.

150 *Hammar, T.*, Democracy, 1990, p. 3. 'Nationality' is sometimes used as a synonym for citizenship in the academic literature. The concept is however also used to denote membership in an ethnic group (*Bauböck, R.*, Citizenship, 2006, p. 17). In order to avoid these terminological ambiguities, the term nationality will be avoided in this work. Only 'citizenship' will be used to describe the legal membership of individuals in the German state.

war.[151] Today, many of these rights and obligations are no longer tied to citizenship but to residence and are therefore shared by long-term foreign residents. Some core obligations and rights, such as the right to vote, however remain the prerogative of citizens.[152] Access to German citizenship and thereby to the full rights and obligations of a citizen is determined by the Citizenship Act (in German: *Staatsangehörigkeitsgesetz; StAG*). It distinguishes between two main contexts in which citizenship can be acquired: at birth via ascription and at later stages in life via naturalization procedures. These two ways of citizenship acquisition will be briefly described in turn.

For children who are born in Germany, the Citizenship Act distinguishes two main modes of citizenship acquisition. They are illustrated in Figure 3. On the one hand (mode 1, left branch of the figure), German citizenship is acquired by descent from a citizen ('ius sanguinis', literally: the law of the blood). All children who are born in Germany and have at least one German parent become German citizens at birth (Article 4(1) StAG).[153]

In addition to German citizenship, these children may also acquire a foreign citizenship at birth, if one or both parents are (also) citizens of a foreign country (1a in Figure 3). In this case, the children become dual citizens at birth. If both parents are German citizens only, no further citizenship is acquired (1b in Figure 3). For the acquisition of the right to vote, it is of no relevance whether the children are dual citizens or not. All children who acquire German citizenship qua ius sanguinis acquire the right to vote once they are 18 years old unless they are disenfranchised on the basis of another membership or competence criterion.

On the other hand (mode 2, right branch of Figure 3), German citizenship can be acquired by birth in Germany ('ius soli', literally: the law of soil). This mode of citizenship acquisition is relatively new. It was only introduced after a reform of

---

151 See *Turner, B. S.*, Erosion, 2001, p. 189 f.; *Masing, J.*, Wandel, 2001, p. 57.

152 See *Diehl, C./Blohm, M.*, Rights, 2003, p. 142 f.

153 Further specific rules apply in individual cases: Children who are born out of wedlock to a foreign mother and a German father only acquire German citizenship if the father officially acknowledges the child as his own or if his paternity is established by court ruling (Art. 4(1) and 5 StAG). A child of unknown parents that is found in Germany acquires German citizenship (Art. 4(2) StAG). Children who are born in a foreign country to German parents who were themselves born abroad may only acquire German citizenship under specific circumstances (Art. 4(4) StAG; for more information see also *Masing, J.*, Wandel, 2001, p. 5 ff.).

the Citizenship Act in 2000. Since that year, children of foreign parents acquire German citizenship at birth if at least one parent has been permanently and lawfully resident in Germany for at least eight years and is in possession of a right of permanent residence. A right of permanent residence may be acquired by foreigners who have been in possession of a temporary residence permit for five years and who fulfil other requirements, for instance in terms of language, employment and law abidingness. Citizens from EU member states, Iceland, Norway and Liechtenstein who are entitled to freedom of movement also have a right to permanent residence. If foreign parents do not fulfil these conditions, their child does not acquire German citizenship at birth but only the foreign citizenship(s) of the parents (2b in Figure 3). These children do not acquire the right to vote when they turn 18, unless they obtain German citizenship via naturalization at some point during their childhood or adolescence. If at least one of the parents fulfils the ius soli-requirements, their children acquire German citizenship at birth (2a in Figure 3). These children are likely to acquire the foreign citizenship(s) of their parents as well, so that they become dual – or even triple – citizens.

In Germany, these children who are born in Germany, have foreign parents and have acquired German citizenship qua ius soli are referred to as 'ius soli-children' (*ius soli-Kinder*), 'ius soli-Germans' (*ius soli-Deutsche*) or 'ius soli-citizens' (*ius soli-Bürger*).[154] In the remainder of this work, these terms will be used interchangeably. German citizens who have acquired citizenship via the ius sanguinis-principle or via naturalization will be referred to as the 'German majority population' in order to distinguish them from ius soli-citizens.

In terms of voting rights, ius soli-children are in a curious position. They acquire the right to vote when they turn 18 years old but may lose this right again. The potential loss of the franchise is triggered by the so-called 'obligation to choose' (*Optionspflicht*): When ius soli-children become 18 years old, they are legally obliged to choose between their German and their foreign citizenship(s) within a period of five years, i.e. until their 23rd birthday.

---

[154] See *Lämmermann, F.*, Ius soli, 2011, p. 2; *Göbel-Zimmermann, R./Eichhorn, A.*, Entwicklungen I, 2010, p. 295.

Figure 3: Acquisition of German citizenship at birth

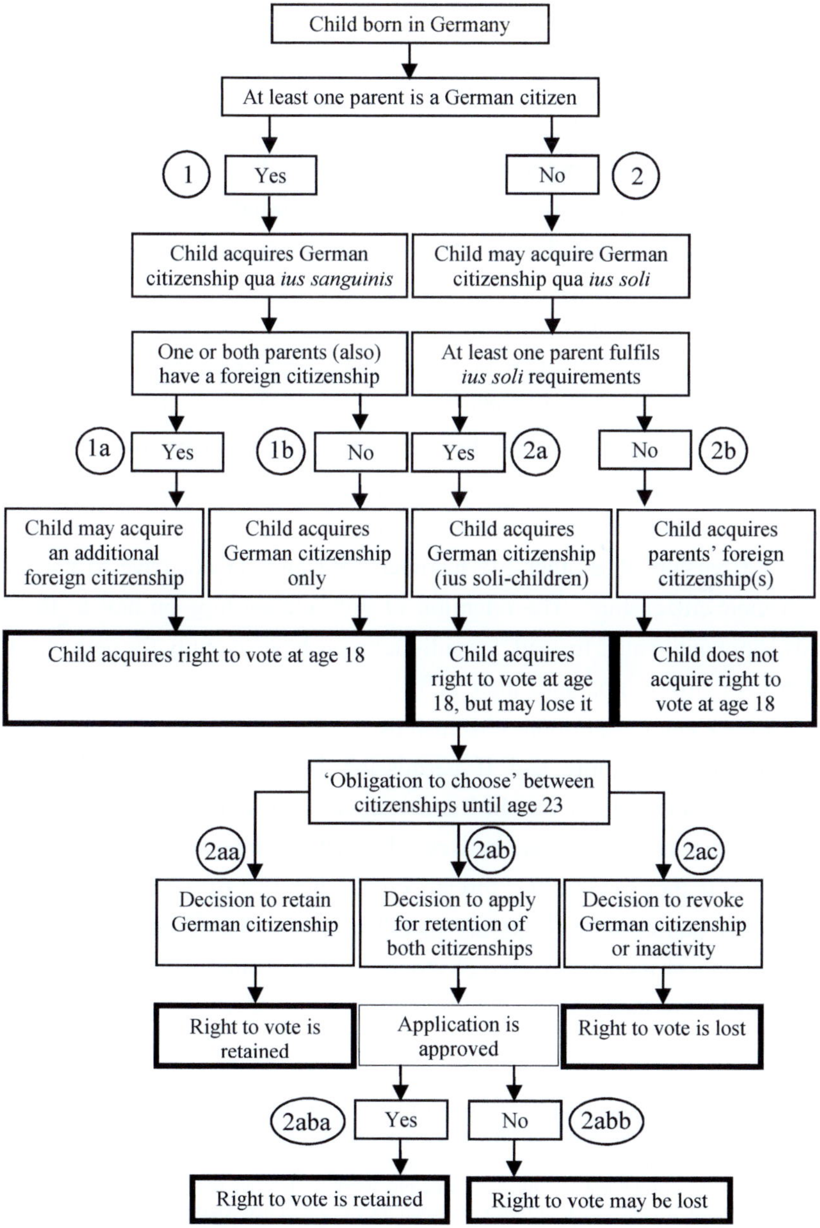

Source: Own illustration based on Citizenship Act.

The German citizenship authorities inform ius soli-children on their 18th birthday of this obligation and the following legal options which apply.[155]
First, ius soli-citizens can retain their German citizenship and the right to vote beyond their 23rd birthday if they provide a proof that they have renounced all other citizenships (2aa in Figure 3). Second, if ius-soli children fail to provide this proof or if they do not make a choice at all, they lose their German citizenship and the right to vote on their 23rd birthday. The same legal consequence applies if they choose to retain their foreign citizenship and revoke the German citizenship (2ac).
Third, in certain cases ius soli-citizens are exempted from the obligation to choose and are entitled to retain both citizenships beyond their 23rd birthday (2ab). This is the case if the other country of citizenship does not allow renunciation of citizenship or attaches unreasonable conditions to it or if the revocation of the foreign citizenship would result in important financial or economic disadvantages. Ius soli-children who are recognized refugees or who hold the citizenship of another EU member state also do not have to choose between their citizenships. The retention of both citizenships on any of these grounds is not automatic. Instead, ius soli-Germans have to apply for permission to retain both citizenships until their 21st birthday. Ius soli-children who fail to apply in time cannot retain both citizenships but have to make a choice. If ius soli-citizens apply in time and if permission is granted, they retain both citizenships and the right to vote in Bundestag elections (2aba). If permission is not granted, they have to choose between their citizenships and only retain the right to vote if they revoke the foreign citizenship (2abb). Overall, ius soli-Germans may therefore be temporary members of the demos only. They only become permanent members of the electorate if they retain German citizenship beyond their 23rd birthday.[156]

---

155 Art. 29 StAG. See also *Masing, J.*, Wandel, 2001, pp. 9 and 13 ff.; *Beauftragte der Bundesregierung für Migration, Flüchtlinge und Integration*, Migrationsbericht, 2010, p. 456 f.

156 German citizenship law thus distinguishes between two groups of dual citizens: Germans who acquire two citizenships via the ius soli-principle (born to foreign parents in Germany) are obliged to choose between their citizenships when they come of age. Germans who acquire two citizenships via the ius sanguinis principle (born to parents with German and a foreign

As stated above, the ius soli-regulation applied as of 1. January 2000. Children who were born in Germany to foreign parents before then could only become members of the German demos via naturalization.[157] One exception however exists: When the ius soli-regulation was introduced in 2000, it provided for a transitory regulation that applied to children of foreign parents who had been born in Germany between 1990 and 1999. The regulation entitled these children to retrospectively acquire German citizenship if at least one parent had fulfilled the ius soli-requirements at the time of birth and still fulfilled them.[158] In order to make use of this legal option, the parents had to apply for citizenship in the name of their children within one year after the enactment of the reform, i.e. until 31. December 2000.[159]

Apart from citizenship acquisition at birth, German citizenship can be acquired at later stages in life through naturalization. Naturalization requirements have been frequently changed during the past twenty years.[160] Until the early 1990s, the naturalization procedure followed the Nationality Act of the German Empire and States, enacted in 1914, and administrative guidelines on naturalization from 1977.[161] The naturalization requirements that were defined by these two legal documents were relatively strict. Foreign residents could only acquire German citizenship if they had legally lived in Germany for at least ten years (exceptions existed, for instance for spouses of German citizens), were integrated into German society and spoke the German language, did not depend on public welfare and were of respectable moral conduct (*unbescholtener Lebenswandel*). The naturalization guidelines of 1977 further required that naturalization applicants renounce their previous citizenship. Exceptions existed in certain cases. Naturalization fees could amount to several thousand Deutsche Mark

---

citzenship) do not share this obligation. They are entitled to retain all citizenships beyond childhood and adolescence (see *Masing, J.*, Wandel, 2001, p. 11).

157 See *Hagedorn, H.*, Einbürgerung, 2001, p. 115.

158 Article 40b StAG.

159 See *Worbs, S.*, Einbürgerung, 2008, p. 12.

160 For a discussion of developments in naturalization law, see *Hagedorn, H.*, Liberale Trends, 1999 and *Hailbronner, K.*, Germany, 2006.

161 Nationality Act of the German Empire and States (in German: *Reichs- und Staatsangehörigkeitsgesetz; RuStAG*) of 22.07.1913; Guidelines on naturalization (in German: *Einbürgerungsrichtlinien*) of 15.12.1977.

(DM). Even if all conditions were fulfilled, no automatic right to naturalization accrued. Instead, each act of naturalization was decided upon discretionarily by the citizenship authorities and was only granted if a 'public interest' in the naturalization of the applicant existed.[162]

This practice slowly changed in the 1990s, when several reforms were enacted. The Aliens Act of 1990 facilitated naturalization requirements for long-term foreign residents and young foreign residents who had grown up in Germany. It also reduced the naturalization fee.[163] In 1993, another legal reform for the first time introduced a right to naturalization for long-term foreign residents. They were entitled to acquire German citizenship in case they met certain requirements, notably a period of legal residence of 15 years, lack of criminal conviction, proof of income security and if they renounced their previous citizenship. Long-term foreign residents no longer had to prove fluency in German or assimilation to German society as a prerequisite for naturalization. Young adults aged 16 to 23 who had grown up in Germany were also given the right to naturalize.[164]

A further reform of the German citizenship law was enacted in 2000. In addition to the introduction of the ius soli-principle (see above), the reform reduced the residence period required for naturalization from 15 to 8 years (it provided for further reductions for specific groups of foreign residents) and increased the number of cases in which the retention of the previous citizenship is tolerated. The law also re-introduced the language requirement as a precondition for naturalization and introduced the requirement that applicants pledge their loyalty to the free and democratic order of the Basic Law. It also raised the naturalization fee. The specific naturalization rules that previously applied to

---

[162] For detailed information see the chapter on historic developments of citizenship law in *Hagedorn, H.*, Einbürgerung, 2001, pp. 35-100; also see *Hailbronner, K.*, Citizenship, 1989, pp. 67-70.

[163] Act to Revise the Aliens law (in German: *Gesetz zur Neuregelung des Ausländerrechts*) of 09.07.1990; see also *Hagedorn, H.*, Einbürgerung, 2001, pp. 57 f. and 89 f.; *Hailbronner, K.*, Germany, 2006, p. 220 f.

[164] Act to Change Regulations on Asylum Procedures, Aliens Law and Citizenship Law (in German: *Gesetz zur Änderung asylverfahrens-, ausländer- und staatsangehörigkeitsrechtlicher Vorschriften)* of 30.06.1993; see also *Rittstieg, H.*, Dual citizenship, 1994, p. 114 f.; *Hagedorn, H.*, Einbürgerung, 2001, pp. 79 and 90.

young foreign residents and long-term foreign residents were cancelled. The new naturalization rules now applied to all foreign residents. Since the reform of 2000, further amendments of the Citizenship Act have been adopted, among them the introduction of integration courses.[165] Overall, the reforms of the citizenship law since 1990 were enacted with the aim of encouraging foreign residents to naturalize and to become members of the German demos.[166]

Under current law, citizenship may be acquired in the following circumstances: Foreign children acquire German citizenship if they are adopted by a German citizen or if one of their parents naturalizes. Adult foreign residents have a right to be naturalized if they have legally lived in Germany for at least eight years, have expressed their commitment to the constitutional order of Germany, possess a right to permanent residence, speak the German language, have proven knowledge of the German legal and political system and society as well as their ability to maintain themselves and their families without recourse to social security benefits.[167] The applicants for naturalization also need to be law abiding and have to renounce their previous citizenship unless one of several exceptions applies to them. The retention of the first citizenship is for instance allowed for refugees and asylum seekers, citizens from other EU countries and from Switzerland, ethnic Germans, persons who are aged 60 or older and persons from countries which do not allow the revocation of citizenship or only allow it under 'unreasonable' conditions. Further, foreign residents who have not yet lived for eight years in Germany can apply for naturalization if they fulfil specific requirements. The naturalization offices decide discretionarily about these applications. Foreign residents who have successfully taken part in an integration course, speak the German language very well, are married to or the life partner of a German citizen as well as former German citizens can (re-)

---

165 See *Hailbronner, K.*, Country report, 2010 and *Göbel-Zimmermann, R./Eichhorn, A.*, Entwicklungen I, 2010 for a detailed discussion of recent changes.

166 Act to Reform the Citizenship Law (in German: *Gesetz zur Reform des Staatsangehörigkeits-rechts – Staatsangehörigkeitsgesetz; StAG*) of 15.07.1999; see also *Hailbronner, K.*, Country report, 2010, pp. 6-8 and 15; *Hagedorn, H.*, Einbürgerung, 2001, pp. 61-64 and 69; *Masing, J.*, Wandel, 2001, pp. 11-19.

167 The requirement that applicants may not depend on social security can be waived in certain cases (see *Worbs, S.*, Einbürgerung, 2008, p. 12).

acquire German citizenship under privileged conditions. If a foreign person has erroneously been considered and treated as a citizen by the German public authorities for twelve years and is not responsible for this, the person may also acquire German citizenship. Finally, ethnic German resettlers and their family members are entitled to acquire German citizenship once they have proven their German descent and knowledge of the German language.[168] Upon acquisition of German citizenship all these different groups of persons acquire the right to vote, provided that they are not disenfranchised by one of the other electoral criteria.[169]

In addition to regulating the acquisition of German citizenship, the Citizenship Act also defines how German citizenship may be lost. Under current law this is possible in the following cases: German citizens can revoke the citizenship if they are in possession of another citizenship and thus do not become stateless. In addition, Germans may be deprived of their citizenship if they voluntarily join the armed forces of another country of which they are also citizens without having been entitled to do so by the German Ministry of Defence. Citizens who voluntarily acquire a foreign citizenship also lose the German citizenship. In the latter case, exceptions exist. The German citizenship is for instance not lost by Germans who acquire the citizenship of another EU country or Switzerland. Germans may also be deprived of their citizenship if they acquired it by fraud. German children who are adopted by a foreign citizen and thereby acquire a foreign citizenship lose the German citizenship. Finally, German citizenship is lost by ius soli-citizen if they revoke it or lose it when coming off age (see above).[170] Persons who lose the German citizenship for any of these reasons thereby lose the right to vote in Bundestag elections. Citizenship and the franchise are thus intricately linked – the acquisition of German citizenship is a prerequisite to become a member of the German demos and loss of citizenship entails exclusion from it.

---

[168] See current version of the StAG of 22.07.1913, last amended by Legal Act of 01.06.2012; also see *Hailbronner, K.*, Country report, 2010.

[169] See *Schreiber, W.*, Handbuch, 2002, p. 262.

[170] See current version of the StAG of 22.07.1913, last amended by Legal Act of 01.06.2012. Also see *Hailbronner, K.*, Country report, 2010, p. 16; *Masing, J.*, Wandel, 2001, pp. 16-18.

2.4. Influence of changing restrictions on the German electorate, 1949-2010

Taken as a whole, the legal reforms of the past sixty years have made the German electorate more inclusive. Since the first Bundestag election of 1949, the right to vote was extended to most criminal convicts and many mentally ill persons, 18- to 20-year old citizens and expatriates. The acquisition of German citizenship and thereby of voting rights has become a right for foreign residents once they fulfil naturalization requirements and for many children born to foreign parents in Germany. In addition, Germans living in the new Länder and citizens in Berlin became eligible to vote in Bundestag elections after German reunification.

While detailed information is available on these legal developments, it is not always possible to quantify how they have shaped the size and age structure of the demos. Comprehensive statistics on the number of persons who were disenfranchised over time and how legal reforms have changed these numbers do not exist. Data on the effect of legal reforms could only be obtained in a few individual cases by consulting population statistics, electoral statistics, crime statistics and birth statistics as well as secondary literature. These data are commented on in the following by considering each electoral restriction in turn.

Information on the number of foreign residents who have been excluded from voting in Bundestag elections over time due to lack of citizenship can be obtained from the population statistics (*Fortschreibung des Bevölkerungsstandes*). These statistics provide data on the size and age structure of the population of Germany at the end of each year. Since 1970, the statistics distinguish between Germans and foreign residents.[171] The data show that the number of foreign residents who are disenfranchised on the basis of the citizenship restriction has increased over time from 2.7 million persons (in 1970) to 7.2 million persons (in 2010) or, expressed as a proportion of the total population, from 4.5% to 8.8% (Figure 4).

---

[171] See *Statistisches Bundesamt*, Fortschreibung, 2008. It has to be noted that the data shown here may not be exact, since the population statistics are subject to several sources of error. For more details on data quality, see Chapter 4.1.3.1.

Figure 4: Size of the foreign population in Germany (all ages) in absolute numbers and as a proportion of the total population, 1970-2010

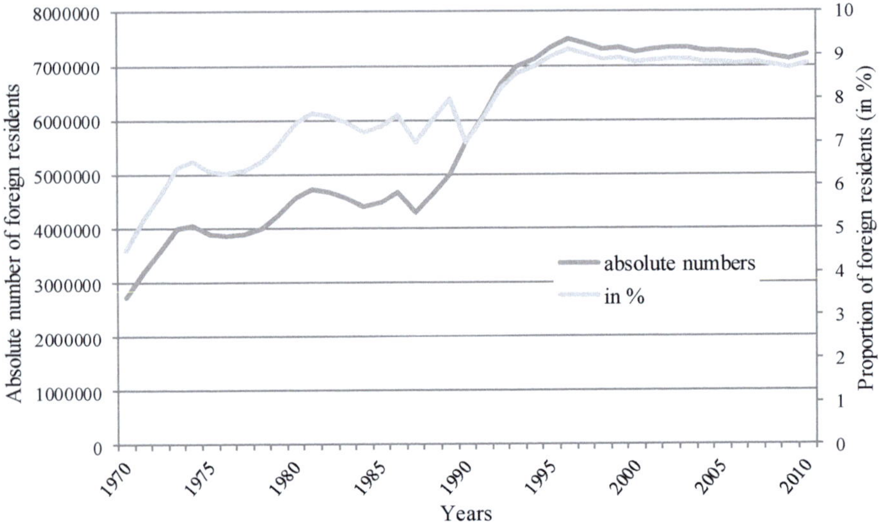

Source: Own calculations based on Population Statistics of 1970-2010, provided by the Federal Statistical Office of Germany.

Note: Data for the years 1970 to 1989 refer to the former West German states only.

Since the citizenship restriction has not been subject to any reform since 1949, developments in the size of this disenfranchised population group must be the result of demographic processes.[172] These processes will be described in more detail in Chapter 3. In addition, changes in citizenship law may have played a role. As was described above, different reforms of the Citizenship Act have been adopted since the early 1990s. These reforms aimed at facilitating naturalization and encouraging foreign residents to acquire German citizenship. The reform may have led to changes in naturalization numbers and thereby reduced the size of the foreign population in Germany.

Figure 5 reveals that the naturalization rate in fact increased after the first reforms of the Citizenship Act in the early 1990s. While only 0.4% of all foreign residents in West Germany became German citizens in 1989, the rate increased

---

172 In addition, statistical factors have had an influence: After the population census in West Germany in 1987, data of the foreign population were found to be too high and were corrected. The drop in the number and proportion of foreign residents in this year is attributable to this effect (*Kohls, M.*, Morbidität, 2011, p. 43).

rapidly to 2.3% in the year 2000. Naturalization numbers and the naturalization rate have declined again thereafter. Nonetheless, they remain at a higher level today than during the 1970s and 1980s.

Figure 5: Naturalization rate of foreign residents (all ages), 1974-2010

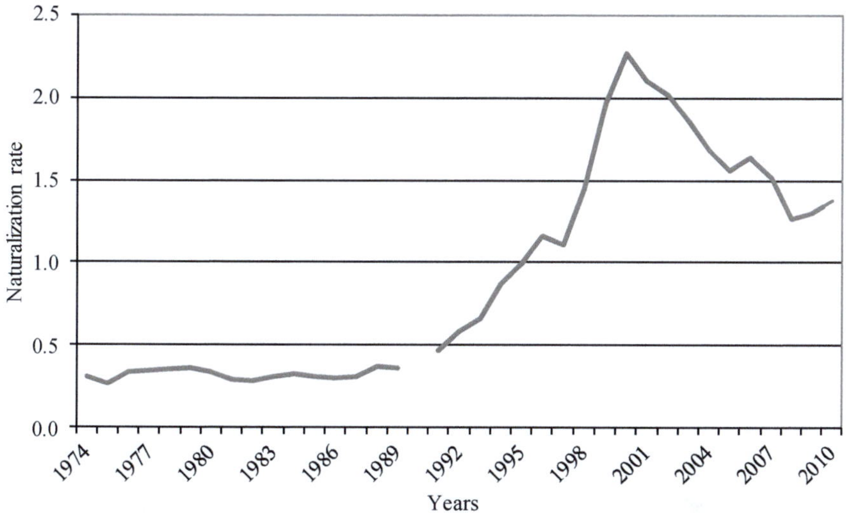

Source: Own calculations based on Naturalization Statistics and Population Statistics of 1974-2010, provided by the Federal Statistical Office.

Note: Data do not include acquisitions of citizenship by ethnic Germans and acquisitions of citizenship at birth based on the ius soli-principle. Data for the years 1974 to 1989 refer to the former West German states only. Value for 1990 was not calculated due to nominator-denominator mismatch: Population data of this year refer to the reunified Germany, while naturalization data refer to West Germany only. Data for the years 2000 to 2010 only refer to naturalization cases among foreign residents who are living in Germany. In earlier years, the statistics include persons who naturalized while living abroad.

At first sight, the naturalization trend thus suggests that the citizenship law reforms were successful in encouraging foreign residents to naturalize especially during the 1990s. However, this conclusion could be premature. Naturalization trends are not only influenced by changes in law, but are also dependent on the composition of the foreign population as well as on economic, social and political developments. Hence, while the different reforms of citizenship law may have influenced the naturalization rate over time, the changing trend may not be the result of legal changes alone. The influence of citizenship law on the number of citizenship acquisitions can be more straightforwardly determined in the case of ius soli citizens: One of the most important elements of the citizenship law reform in the year 2000 was the introduction of the ius soli-principle and the transitory rule which allowed children of foreign parents born between 1990 and 1999 to acquire German citizenship retrospectively. Around 49.000 children made use of the transitory rule and between 29.000 and 41.000 children became German citizens at birth each year between 2000 and 2010 (Figure 6). Overall, around 444.000 children have so far become German citizens based on the ius soli-principle.

Figure 6: Number of ius soli-children born between 1990 and 2010

Source: Birth Statistics and Naturalization Statistics of 2000-2010, provided by the Federal Statistical Office.

When they come of age, these ius soli-Germans acquire the right to vote. Whether they will retain this right in the long term depends on whether they will remain German citizens after their 23rd birthday. So far, only the first ius soli-cohorts born between 1990 and 1994 have come of age and have been informed of the obligation to choose between their citizenships. The first cohort of ius soli-citizens born in 1990 will have to make their decision until 2013. Comprehensive data on their decision-making behaviour will only be available in 2014. Starting from then, the number of individuals who acquired German

citizenship and thereby the right to vote as a result of citizenship reform of 2000 can be more precisely quantified. So far, it is only possible to quantify the number of ius soli-citizens who are potential future members of the demos.
It is also difficult to quantify the influence of the second membership criterion, residence, on the development of the German demos. As was described in the previous chapter, expatriates could not vote during the first Bundestag election in 1949. Over time successive legal reforms led to the enfranchisement of all German expatriates who have lived in Germany for more than three consecutive months. The number of expatriates who thereby obtained the right to vote is unknown since statistics of expatriates are not compiled in Germany. The only data that are available show the number of expatriates who have registered to receive election documents by mail. These data thus show the number of *registered* expatriate voters, not the number of *eligible* expatriate voters.[173] During the elections of 1987, 1990 and 1994, between 31.600 and 34.100 expatriates received election documents. After the reform of 1998, which extended voting rights of Germans living outside the Council of Europe area, the number of registered expatriates increased. Between 48.000 and 55.000 expatriates received election documents for the elections of 1998, 2002 and 2005. After the latest legal reform in 2008, around 66.000 persons participated during the Bundestag election of 2009.[174] Today, adult expatriates only remain disenfranchised if they have not lived in Germany for at least three consecutive months. The number of persons affected by this is not known.
While changes in electoral law may in part explain the increase in registered expatriate voters over time, demographic trends may also have played a role. The increase in registered voters may for instance reflect an increase in the number of German citizens who move abroad. In the absence of comprehensive statistics on the number of German expatriates, the respective influence of demography and law cannot be disentangled.

[173] Schreiber estimates that only a small proportion of all expatriates who would be eligible to participate in Bundestag elections actually makes use of this right. See *Schreiber, W.*, Handbuch, 2002, p. 277.

[174] The data are taken from *Schreiber, W.*, Handbuch, 2002, p. 277; *Schorn, K./von Schwartzenberg, M.*, Grundlagen, 2005, p. 872; *Gisart, B.*, Grundlagen, 2009, p. 750 and *Bundeswahlleiter*, Wahl, 2010, p. 32.

Comprehensive statistical data on the number of persons who were affected by changes of the third membership criterion, law abidingness, are also not available. Therefore, it is not known how many individuals were disenfranchised during the Bundestag election in 1949 in the context of denazification procedures. Similarly, information on the number of persons who were undergoing custodial measures of rehabilitation or incapacitation when this group was disenfranchised in 1953 could not be obtained. Data on the number of prison inmates who were disenfranchised between 1949 and 1956 are also not available.[175] Only few pieces of information can be extracted from secondary literature and criminal statistics. Data presented by Heinz reveal that around 500 persons were held in preventive detention or placed in detoxification clinics in 1974.[176] These two groups of persons became eligible to vote through an electoral reform in that same year.

Today, persons who have lost the right to vote by court judgement as well as persons who have been placed in psychiatric hospitals by court ruling based on criminal law remain disenfranchised. The number of persons who have lost the franchise for the first reason is negligible: Only eight persons were disenfranchised through judicial sentence during the past five years.[177] Exact data on the number of persons who are disenfranchised for the latter reason are not available. Statistics reveal that 6.600 persons were accommodated in psychiatric hospitals on the basis of court rulings in 2010.[178] However, not all of these individuals lose their right to vote. Since 1985, only inmates of psychiatric hospitals who have committed a crime in a state of insanity and are judged to be a danger to society are disenfranchised. Separate data on the number of persons who fall under this category could not be obtained. It is clear, however, that not more than a four-digit number of cases can be concerned. In quantitative terms,

---

175 Data on the number of imprisoned persons in Germany are only available from 1961. This information was obtained via e-mail on 01.11.2011 from Ralph Kaiser, Federal Statistical Office of Germany.

176 *Heinz, W.*, Sanktionensystem, 2012, p. 170.

177 Data are taken from *Statistisches Bundesamt*, Rechtspflege, 2003-2011; for more information on the statistics, see *Statistisches Bundesamt*, Strafverfolgungsstatistik, 2011.

178 Data are taken from *Statistisches Bundesamt*, Maßregelvollzug, 2011.

the law abidingness restriction therefore only has a small influence in restricting membership in the demos today.

In comparison to this, the age criterion has a much stronger influence in shaping the electorate. The population statistics reveal that 18.2 million German children and adolescents lived in Germany in 1970 (29.8% of the population). Since then, both the number and the proportion of underage German citizens among the total population have decreased (Figure 7). This decrease was especially pronounced in 1972 when the minimum voting age was lowered. Around 2.2 million 18- to 20-year-old adolescents obtained the right to vote in this year.[179] The proportion of electors among the resident population rose by nearly 4 percentage points and the median age of the electorate decreased from 47.0 years to 45.4 years.[180]

Figure 7: Size of the population of underage German citizens (ages 0-17) in absolute numbers and as proportion of the total population, 1970-2010

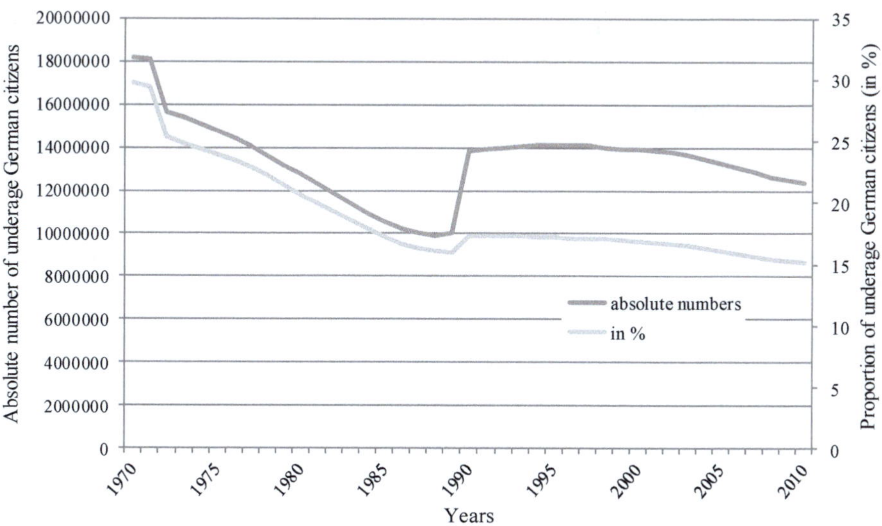

Source: Own calculations based on Population Statistics of 1970-2010, provided by the Federal Statistical Office of Germany.

Note: Data for the years 1970 to 1989 refer to the former West German states only.

179 For this data point, see also *Statistisches Bundesamt*, Wahlberechtigte, 2010.

180 Data are not shown in Figure 7. Own calculations based on *Statistisches Bundesamt*, Wahlberechtigte, 2010, and *Statistisches Bundesamt*, Bevölkerung, 1951-2011.

The decline in the number and proportion of German children and adolescents during the rest of the time period shown in Figure 7 is the result of demographic developments, especially of changes in fertility.[181] The trend was only interrupted in 1990 upon German reunification when the number of German children and adolescents increased from 10.0 to 13.8 million individuals. The proportion of minors among the total population also increased somewhat from 16.0% to 17.4% since the population in East Germany had a younger age structure than in West Germany. During the last ten years, the decline in the number and proportion of German minors has continued. In 2010, 12.4 million German children and adolescents lived in Germany. They constituted 15.4% of the total population. The age restriction to the franchise thus applies to fewer individuals today than in 1970. Nonetheless, it remains the most important electoral restriction in terms of the number of persons who are affected by it.

Complete data on the number of persons who have been excluded from the franchise by the second competence criterion, mental health, could not be obtained. Only for individual reforms, rough estimates exist. Schreiber for instance estimates that around 4.000 persons were placed in psychiatric institutions in 1985 by judicial decision based on Länder law.[182] These persons gained the right to vote as a consequence of the electoral reform of the same year. A larger number of persons appear to have benefited from the next electoral reform of 1990. It is estimated that around 60.000 adult persons were under disability and around 190.000 adults were under guardianship in 1988.[183] These individuals were not entitled to vote in Bundestag elections at the time. The reform of 1990 abolished these restrictions and replaced them by the regulation that persons for whom a custodian has been appointed to administer all their affairs are disenfranchised. Individuals under guardianship gained the right to vote through this reform, provided that they fulfilled all other electoral criteria.[184] The change in law in 1990 is therefore likely to have affected around 190.000 persons.

181 See Chapter 3.3.1.1.
182 *Schreiber, W.*, Handbuch, 2002, p. 306.
183 See BT-Drs. 11/4528 of 11.05.1989, p. 43 and *Deinert, H.*, Handbuch, 1994, p. 494.
184 See *Schreiber, W.*, Handbuch, 2002, p. 304.

Comprehensive statistics on the number of individuals who are disenfranchised on the basis of the mental health restriction today do not exist. It is known that 1.3 million persons were placed under custody in late 2009.[185] Many of these persons however retain legal responsibility for some aspects of their lives and are therefore not disenfranchised. In a recent study, Palleit estimates that only a very small fraction of all 1.3 million custody cases are put under full custody and thereby lose the right to vote.[186]

Apart from legal changes, German reunification in 1990 has affected the size and age structure of the demos. This effect can very roughly be estimated on the basis of population data of late December 1989. At this point, 16.4 million persons were living on the territory of the former German Democratic Republic, 12.7 million of which were of adult age. 2.1 million persons were living in West Berlin during the same year, 1.8 million of which were aged 18 or older. These adult persons became eligible to vote during Bundestag elections after reunification, provided that they were German and fulfilled the other electoral criteria. The demos of Germany thus increased by roughly 14.5 million persons.[187]

The inclusion of adult Eastern Germans into the demos also slightly reduced the median age of the electorate, since the East German population had a somewhat younger age structure than the West German population. Again, the effect can roughly be estimated with East and West German population data of late 1989. At this point in time, the median age of the (West German) electorate measured 46.3 years. By including adult East Germans into the electorate, the median age declined to 46.0 years.[188]

---

185 See *Palleit, L.*, Wahlrecht, 2011, p. 14.

186 *Palleit, L.*, Wahlrecht, 2011, p. 14.

187 Data taken from *Statistisches Bundesamt*, Bevölkerung, 1951-2011 and *Amt für Statistik Berlin-Brandenburg*, Bevölkerung, 1971-1990. The numbers calculated on the basis of these data may misestimate the effect of reunification on the electorate. One the one hand, Eastern Germans started to move to West Germany during 1989. In the population statistics of late 1989, these East-West migrants would be registered as West Germans. On the other hand, the population statistics of the GDR do not distinguish between Germans and foreign residents. Therefore, some of the 14.5 million adult residents of Eastern Germany may not have acquired the right to vote due to lack of citizenship.

188 Own calculations based on *Statistisches Bundesamt*, Bevölkerung, 1951-2011 and *Amt für Statistik Berlin-Brandenburg*, Bevölkerung, 1971-1990.

All of these legal and territorial changes had an influence on the size and age structure of the German electorate. Between the Bundestag elections of 1949 and 2009, the size of the electorate has increased both in terms of absolute numbers and as a proportion among the total population (Figure 8). The number of eligible voters doubled from 31 million to 62 million persons during this time, while the proportion of eligible voters increased from 63.5% in 1953 to 75.8% in 2009.

Figure 8: Size of the electorate in absolute numbers and as a proportion of the total population, 1949-2010

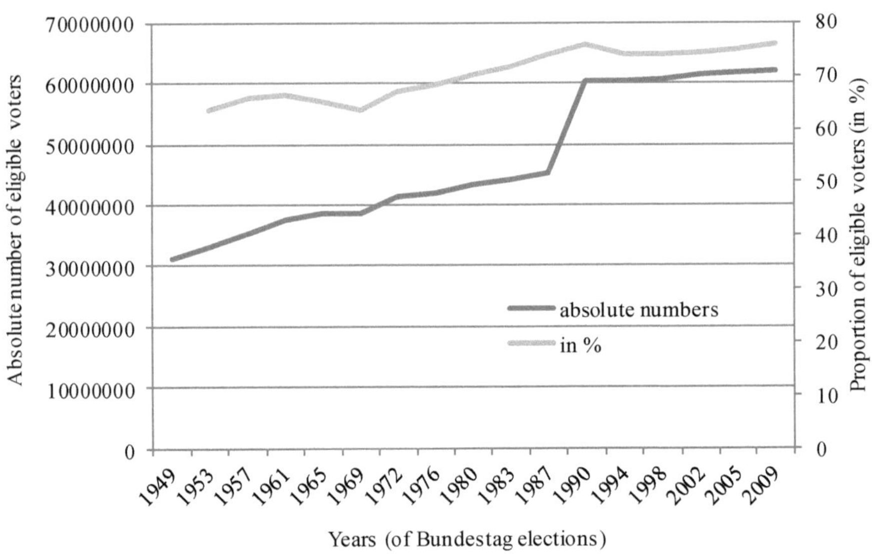

Source: Statistics on eligible voters of 1949-2009, obtained from the Federal Returning Officer (*Bundeswahlleiter*).

Note: Data for the years 1949 to 1989 refer to the former West German states only.

The median age of the electorate changed less strongly over time (Figure 9). Between the elections of 1953 and 1990, it oscillated between 45 and 47 years. Only in recent years, it started to increase from 48.2 years in 2002 to 49.9 years in 2009.

Figure 9: Median age of electorate, 1953-2009

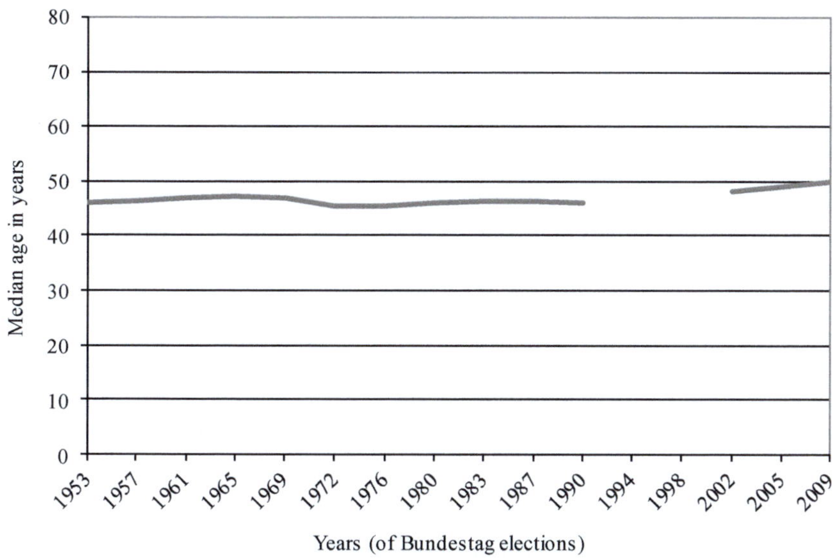

Source: Statistics on eligible voters, 1949-2009, obtained from the Federal Returning Officer.
Note: Data for the years 1953 to 1989 refer to the former West German states only. Data on the age structure of the electorate are not available for the years 1994 and 1998.

The changes in electoral law and spatial application which were described above contributed to these developments. Especially the voting age reform of 1972 and German reunification in 1990 increased the size of the electorate by several millions of persons and lowered the median age. As far as available data suggest, the other changes in electoral law led to the enfranchisement or disenfranchisement of fewer persons and therefore had less influence on the development of the electorate.

Today, age and citizenship/ethnicity restrictions are the most important criteria to restrict membership in the demos, since the largest numbers of persons are disenfranchised on their basis. Later parts of this study in which the electorate will be projected into the future will exclusively focus on these two restrictions. While it is acknowledged that persons may also be disenfranchised on the basis of mental health or law abidingness restrictions in the future, the number of these disenfranchisements is highly likely to be of a much smaller scale than the number of disenfranchisements based on citizenship and age. The rest of this study will also exclude expartriates from the analyses. It is acknowledged that adult German citizens who are living abroad are today entitled to vote in Bundestag elections and therefore form part of the demos. Nonetheless, this study is primarily interested in the degree to which members of the resident population ('Wohnbevölkerung') are entitled to participate in elections. Since expatriates do not form part of the resident population of Germany, they are not of central interest for the research questions that shall be answered here. In addition, reliable data on the number of expatriates who enjoy the franchise do not exist, as was explained above. Therefore, it is also not feasible at this point to do any serious analyses and projections of this group of individuals.[189]

Overall, changes in law help to explain developments of the electorate, but they cannot account for all changes in their entirety. Changes in law influence the size and age structure of the demos in the moment in which they become legally effective. Figure 8 and Figure 9 however reveal that the size and median age of the electorate have changed continuously over time even during periods in which electoral restrictions were not subject to reform. These changes were caused by demographic trends.[190] To these demographic processes and their influence on the German demos we will turn in the next chapter.

---

[189] Political scientists debate controversially whether expatriate citizens should be entitled to vote at all, since they are not immediatelly affected by most of the decisions made by elected policy makers. For more information see for example *Bauböck, R.*, Stakeholder citizenship, 2007.

[190] Changes in the health status of population members and changes in criminal behaviour may also have influenced the numbers of persons who were excluded from the franchise due to the mental health and law abidingness restrictions.

Chapter 3. The influence of demographic changes on the development of the electorate

3.1. Demographic trends across space and time

In demographic terms, a population can be defined as a collectivity of individuals "that persists through time even though its members are continuously changing through attrition and accession".[191] Attrition, the process of leaving a population, is only possible via death or emigration. Accession, the process of joining a population, is possible via birth or immigration (Figure 10).[192] If one considers the population of a country, cases of immigration and emigration only contribute to population change if they cross its external borders, i.e. if they are cases of international migration. Migration which takes place within the borders of a country – so called internal migration – may change the population size of different regions, but does not have an effect on total population size.

Figure 10: Demographic factors which change the size of a population over time

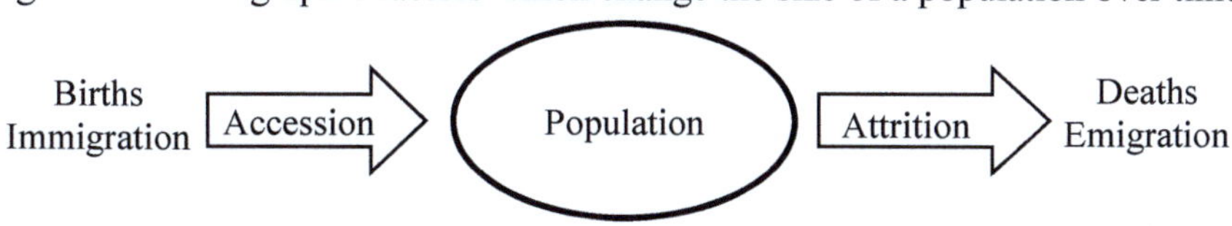

Source: Own illustration

All increases or decreases in population size over time can be explained in terms of attrition and accession: If processes of attrition are lower than processes of accession, a population increases in size. Conversely, if attrition is higher than accession, the population size declines. Processes of attrition and accession also influence the age structure of a population: If processes of attrition or accession

[191] *Preston, S. H./Heuveline, P./Guillot, M.*, Demography, 2001, p. 1.
[192] See *Preston, S. H./Heuveline, P./Guillot, M.*, Demography, 2001, p. 2.

result in a relative increase of younger age groups, the median age declines. If older age groups become relatively stronger in size, the median age rises.[193]
The impact of different demographic factors varies strongly by age: Migration has the biggest impact on young adult age groups, since they are most prone to migrate. Cases of death decimate especially the oldest age groups among a population and the likelihood of giving birth is usually highest among women aged 20 to 35. Similarly, the impact of death and migration differs by sex: Women live longer than men and have traditionally been less prone to migrate, although this has changed during the last decades. In order to capture these differences, the impact of demographic factors may be measured separately for different age- and sex-groups (Figure 11).[194]

Figure 11: Demographic factors which change the size and age structure of a population over time

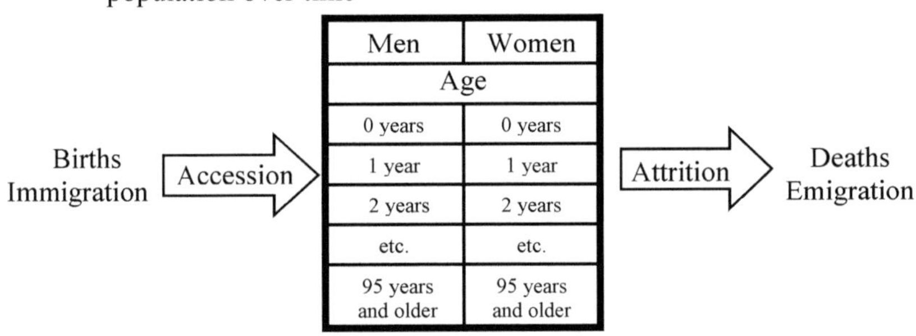

Source: Own illustration

The influence of birth, death and migration on population size may also be studied for further differentiated subgroups of a population, for example groups with different marital status or educational attainment. For such a more detailed analysis, the influence of births, deaths and migration is calculated separately for each of these specific subgroups. In addition to births, deaths and migration,

---

193 See *Birg, H./Flöthmann, E.-J.*, Bevölkerungsprojektionen, 1993, p. 3; *Preston, S. H./Heuveline, P./Guillot, M.*, Demography, 2001, p. 2. As was already stated in the previous chapter, changes in the national borders of a state may also lead to changes in the size or age structure of a population.

194 See *Vallin, J.*, Population, 2006, p. 13; *Lutz, W./Goujon, A./Doblhammer-Reiter, G.*, Demographic dimensions, 1998, p. 42 f.

changes in group membership may affect the size and age structure of different subgroups over time (Figure 12).[195]

Figure 12: Demographic factors which change the size and age structure of population subgroups over time

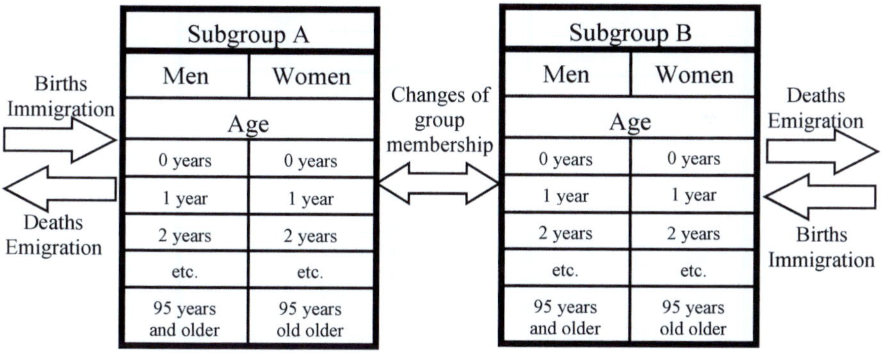

Source: Own illustration

Chapter 2 concluded that age and citizenship are the most important restrictions which currently delimit membership in the electorate in Germany and other European countries, since they affect the largest numbers of individuals. In order to analyse the impact of demographic processes on the size and age structure of the demos, the population of these countries therefore has to be disaggregated by citizenship, in addition to age and sex (Figure 13). Only citizens aged 18 and older form part of the demos in most countries (see highlighted areas in Figure 13). Over time, the size and age structure of each citizenship group is influenced by cases of birth, death and migration, as well as by changes of citizenship. These different demographic factors ultimately influence the size and age structure of the electorate as well.

[195] See *Lutz, W./Goujon, A./Doblhammer-Reiter, G.*, Demographic dimensions, 1998, p. 43 ff.; *Shryock, H. S./Siegel, J. S.*, Demography 2, 1971, p. 387.

Figure 13: Demographic factors which change the size and age structure of citizenship groups

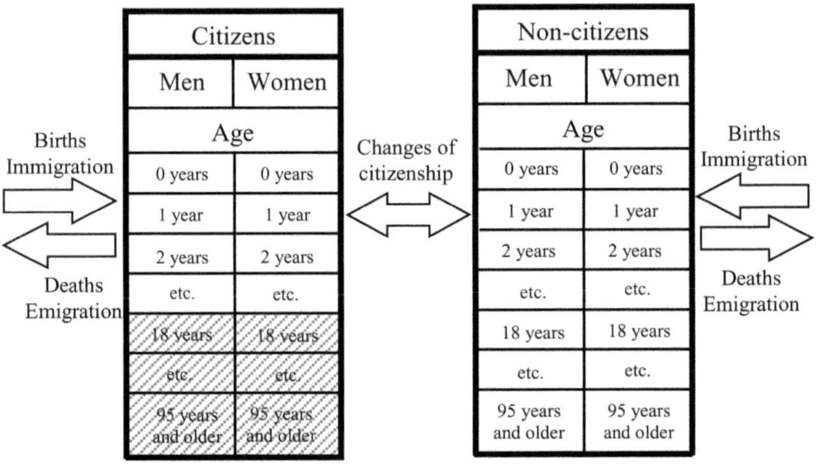

Source: Own illustration

3.2. Influence of demographic trends on electorates across space and time

In order to make demographic behaviour comparable across time and space, it is commonly measured in terms of so-called period rates.[196] Period rates are calculated by dividing the number of demographic events that happen during a specific period of time by the population which is 'at risk' of causing them. The population 'at risk' of causing a demographic event is the population to whom a vital event may occur. Women at a certain age range are for instance at risk of giving birth. Period rates are most often calculated for years. The demographic events that occur during a given year are therefore related to the population at risk of causing them during that year. The latter indicator is usually expressed as the population alive at the middle of the particular year, the so-called midyear population.[197]

---

196 Cohort rates may also be calculated: *Preston, S. H./Heuveline, P./Guillot, M.*, Demography, 2001, pp. 16-18.

197 See *Caselli, G./Vallin, J.*, Population dynamics, 2006, p. 37; *Shryock, H. S./Siegel, J. S.*, Demography 1, 1971, p. 7. For a discussion on how to measure the size of the population which

Since demographic behaviour varies by age and sex and may also differ by citizenship, demographic rates can be calculated by taking these factors into consideration. Age-, sex- and citizenship-specific rates are calculated by dividing the number of demographic events which occur among an age-, sex- and citizenship-specific population group by the midyear size of the same population group. Fertility, mortality and naturalization rates can be calculated in this form.

Fertility rates measure the extent to which a population reproduces itself by relating the number of births during a year to the number of women of childbearing ages (15 to 50 years of age).[198] In order to calculate age- and citizenship-specific fertility rates, the annual number of children born by women of a specific age and citizenship is divided by the midyear population of women of the same specific age and citizenship:[199]

$$ {}_{n}F_{x}^{y}\,[0,T] = \frac{\text{Births to women aged x to x + n of citizenship y between time 0 and T}}{\text{Midyear population of women aged x to x + n of citizenship y between time 0 and T}} $$

By adding all age-specific fertility rates of a particular citizenship group, the so-called period total fertility rate (TFR) is calculated. The period TFR shows how many children a woman of that citizenship group would on average bear during her lifetime if the fertility behaviour observed during the year under consideration were to remain constant and if the woman would reach the end of her reproductive period.[200] For example, the TFR value of 1.36, measured for German women in 2010, indicates that each woman would on average bear 1.36 children during her reproductive years if fertility rates were to remain constant.

is at risk of causing demographic events, see *Preston, S. H./Heuveline, P./Guillot, M.*, Demography, 2001, p. 15.

198 Fertility rates could be constructed in the same way by relating births to the midyear population of men. Nonetheless, most often fertility rates are calculated for women, since information about the number of children ever born to women are more reliable than comparative data for men (*Preston, S. H./Heuveline, P./Guillot, M.*, Demography, 2001, pp. 92-94).

199 Formula taken and adjusted from *Preston, S. H./Heuveline, P./Guillot, M.*, Demography, 2001, p. 93 f.

200 See *Bongaarts, J./Feeney, G.*, Quantum, 1998, p. 271; *Preston, S. H./Heuveline, P./Guillot, M.*, Demography, 2001, p. 95.

In order for a population to reproduce itself in the absence of migration, a TFR of 2.1 is required.[201]

The TFR is a simplified construct, since fertility patterns do not necessarily remain stable over long periods of time. Instead, the number of children that women bear and the age at which they have them may change. If such changes occur, women may have more or fewer children during their lives than the TFR value of a specific year suggests.[202] Despite this drawback, the TFR provides useful information about trends in fertility over time as well as about the long-term consequences of prevalent fertility patterns.

Mortality rates measure the impact of deaths on population change. In order to calculate age-, sex- and citizenship-specific mortality rates for a certain year, the number of deaths occurring among male or female members of a citizenship group and a specific age range is divided by the number of persons alive in that same group at the middle of the year:[203]

$$_{n}M_{x}^{y}\ [0,T] = \frac{\text{Deaths to men|women aged x to x + n of citizenship y between time 0 and T}}{\text{Midyear population of men|women aged x to x + n of citizenship y between time 0 and T}}$$

If age-specific mortality rates are available across the entire age range of a citizenship group, a so-called life table may be calculated. Among other indicators, life tables show the remaining life expectancy of individuals at different ages. This indicator measures "the average number of additional years a person could expect to live if current mortality trends were to continue for the rest of that person's life".[204] The remaining life expectancy of a newborn child for instance indicates the age that the child can expect to reach if mortality conditions remain constant in the future.

---

201 See *Preston, S. H./Heuveline, P./Guillot, M.*, Demography, 2001, p. 115.

202 See *Bongaarts, J./Feeney, G.*, Quantum, 1998, p. 271. The inaccuracies of the period TFR may be avoided by calculating the so-called cohort TFR. It is a retrospective indicator and better suitable to study past than current fertility developments. For more information see *Bongaarts, J.*, Fertility transition, 2002, p. 421; *Kreyenfeld, M./Konietzka, D.*, Wandel, 2008, p. 126 f.

203 See *Haupt, A./Kane, T. T.*, Handbook, 2004, p. 59. The formula is taken and adjusted from *Preston, S. H./Heuveline, P./Guillot, M.*, Demography, 2001, p. 21.

204 *Haupt, A./Kane, T. T.*, Handbook, 2004, p. 58. For a detailed explanation of the calculation of life tables, see *Preston, S. H./Heuveline, P./Guillot, M.*, Demography, 2001, p. 49.

The assumption that currently observed mortality conditions will remain stable in the future is very simplified. De facto, mortality conditions tend to change over time. During the past century, for instance, mortality has decreased across Western Europe and life expectancy increased. If the decline in mortality will continue in the future, members of a population are likely to live longer than is suggested by a life table based on current mortality data. Life expectancy values that are calculated on the basis of life tables are therefore somewhat artificial devices. As long as mortality is declining, they are a conservative estimate of the additional number of years that members of the population are likely to live.[205]

Naturalization rates measure the proportion of individuals who change their citizenship during a year. They are calculated by relating the number of naturalization cases among an age-, sex- and citizenship-specific population group to the midyear size of that same population group[206]:

$$ {}_{n}N_{x}^{y}\,[0,T] = \frac{\text{Number of men|women aged x to x + n who change citizenship y for citizenship z between time 0 and T}}{\text{Midyear population of men|women aged x to x + n of citizenship y between time 0 and T}} $$

In contrast to other demographic factors, migration is generally not measured in terms of period rates, but in terms of net migration numbers, i.e. by subtracting annual emigration numbers from immigration numbers.[207] Since the propensity to migrate varies by age, sex and citizenship, net migration values are often calculated for age-, sex- and citizenship-specific subgroups of the population:

$$ {}_{n}Mi_{x}^{y} = \text{Immigration by men or women aged x to x+n of citizenship y between time 0 and T} - \text{Emigration by men or women aged x to x+n of citizenship y between time 0 and T} $$

Net migration numbers indicate "the net effect of immigration and emigration on an area's population in a given time period, expressed as an increase or

205 See *Buttler, G.*, Steigende Lebenserwartung, 2002, p. 91.

206 Strictly speaking, it would be more adequate to divide the number of naturalization cases by the number of persons who fulfil naturalization requirements. After all, demographic rates relate demographic events to the population which is 'at risk' of causing them and not all foreign residents living in a country are eligible and thus 'at risk' of naturalizing. Statistics on the number of persons who are eligible to naturalize are however difficult to obtain. Therefore, naturalization rates are most commonly constructed in the form shown above.

207 See *Shryock, H. S./Siegel, J. S.*, Demography 2, 1971, pp. 603 and 605.

decrease".[208] If the numbers are negative, migration contributes to population decline. If numbers are positive, migration contributes to population increase. Changes in fertility, mortality and naturalization rates as well as migration numbers may influence the size and age structure of electorates in democratic states. The effect of such changes is not necessarily direct and immediate, but may only become visible over time. It also depends on which citizenship or age groups change their demographic behaviour most strongly. To illustrate this, consider a population in which age-specific fertility, mortality and naturalization rates of citizens and foreign residents as well as their migration behaviour have remained constant for more than a century. Over time, the constancy of demographic behaviour leads to a constant age structure of the population. In other words, the proportionate size of different age groups remains stable. A population that has reached such a stable structure is called a 'stable' population.[209] It might look as in Figure 14.

Figure 14: Hypothetical stable population

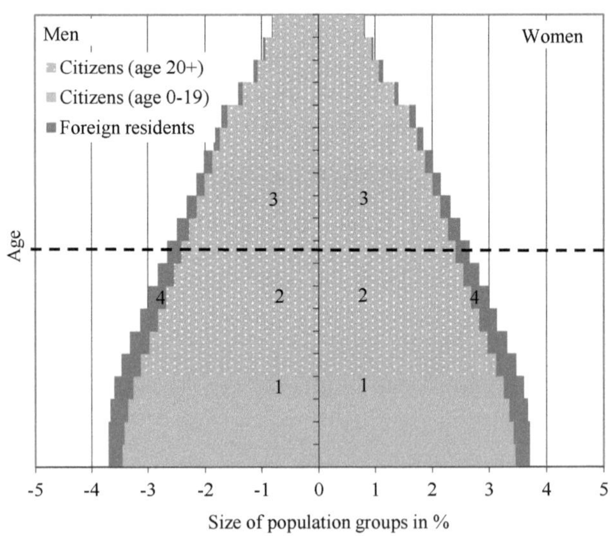

Source: Own illustration

[208] *Haupt, A./Kane, T. T.*, Handbook, 2004, p. 60.
[209] See *Preston, S. H./Heuveline, P./Guillot, M.*, Demography, 2001, pp. 53 and 138-147.

The vertical axis in this figure shows different age groups of the population, with younger age groups located at the lower end of the axis, and older age groups at the top. The horizontal axis shows the relative size of the different age groups. The figure also distinguishes between men (left side) and women (right side) as well as between citizens (lighter grey parts of bars) and foreign residents (dark grey parts). In this hypothetical model population, it might be assumed that the minimum voting age is 20 years and that foreign residents are not enfranchised. Under these conditions, the proportion of eligible voters among the population would amount to around 75% (highlighted areas in the Figure). The median age of the electorate would lie between 45 and 50 years (visualized by dashed line in the figure).

In order to assess the effect of demographic changes on the proportion of electors among the population and on the median age of the electorate, it is important to know which population groups would be most strongly affected by the changes. Four different population groups are of interest: First, male and female citizens below voting age (groups 1 in Figure 14); second, male and female citizens above minimum voting age, but below the median age (groups 2); third, male and female citizens above the median age (groups 3); and fourth, male and female foreign residents of all age groups (groups 4). Below, they will be referred to as the population of 'underage citizens', 'younger electors', 'older electors' and 'foreign residents'.

In the hypothetical stable population shown above, any change in demographic behaviour that would lead to a relative increase of the population of underage citizens (groups 1) would imply a decline in the proportion of electors in the short term: Since children do not enjoy the right to vote, an increase in the size of this group would increase the proportion of disenfranchised population members relative to enfranchised population members. This effect would only be short-term in nature. In the longer term, as the bigger child cohorts age, they join the electorate and the proportion of enfranchised residents would increase again (see illustration in Figure 15). The converse effect would take place if the relative size of the child population were to decrease. In this case, the proportion

of eligible voters would increase in the short term but reverse once the quantitatively small child cohorts would pass the minimum voting age.
The median age of the demos would not be affected by increases or decreases of the child population in the short term. Only once the quantitatively stronger or weaker cohorts pass the minimum voting age would the demographic change have an impact. If the cohorts who reach the minimum voting age are numerically strong, this would initially have a depressing effect on the median age of the demos, since younger electors would gain a stronger relative weight among the electorate. Conversely, if the cohorts who reach the minimum voting age are small, this would initially put an upward pressure on the median age. As the numerically strong or weak cohorts reach older age, the effect would disappear.

Figure 15: Effects of an increase of the child population over time

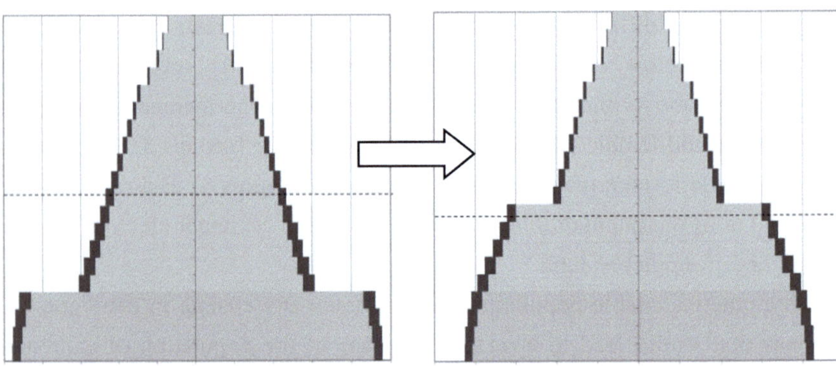

Source: Own illustration

Demographic changes which affect the population of young electors and older electors (groups 2 and 3) have a more immediate effect: If the proportion of younger electors among the population increases, the median age would decline immediately. Over time, as the quantitatively big cohorts would become older, this effect would disappear (Figure 16).

Figure 16: Effects of an increase of the population of younger electors over time

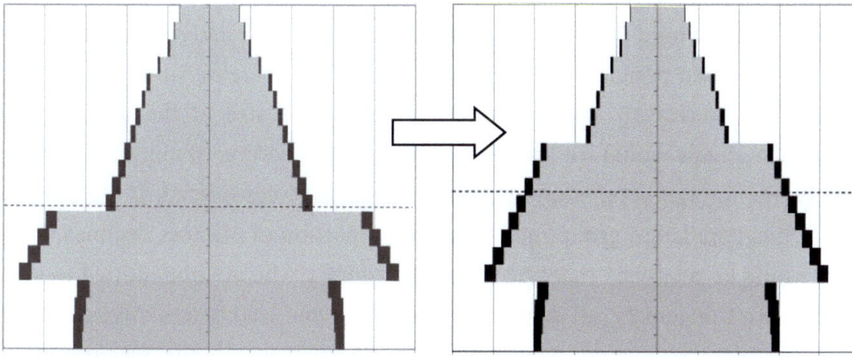

Source: Own illustration

The reverse effect would occur if the proportion of younger electors among the population would decrease. Such a change would initially put an upward pressure on the median age, which would disappear over time. Any demographic trend that would change the size of the population group of older electors would have the opposite effect in a stable population: An increase would rise the median age of the electorate (Figure 17); a decrease would lower it.

Figure 17: Effects of an increase of the population of older electors over time

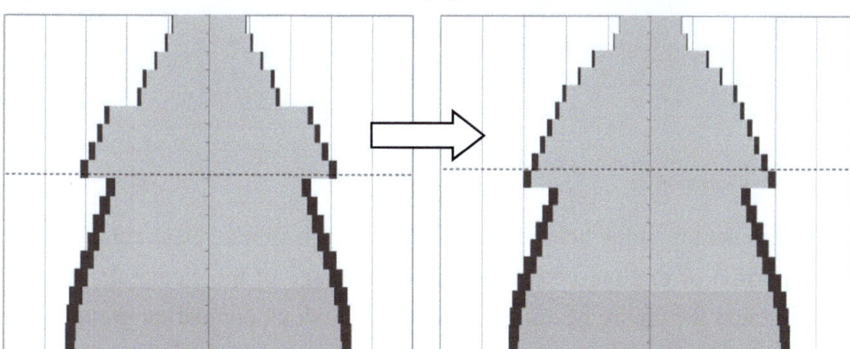

Source: Own illustration

While increases or decreases in the population of younger and older electors have contrasting effects on the median age, the effect on the proportion of eligible voters would be the same: Any increase in the relative size of one or both of these two population groups would entail an increase in the proportion of electors. Conversely, any decrease in the relative size of the one or both population groups would lead to a decrease in the proportion of eligible voters.

Finally, the foreign population (groups 4) needs to be considered. If the relative size of this population group increases, the proportion of electors declines since there would be relatively more people in the country who are not entitled to vote (Figure 18). Conversely, all demographic changes that lead to a relative decrease of the foreign population would result in an increase in the proportion of electors. Since foreign residents do not form part of the electorate, any changes in the size of this group would have no effect on its median age.

Figure 18: Effects of an increase of the foreign population

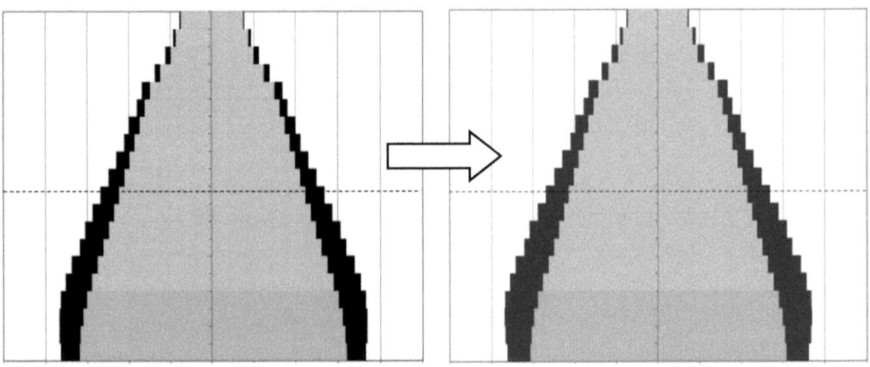

Source: Own illustration

Changes in demographic behaviour thus do not have simple, clear cut effects on the proportion of eligible voters and the median age of the electorate. Instead, the extent and the nature of the effect depend on which population groups grow or decline in size due to demographic changes.

Table 3: Effects of changes in the size of different population groups on the proportion of eligible voters and the median age of the electorate

			Proportion of electors	Median age of electorate
1	Underage citizens	increase in relative size	- +	(- +)
2		decrease in relative size	+ -	(+ -)
3	Younger electors	increase in relative size	+	- +
4		decrease in relative size	-	+ -
5	Older electors	increase in relative size	+	+
6		decrease in relative size	-	-
7	Foreign residents	increase in relative size	-	no effect
8		decrease in relative size	+	no effect

+ increase   + - first increase, then decrease   ( ) effect appears with delay
- decrease   - + first decrease, then increase

Source: Own illustration

Table 3 summarizes the main insights described above and helps to estimate the effect of individual demographic trends: Changes in the fertility rate of citizens influence the number of underage citizens. If fertility among citizens decreases, the proportion of children among the population declines (see row 2 in Table 3). As a result, the proportion of eligible voters increases in the short run, but will decrease again in the longer run when the smaller cohorts reach voting age. At that point in time, the median age of the electorate will also increase. It will later decrease again once the small cohorts reach higher age groups. An increase in fertility will have the opposite consequences (row 1). An increase in fertility among foreign residents will have the same consequences, provided that their children acquire the citizenship of the country of residence upon birth. If the children acquire the foreign citizenship of the parents only, any changes in fertility of foreign residents will increase or decrease the proportion of foreign residents among the total population. The effects described in rows 7 and 8 will be the consequence. For instance, if increased fertility levels lead to an increase in the proportion of the foreign population (row 7), there will be relatively more residents who are not eligible to vote. Consequently, the proportion of eligible voters will decline. A decrease in fertility that will lead to a decrease in the proportion of foreign residents will have the opposite effect (row 8). The median age of the electorate is not affected by changes in the proportion of foreign residents.

Changes in mortality can in principle affect all age groups of a population alike. If mortality among citizens declines, the effect depends on which age group profits most strongly. For instance, if mortality rates decline especially among elderly citizens, this will increase the relative size of the population of older electors. The consequences shown in row 5 of the table would be the result: The proportion of eligible voters will increase and the relatively larger number of older electors will put an upward pressure on the median age of the electorate. Changes in mortality among foreign residents in an otherwise stable population would entail the consequences displayed in rows 7 and 8. A decrease in mortality rates among foreign residents for instance implies that more foreign residents will survive to higher ages. This will increase the relative proportion of foreign residents among the total population. The proportion of eligible voters would consequently decline.

Migration and naturalization also in principle affect all age groups alike. Nonetheless, it has been shown that young adults and, to a lesser degree, children are most likely to migrate and change their citizenship.[210] Therefore, any changes in migration and naturalization behaviour should primarily affect the population of young electors and underage citizens as well as foreign residents. An increase in immigration might for instance lead to an increase in

[210] See *Rogers, A.*, Population dynamics, 1986, p. 49; *Sartori, F.*, Citizenship, 2010, p. 6.

the foreign population. Since a relatively larger number of disenfranchised residents would then live in the country, the proportion of eligible voters would decline (row 7).

So far, the discussion of demographic changes has been restricted to a hypothetical stable population in which only one demographic component changes while the others remain stable. Reality, of course, is much more complex. For one, populations in industrialized countries are not stable but have been undergoing profound demographic changes during the past decades.[211] Demographic components also do not change one at a time. Instead, changes in fertility, mortality, migration and naturalization may occur simultaneously and may have contrasting effects on the size and age structure of a population and its electorate. Demographic factors also do not necessarily either increase or decrease over longer periods of time, but may fluctuate. These fluctuations, again, may have contrasting effects. Further, the impact of demographic changes has so far been discussed with a special focus on age groups that are most concerned by them. In reality all age groups of the population can change their behaviour simultaneously. Finally, changes in one population group may not occur in isolation but have implications for other groups. For instance, an increase in the population of young electors through positive net migration may affect the size of the child population, if the immigrants have high fertility levels. In any of these cases, the influence of demographic changes on the electorate may be much more complex than sketched above.

Analysing the effect of demographic changes on the size and age structure of the electorate is therefore an inherently complex endeavour. This will be illustrated in the following by turning Germany. First, fertility, mortality, migration and naturalization trends of the past decades will be described. Then, it will be illustrated to which extent these developments have become visible in the population structure and how they have shaped the electorate.

[211] For an overview, see *European Commission*, Demography report, 2011.

3.3. Demographic trends in Germany, 1949-2010

It was concluded in Chapter 2 that three citizenship groups have to be distinguished for the purposes of this study and on the basis of current citizenship law: German citizens (majority population), ius soli-children and foreign residents. Each group has different access to voting rights: German citizens acquire the right to vote when they turn 18 and only lose this right under the very restricted conditions described in Chapter 2.3.2. Ius soli-citizens acquire the franchise when they come of age, but have to decide between their German and their foreign citizenship between age 18 and age 23. They only keep the right to vote in Germany if they retain their German citizenship. Foreign residents do not enjoy the right to vote in Bundestag elections and only obtain it by acquiring German citizenship. The three citizenship groups as well as the demographic factors which may change their size and composition over time are visualized in Figure 19. The age- and citizenship-specific population groups which form the electorate are highlighted in grey.
The size and age structure of the three groups continuously change due to births, deaths, immigration and emigration. These demographic factors are measured in terms of fertility rates, mortality rates and net migration numbers. The extent to which births contribute to the growth of individual citizenship groups does not only depend on fertility, but also on German citizenship law. As was explained in Chapter 2.3.3., children born to foreign mothers acquire the German citizenship qua ius sanguinis if their father is a German citizen or qua ius soli if one parent fulfils the relevant conditions. These children thus contribute to the size of the German population groups (majority population and ius soli population) rather than to the foreign population.
The size and age structure of the three citizenship groups also changes over time due to changes of citizenship. The different ways in which individuals may change their citizenship are indicated by arrows in Figure 19. Members of the German majority population (German citizens) may lose their citizenship under certain conditions. Foreign residents may acquire German citizenship via naturalization. Ius soli-citizens have to choose between their citizenships until

their 23rd birthday. Depending on their choice, the German state treats them either as German citizens or as foreign residents thereafter. An opposite change of citizenship is not possible: German citizens and foreign residents cannot become ius soli-citizens during their life course, since this status is only acquired at birth. The transitory regulation that allowed children born to foreign parents between 1990 and 1999 to acquire German citizenship qua ius soli retrospectively is the only exception (see Chapter 2.3.3.).

Figure 19: Demographic factors which change the size and age structure of citizenship groups in Germany over time

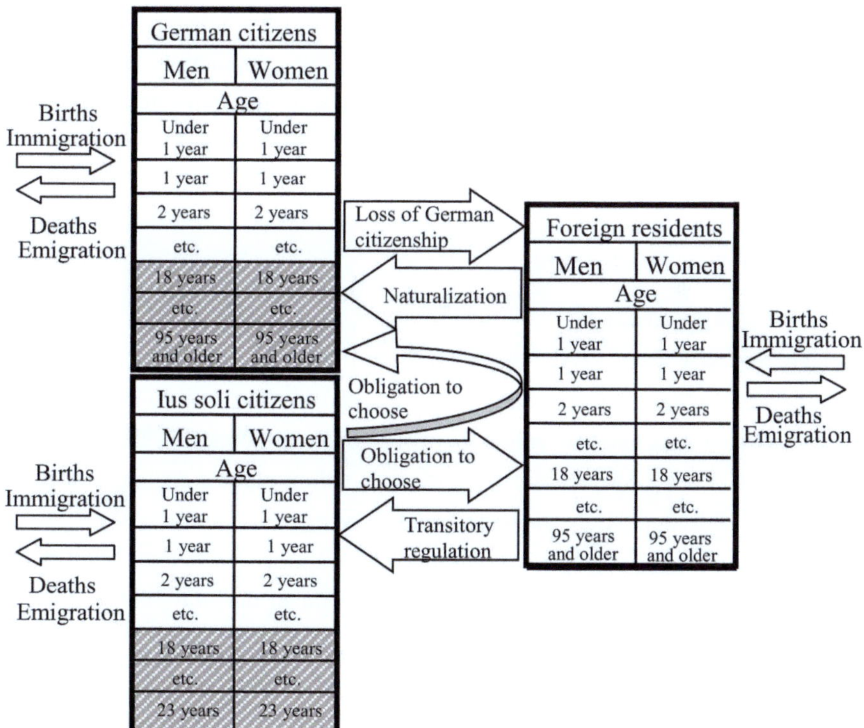

Source: Own illustration

The following subchapters describe how fertility, mortality, migration and trends in citizenship loss and acquisition have changed in Germany during the past decades. The statistics on births, deaths and migration which are used for this purpose only allow a separate analysis of the behaviour of Germans and foreign residents. The statistics define 'Germans' as individuals who are in possession of German citizenship. This includes ius soli-citizens. 'Foreign residents' are defined as all individuals who are registered as living in Germany but do not possess German citizenship. A further differentiation is not possible. In other words, while the present study is interested in tracing the development of the ius soli-population and the German majority population separately, most official statistics merge the two groups into one. Separate analyses of demographic behaviours cannot be undertaken. In the following, different demographic trends will therefore be discussed by distinguishing between German citizens (including the German majority population and ius soli-citizens) and foreigners only. Separate analyses of ius soli-citizens are only possible with regard to the acquisition and loss of citizenship. These data will be presented at the end of Chapter 3.3.[212]

3.3.1. Fertility developments

3.3.1.1. German citizens

During the past sixty years, the period total fertility rate (TFR) of German women has changed substantially. After the end of the Second World War, it first increased and reached values between 2.0 and 2.5 during the 1950s and early 1960s. Young couples married earlier than their parents during these years, had more children and bore them at a younger age.

This period of high fertility – commonly referred to as the 'baby boom' period or the 'golden age of marriage' – came to an end in the mid-1960s. Within a period of ten years, the TFR nearly dropped by half to reach a level of 1.3 in 1975 (Figure 20). It oscillated between 1.26 and 1.4 until German reunification

[212] In addition to distinguishing by citizenship groups, the following chapters on mortality, migration and changes of citizenship comment on gender differences in demographic behaviour. The data obtained from the population projections, which are presented in later chapters, also partly distinguish by gender. Despite the availability of these data, it would be beyond the scope of this study to discuss the effects of demographic and legal changes on the gender balance of the electorate in depth. Readers who are interested in such questions, however, may find the gender-specific data and projection results of this study useful as a starting point for their research. The complete set of gender-specific projection files is readily available upon request.

in 1990 and dropped to a level of 1.1 in 1994/95, but recovered during the years that followed. In 2010, the TFR of German women reached a level of 1.36, the highest value measured since reunification.

Figure 20: Total fertility rate of German women, 1972-2010

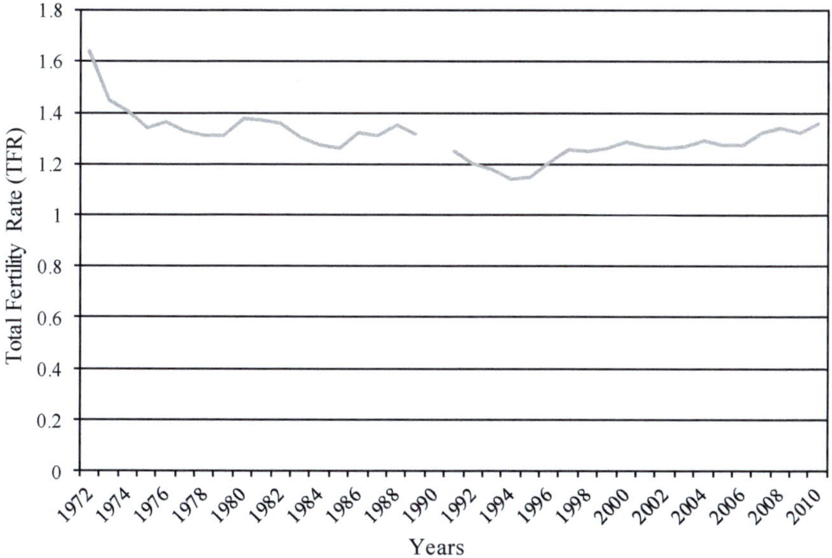

Source: Own calculations based on Birth Statistics and Population Statistics of 1972-2010, provided by the Federal Statistical Office.

Note: Data for the years 1972 to 1989 refer to the former West German states only. Value for 1990 was not calculated due to nominator-denominator mismatch: Population data of this year refer to the reunified Germany, while birth data refer to West Germany only.

The decline of the TFR during the 1960s and 1970s and the low fertility levels during the following decades have been the result of two simultaneous processes: First, the average number of children born by German women has declined over time.[213] Second, women have started to bear children at increasingly higher ages. Figure 21 shows the age-specific fertility rates of German women between 1972 and 2010. As can be seen, age-specific fertility reached its peak at ages 24 to 26 in 1972. Over time, the peak of the fertility curve shifted to higher ages. In 2010, the highest age-specific fertility value was

213 See *Pötzsch, O.*, Geburtenentwicklung, 2010; *Schulze, A.*, Konsequenzen, 2009, p. 26.

reached at age 31. The processes of decline and postponement of childbearing are referred to in the literature as the 'quantum' and the 'tempo' aspects of the fertility decline, respectively.[214]

Figure 21: Age-specific fertility rates of German women, selected years

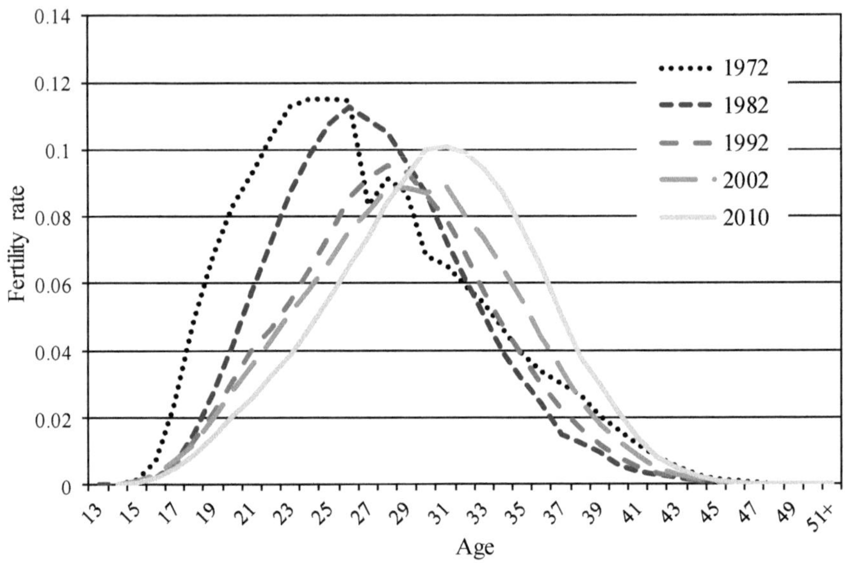

Source: Own calculations based on Birth Statistics and Population Statistics of 1972-2010, provided by the Federal Statistical Office.

Note: Data for the years 1972 and 1982 refer to the former West German states only.

The question why German women began to have fewer children and why they postponed childbearing to higher ages has been strongly debated among demographers and social scientists. Most approaches to explain these developments have taken a socio-cultural or an economic perspective.[215]

Socio-cultural approaches stress that values and norms regarding family formation and childbearing have changed in Germany and other Western

---

214 For a discussion of the impact of tempo and quantum changes on the TFR, see *Bongaarts, J./Feeney, G.*, Quantum, 1998 and *Frejka, T./Sobotka, T.*, Fertility, 2008.

215 See *Kreyenfeld, M./Konietzka, D.*, Wandel, 2008, p. 122 f. and *Ehrhardt, J., et al.*, Theorien, 2012.

European countries since the mid-1960s.[216] Life-long marriage and childbearing have lost their role as necessary parts of adult life and have become options that compete with other life choices. This is particularly true for women. While it was still common in the 1960s that women stopped working after marriage to focus on housework and childrearing, more women have gained academic degrees from the 1960s and 1970s. Their employment rates have risen, leading to higher financial and economic independence and opening up new roles and life models.[217] In addition, the introduction of reliable contraceptives in the early 1960s allowed women to prevent pregnancies and to plan childbearing in accordance with career and other life plans. Entry into marriage and childbearing has been postponed, unions have become more unstable and divorce rates have increased. Voluntary childlessness has also become more frequent and increasingly socially accepted. Today, it is estimated that up to 30% of West German women born during the late 1960s may remain childless. While voluntary childlessness increases, not all of these cases are the result of a conscious choice. Childlessness may also be an involuntary state, caused by the lack of a suitable partner or infecundity.[218]

Economic approaches stress the changing costs and benefits of childrearing. During long parts of history, children contributed to the family income and supported their parents in old age. Since the abolishment of child labour and the introduction of state welfare schemes, childbearing is no longer connected to such financial or material benefits. Instead, the benefits that parents receive from having children are largely social and emotional in character.[219] At the same time, the financial costs of raising children are high and put a strain on many families. Child-rich families and single parents have a high poverty risk in Germany today. Petersen and Lübcke suggest that the costs of childrearing may negatively influence the decision to have a(nother) child among persons with

---

[216] Lesthaeghe and van de Kaa refer to these changes as the 'second demographic transition'. The concept of the 'first demographic transition' refers to demographic changes that occurred in Europe since the late 18th century. See *van de Kaa, D. J.*, Fertility preferences, 2001, p. 300; *Lesthaeghe, R.*, Second demographic transition, 2010.

[217] See *Keyfitz, N.*, Knowledge, 1982, p. 733.

[218] See *Dorbritz, J.*, Germany, 2008, p. 569; *Eckhard, J.*, Kinderlosigkeit, 2006, p. 119 f.

[219] See *Petersen, T./Lübcke, B.*, Elternschaft, 2006, pp. 190-198.

low income or living in economically insecure living conditions.[220] Apart from the direct costs, indirect or opportunity costs of childrearing have been discussed as factors to explain low fertility levels. If parents, most often women, have to stop or at least reduce work in order to care for their children, they lose parts or the entirety of their income and may accumulate fewer pension entitlements. The decision to work less or to temporarily drop out of the labour force may also lower career prospects in the future. Opportunity costs may be reduced if childcare facilities are available that allow the reconciliation of family and work obligations. Even where childcare is available, however, parents may be disadvantaged if they work in professions that require flexibility, geographic mobility and the willingness to work long hours.[221] High opportunity costs and problems of combining professional and family obligations have been adduced as reasons for why highly educated women in Germany are particularly likely to postpone childbearing or to remain childless.[222]

While the decline and subsequently low fertility levels of the 1970s and 1980s are usually explained by economic factors or ideational changes, the sharp drop in the TFR after German reunification is attributed to the radical change in contextual conditions. Eastern German women postponed childbearing in the early 1990s to avoid long-term commitments in an environment that was characterised by rapid economic, political and social change.[223] As the economic and political conditions in East Germany stabilized during the mid- to late 1990s, the fertility of East German women increased again. Today, they even appear to surpass the fertility of West German women.[224] It has as yet not been conclusively shown to what extent the slight increase in the TFR during recent years is the result of this recuperation process or whether family policies or other factors have also played a role.

---

220 *Petersen, T./Lübcke, B.*, Elternschaft, 2006, p. 199. See also *Dorbritz, J.*, Germany, 2008, p. 592 f.; *Frejka, T., et al.*, Summary, 2008, p. 8; *Kohler, H.-P./Billari, F. C./Ortega, J. A.*, Lowest-low fertility, 2002, p. 655.

221 See *Avramov, D./Cliquet, R.*, Economy of time, 2003, p. 376; *Enquete-Kommission 'Demographischer Wandel'*, Zwischenbericht, 1998, p. 59; *Dorbritz, J.*, Germany, 2008, p. 591.

222 See *Wirth, H./Dümmler, K.*, Childlessness, 2005, p. 329 f.; *Dorbritz, J.*, Kinderlosigkeit, 2005.

223 See *Witte, J. C./Wagner, G. G.*, Fertility, 1995, p. 388; *Dorbritz, J.*, Germany, 2008, p. 562 f.; *Conrad, C./Lechner, M./Werner, W.*, East German fertility, 1996, p. 342.

224 See *Goldstein, J. R./Kreyenfeld, M.*, Der Osten, 2011.

3.3.1.2. Foreign residents

The TFR of foreign women in Germany has consistently been higher than the TFR of German women during the last decades (Figure 22). The difference was especially strong in 1972, the first year in which the birth statistics included information on the citizenship of mothers. While the TFR of German women had already declined to a level of 1.6 by then, the TFR of foreign women stood at 2.6. Over time, the TFR values approached each other, but a complete convergence has not taken place. The TFR of foreign women had a value of 1.6 in 2010, 0.2 points higher than the German TFR.

Figure 22: Total fertility rate of German women and foreign women, 1972-2010

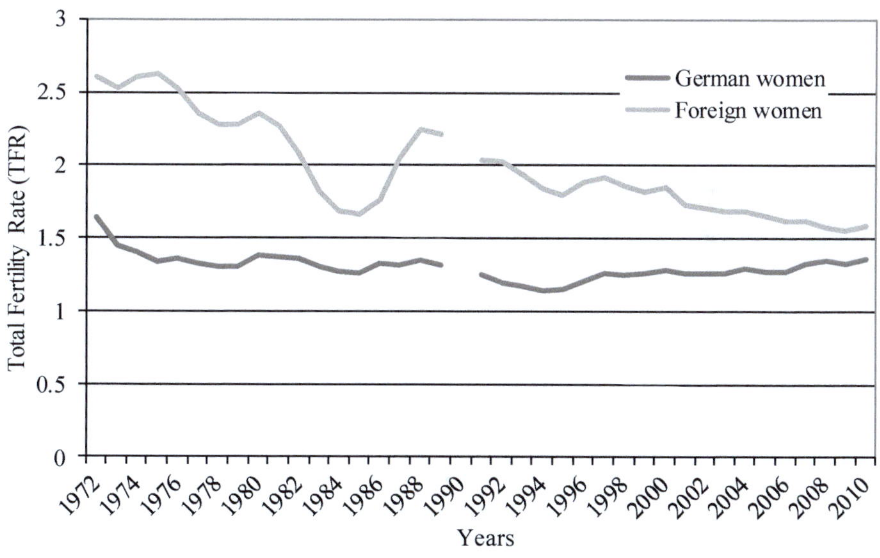

Source: Own calculations based on Birth Statistics and Population Statistics of 1972-2010, provided by the Federal Statistical Office.

Note: Data for the years 1972 to 1989 refer to the former West German states only. Values for 1990 were not calculated due to nominator-denominator mismatch: Population data of this year refer to the reunified Germany, while birth data refer to West Germany only.

The decline in the TFR of foreign women has been the result both of a decrease in the number of children born per woman (quantity) and of a postponement process (timing). This is visualised in Figure 23. The figure shows the age-specific fertility rates of foreign women in Germany between 1972 and 2010. In 1972 and 1982, the fertility rates of foreign women were highest at age 22. Over time, foreign women postponed childbearing to increasingly higher age. In 2010 the rate was highest at age 30, only one year below the peak of the German age-specific fertility curve (see Figure 21 in Chapter 3.3.1.1.). Besides shifting to higher age, age-specific fertility rates of foreign women also declined between 1972 and 2010, reflecting changes in the quantum of children.

Figure 23: Age-specific fertility rates of foreign women, selected years

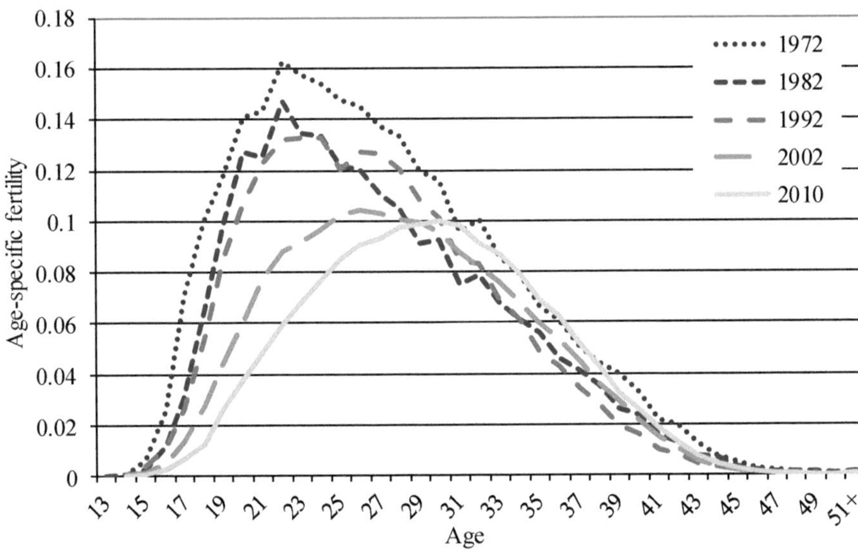

Source: Own calculations based on Birth Statistics and Population Statistics of 1972-2010, provided by the Federal Statistical Office.

Note: Data for the years 1972 and 1982 refer to the former West German states only.

Despite the gradual approach of foreign women's fertility patterns to those of German women, differences remain: The TFR of foreign women was still somewhat higher in 2010 and they still had children at somewhat younger age than German women.

Demographers and social scientists have discussed several hypotheses to explain these long-term differences in reproductive behaviour. Some demographers such as Schmid and Kohls point out that many foreign women come from countries with family-oriented values that encourage high fertility and maintain these attitudes at least initially after migration. In addition, demographers such as Milewski have suggested that some immigration to Germany in fact occurs for the purposes of marriage and family formation and that somewhat elevated fertility rates among young foreign women in Germany are therefore to be expected. Also, socio-economic differences between Germans and foreign residents have been adduced to explain differences in fertility behaviours.[225]

These various hypotheses are not necessarily mutually exclusive, but may complement each other. The population of foreign residents in Germany is highly heterogeneous and fertility rates of foreign women differ by country of origin. Women from some European countries, for instance, have even lower fertility levels than German women, while women from Turkey, Africa and Asia have higher fertility levels. Differences in fertility behaviour also exist between foreign women who have immigrated to Germany and their daughters who were born and raised there as well as between foreign women of different socio-economic status.[226] Each of the different hypotheses may help to explain the fertility behaviour of some groups of foreign women in Germany while being less helpful in explaining others.

Some demographers have focused on explaining the gradual approach in the fertility behaviour of German and foreign women over time rather than the continuing differences. In the 1980s, the fertility of foreign women changed especially drastically within few years, first declining to a level of 1.7 between 1980 and 1984, then increasing again until 1988. Demographers explain this down- and upturn by changes in migration behaviour: Many foreign residents returned to their countries of origin during the economic recession of the early 1980s or moved to third countries. Fewer foreign residents formed unions or families during these years. After 1984, immigration numbers sparked again and

---

225 For these and other hypotheses see *Schmid, S./Kohls, M.*, Generatives Verhalten, 2011, pp. 34-37 and 46; *Milewski, N.*, First child, 2007, p. 862; *Sobotka, T.*, Rising importance, 2008, p. 234 f.

226 See *Sobotka, T.*, Rising importance, 2008, p. 233; *Schoorl, J.*, Fertility trends, 1995, p. 103; *Enquete-Kommission 'Demographischer Wandel'*, Zwischenbericht, 1998, p. 55; *Schmid, S./Kohls, M.*, Generatives Verhalten, 2011, especially pp. 54-57, 167 and 174.

an increasing number of foreign residents started families in Germany. Birg and Flöthmann suggest that a change in family policy may also have contributed to the increase in fertility rates in the mid-1980s: Child allowance was only paid for children who were growing up in Germany. This may have induced foreign residents to found families there rather than in their countries of origin. Finally, the increase in fertility rates around the year 1987 is partly the result of a statistical effect. The population census conducted in that year revealed that the size of the foreign population had been overestimated and was corrected downward. This somewhat increased the fertility rate which was calculated with the new data in 1987.[227]

In addition to the preceding hypotheses, researchers have also argued that the increasing similarity between foreign and German fertility behaviours is a sign that the foreign population is taking on the norms, values and habits of the German population and is adapting to contextual factors such as family policies, economic and labour market conditions.[228] Finally, Münz and colleagues stress that fertility rates have also declined in many countries of origin such as Spain, Italy or Turkey since the 1970s. Foreign residents who immigrated to Germany from these countries in recent years therefore no longer have the same average number of children as immigrants who came to Germany in the 1960s and 1970s.[229] It remains to be seen whether these factors will eventually lead to a complete convergence in the fertility behaviour of German and foreign women or whether differences will persist over time.

---

[227] *Birg, H./Flöthmann, E.-J.*, Bevölkerungsprojektionen, 1993, p. 5. See also *Enquete-Kommission 'Demographischer Wandel'*, Zwischenbericht, 1998, p. 55; *Münz, R./Seifert, W./Ulrich, R.*, Zuwanderung, 1999, p. 71. For a debate on the quality of fertility data and the implication of data inaccuracies on TFR calculations, see *Schmid, S./Kohls, M.*, Generatives Verhalten, 2011, p. 162.

[228] See *Milewski, N.*, First child, 2007, pp. 862 f. and 884; *Schmid, S./Kohls, M.*, Generatives Verhalten, 2011, pp. 38 ff. and 45 ff.; *Frejka, T., et al.*, Summary, 2008, p. 11. Foreign women who are married to a German man and foreign women who were born and raised in Germany or migrated there as young children appear to adapt to fertility behaviours of German women at a faster pace than women who migrated to Germany at older ages.

[229] *Münz, R./Seifert, W./Ulrich, R.*, Zuwanderung, 1999, p. 70. See also *Schoorl, J.*, Fertility trends, 1995, tables on pp. 105-112; *Milewski, N.*, First child, 2007, p. 868 f.

3.3.2. Mortality developments

3.3.2.1. German citizens

Not only fertility, but also mortality trends have changed profoundly in Germany. As in other industrialized countries, life expectancy at birth has increased steadily for more than a century.[230] This process was only interrupted during the two world wars of the 20th century. Between 1871 and 1881, a newborn male child could expect to reach 36 years of age, a female child 38 years.[231] Until 1931-33, life expectancy at birth increased by nearly 70% to measure 60 years for men and 63 years for women. After a brief drop during the Second World War, the increase continued. The development in life expectancy during the past thirty years is visualised in Figure 24.

Figure 24: Life expectancy at birth of German men and women, 1980-2010

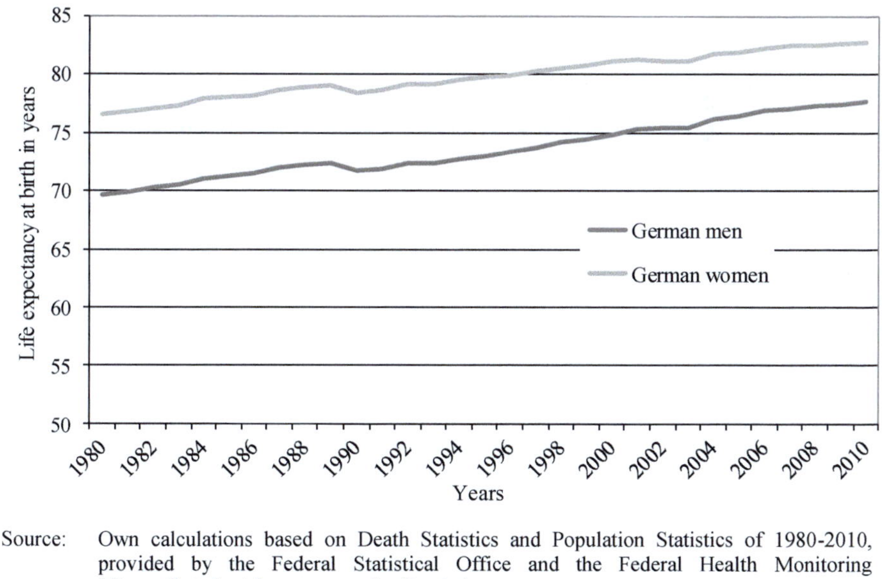

Source: Own calculations based on Death Statistics and Population Statistics of 1980-2010, provided by the Federal Statistical Office and the Federal Health Monitoring (*Gesundheitsberichterstattung des Bundes*).

Note: Data for the years 1980 to 1989 refer to the former West German states only.

---

[230] See *Tuljapurkar, S./Li, N./Boe, C.*, Mortality decline, 2000, p. 789. The focus of this article is on the years 1950 to the early 1990s.

[231] See *Enquete-Kommission 'Demographischer Wandel'*, Zwischenbericht, 1998, p. 73.

In 1989, German men had a life expectancy of 72 years at birth, German women a life expectancy of 79 years. After German reunification in 1990, these values slightly declined, but then continued to rise. Between 1990 and 2010, the life expectancy of newborns has increased in an almost linear manner by an additional six years for men and five years for women to reach 78 years and 83 years in 2010, respectively.The steady gains in longevity during the past century were initially the result of a decrease in infant and child mortality as well as of maternal mortality. During the first decades of the 20th century, better hygiene in hospitals and increasing provision of maternal, infant and child care reduced the number of deaths among infants, children, and among women before and after childbirth. Biomedical advances such as the discovery of antibiotics and vaccinations reduced the number of deaths caused by infectious and parasitic diseases. Since the 1950s, mortality has also declined at middle and old ages. Advances in medical treatment, increased safety at the workplace, healthier life styles and nutritional habits, among other factors, have contributed to mortality decline among these age groups.

The temporary decline in life expectancy after German reunification was the result of a statistical effect. Starting from 1991, life expectancy values have been calculated for the reunified Germany, i.e. including mortality data from East Germany. Since life expectancy values of East Germans were somewhat lower than those of West Germans at this point in time, the calculation of joint life tables initially led to a decrease in German life expectancy values.[232] During the last two decades, the mortality gap between the Eastern and Western parts of Germany has started to close. Vogt and Klüsener as well as Nolte and colleagues suggest that this approximation is attributable to the rapid incorporation of the East German population into the West German health care system. The availability of better diet and increases in living standards, as well as the more advanced medical equipment and pharmaceuticals that were made available in East Germany soon after reunification also reduced mortality rates. Especially mortality caused by cardiovascular diseases and certain types of cancer

[232] See *Luy, M.*, Sterblichkeitsentwicklung, 2004, p. 30 f.

decreased during the past twenty years.[233] Figure 25 illustrates how declines in mortality affected different age groups at different points in time. It shows the age-specific mortality rates of German men in 1956, 1983 and 2010 on a logarithmic scale.

Figure 25: Age-specific mortality rates of German men, selected years

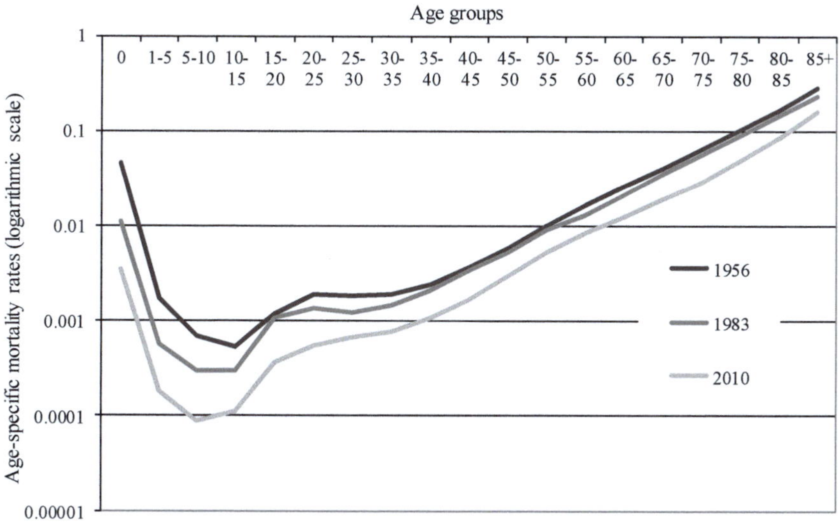

Source: Mortality rates for 1983 and 2010: Own calculations based on Death Statistics and Population Statistics obtained from the Federal Statistical Office. Mortality rate of 1956: Own calculations based on Death Statistics provided by the Human Mortality Database (www.mortality.org) and Population Statistics provided by the Federal Statistical Office.

Note: Data for 1956 do not distinguish between Germans and foreign residents. The mortality rate for this year therefore applies to the entire male population living in Germany in this year. Data for the years 1956 and 1983 refer to the former West German states only.

As can be seen, the shape of the mortality curve has remained relatively stable over time. Mortality is high among infants, declines rapidly and stays at a very low level through childhood ages. The mortality bump around age 18 is attributable to deaths resulting from traffic accidents. Mortality stays relatively stable during young adulthood until around age 35. From that age onwards,

[233] This is not visible in Figure 24. For more information see *Vogt, T./Klüsener, S.*, Mortality decline, 2011; *Vogt, T./Vaupel, J.*, Health care, 2012; *Nolte, E./Shkolnikov, V. M./McKee, M.*, Mortality patterns, 2000, pp. 899, 902 f. and 905; but: *Luy, M.*, Sterblichkeitsentwicklung, 2004, p. 48.

mortality continuously increases. Figure 25 also shows that the level of mortality among German men has decreased over time. Between 1956 and 1983, mortality particularly declined among infants and children and somewhat among young adults. Between 1983 and 2010, mortality has also declined among older age groups.

The characteristics and development of age-specific mortality rates of German women resemble those of German men (not shown in Figure 25). Age-specific mortality rates of German women however have been lower than those of men during past decades and their life expectancy has been higher. The gap in mortality rates has slightly closed since 1990, but the difference in male and female life expectancy at birth still amounted to around five years in 2010 (see Figure 24). These differences are caused by biological and behavioural factors: Women seem to be more resistant to certain kinds of diseases due to genetic, anatomic, physiological and hormonal characteristics. In addition, studies have revealed that men are more likely to engage in health-risky behaviour such as smoking, high alcohol consumption or ruthless car driving and seem to be more susceptible to cardiovascular deaths caused by stress. It has also been debated whether the higher mortality of older men in Germany is a remnant of the comparatively higher health risks and stress that they experienced as soldiers during the Second World War and as prisoners of war in the after-war period.[234] The persistence of sex-specific differences in life expectancy over time however suggests that war-related health deficiencies cannot be the sole explanatory factor for female advantages in life expectancy.

3.3.2.2. Foreign residents

While detailed information is available about past developments in life expectancy among the German population, less is known about mortality and life expectancy trends among foreign residents.[235] The main reason for this knowledge gap is a lack of reliable statistics: In order to calculate mortality rates and life expectancy values, data are required on the annual number of deaths and

---

234 See *Luy, M.*, Sterblichkeitsentwicklung, 2004, p. 26 f.

235 See *Razum, O., et al.*, Mortality, 1998, p. 298.

the annual size of a population group.[236] Both types of statistics exist for the foreign population in Germany, but they are not considered to be reliable. The statistics on cases of death underestimate the annual number of deaths among foreign residents: If foreign residents die while they are abroad, for instance during a visit in their country of origin, these deaths are often not registered in the German statistics or are only registered with delay.[237] For the same reason, population statistics are likely to overestimate the size of the foreign population in Germany: If foreign residents die while staying abroad and if their death is not registered, these individuals continue to be counted as living in Germany after their death. They become 'statistically immortal'. The population statistics also do not capture illegal immigration. Finally, if foreign residents emigrate from Germany and do not inform the German registration offices about their departure, these individuals continue to be counted as living in Germany and inflate the population statistics.[238]

Errors in the population statistics can only be systematically detected with the help of a census. In Germany, the last census was held in May 2011, but the results were not yet available at the time of writing.[239] Once they will be published, the current size of the foreign population can be estimated more reliably. At the moment, however, the exact size of error in the population statistics is not known.

To overcome these data limitations, some demographers have estimated the mortality of foreign residents by comparing and combining data from different sources (e.g. German pension data, data from health insurances) and by applying estimation procedures. Most of these studies have concluded that the mortality of foreign residents is somewhat lower than that of German citizens. This finding, however, does not apply equally across all age groups. While especially

---

[236] See Chapter 3.2.

[237] See *Kohls, M.*, Healthy-migrant-effect, 2008, p. 13 f.

[238] See *Kohls, M.*, Healthy-migrant-effect, 2008, p. 14; *Kibele, E./Scholz, R./Shkolnikov, V. M.*, Migrant mortality, 2008, p. 389 f.; *Kohls, M.*, Mortalität, 2008, p. 31. It has been assumed that the population statistics of German citizens are also somewhat affected by these sources of error, but since the German population is much bigger in size, the distortion is considered to be of a relatively smaller nature.

[239] See *Kohls, M.*, Morbidität, 2011, p. 36.

adult and old age foreign residents appear to have a mortality advantage, the mortality of foreign infants and children exceeds that of their German peers.[240]
Several reasons are discussed to explain the mortality advantage of adult foreign residents, among them the so-called 'healthy-migrant effect'. This effect refers to the observation that individuals who migrate are on average younger and healthier than non-mobile persons. In Germany, foreign immigrants were of particularly sound constitution during the guest worker period of the 1960s and 1970s, since they had to pass health examinations before immigration. This positive selection in terms of health is assumed to explain at least in part why mortality rates of foreign residents have been lower in many age groups than those of the German population.[241]
It has also been suggested that some old or critically ill foreign residents return to their countries of origin in order to spend the rest of their lives there. This selective re-migration is referred to as the 'salmon bias effect' in the literature, a term coined in analogy to salmon fish which die at their place of birth after having returned there to spawn. Again, this effect leads to a positive selection of the foreign population in Germany in terms of health.[242] Foreign residents who migrated to Germany as children or young adults may also adhere to healthier life styles and dietary habits than Germans, which could advantage them in terms of mortality.[243]
Some researchers argue that mortality advantages of foreign residents should diminish over time. Foreign residents have a lower average socio-economic status than Germans, e.g. in terms of job ratings, income and educational levels.

---

240 See for example *Kohls, M.*, Mortalität, 2008; *Razum, O., et al.*, Mortality, 1998; *Altenhofen, L./Weber, I.*, Mortalität, 1993. On age patterns see *Kohls, M.*, Morbidität, 2011, p. 72 f.; *Razum, O./Zeeb, H./Rohrmann, S.*, Healthy migrant effect, 2000, p. 191. But, regarding old age migrants, see deviating findings in *Kibele, E./Scholz, R./Shkolnikov, V. M.*, Migrant mortality, 2008, p. 391. Mortality differences also appear to exist between foreign residents from different countries of origin and between foreign residents who migrated to Germany and their children who were born there (*Kohls, M.*, Healthy-migrant-effect, 2008, p. 20; *Linke, W.*, Mortality trends, 1995, p. 124 f.).

241 See *Linke, W.*, Mortality trends, 1995, p. 124; *Kohls, M.*, Morbidität, 2011, pp. 78-85.

242 See *Altenhofen, L./Weber, I.*, Mortalität, 1993, p. 228 f.; *Razum, O./Sahin-Hodoglugil, N. N./Polit, K.*, Health, 2005, p. 733 f.; more critical: *Kohls, M.*, Healthy-migrant-effect, 2008, p. 20 f.

243 See *Razum, O.*, Commentary, 2006, p. 920; *Razum, O., et al.*, Mortality, 1998, p. 301.

They also have higher rates of accidents at the workplace and are more likely to be unemployed. All of these factors are associated with higher morbidity, increased incidences of chronic disease and with comparatively higher mortality risks. Foreign residents from poorer world regions might also not have enjoyed innovative preventive treatments in their childhood or might have experienced deprivation. This may increase the risk to suffer from certain diseases such as stomach cancer during adulthood. Finally, foreign residents tend to have poorer access to the health care system than Germans in case of sickness due to cultural and language barriers.[244] All of these factors could potentially reduce the mortality advantages of long-term foreign residents over time.

Recent studies suggest that the hypothesis according to which the mortality advantage of foreign residents should diminish over time is correct. Their mortality rates even appear to have reached higher levels than those of Germans among certain age groups.[245] Nonetheless, due to the lack of reliable data, conclusive evidence is lacking.

3.3.3. Migration developments

3.3.3.1. German citizens

During the past fifty years, the number of Germans who immigrated to Germany has nearly constantly been higher than the number of Germans who moved away. This is visible in Figure 26 which shows annual immigration and emigration numbers as well as net migration numbers between 1954 and 2010. As can be seen, net migration numbers only turned negative in recent years.[246]

---

[244] See *Kibele, E./Scholz, R./Shkolnikov, V. M.*, Migrant mortality, 2008, p. 392; *Kohls, M.*, Healthy-migrant-effect, 2008, p. 24; *Razum, O., et al.*, Mortality, 1998, p. 298; *Razum, O./Twardella, D.*, Time travel, 2002, p. 8; *Kohls, M.*, Morbidität, 2011, pp. 10-13 and 63-69.

[245] See *Kibele, E./Scholz, R./Shkolnikov, V. M.*, Migrant mortality, 2008; *Kohls, M.*, Mortalität, 2008, p. 44.

[246] It is likely that the migration statistics do not capture all cases of migration, since not all Germans who move abroad or move back to Germany comply with their duty to deregister and (re)-register at the local registration offices (*Einwohnermeldeamt*). For more information see *Bundesamt für Migration und Flüchtlinge*, Migrationsbericht 2008, 2010, p. 162; *Schupp, J./Söhn, J./Schmiade, N.*, Internationale Mobilität, 2005, p. 280.

Figure 26: Migration trends of German citizens, 1954-2010

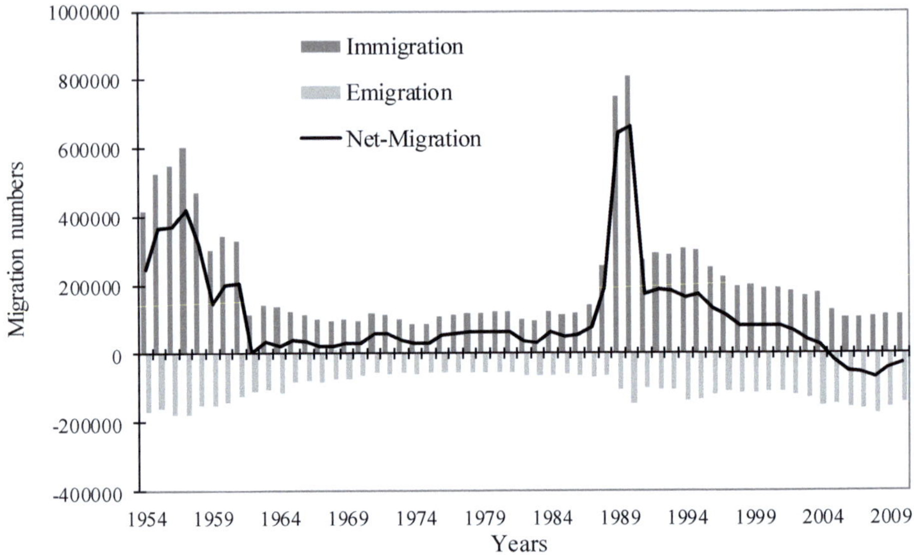

Source: Migration Statistics of 1954-2010, provided by the Federal Statistical Office.
Note: Data for the years 1954-1990 refer to the former West German states only and include migration to and from the GDR. From 1991, data refer to the reunified Germany and do not include migration between East and West Germany. Before 1957 data do not include migration to and from Saarland.[247]

Immigration numbers surpassed emigration numbers particularly strongly during the 1950s and until the construction of the Berlin Wall in 1961. Between 300.000 and 600.000 Germans moved to Germany each year. Many of these immigrants were citizens of the German Democratic Republic (GDR) who moved to the Federal Republic of Germany (FRG) for political reasons, for the purpose of family reunification and because of better prospects on the job market. Resettlers of ethnic German origin were another important group of immigrants during this period. They came from territories in Central and Eastern Europe, parts of which had belonged to the German Reich before the Second World War and had become part of Poland or Russia after the war.

Not all GDR citizens and resettlers remained in the FRG after their immigration. Some moved on to third countries and thus contributed not only to immigration

[247] See *Bundesamt für Migration und Flüchtlinge*, Migrationsbericht 2008, 2010, p. 170.

but also to emigration numbers. Other groups of German emigrants during this period were persons who moved to the GDR because they preferred to live in a socialist system as well as German women who had married allied soldiers in the after war period and followed them to their countries of origin. Some Germans also moved abroad for work. Overall, between 120.000 and 180.000 persons emigrated from Germany each year during the 1950s and early 1960s.

Immigration numbers abruptly declined from 330.000 persons in 1961 to 110.000 persons in 1962 and stayed at comparatively low levels until the late 1980s (see Figure 26). This was particularly the result of the construction of the Berlin Wall in 1961 which blocked almost all migration between the GDR and the FRG. In addition, the number of ethnic Germans who moved to Germany was low during this period, since communist countries in Eastern Europe restricted travel and migration of their citizens, including of ethnic Germans. Ethnic Germans who did move to Germany between the early 1960s and late 1980s often profited from bilateral agreements between the German government and governments of Central and Eastern European countries. Other groups which contributed to immigration numbers during this period were German expatriates who returned to Germany after having lived abroad as well as children of German citizens who were born abroad.[248] Emigration numbers remained at low levels between the early 1960s and late 1980s. Between 55.000 and 110.000 Germans left Germany each year.

Towards the end of the 1980s, the number of immigrants increased drastically and reached its peak after the fall of the Berlin Wall. More than 809.000 German migrants moved to the Federal Republic in 1990. Many of these immigrants were citizens of the former GDR who moved to West Germany as soon as the borders opened. Migration between the old and new Länder continued at a large scale throughout the 1990s. Since 1991, however, this type of migration is registered as internal migration and no longer appears in the international migration statistics.

---

[248] See *Münz, R./Seifert, W./Ulrich, R.*, Zuwanderung, 1999, pp. 31 f. and 37; *Münz, R./Ulrich, R.*, Immigration, 1999, p. 23 f.; *Ette, A./Sauer, L.*, Auswanderung, 2010, p. 56 f.

Central and Eastern European countries also lifted travel restrictions for ethnic Germans after the fall of the iron curtain. As a consequence, the number of ethnic German immigrants increased substantially. The German government reacted by restricting migration rules for this group of people from the early 1990s.[249] As a consequence, the immigration numbers of ethnic Germans dropped during the years after reunification. While in 1990 nearly 400.000 ethnic Germans had moved to Germany, only 4.400 did so in 2008. Apart from increasing legal requirements, this drop in numbers reflects a decline in the stock of individuals who are both willing and eligible to move to Germany. It is also thought to reflect improvements in living conditions of ethnic Germans in Eastern European countries.[250]

Overall, immigration numbers have declined since the early 1990 and have only slightly increased again since 2006. German citizens who are moving to Germany today are mainly citizens who return after having lived abroad, for instance students, researchers, retirees, managers or merchants as well as their family members. German children who were born abroad are also registered as German immigrants when they first come to Germany.[251] Migration statistics have also reported a gradual increase in the number of Germans emigrants from around 99.000 in 1991 to 175.000 in 2008. Recent studies reveal that many of these emigrants move abroad to work or study, to join family members or – to a smaller degree – to live in countries with a warmer climate or lower costs of living after retirement. Many emigrants do not permanently settle down abroad, but eventually move back to Germany.[252] Because of the increase in emigration and the parallel decrease in immigration, net migration numbers turned negative for the first time in 2005 and have remained so until 2010.

---

249 See *Bundesamt für Migration und Flüchtlinge*, Migrationsbericht 2008, 2010, p. 56 f. See also *Münz, R./Seifert, W./Ulrich, R.*, Zuwanderung, 1999, pp. 34 and 37; *Bade, K. J./Oltmer, J.*, Einwanderungsland, 2003, p. 290 ff.; *Münz, R., et al.*, Migrationsmuster, 1997, p. 34.

250 See *Bundesamt für Migration und Flüchtlinge*, Migrationsbericht 2008, 2010, p. 56 ff.

251 See *Bundesamt für Migration und Flüchtlinge*, Migrationsbericht 2008, 2010, pp. 161-163; *Sauer, L./Ette, A.*, Auswanderung, 2007, p. 30.

252 See *Sauer, L./Ette, A.*, Auswanderung, 2007, pp. 47-68 and 71-73; *Bundesamt für Migration und Flüchtlinge*, Migrationsbericht 2008, 2010, p. 170 ff.

Figure 27 shows the number of German immigrants and emigrants per age group as well as net migration values in 2010. As can be seen, large numbers of immigrants and emigrants were of very young ages (0 to 5 years) and of young adult ages (20 to 45 years). This age pattern has been similar in previous years. The proportion of women among migrants has been slightly higher than the proportion of men until German reunification (between 50% and 55%; not shown in Figure 27) Since then, this has changed and the proportion of male migrants (between 50% and 60%) has somewhat surpassed that of women.[253]

Figure 27: Age-specific migration numbers of German citizens, 2010

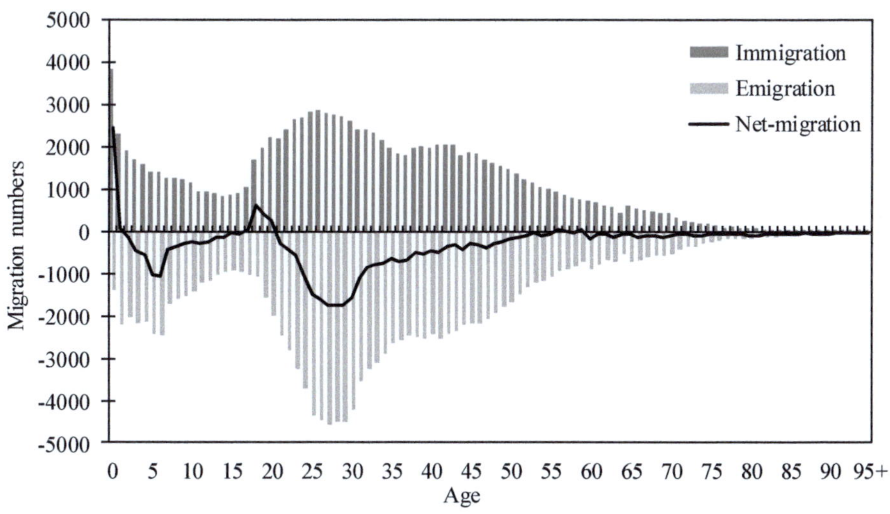

Source: Migration Statistics of 2010, provided by the Federal Statistical Office.

3.3.3.2. Foreign residents

Whereas net migration numbers of German citizens have been positive during most of the last six decades, migration behaviours of foreigners have been subject to greater variation. Between the mid-1950s and the mid-1990s, periods of high positive net migration were interrupted by years with negative net migration numbers (Figure 28). Since the late 1990s immigration and emigration

253 Own calculations based on Migration Statistics obtained from the Federal Statistical Office.

numbers have become more stable, with immigration numbers slightly exceeding emigration numbers in most years.

Figure 28: Migration trends of foreign residents, 1954-2010

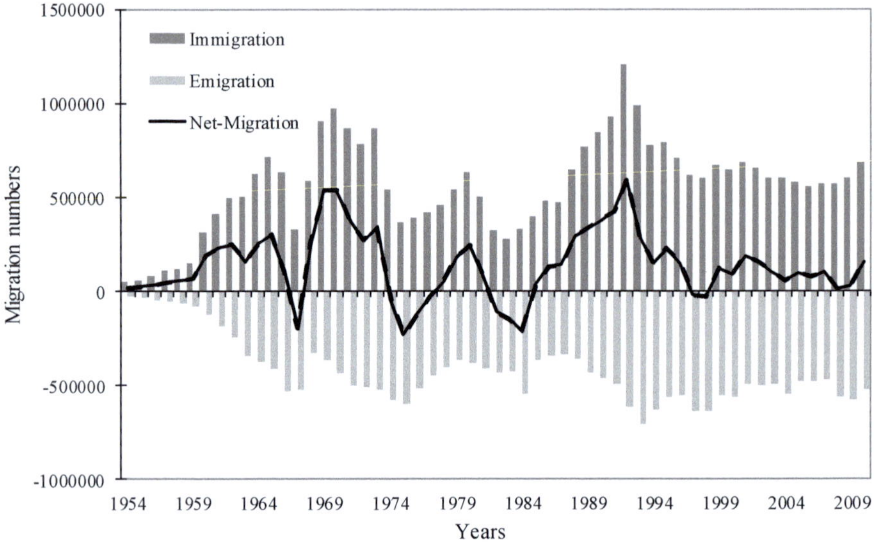

Source: Migration Statistics of 1954-2010, provided by the Federal Statistical Office.
Note: Data for the years 1954-1990 refer to the former West German states only and include migration to and from the GDR. From 1991, data refer to the reunified Germany and do not include migration between East and West Germany. Before 1957 data do not include migration to and from Saarland.

In order to explain the fluctuations in migration numbers over time, economic and social as well as political factors are discussed: Until the early 1970s, migration trends were predominantly characterized by the massive recruitment of mostly male foreign workers. The recruitment process was a direct consequence of the economic boom in Germany in the post-war period. While the resident German population as well as immigrants from the GDR and ethnic German resettlers could meet the increasing demand for workers until the mid-1950s, the recruitment of additional workers then became necessary in order to prevent a slow down of the economic boom. In 1955, the German government signed a first bilateral recruitment agreement with Italy. Further agreements with Spain, Greece, Turkey, Morocco, Tunisia and Yugoslavia followed during the

1960s.[254] The number of foreign immigrants increased more than tenfold from 60.000 in 1954 to 870.000 in 1965. The massive recruitment of foreign workers was only interrupted in 1966 and 1967 when the German economy went into recession. During these years, net migration numbers turned negative.[255]

Foreign workers who came to Germany on the basis of recruitment agreements were not expected to settle down, but to return to their countries of origin after a limited period of residence and employment in Germany.[256] This 'rotation principle' is reflected in the increase in emigration numbers in the 1960s. Towards the end of the 1960s, the rotation principle became increasingly criticized by the German industry and by migrants who wanted to work in Germany for longer periods of time. The German government reacted and facilitated longer terms of employment of guest workers from the early 1970s.[257]

After the OPEC oil crisis of 1973 the German economy went into recession and the government stopped recruiting foreign workers. Migrant workers were left with the choice of returning to their countries of origin or staying and settling down in Germany. Some migrants chose the first option. As a consequence, net migration numbers turned negative between 1974 and 1977. The majority of guest workers, however, decided to stay and many brought family members to Germany. Due to this family migration, the number of immigrants began to surpass the number of emigrants again from 1978. Asylum seekers were another, albeit quantitatively less prominent group of immigrants during the late 1970s and early 1980s. These migrants moved to Germany especially from Turkey and Poland.[258]

A further period of negative net-migration was recorded between 1982 and 1984 after the second oil crisis. In these years, the German economy was again affected by an economic downturn and unemployment rates increased. The

---

254 See *Bade, K. J./Oltmer, J.*, Einwanderungsland, 2003, p. 283; *Münz, R., et al.*, Migrationsmuster, 1997, p. 17.

255 See *Münz, R./Seifert, W./Ulrich, R.*, Zuwanderung, 1999, p. 47; *Hammar, T.*, Democracy, 1990, p. 18.

256 See *Castles, S.*, Guest worker, 1986, p. 768 f.

257 See *Enquete-Kommission 'Demographischer Wandel'*, Zwischenbericht, 1998, p. 753.

258 See *Münz, R., et al.*, Migrationsmuster, 1997, p. 2; *Castles, S.*, Guest worker, 1986, p. 769; *Münz, R./Seifert, W./Ulrich, R.*, Zuwanderung, 1999, p. 54 ff.

government reacted by offering financial incentives for migrants to return to their countries of origin.[259]

With the end of the Cold War a new period of high net migration started which lasted until the mid-1990s. It was characterized by the migration of asylum seekers and refugees who moved to Germany from the Balkan area, Turkey, Eastern Europe, Iraq and Iran.[260] In addition, an increasing number of foreign workers moved to Germany. In contrast to the work migration of the 1960s and early 1970s, these migrant workers came predominantly from Eastern Europe. They generally stayed in Germany for limited periods of time only and worked in economic areas with labour deficits or as seasonal workers.[261]

The increase in migration numbers was especially drastic between 1988 and 1992. During these five years, the number of immigrants more than doubled from 470.000 persons to 1.200.000 persons. The German government reacted by restricting the possibilities to apply for asylum in 1993. The number of immigrants to Germany began to decline again thereafter.[262] In the second half of the 1990s, refugees who had fled from the conflicts in the former Yugoslavia also started to return to their home regions. Mainly due to this process of return migration, net migration numbers turned negative in 1997 and 1998.[263]

Since the end of the 1990s, immigration and emigration trends in Germany have become somewhat more stable, with emigration numbers being slightly lower than immigration numbers throughout the period. The relatively balanced immigration and emigration numbers reflect an increase in temporary migration. Especially seasonal workers, foreign students and qualified workers often stay in Germany for limited periods of time only, either by choice or by requirement.[264] Immigrants who move to Germany for the purposes of family (re)unification or

---

259 See *Münz, R./Seifert, W./Ulrich, R.*, Zuwanderung, 1999, p. 50; *Hagedorn, H.*, Einbürgerung, 2001, p. 110.

260 See *Münz, R./Seifert, W./Ulrich, R.*, Zuwanderung, 1999, p. 54; *Bade, K. J./Oltmer, J.*, Einwanderungsland, 2003, p. 288.

261 See *Münz, R., et al.*, Migrationsmuster, 1997, p. 21; *Kemper, F.-J.*, Wanderungen, 2006, p. 397.

262 See *Münch, U.*, Asylpolitik, 1993, p. 10 f.; *Zlotnik, H.*, Migration, 1998, p. 442; *Münz, R./Ulrich, R.*, Wachstum, 1997, p. 15.

263 See *Kemper, F.-J.*, Wanderungen, 2006, p. 391.

264 See *Bundesamt für Migration und Flüchtlinge*, Migrationsbericht 2008, 2010, p. 38 f.; *Kemper, F.-J.*, Wanderungen, 2006, p. 395.

asylum are further important migrant groups. During recent years the number of asylum applications has also increased again. In 2010, around 41.300 asylum applications were filed, twice as many as in 2007, with applicants coming especially from Afghanistan, Iraq, Serbia, and Iran.[265] Preliminary statistics for the years 2011 and 2012 suggest that the number of asylum applications has further increased since then, triggered among other factors by the social and political upheavals in Northern Africa.[266]

Figure 29: Age-specific migration numbers of foreign residents, 2010

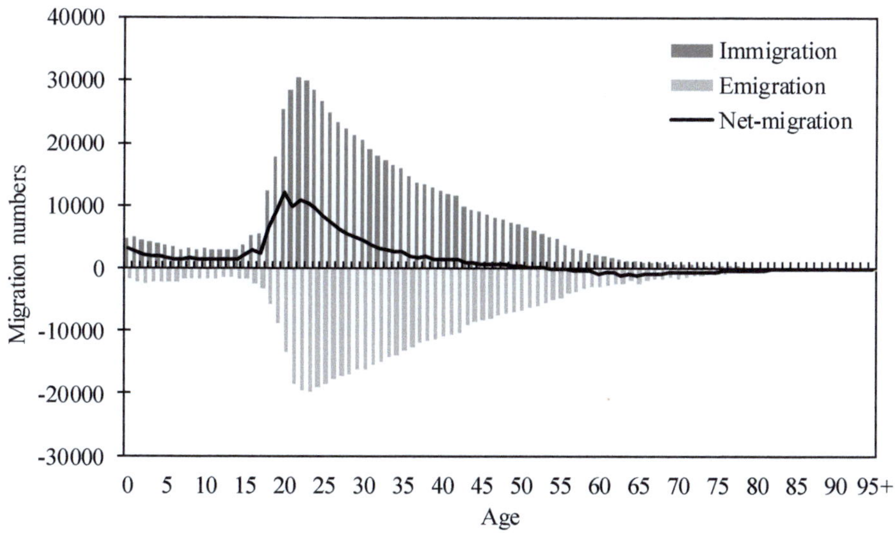

Source: Migration Statistics of 2010, provided by the Federal Statistical Office.

During the last five decades, foreign residents who have migrated to and from Germany have predominantly been of young adult ages. Figure 29 shows the total number of male and female foreign immigrants and emigrants by age group, as well as net migration values for the year 2010. As can be seen, immigration and emigration numbers rise sharply between ages 15 and 20, remain at high levels until age 25 and then decline progressively. In previous

265 See *Bundesamt für Migration und Flüchtlinge*, Migrationsbericht 2010, 2011, p. 94 f.

266 See *Bundesamt für Migration und Flüchtlinge*, Aktuelle Zahlen, 2012, p. 3 f.

years, migration numbers followed a similar age pattern. The proportion of men among migrants has been somewhat higher than the proportion of women in recent years (around 60% vs. 40%).

3.3.4. Citizenship acquisition at birth

3.3.4.1. Children born to German citizens

All children born to a German mother have acquired the German citizenship at birth since 1975 on the basis of the ius sanguinis principle. Since 2000, this includes children born to mothers who are ius soli-citizens. Before 1975, children born in a mixed marriage of a German woman and a foreign man generally acquired the foreign citizenship of their father only. They could exceptionally acquire the German citizenship if they would otherwise have become stateless. Since 1975, a change in law has made it possible for German women to pass their citizenship on to their children.

3.3.4.2. Children born to foreign residents

The statistics on children born to foreign mothers reflect the more complex rules on citizenship acquisition which apply to them. The trends over time are displayed in Figure 30.

In 1972, only 10% of the children born to foreign mothers acquired German citizenship qua ius sanguinis, i.e. because they had a German father. All other children were born to two foreign parents or to a foreign mother and a German father whose paternity was not established and therefore acquired a foreign citizenship at birth only. Over time, the proportion of children who acquired German citizenship qua ius sanguinis increased, first gradually to reach 25% in 1999 and then more strongly from 30% in 2000 to 44% in 2007. Since then, the increase has levelled off.

The increase in the proportion of children to whom the ius sanguinis principle applies is the result of changing union formation trends in Germany. During recent years, the number of 'mixed' partnerships and marriages in Germany, i.e. relationships between foreign residents and Germans citizens, has increased. The German citizens in these relationships may be 'native' Germans. A recent study of Haug however suggests that interethnic marriages and partnerships are still relatively rare in Germany.[267] It is therefore likely that many of the mixed partnerships are in fact unions between a foreign resident and a German citizen of foreign ethnic origin who naturalized in Germany. Since comprehensive data on the ethnicity or country of origin of parents are not collected in the birth statistics, however, this is only a hypothesis which cannot be verified here.

Figure 30: Citizenship acquired by children born to foreign women in Germany, 1972-2010

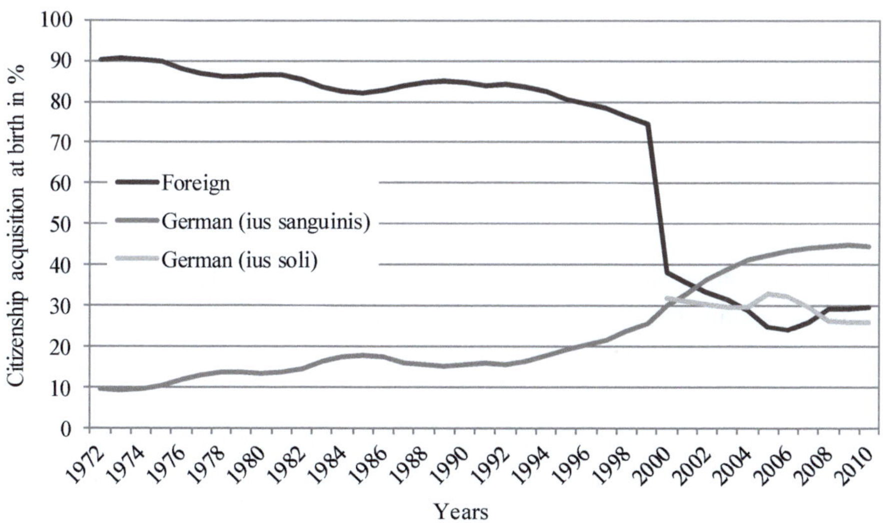

Source: Own calculations based on Birth Statistics of 1972-2010, provided by the Federal Statistical Office.
Note: Data for the years 1972 to 1990 refer to the former West German states only.

Since 2000, an additional 25% to 31% of each cohort born to foreign mothers have acquired the German citizenship qua ius soli. These children have foreign parents of which at least one fulfilled the ius soli-requirements. Overall, more

[267] See *Haug, S.*, Interethnische Kontakte, 2010, p. 47 f.

than two thirds of all children born to a foreign mother have acquired the German citizenship at birth since the year 2000.[268]

3.3.5. *Changes of citizenship during the life course*

3.3.5.1. German citizens (majority population)

German citizens can under certain conditions revoke or lose their German citizenship even while living in Germany (see Chapter 2.3.3.). In practice, it is not clear if and how many Germans lose their citizenship each year, since a comprehensive federal-level statistics on this topic does not exist.[269]

Only few individual data points are available. It has for instance been estimated that around 40.000 persons of Turkish origin who had naturalized in Germany after the year 2000 lost their German citizenship again.[270] These naturalized Turks had first revoked their Turkish citizenship in order to comply with German naturalization requirements, and had reacquired their Turkish citizenship immediately after their successful naturalization in Germany. Before 2000, this revocation and subsequent reacquisition of the Turkish citizenship had been lawful. The reform of the Citizenship Act in the year 2000, however, abolished this option. A regulation was introduced into German citizenship law which provides that German citizenship is lost if German citizens (re-)acquire a foreign citizenship. Many Turkish persons were apparently not aware of this change in law and lost their German citizenship during the first years after the reform when they maintained the previous practice of reacquiring the Turkish citizenship after naturalization.

Apart from this exception, the number of Germans who lose their citizenship each year seems to be small. During a minor interpellation in the Bundestag in May 2008, the German government stated that it was aware of only 84

[268] See *Bundesamt für Migration und Flüchtlinge*, Migrationsbericht 2008, 2010, pp. 245-248 for more information on citizenship acquisition at birth.

[269] Information obtained via e-mail from the Federal Ministry of the Interior on 7. June 2011; see also *Waldrauch, H.*, Statistics, 2006, p. 310.

[270] See *Hailbronner, K.*, Germany, 2006, p. 233; *Ersanilli, E./Koopmans, R.*, Rewarding integration, 2010, p. 778.

individuals who had been deprived of the German citizenship between 2002 and 2005.[271]

3.3.5.2. Ius soli-citizens

Ius soli-Germans are legally obliged to choose between their citizenships within a period of five years after reaching majority age, unless they obtain the official permission to keep both citizenships. Thus, after age 23, ius soli-citizens are either regarded as foreign residents by the German state if they revoke their German citizenship or as German citizens if they retain their German citizenship. The first cohort of ius soli-citizens was born in 1990. They turned 18 in 2008. This cohort encompasses around 3.300 persons (Figure 31).

Figure 31: Number of ius soli-children born between 1990 and 2010

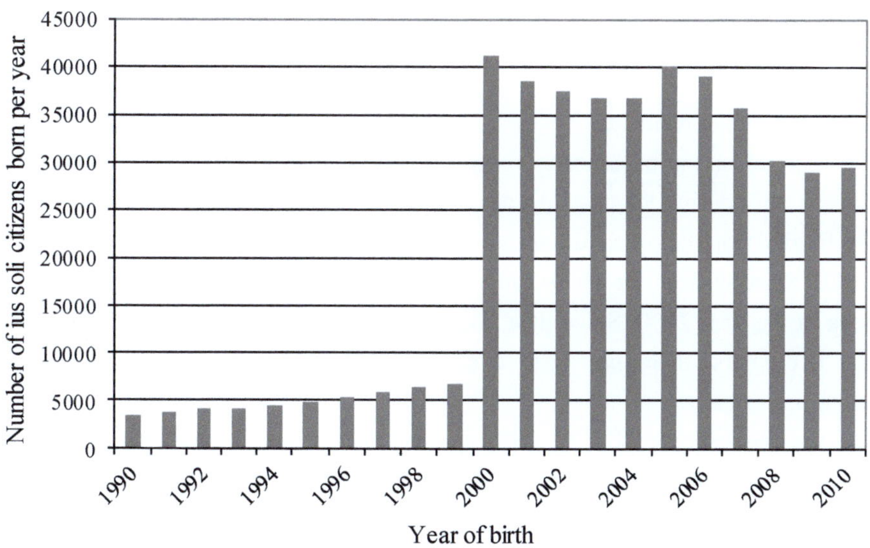

Source: Birth Statistics and Naturalization Statistics of 2000-2010, provided by the Federal Statistical Office.

The cohorts born between 1991 and 1994, around 4.000 persons each, have also reached or are currently reaching majority age and have entered the consideration period during which they have to decide between their

271 See BT-Drs. 16/9265 of 26.05.2008, p. 7.

citizenships. The quantitatively bigger cohorts born after the enactment of the citizenship law in 2000 will only start to reach majority age in 2018. Since none of the cohorts has reached age 23 at the time of writing, complete statistics about their decision-making behaviour are not yet available. Only preliminary data and anecdotal evidence from some German municipalities exist. According to Lämmermann, many ius soli-citizens appear to postpone the obligation to choose between their citizenships. In the Southern regions of Hessen, for example, only 108 out of 263 ius soli-citizens of the 1990 cohort had opted between their citizenships by June 2010. Among these 108 individuals, only two decided to retain their foreign citizenship. The other 106 individuals revoked their foreign citizenship or were entitled to keep both. Similar experiences have been reported from other regions and municipalities.[272] It is not clear whether the ius soli-citizens who have so far not made a choice will opt for the German citizenship in as large numbers.

3.3.5.3. Foreign residents

The naturalization behaviour of foreign residents in Germany has changed substantially during the past decades. Figure 32 shows that only around 0.4% of the foreign population acquired the German citizenship each year until the late 1980s. Starting from the 1990s, the naturalization rate increased and reached its peak in the year 2000. Since then, the rate has declined again. Only during the last two years, there has been a change in trend a slight increase in the naturalization rate.

Social scientists have discussed different factors to explain these changes of the naturalization rate. The low naturalization rate during the 1970s and 1980s has been attributed to the strict naturalization requirements of the time (see Chapter 2.3.3.). Especially the obligation to revoke the previous citizenship has been mentioned as a factor which presumably deterred foreign residents from naturalizing. Anil and others have argued that many foreign residents who moved to Germany during the 1950s and 1960s retained a strong attachment to

---

[272] See *Lämmermann, F.*, Ius soli, 2011, p. 2 f.; *Göbel-Zimmermann, R./Eichhorn, A.*, Entwicklungen I, 2010, p. 296; *Weinmann, M./Becher, I./Babka von Gostomski, C.*, Einbürgerungsverhalten, 2012, p. 8.

their home country and fostered the idea of returning there in old age. Giving up the citizenship of their home country might have entailed the loss of important rights, such as the right to move and settle there without limitation or the right to own or inherit property.

Figure 32: Naturalization rate of foreign residents, 1974-2010

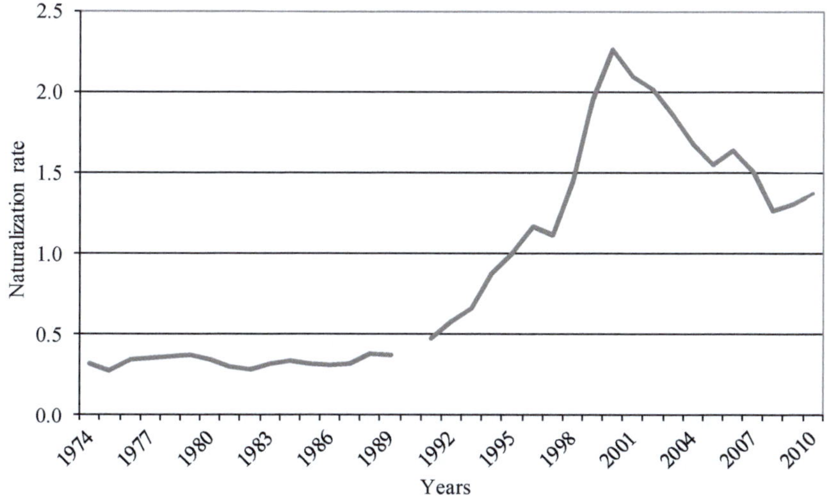

Source: Own calculations based on Naturalization Statistics and Population Statistics of 1974-2010, provided by the Federal Statistical Office.

Note: Data do not include acquisitions of citizenship by ethnic Germans and acquisitions of citizenship at birth based on the ius soli-principle. Data for the years 1974 to 1989 refer to the former West German states only. Value for 1990 was not calculated due to nominator-denominator mismatch: Population data of this year refer to the reunified Germany, while naturalization data refer to West Germany only. Data for the years 2000 to 2010 refer to naturalization cases among foreign residents who are living in Germany only. In the years before that, persons who naturalize while living abroad are also included.

The acquisition of the German citizenship, by contrast, would have entailed few additional rights for long-term guest workers. After having obtained an unlimited residence permit in Germany, they could only be expulsed in very restrictive circumstances and had access to almost all jobs and the social security system. Only the right to vote and access to some jobs in the public sector remain the prerogative of German citizens. Hammar has argued that these few benefits of naturalization did not outweigh the financial and emotional costs of giving up the previous citizenship and that many foreign residents therefore refrained from applying for naturalization. High fees and the fact that naturalization was not a right but depended on the discretion of naturalization offices are also considered to have deterred foreign residents from naturalizing during the 1970s and 1980s. In addition, it has been suggested that some foreign residents may have refrained from naturalizing because they experienced discrimination or social rejection in Germany or because they did not identify with the German culture.

The increase of the naturalization rate in the early and mid-1990s has been attributed to reforms of the Citizenship Act which were enacted during these years. The reforms facilitated naturalization for young foreign residents who had grown up in Germany and adult foreign residents who had lived there for long periods of time. If these groups fulfilled naturalization requirements, they gained the right to acquire the German citizenship and did not depend on the discretionary decision of naturalization offices any more.[273]

After a brief decline in 1997, the naturalization rate increased even stronger until 2000, when more than 2.3% of the foreign population acquired German citizenship. In the academic discussion, this increase has been attributed to a highly controversial public debate surrounding the major citizenship reform which was enacted in 2000. After the red-green coalition had won the Bundestag elections in 1998, they proposed a draft for a new citizenship law, which among other points provided for the general acceptance of dual citizenship upon naturalization. The conservative parties CDU/CSU launched a public campaign against the draft law in general and the acceptance of dual citizenship in particular. The media, churches and many interest groups were in favour of allowing dual citizenship, but the German population was overall sceptic. The political parties in the Bundestag were also deeply divided over the topic.[274] The citizenship reform was finally adopted in 1999 after a compromise between the

---

273 See Chapter 2.3.3.

274 The controversial debates are even held to be partly responsible for the outcome of Landtag elections in Hesse during this year. The CDU won the elections and as a consequence the federal red-green coalition government lost its majority in the Bundesrat. See *Hailbronner, K.*, Germany, 2006, p. 230 and *Münz, R./Ulrich, R.*, Immigration, 1999, p. 14.

government and the opposition parties had been reached. The general acceptance of dual citizenship was not retained. Nonetheless, the reform extended the number of exceptions in which dual citizenship is tolerated.

It has been suggested that the prominence of the citizenship reform in the public discussion prompted foreign residents to consider naturalizing and contributed to the increase in the naturalization rate in the late 1990s.[275] In addition, it has been argued that specific elements of the draft citizenship law may have led foreign residents to apply for naturalization. Most notably, the citizenship reform of 2000 re-introduced the requirement that naturalization applicants must speak German. Anil and Wüst assume that some foreign residents applied for naturalization before this new requirement became effective, because they feared that they might not be able to pass language tests.[276]

Although the reform of 2000 was intended to encourage foreign residents to naturalize, naturalization rates started to drop after its enactment and nearly constantly declined until 2008. This development is controversially discussed in the literature. Some authors attribute it to the language requirement and to other naturalization requirements that were introduced during the last years which may have deterred some foreign residents.[277] Other researchers interpret the decline in the naturalization rate as a sign of a 'saturation effect'.[278] According to this view, naturalization rates declined after 2000 because most migrants who were eligible and willing to naturalize had made use of their right when the topic was in the headlines around the turn of the century.

---

[275] See *Hagedorn, H.*, Einbürgerung, 2001, p. 126; *Böcker, A./Thränhardt, D.*, Multiple citizenship, 2006, p. 80.

[276] *Anil, M.*, Citizenship law, 2006, p. 458; *Wüst, A.*, Naturalized citizens, 2004, p. 343.

[277] See *Ersanilli, E./Koopmans, R.*, Rewarding integration, 2010, p. 778; *Göbel-Zimmermann, R./Eichhorn, A.*, Entwicklungen I, 2010, p. 300.

[278] *Özcan, V.*, Deutschland, 2005, p. 1. The declining naturalization rate has also been attributed to a statistical effect: The Citizenship Law of 2000 allowed children under 10 years of age to apply for German citizenship under the new *ius soli*-regulation until 2001 (see Chapter 2.3.3.). Some researchers have suggested that these cases of citizenship acquisition temporarily boosted the naturalization rate and that the rate was bound to decline once all cases were processed (*Diehl, C./Blohm, M.*, Entscheidung, 2008, p. 439; *Worbs, S.*, Einbürgerung, 2008, p. 17 f.). Naturalization data however show that this effect does not explain the overall decline in the naturalization rate. When only naturalizations by persons aged 10 or older are considered, the drop in the naturalization rate between 2000 and 2008 nevertheless amounts to more than 43% (Own calculations based on naturalization statistics obtained from the Federal Statistical Office).

Some academics discuss the drop in the naturalization rate with a special focus on Turkish residents. As was already mentioned before, the Turkish government had allowed Turks in Germany to first revoke their Turkish citizenship in order to comply with German naturalization regulations and then to reacquire their Turkish citizenship immediately after successful naturalization in Germany. Since the reform of 2000, this legal option does not exist anymore. The naturalization rate of Turkish citizens in Germany dropped since 2000 and it has been suggested that this may have been a direct reaction to the legal change.[279]
Finally, the rejection of dual citizenship continues to be discussed as one of the main reasons for the low naturalization propensity of foreign residents. In surveys, foreign residents still mention their desire to retain their previous citizenship as one of the main reasons against naturalization. Worbs has pointed out that this is somewhat surprising, given that the citizenship reform of 2000 increased the number of exceptions in which dual citizenship upon naturalization is accepted. She suggests that this somewhat paradoxical finding may be the result of misinformation: Many foreign residents may not be fully aware of the many exceptions in which dual citizenship is tolerated and for fear of having to give up their previous citizenship do not apply.[280] During the last two years, the naturalization rate has slightly increased again.
In 2010, the naturalization rate reached 1.4%, a level comparable to the rate of 1998. In terms of their demographic characteristics, foreign residents who naturalized in the last ten years were predominantly of young age. Figure 33 shows the age-specific naturalization rate in 2010. As can be seen, especially children, adolescents and young adults acquired the German citizenship during this year. Persons aged 18 to 21 were particularly likely to naturalize. The proportion of men and women who decided to naturalize in 2010 and previous years has been relatively balanced.[281]

279 See *Thränhardt, D.*, Einbürgerung, 2008, p. 12.
280 *Worbs, S.*, Einbürgerung, 2008, p. 37.
281 See *Worbs, S.*, Einbürgerung, 2008, p. 19.

Figure 33: Age-specific naturalization rate of foreign residents, 2010

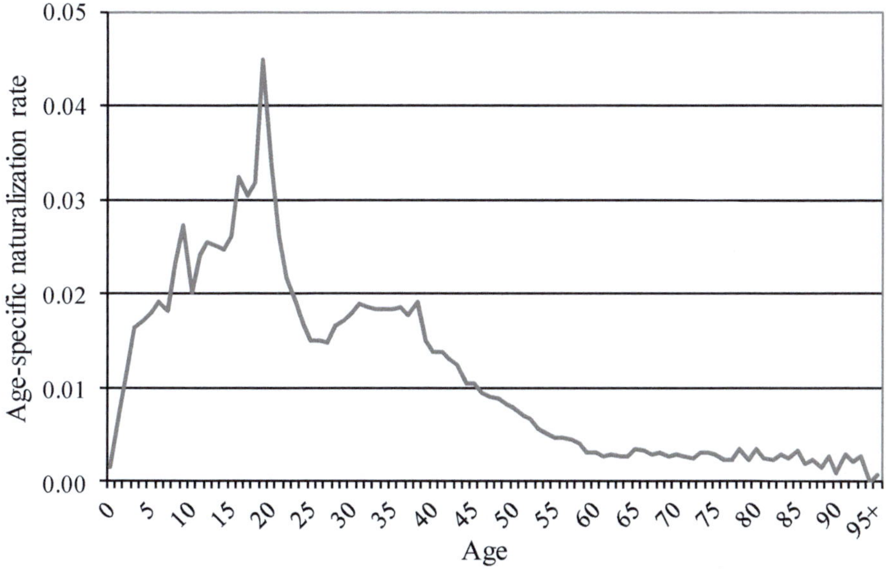

Source: Own calculations based on Naturalization Statistics and Population Statistics of 2010, provided by the Federal Statistical Office.

3.4. Influence of demographic trends on the German electorate, 1949-2010

Among the demographic components described above, fertility trends among German and foreign women, mortality trends among the German population and migration trends among the foreign population were quantitatively most important for the development of the population in Germany and its demos. This appears from Figure 34 which shows the number of individuals who have joined or left different citizenship groups in Germany through various forms of attrition and accession between 1974 and 2010.[282]

The data show that German women (including ius soli-citizens) have given birth to more than 20.8 million children since 1974. Nearly all of these children acquired German citizenship, making them eligible voters of the future. Only

[282] More distant years could not be considered here, since data were not available for all demographic factors.

11.619 children who were born in 1974 to German mothers and foreign fathers did not acquire German citizenship due to the prevalent citizenship legislation at the time. These children were legally considered foreign residents of Germany by the German state and unless they naturalized during a later stage of their lives, they did not obtain the right to vote. In addition, more than 28 million Germans died between 1974 and 2010. This figure includes cases of death among ius soli-citizens. Migration was of quantitatively smaller scale: The number of German immigrants surpassed the number of German emigrants by more than 2.9 million persons since 1974. Again, this number includes cases of migration of ius soli-children.

The size of the foreign population in Germany (right side of Figure 34) was most strongly influenced by international migration. Between 1974 and 2010, the number of foreign immigrants surpassed the number of emigrants by a net value of 3.5 million persons. In addition, more than 3.8 million children were born to foreign women since 1974. Almost 2.5 million of these children acquired the foreign citizenship(s) of their parents only and thus entered the statistics as new members of the foreign population. Nearly 950.000 children born to foreign women acquired German citizenship at birth because they had a German father. A further 395.000 of the children born to foreign mothers acquired German citizenship qua ius soli since the year 2000. Naturalization and death decimated the foreign population. More than 2.2 million foreign residents acquired German citizenship since 1974 and 49.000 foreign children who were born between 1990 and 1999 made use of the transitory ius soli-regulation and acquired German citizenship retrospectively. In addition, more than 430.000 cases of death by foreign residents were registered in Germany.

These different demographic components shaped the development of the population structure in Germany over time. Figure 34 shows the structure of the population of Germany in 1974, 1986, 1998 and 2010 in the form of population pyramids which distinguish by age, sex and citizenship. The dark grey areas represent the foreign population in Germany, the light grey parts the German population. In the last population pyramid of 2010, the mid-grey areas visualize the population of ius soli-children. The German adult population aged 18 and older formed the electorate during the different years (highlighted population groups in the Figure).

Figure 34: Demographic factors which have changed the size and age structure of citizenship groups in Germany, 1974-2010

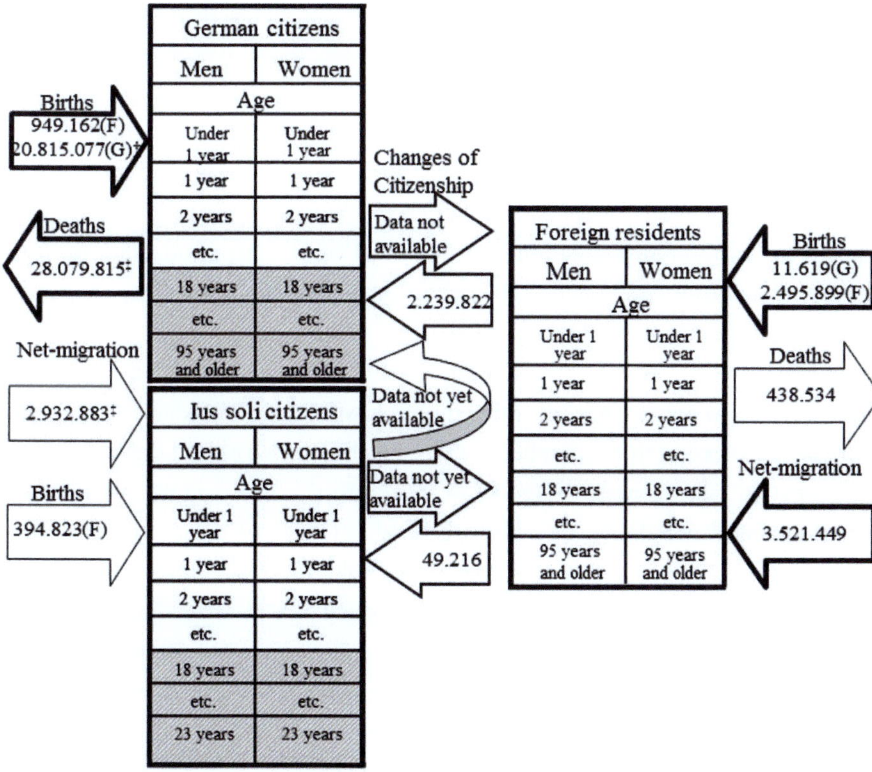

‡ Data include demographic events of German citizens and ius soli citizens, separate data not available. Abbreviations: G= Births by German women; F = Births by foreign women

Source: Own illustration. Calculations based on Birth Statistics, Death Statistics, Migration Statistics and Naturalization Statistics of 1974-2010, provided by the Federal Statistical Office.

Note: Data for the years 1974 to 1989 refer to the former West German states only. The year 1990 was excluded from the overview, since some statistics for this year cover the reunified Germany and others are restricted to the former West German states.

In 1974, the age structure of the German population was uneven. Towards the bottom of the population pyramid, the high fertility of the 1950s and 1960s had created a bulge of quantitatively strong age cohorts. The indentations around ages 29, 42 and 57 were the result of sharp fertility declines during the two world wars and the economic crisis of the early 1930s. The wars had also led to population losses which account for the larger number of women than men in higher age groups. The number of foreign residents was highest among ages 20 to 45 and the number of foreign men was somewhat higher than the number of foreign women. This was the result of the guest worker migration period, which had brought especially young male migrants to Germany. In 1974, around 69% of all members of the resident population were in possession of German citizenship, aged 18 years or older and therefore entitled to vote. The median age of the electorate was between 44 and 45 years.

By 1986, the foreign population had increased in size especially due to high fertility rates of foreign women. Most children born to foreign mothers acquired a foreign citizenship at birth only and thus became members of the foreign population. The size of the second disenfranchised population group in Germany, underage citizens, declined due to low fertility levels among German women. The decline in the number of German children surpassed the increase in the size of the foreign population. Therefore, the overall number of disenfranchised population members declined between 1974 and 1986 and the proportion of eligible voters increased from 69% to 76%. Most of the baby-boom generations had passed the minimum voting age in 1986. This increased the number of younger electors. Nonetheless, reductions in old age mortality led to a parallel increase in the number of older electors. The median age of the electorate therefore did not decrease as might have been expected but by contrast slightly increased to between 45 and 46 years.

By 1998, the German population had increased in size from around 62.7 million to around 79.8 million persons especially due to German reunification. The overall shape of the population pyramid, however, had not changed. The base of the population pyramid remained small and had in fact shrunk further because of the short-term decline in fertility after German reunification. The foreign population in Germany had further increased in size, especially due to high positive net migration numbers during the early 1990s.

Figure 35: Structure of the population in Germany by age, sex and citizenship in 1974, 1986, 1998 and 2010

1974

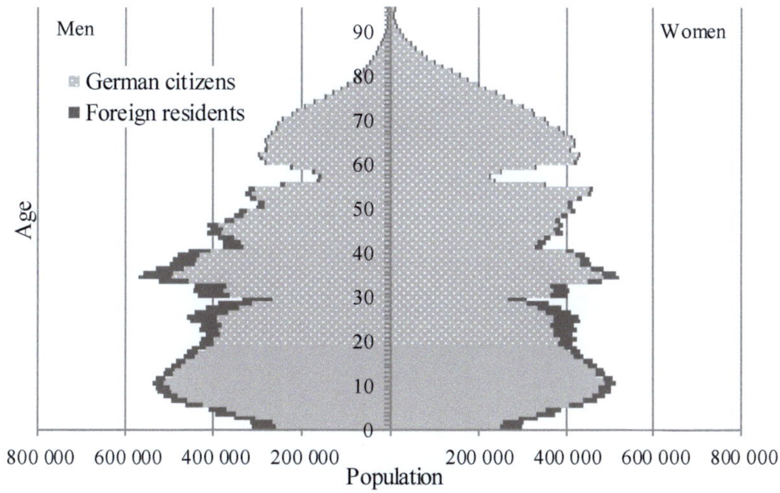

1986

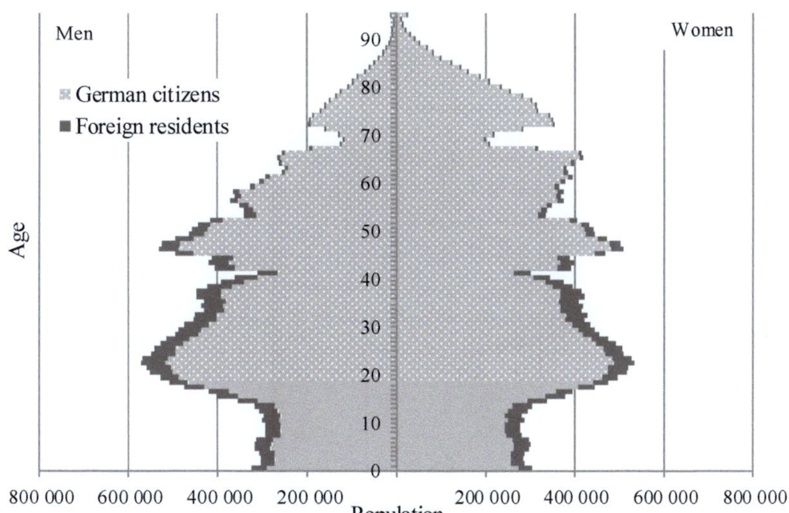

Source: Own illustration based on Population Statistics of 1974 and 1986, obtained from the Federal Statistical Office.

Note: Data for the years 1974 and 1986 refer to the former West German states only.

Figure 35 (cont.): Structure of the population in Germany by age, sex and citizenship in 1974, 1986, 1998 and 2010

1998

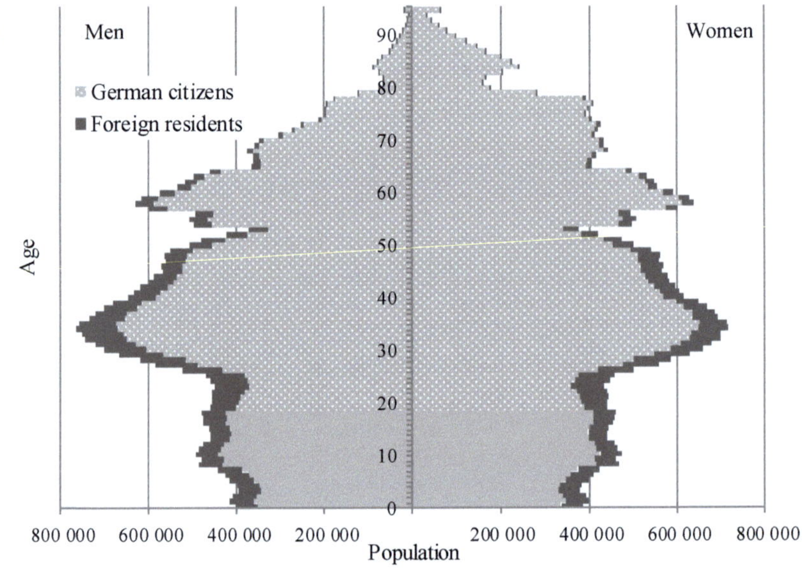

2010

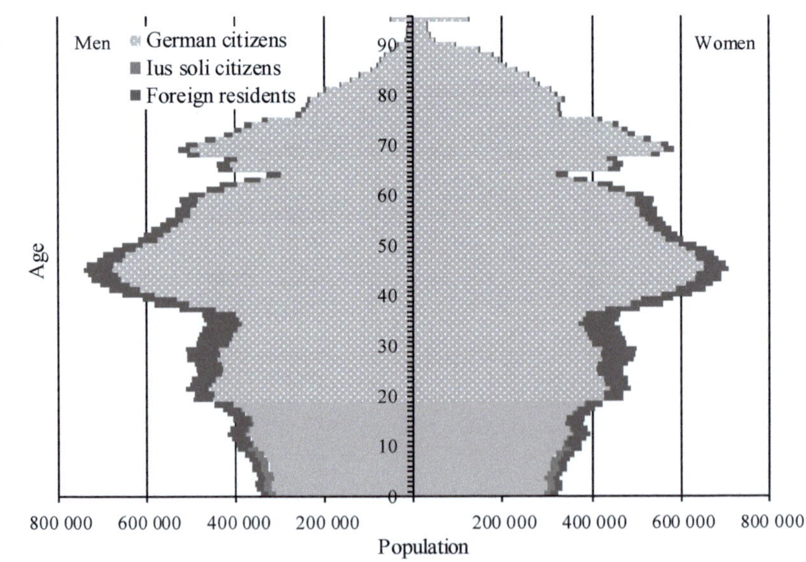

Source: Own illustration based on Population Statistics of 1998 and 2010, obtained from the Federal Statistical Office.

A larger number of foreign residents had naturalized and thus joined the German population during this period. Nonetheless, this process was not high enough to stop the increase of the foreign population. This increase would have resulted in a decrease in the proportion of electors, if the decline in the number of underage citizens had not balanced this trend. Due to the two contrasting trends, the proportion of eligible voters remained relatively stable at 74%. The median age of the electorate also remained relatively stable at 46 to 47 years since the number of younger electors and older electors increased to a roughly equal degree through German reunification, migration, the ageing of the baby boomer generation and declines in mortality.

In the most recent year considered here, 2010, the size of the population of underage citizens has further decreased due to continuing low fertility levels among German women. The fact that between 24% and 45% of all children born to foreign mothers acquired German citizenship between 1998 and 2010 and thus replenished the German population could not counteract this trend. Children born to foreign mothers could also acquire the German citizenship qua ius soli since 2000. In mid-grey, the population pyramid reveals the size of the first ius soli-cohorts. As can be seen, they formed a small minority among the total population of Germany. The foreign population slightly declined in size between 1998 and 2010 from 7.3 million to 6.8 million individuals since different modes of accession – birth and migration – were lower than forms of attrition – death and naturalization. Due to the declining size of both the population of underage German citizens and the foreign population, the number of disenfranchised population members decreased and the proportion of eligible voters increased from 74% to 76%. The median age of the electorate also increased between 1998 and 2010 to between 49 and 50 years. This increase can be attributed to the ageing of the baby boom cohorts. In addition, the cohorts who joined the electorate after reaching majority age during this period were relatively small.

The population pyramids of the last decades reveal how complex the influence of demographic trends on the size and structure of the population in Germany and its electorate has been: Not all demographic factors had an equally strong influence and different demographic factors were influential at different points in time. Demographic trends have also counteracted each other, for instance when some trends pushed the median age upward while others exerted a downward pressure. When projecting the influence of demographic trends on the future development of the electorate, the large number of demographic factors that may play a role has to be taken into consideration as well as possible fluctuations, age-, sex- and citizenship-specific differences, the simultaneity with which various trends may evolve and their interplay.

Overall, the two preceding chapters showed that electoral law and demographic trends have both shaped the size and age structure of the German electorate during the past decades. While electoral reforms changed the size and composition of the electorate on the specific day of their enactment, demographic trends developed gradually over time and thus continuously influenced the development of the electorate. With these findings in mind, the following chapters will set out to project the electorate of Germany into the future.

Part 2: Estimating the German electorate, 2010-2030

Will the proportion of eligible voters be larger or smaller in the future? To what extent will the median age of the electorate increase? In order to answer these questions, information is needed on the future composition of the population in Germany in terms of age and citizenship. Multi-state population projections and policy scenarios can provide this type of information. Both tools will be used in Part II of this study to investigate how the German electorate will develop in the future.

In Chapter 4, population projection methodology will be introduced. In addition, it will be explained how the policy scenarios for this study were defined. The data and software used for the demographic projections and policy scenarios will also be presented. In Chapter 5, a base-year projection will be calculated. In this projection, it was assumed that current demographic behaviour and the current legal definition of membership in the demos will remain unchanged until 2030. The projection thus shows the longer-term consequences of current behaviours and law. In Chapter 6 and Chapter 7, the effect of different demographic trends and policy changes on the future development of the electorate will be estimated. For this purpose, assumptions on probable future fertility, mortality, migration and naturalization trends as well as assumptions on possible future legal changes were defined. These demographic and policy assumptions were then combined to form demographic scenarios and policy scenarios. The findings gained from the demographic projections and policy scenarios will be presented at the end of Chapter 6 and Chapter 7, respectively.

Chapter 4. Methods, data and software

4.1. Demographic projections

4.1.1. Method

Population projections are today mostly based on the so-called 'cohort component method'.[283] This method was developed in the 1930s and 1940s and has not been substantially changed since then. It allows for the projection of populations by age and sex. For this purpose, the population that should be projected is subdivided by sex and into age groups of equal size. The age groups can cover 5 or 10 ages, but also projections of single-year age groups are possible. Such a single-year disaggregation will be used in this study. Only the oldest male and female age groups are of a bigger size as they are open-ended, i.e. they include all persons aged 95 and older. Each of the age- and sex-specific subgroups of the population is separately projected into the future. The time intervals of the projection are of equal length as the size of the age groups, so that each age group can be projected as one discrete unit in each projection step. In this study, the population is projected in single-year steps, since it is disaggregated into single-year age groups.[284]

The cohort component method depends on two types of input: base-year data and assumptions. The base-year is the year in which the population projection begins. Base-year data are therefore data on demographic conditions in the starting year of the population projection, notably information on the size and the age- and sex-structure of the population[285], as well as information on fertility, mortality and migration behaviours of the different population groups.

---

283 See *Preston, S. H./Heuveline, P./Guillot, M.*, Demography, 2001, p. 119; *Wilson, T./Rees, P.*, Recent developments, 2005, p. 338.

284 See *Lutz, W./Goldstein, J. R./Prinz, C.*, Alternative approaches, 1996, p. 14 f. For a description of the mathematical formulas and notations underlying this method, see *Preston, S. H./Heuveline, P./Guillot, M.*, Demography, 2001, pp. 118-130; *Goujon, A.*, Education, 2003, p. 42 f.

285 The base-year population has also been referred to as the 'jump-off population' in the literature, for instance by *Alho, J.*, Probabilistic forecasts, 1984, p. 100.

Assumptions are hypotheses about how future demographic trends might develop. Age- and sex-specific fertility, mortality and migration assumptions have to be defined for each projection year. These assumptions need to be well-justified, since the outcome of the projection depends on them to a large degree.[286]

Once base-year data and assumptions are prepared, the population can be projected into the future. Each age- and sex-specific population subgroup is individually projected by multiplying it with the appropriate age- and sex-specific mortality rate. Thereby, the group is reduced by the number of deaths. In addition, age- and sex-specific net migration numbers are added or subtracted from each population group.[287] These calculation steps are repeated for each projection year. The size of the youngest male and female age groups of the population is determined by the number of births during each projection year, the mortality of the newborns as well as by the number of migrants. The proportion of male and female children among all newborns is determined by a predefined ratio.[288]

For many research questions, the information that is derived from age- and sex-specific population projections is sufficient. However, if the projections are not only meant to provide information on the future age- and sex-composition of a population but also on additional characteristics, a more complex approach is necessary. In the 1960s and 1970s, Andrei Rogers developed the multistate population projection approach to meet such more specific research demands.[289] It is an extended version of the cohort component method and can be used to project a population which is not only disaggregated by age and sex, but also by a third characteristic, referred to as a 'state'. Such states may for instance be

[286] See *Preston, S. H./Heuveline, P./Guillot, M.*, Demography, 2001, p. 121; *Lutz, W./Goldstein, J. R./Prinz, C.*, Alternative approaches, 1996, p. 14 f.

[287] See *Babel, B.*, Bevölkerungsvorausberechnungen, 2007, p. 71 ff.

[288] See *Goujon, A.*, Education, 2003, p. 42 f. In most population projections, it is assumed that half of all newborns will be male and half will be female.

[289] See *Rogers, A.*, Population dynamics, 1986. See also *Lutz, W./Goldstein, J. R./Prinz, C.*, Alternative approaches, 1996, p. 15 f.

educational attainment, marital status, geographical regions or – as in this study – citizenship.[290]

Figure 36: Projection of age groups 1 to 94

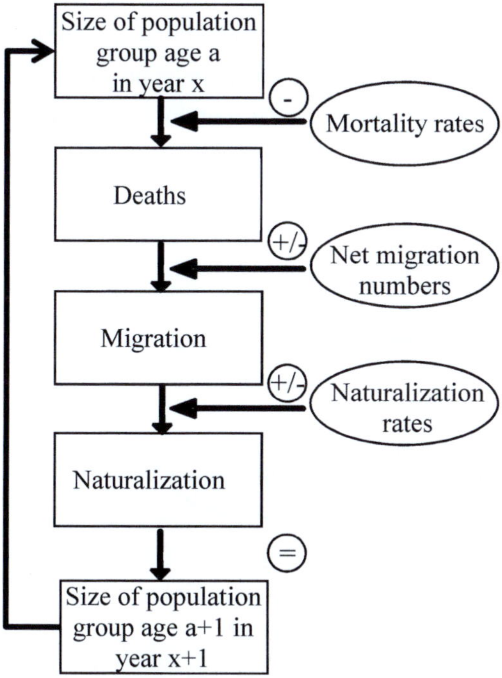

Source: Own illustration based on *Weitbrecht, K.*, Bevölkerung Deutschlands, no year given, p. 6.

The input requirements of a multistate population projection are similar, but more complex, than those of projections which only distinguish by age and sex. For a multistate population projection which focuses on citizenship, base-year population data and base-year fertility, mortality and migration data ideally have to distinguish by age, sex and citizenship. Fertility, mortality and migration assumptions also have to be defined for age-, sex-, and citizenship-specific population groups in each projection year. In addition, naturalization rates have to be defined for each age-, sex- and citizenship-specific population group to

[290] See *Lutz, W./Goujon, A./Doblhammer-Reiter, G.*, Demographic dimensions, 1998, p. 47.

account for changes in citizenship during each projection step.[291] Finally, assumptions have to be made about the citizenship which newborn members of the population acquire at birth in each projection year.

The age-, sex- and citizenship-specific population groups are projected from one year to the next by subtracting cases of death and adding or subtracting cases of migration and naturalization. The size of the population group which results from these calculations in each projection year then forms the basis for the next projection step (Figure 36).

Figure 37: Projection of age group 0

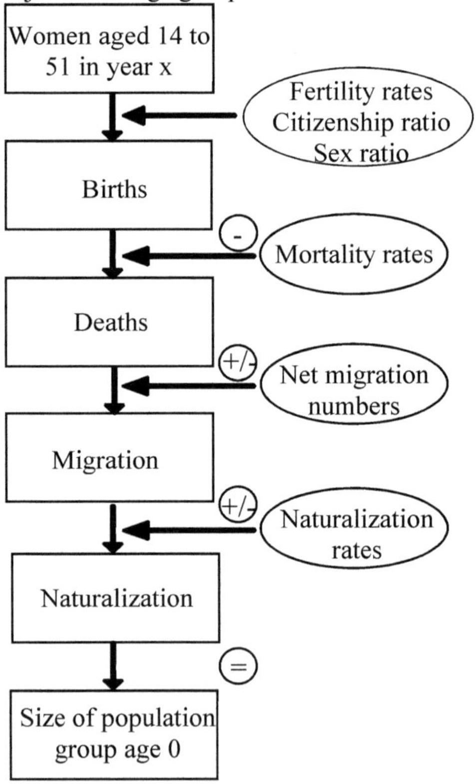

Source: Own illustration based on *Weitbrecht, K.*, Bevölkerung Deutschlands, no year given, p. 6.

[291] See *Goujon, A.*, Education, 2003, p. 43 f.; *Lutz, W./Goujon, A./Doblhammer-Reiter, G.*, Demographic dimensions, 1998, p. 48 f. Instead of citizenship, these studies focus on education and transitions from one educational 'state' to another.

Only the calculations for the youngest (0 years) and oldest (94/95 years and older) age groups of the population follow somewhat different rules (see Figure 37 and Figure 38).

Figure 38: Projection of age group 95 and older

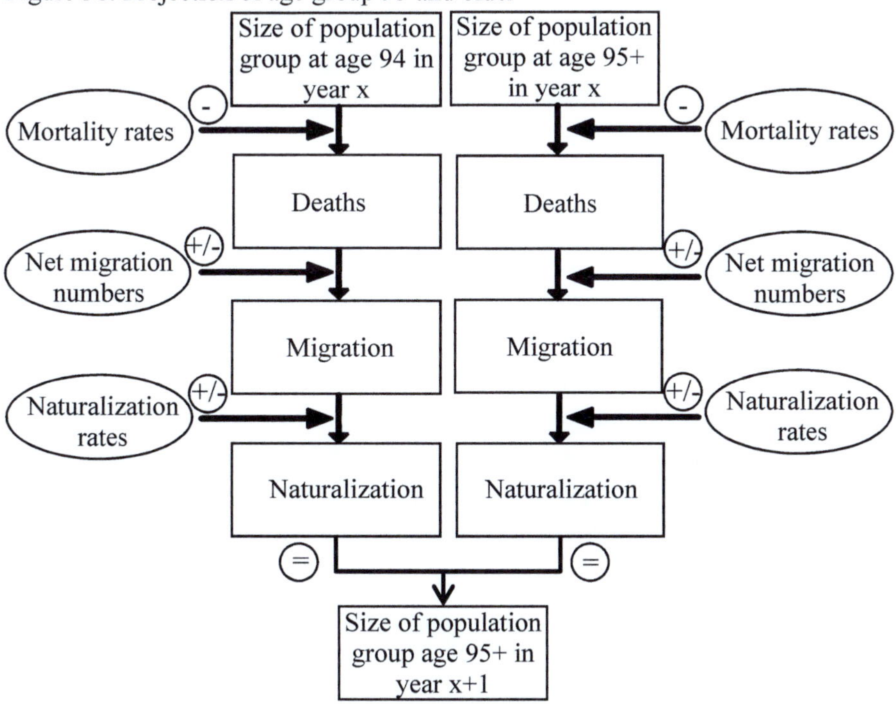

Source: Own illustration based on *Weitbrecht, K.*, Bevölkerung Deutschlands, no year given, p. 6.

The size of the youngest age-, sex- and citizenship-specific groups is determined by the number of children born during the projection year by women in childbearing age (ages 14 to 51). The births are allocated to the various sex- and citizenship-specific population groups by means of a pre-defined sex-ratio and pre-defined assumptions on citizenship acquisition at birth. Further, the number of children in the youngest population groups depends on assumptions on their survival, their migration and their naturalization behaviour. The oldest sex- and citizenship-specific groups are composed of persons who reach age 95 in a given

projection year and of persons who have already been 95 years or older during the previous projection step. Both age groups are separately projected by taking mortality, migration and naturalization into account before they are added at the end of each projection step.
By projecting a population along these lines, multistate projections provide information on the size of all age-, sex- and citizenship-specific population groups in each projection year. These data can be aggregated to calculate the size of the total population or to derive information on other indicators of interest, such as the size and median age of the electorate.

4.1.2. Uncertainty

The accuracy of population projections depends on the quality of its underlying assumptions.[292] Only if the assumptions predict future demographic trends correctly will the size and structure of the projected population accord with de facto developments. Defining assumptions is therefore the most important step of a population projection. At the same time it is the most challenging task since it requires that precise and testable hypotheses are developed about future demographic trends which are inherently uncertain. In particular, two sources of uncertainty have to be taken into consideration:
First, demographic developments depend on the behaviour of population members. Decisions of individual persons about how many children to bear, whether to smoke or exercise regularly or whether to move to another country influence future fertility and mortality trends as well as migration numbers. Such behaviour of human beings is, however, difficult to predict. Booth acknowledges: "Demographic behaviour, like most human behaviour, is too complex to be easily modelled and forecast; indeed, it may be inherently unpredictable."[293]
Second, external factors are a source of uncertainty in population projections. Future wars, epidemics, economic up- or downturns, natural disasters and

---

[292] See *Birg, H.*, Bevölkerungsentwicklung, 2000, p. 16; *Lutz, W./Goldstein, J. R./Prinz, C.*, Alternative approaches, 1996, p. 16.

[293] *Booth, H.*, Demographic forecasting, 2006, p. 571; see also *Lutz, W./Sanderson, W. C./Scherbov, S.*, Population projections, 1998, p. 142.

medical advances might all affect future fertility, mortality, migration and naturalization trends but are difficult to predict and to incorporate in population projections. Especially future migration levels are notoriously challenging to estimate as they can be influenced by a range of external factors. Developments in migration policies in the countries of origin and destination, for instance, or economic, environmental and political developments may all change migration numbers from one year to the next.[294]

According to Swanson and Tayman, population projections almost certainly fail to exactly predict population trends due to these sources of uncertainty: "Forecasts are inherently 'inaccurate'".[295] In the face of this challenge, demographers have made the question of how to define assumptions and how to deal with different sources of uncertainty one of the main topics of discussion.

One strategy to deal with uncertainty is to base assumptions on as much information as possible. De Beer for instance recommends that "all relevant information available [...] is taken into account, at least to the extent that the availability of resources permits this".[296] Three different sources of information can be distinguished which are commonly used – either individually or in combination – for the formulation of assumptions.[297]

First, past demographic trends can be studied and extrapolated into the future. This approach relies on the observation that some demographic components do not change radically from one year to the next, but tend to develop gradually over time. Most notably, this is the case for fertility and mortality.[298] Past mortality and fertility trends, however, can only function as an instructive source of input if reliable quantitative data are available. If data over- or underestimate past demographic trends, they may introduce errors into the projection.

---

294 See *Lee, R. D.*, Probabilistic approaches, 1998, p. 159; *Borchers, K.*, Datenlage, 2008, p. 10; *Enquete-Kommission 'Demographischer Wandel'*, Zwischenbericht, 1998, p. 124.

295 *Swanson, D. A./Tayman, J.*, Demographic forecasts, 1995, p. 239; see also *Booth, H.*, Demographic forecasting, 2006, p. 548; *Keyfitz, N.*, Limits, 1981, p. 579.

296 *de Beer, J.*, Conceptual framework, 1995, p. 330. De Beer makes his recommendation for migration assumptions in particular.

297 See *Booth, H.*, Demographic forecasting, 2006, p. 550 ff.; *Lutz, W./Sanderson, W. C./Scherbov, S.*, Expert opinion, 1996, p. 399 f.

298 Even though abrupt changes in mortality and fertility have been observed in the past, this generally only happened in exceptional circumstances, e.g. in times of war.

Migration and naturalization developments are more difficult to extrapolate on the basis of past trends than fertility and mortality since they are more prone to fluctuate over time.[299]

A second source of information for assumptions is expert knowledge and research findings.[300] Academic publications which deal with past demographic trends may provide insights into how and why trends have changed over time. This type of knowledge is helpful to estimate future changes in demographic behaviour. In Germany, demographic research has especially focused on explaining fertility trends of past decades, but publications on mortality developments are also available. Analyses of past migration and naturalization trends have been published especially by political scientists and sociologists. Apart from analysing and explaining past trends, some publications contain explicit predictions or hypotheses about how different demographic components might develop in the future. By comparing hypotheses of different researchers, demographic trends that are considered most likely may be identified and taken into consideration when formulating assumptions.

Third, population projections which were published in past years can be consulted to see which assumptions about demographic developments were made, how they were justified and how accurate they have been. This type of ex-post analysis can help to detect which demographic components were most prone to be misestimated and which factors have led to unexpected developments.[301]

In this study, demographic assumptions were derived on the basis of all three types of qualitative and quantitative information.[302]

---

299 See *Lutz, W./Scherbov, S.*, Future changes, 1999, p. 2 f.; *Lee, R. D.*, Probabilistic approaches, 1998, pp. 156 and 158; *Booth, H.*, Demographic forecasting, 2006, p. 550 f.

300 Especially Lutz and colleagues have used expert opinion for projections. They derived assumptions for projections by interviewing experts based on the Delphi-method. See *Lutz, W./Goldstein, J. R./Prinz, C.*, Alternative approaches, 1996, pp. 17 and 28-30. Critical reflections on the use of expert opinion in projections: *Lee, R. D.*, Probabilistic approaches, 1998, pp. 167-170. See also *Booth, H.*, Demographic forecasting, 2006.

301 See *Lutz, W./Goldstein, J. R.*, Introduction, 2004, p. 2; *de Beer, J.*, Conceptual framework, 1995, p. 340 f.

302 See Chapter 4.1.3.2. for an overview of the data and information sources that were used. Bijak refers to scenarios which are based on quantitative and qualitative argumentation as "judgemental scenarios" (*Bijak, J.*, Forecasting, 2006, pp. 19 and 44).

Demographers have also tried to account for the uncertainty of demographic projections by defining not only one assumption on future fertility, mortality and migration trends respectively, but several. Most commonly, up to three assumptions are defined per demographic component to capture different possible trends (so-called 'high', 'medium' and 'low' assumptions). These assumptions are then combined to demographic scenarios.[303] A demographic scenario describes an if-then calculation; it is "a consistent set of fertility, mortality and migration assumptions that provide a comprehensive picture of what the future might be".[304] A comparison of different scenarios can reveal how various combinations of possible fertility, mortality and migration trends would influence the development of a population. It may also help to identify the demographic factors which have the strongest influence on projected population outcomes.

Given the large number of demographic components considered in this study, only one or two different assumptions were defined per demographic component. A larger number of assumptions would have resulted in too many possible combinations and therefore too many scenarios. The assumptions in this study describe future fertility, mortality, migration and naturalization trends that appear most plausible given currently available information. These assumptions were combined into sixteen demographic scenarios and then calculated. Each scenario shows the effect of different combinations of demographic assumptions on the future development of the German population and its electorate. A description and discussion of the assumptions and scenarios is provided in Chapter 6.

---

303 In recent years, demographers have also developed and applied stochastic methods for population projections. The projection results are presented in the form of predictive intervals with probability distributions (see *Booth, H.*, Demographic forecasting, 2006, pp. 563-567; *Lee, R. D.*, Probabilistic approaches, 1998, p. 170 ff.; *Keilman, N./Pham, D. Q./Hetland, A.*, Population forecasts, 2002; *Lutz, W./Sanderson, W. C./Scherbov, S.*, Expert opinion, 1996, p. 401 f.). So far, these approaches have primarily been used for single-state projections (see for instance *Lutz, W./Scherbov, S.*, Bevölkerungsprognosen, 1998). Multistate projections that were published in recent years as well as projections that seek to estimate the effect of policies continue to use scenarios (see for instance *Goujon, A., et al.*, New times, 2007; *Kaufmann, E./Goujon, A./Skirbekk, V.*, Political affiliation, 2012; *Wilson, T./Rees, P.*, Recent developments, 2005, pp. 350 and 353).

304 *Ahlburg, D. A./Lutz, W.*, Introduction, 1998, p. 10.

Finally, demographers have discussed the length of the projection period as a source of uncertainty. Lutz and colleagues have argued that population projections should not extend beyond four of five decades, since it becomes too difficult to make accurate assumptions about demographic behaviour beyond this time:

> "From a psychological perspective, there may be reasons for being suspicious of projections that forecast further than 40 or 50 years into the future, a little less than two generations. [...] When we specify demographic rates beyond this, not only must we forecast the behaviour of individuals whom we will probably never meet, but we must deal with individuals who are more distant, in generational terms, than anyone we have met in our lives."[305]

Keyfitz goes beyond this by stating that population projections become unreliable beyond a time horizon of twenty years. The range of demographic developments that appears possible becomes wider and the likelihood that unexpected factors influence the demographic behaviour of individuals increases.[306] For the projections in this study, it was decided to follow Keyfitz' suggestion and cover a period of twenty years only. The projections start in the year 2010 and end in 2030. Except for the youngest 20 cohorts, all age cohorts alive in 2030 were already born in 2010. The size of these age cohorts in the base-year is therefore known and data concerning their previous demographic behaviour are available.[307]

Even though this study tries to account for uncertainty in the manner described above, it has to be stressed that the demographic projections are not likely to predict the development of the electorate with precision. Too many factors may affect the development of the population and lead to different trends than those that were assumed here. Nonetheless, the projections offer important insights.

---

305 *Lutz, W./Goldstein, J. R./Prinz, C.*, Alternative approaches, 1996, p. 6; see also *Enquete-Kommission 'Demographischer Wandel'*, Zwischenbericht, 1998, p. 123 f.

306 *Keyfitz, N.*, Limits, 1981, p. 583. Lee disagrees with this view. He argues that as long as the uncertainty of projections is made clear, longer-term projections are not misleading for users (*Lee, R. D.*, Probabilistic approaches, 1998, p. 157).

307 See *Enquete-Kommission 'Demographischer Wandel'*, Zwischenbericht, 1998, p. 124.

Most importantly, while they cannot claim to describe the de facto future development of the electorate, they show a range of possible developments. In addition, they highlight which demographic factors appear to have the strongest impact on future developments.[308]

4.1.3. Data

Chapter 2 concluded that age and citizenship are currently the most important restrictions to the franchise, and this is likely to remain the case in the near future. In terms of citizenship, three groups have to be distinguished in Germany: German citizens who acquire the right to vote when they turn 18; ius soli-children who are obliged to choose between their citizenships upon reaching majority age and who only retain the right to vote beyond their 23rd birthday if they retain the German citizenship; and foreign residents who do not enjoy the right to vote in Bundestag elections. These three citizenship groups will be separately projected by age and sex in order to gain information on the number of persons in Germany who will form the electorate in the future. Table 4 gives an overview of the data which are needed as input for such a projection. The necessary base-year data could be obtained from the Federal Statistical Office. Furthermore, the Statistical Office provided time-series data on past trends in fertility, mortality, migration and changes of citizenship. In addition to research findings and population projections published in past years, these demographic data were used to define assumptions for the years 2011 to 2030. The quality of the data sources will briefly be discussed in the following.

4.1.3.1. Data for the base-year 2010

The number of residents living in a state or region in the base-year of a projection (Point 1 in Table 4: Base-year population data) is most precisely estimated with the help of a census. As was stated above, the last census in Germany took place in May 2011, but the results were not available at the time of writing and could therefore not be used as input for this study. Instead, data on the base-year population were taken from the population statistics

---

[308] See *Kosow, H./Gaßner, R.*, Scenario analysis, 2008, p. 21 for a discussion on the value and limitations of scenarios.

(*Bevölkerungsfortschreibung*), the birth statistics (*Statistik der Geburten*) and the statistics on foreigners (*Ausländerstatistik*), all provided by the Federal Statistical Office.

Table 4: Data requirements for population projections by age, sex and citizenship

Data for the base-year 2010: 1. Base-year population data: the number of German citizens (German majority population), ius soli-citizens and foreign residents living in Germany by age and sex; 2. Base-year fertility rates for all three citizenship groups by age; 3. Base-year mortality rates for all three citizenship groups by age and sex; 4. Base-year net migration data for all three citizenship groups by age and sex; 5. Base-year data on citizenship acquisition at birth for all three citizenship groups by sex; 6. Base-year rates on changes of citizenship for all three citizenship groups by age and sex.
Assumptions for the years 2011-2030: 1. Assumptions on fertility rates for all three citizenship groups by age; 2. Assumptions on mortality rates for all three citizenship groups by age and sex; 3. Assumptions on net migration numbers for all three citizenship groups by age and sex; 4. Assumptions on citizenship acquisition at birth for all three citizenship groups by sex; 5. Assumptions on changes of citizenship for all three citizenship groups by age and sex.

Source: Own illustration

Data on the size, age- and sex-structure of the German population were taken from the population statistics. The statistics provide data on the number of persons who are officially registered as living in Germany on 31 December of each year. Since the population projection in this study takes the 1 January 2010 as its starting date, the population statistics of 31 December 2009 was used as input data. The data distinguish by age, sex and citizenship of the population members. In terms of citizenship, the statistics distinguish between Germans and foreign residents. All persons who fall under the scope of Article 116(1) of the Basic Law are counted as Germans, i.e. including ius soli-children and other persons with dual German-foreign citizenship. All persons who do not qualify as Germans under this article are counted as foreign residents.[309] The population statistics are based on the census that was conducted in the Federal Republic of Germany in 1987 and on the register of residents of the former German Democratic Republic of 1990. Each year, the census and register data are updated by deducting cases of death and emigration which occurred during the year and by adding cases of birth and immigration. Further adjustments are made to account for changes of citizenship.[310]

Some adjustments had to be made since the population statistics do not distinguish between ius soli-citizens and the German majority population as would be needed for this study. The number of ius soli-citizens in the base-year is not known since no statistics on this population group are published. It can only be estimated with the help of birth statistics and naturalization statistics. These statistics provide data on the number of ius soli-children who were born each year since 2000 and on the number of children born between 1990 and 1999 who acquired the German citizenship on the basis of the transitonal ius soli-regulation (see Chapter 2.3.3.). It was assumed here that all ius soli-citizens who were born since 2000 and who made use of the transitory agreement were still living in Germany in 2010. This assumption is somewhat simplistic since some ius-children may have died or migrated to other countries since their birth or naturalization. In the absence of other data sources, however, this was the

309 See *Statistisches Bundesamt*, Fortschreibung, 2008, p. 3 f.

310 See *Statistisches Bundesamt*, Fortschreibung, 2008, p. 4; *Kohls, M.*, Morbidität, 2011, p. 38 f.

only available option to estimate the size of the ius soli-population in Germany. The estimated number of ius soli-citizens was then deducted from the total number of Germans as stated in the population statistics. The number of Germans remaining in each age group after this calculation step formed the base-year population of German citizens who have acquired the German citizenship qua ius sanguinis or naturalization (German majority population).

The size, age- and sex-structure of the foreign population can in principle also be estimated with the help of the population statistics. Nonetheless, researchers have cautioned that especially the data on the adult foreign population in the statistics are not reliable. The reliability of the population statistics depends crucially on the accuracy of the birth, death, migration and naturalization statistics on which the annual update is based. Social scientists have pointed out that especially the birth and death statistics do not capture all demographic events that occur among the foreign population of Germany – see later sections. It is therefore assumed that the population statistics do not accurately reflect the size and structure especially of the adult foreign population.[311] The extent to which the population statistics over- or underestimates the size of the foreign population will be known when the results of the 2011 census become available. Due to these potential data inaccuracies, an alternative data source was consulted to estimate the number of foreign residents living in Germany in the base-year: the statistics on foreigners. This statistics is based on the Central Register of Foreigners (*Ausländerzentralregister – AZR*).[312] The register contains personalized data on all foreign residents who stay in Germany for at least three months. It provides information for instance on age, sex and citizenship of the registered individuals.[313] Between 2000 and 2004, the data included in the AZR have been comprehensively revised and updated and have

311 See *Kohls, M.*, Morbidität, 2011, p. 40; *Statistisches Bundesamt*, Fortschreibung, 2008, p. 5.

312 See *Opfermann, H./Grobecker, C./Krack-Roberg, E.*, Bereinigung, 2006; *Kohls, M.*, Healthy-migrant-effect, 2008, p. 35; *Statistisches Bundesamt*, Ausländerstatistik, 2009, p. 5. It has to be noted that the population statistics and the statistics on foreigners measure the foreign population in slightly different terms and are therefore not entirely comparable. Foreign residents enter the population statistics if they are registered as living in Germany. The AZR in general registers foreign residents only if they stay in Germany for a minimum duration of three months.

313 See *Statistisches Bundesamt*, Ausländerstatistik, 2009; *Siegert, M.*, Integrationsmonitoring, 2006, p. 13.

since then been checked for their plausibility on an annual basis. Therefore, at least the data on the adult foreign population are considered more reliable than the data included in the population statistics. Data on the population of foreign children and adolescents (0 to 16 years of age), by contrast, are less reliable. Children who are born in Germany to foreign parents are only counted in the AZR if parents report the birth to the foreign offices. This may sometimes happen with many years of delay. The AZR therefore underestimates the number of foreign children and teenagers living in Germany. The population statistics capture the number of underage foreign children in Germany more accurately, since they are based on the birth statistics which incorporate all births registered in Germany.[314]

In order to use the most reliable data possible for the population projection, the AZR and the population statistics were combined. Data on the size, age- and sex-structure of the foreign population aged 17 and older in the base-year were taken from the AZR statistics of 31.12.2009. Data on the size, age- and sex-structure of the foreign population aged 0 to 16 were taken from the population statistics.

Age- and citizenship-specific fertility rates for 2010 (base-year fertility rates) were calculated on the basis of the birth statistics of 2010, provided by the Federal Statistical Office. The birth statistics contain data on the number of children born in Germany in 2010 and provide information on the age and citizenship of mothers.[315] It is estimated to be of high quality. Gaps in the birth statistics may arise if German or foreign women who normally live in Germany give birth to a child while they are staying abroad. These births are only included in the statistics if the parents register the birth at the civil registry office after their return to Germany. Since the eligibility for child benefits depends on the official registration of births, it is assumed that most mothers who give birth

314 See *Opfermann, H./Grobecker, C./Krack-Roberg, E.*, Bereinigung, 2006, p. 490.

315 See *Statistisches Bundesamt*, Geburten, 2010, p. 5. The fertility rates were calculated on the basis of the forumula for fertility rates introduced in Chapter 3.2.

in another country will in fact register the birth of their children. Overall, gaps in the birth statistics should therefore be small.[316]

The birth statistics only distinguish between mothers who hold the German citizenship and foreign mothers. Hence, children born by women who belong to the ius soli-population are not separately registered but are included in the statistics as births to German women. The calculation of separate fertility rates for ius soli-Germans is therefore not possible. Only two sets of age-specific fertility rates were therefore calculated for the base-year, one for German women and one for foreign women. The fertility rates calculated for German women were used as base-year input for the ius soli-population and the German majority population.

Age-, sex- and citizenship-specific mortality rates for the base-year (base-year mortality rates) were calculated on the basis of the statistics on deaths (*Statistik der Sterbefälle*) of 2010, obtained from the Federal Statistical Office. The statistics distinguish by age, sex and citizenship of the deceased persons. The statistics are thought to be of high quality, since they include all deaths which are reported in Germany. The data are also checked continuously for plausibility.[317]

One possible source of error, however, exists: German citizens or foreign residents who die while they are abroad are only registered in the statistics if the relatives of the deceased inform the German civil registry office of the death. Not all relatives appear to comply with this obligation, but the exact extent of underestimation is not clear. It is estimated to be of a larger scale for the foreign than for the German population.[318] In fact, mortality rates which are calculated

[316] Births to women who are not registered as living in Germany, e.g. tourists, are not included in the statistics. See *Schmid, S./Kohls, M.*, Generatives Verhalten, 2011, p. 84 f.

[317] See *Statistisches Bundesamt*, Sterbefälle, 2010, p. 4. Mortality rates were calculated on the basis of the formula introduced in Chapter 3.2.

[318] See *Statistisches Bundesamt*, Sterbefälle, 2010, p. 5; *Kohls, M.*, Healthy-migrant-effect, 2008, p. 13 f. If persons die in Germany who are not registered as residents, e.g. tourists, these cases of death are not included in the statistics. Data on the annual number of deaths among the foreign population of Germany can also be obtained from the Central Register of Foreigners (AZR). Many researchers consider these data to be more reliable than the statistics on deaths. Kohls as well as Hannemann for instance recommend using AZR data to analyse the mortality of adult foreigners in Germany (*Kohls, M.*, Healthy-migrant-effect, 2008, p. 41; *Hannemann, A./Scholz, R.*, Mortality, 2009, p. 24). A comparison of the statistics on deaths and AZR data for the years

on the basis of the statistics on deaths of 2010 result in unreliable mortality and life expectancy values for the foreign population. According to the calculations, 95-year-old foreign men have a remaining life expectancy of 13 years and foreign women of the same age can expect to live six more years.[319] These remaining life expectancy values are twice as high as those of German men and women of the same age and are not likely to reflect true mortality conditions among foreign residents.

In order to correct for this overestimation of life expectancy, the mortality rates of foreign residents were modelled using the Heligman-Pollard model of mortality. Since mortality data are considered to be especially unreliable for elderly migrants, only the oldest age groups were modelled (age groups 60 and older for men and age groups 85 and older for women).[320] This procedure resulted in more plausible life expectancy values: Foreign men born in 2010 would then have a life expectancy of 79 years at birth and a remaining life expectancy of 3 years at age 95. The life expectancy of women at birth would be 85 years, and they could expect to live another 4 years at age 95. These values are closer to the life expectancy values measured for German men and women at birth (78 years for men/83 years for women) and at age 95 (6 years for men/3 years for women), but still reflect the mortality advantage that demographers expect among foreign residents.[321]

The mortality rates for the German population were not smoothed or modelled, since data on this group are considered to be accurate.[322] As was the case with fertility statistics, the death statistics only distinguish between German citizens and foreign residents, and do not subdivide the German population into ius soli-

---

2005 to 2009 however revealed that the annual registered number of deaths among foreigners is higher in the death statistics than in the AZR statistics, indicating that the AZR data fail to capture some cases of death. For this reason, the statistics on deaths were used to calculate mortality rates both of German citizens and foreign residents for this study.

319 Own calculations based on the mentioned data sources from the Federal Statistical Office. Calculations are not shown here. They are available upon request.

320 The calculations and data are not shown here, but are available upon request. See *Preston, S. H./Heuveline, P./Guillot, M.*, Demography, 2001, p. 194 for more information on the Heligmann-Pollard model. Also see *Kohls, M.*, Mortalität, 2008, p. 20 ff.; *Kohls, M.*, Morbidität, 2011, p. 125.

321 For information on the academic debate on mortality of foreign residents, see Chapter 3.3.2.2.

322 See *Kohls, M.*, Morbidität, 2011, p. 34.

Germans and the German majority population. A separate calculation of mortality rates for these two groups was therefore again not possible. Only one set of mortality rates was calculated and used as base-year input both for the ius soli-population and the German majority population.

The base-year migration data for the projection were taken from the migration statistics (*Wanderungsstatistik*) of 2010, also obtained from the Federal Statistical Office. The statistics provide information on the number of immigration and emigration cases across the external borders of Germany that are registered by the German registration offices. The statistics provide information on age, sex and citizenship of migrants. Cases of immigration are only registered in the statistics if they lead to the uptake of a principal residence in Germany and, conversely, cases of emigration are only included if they imply that the principle residence in Germany is given up. In addition, some Länder only include immigration cases in the statistics if migrants remain in Germany for a minimum period of time (e.g. longer than two months).[323]

The quality of the migration statistics depends crucially on the extent to which migration cases in Germany are officially registered. When German citizens and foreign residents immigrate to or emigrate from Germany, they are in principle required to register or deregister themselves at the municipal population registers.[324] In case of full compliance with this obligation, the migration statistics would reflect migration trends accurately. Demographers, however, assume that many migrants do not comply with their duty to register their move. Illegal immigrants who immigrate to Germany without the appropriate documentation by nature do not inform municipal registration offices. Persons who emigrate from Germany may also not always deregister themselves if they expect to remain abroad for a short term only. This might for instance concern university students who go abroad for only a few months to study. But also persons who permanently move to a foreign country do not always deregister themselves because they are not aware of their duty or because they forget.

323 See *Statistisches Bundesamt*, Wanderungsstatistik, 2008, p. 3 f.

324 See *Bundesamt für Migration und Flüchtlinge*, Migrationsbericht 2008, 2010, p. 9; *Statistisches Bundesamt*, Wanderungsstatistik, 2008, p. 6.

Foreign residents from countries outside the European Union might consciously refrain from informing the registration offices in order to keep their German residence permit. The exact extent to which this occurs is not known.[325]

A main advantage of the migration statistics is that it allows for long-term analyses of migration trends over time. Data on the number of migration cases by age, sex and citizenship could be obtained for the years 1954 to 2010. Like the statistics on births and deaths, these statistics do not distinguish between ius soli-citizens and the German majority population. Separate net migration numbers are, however, required for the population projection. They were estimated by proportionately allocating the net migration number of Germans in 2010 to ius soli-citizens and the German majority population according to the relative size of the two population groups. This procedure implicitly assumes that ius soli-citizens have the same likelihood of migrating as other German citizens.

In addition to fertility, mortality and migration data, the projections in this study require base-year data on citizenship acquisition at birth. The population projection software that is used in this study (see Chapter 4.3.) by default allocates newborn children to the same citizenship group as their mothers. As was described in previous chapters, this assumption holds true for children born to German women, since all children born to a German mother acquire German citizenship qua ius sanguinis. The default assumption is however not correct in the case of children born to foreign women. These children may either acquire German citizenship qua ius sanguinis if their father is a German citizen or qua ius soli if at least one parent fulfils the relevant legal requirements. In order to reflect current citizenship law, base-year data on the proportion of children born to foreign mothers who acquired German citizenship at birth in 2010 are incorporated into the projection. These data were obtained from the birth statistics of 2010 which was described above.[326]

---

325 See *Sauer, L./Ette, A.*, Auswanderung, 2007, p. 17; *Wahl, S.*, Deutschland, 2004, p. 2; *Bundesamt für Migration und Flüchtlinge*, Migrationsbericht 2008, 2010, p. 10.

326 See *Statistisches Bundesamt*, Geburten, 2010, p. 5.

Finally, age-, sex-, and citizenship-specific rates on changes of citizenship during the life course are needed as input for the base-year. Two types of rates are of particular interest: the naturalization rate of foreign residents and the proportion of ius soli-citizens who decide to retain German citizenship or their foreign citizenship after age 23.

The naturalization rate was calculated on the basis of the naturalization statistics of 2010 (*Einbürgerungsstatistik*), provided by the Federal Statistical Office. The statistics provide information on the number of foreign citizens who acquire German citizenship each year and distinguish by age and sex of the naturalized persons. They are estimated to be of high quality.[327] The statistics include all naturalization cases, irrespective of whether the naturalized persons live in Germany or abroad. Since this study is interested in foreign persons living in Germany, only the numbers of naturalizations occurring in Germany are of interest. A separate statistical evaluation could be obtained from the Federal Statistical Office for the years 2000-2010 which restricts the data to naturalization cases in Germany. For previous years, such an evaluation was not possible. The adjusted naturalization statistics of the year 2010 was used to calculate base-year naturalization rates for the projection.

Complete data on the decision-making behaviour of ius soli-citizens are not available. As discussed in Chapter 3.3.5.2., the first cohorts of ius soli-citizens born between 1990 and 1994 have turned 18 since 2008 and are now in the transition period during which they have to make their decision. Statistics on their decision-making behaviours will only be available starting from 2014. For simplicity's sake, it was assumed here that all ius soli-citizens will retain both of their citizenships until their 23rd birthday. Following this assumption, the first cohort of ius soli-citizens would choose between their citizenship in 2013. For the population projection this means that assumptions about their decision

[327] See *Statistisches Bundesamt*, Einbürgerungsstatistik, 2012, pp. 3-6. Children of foreign parents who acquire German citizenship qua ius soli are not included in the naturalization statistics (see *Siegert, M.*, Integrationsmonitoring, 2006, p. 28). Ethnic Germans who acquire German citizenship are also not counted in the naturalization statistics (see *Statistisches Bundesamt*, Einbürgerungsstatistik, 2012, p. 6).

behaviour have to be included for the projection years 2013 to 2029 only and that no data are required for the base-year 2010.

In principle, German citizens may also lose or be deprived of their citizenship. As was stated previously, national-level statistics on these cases do not exist. Anecdotal evidence, however, suggests that the number of Germans who lose or are deprived of their citizenship each year is likely to be very small (see Chapter 3.3.5.1.). It was therefore assumed in this study that no German citizen lost the German citizenship during the base-year.

4.1.3.2. Assumptions for the years 2011-2030

In addition to base-year data, assumptions about demographic trends between 2011 and 2030 are needed as an input for the population projections. Age-, sex- and citizenship-specific assumptions have to be defined on future fertility, mortality, and migration trends as well as on future changes of citizenship. The substantive content of these assumptions is presented in Chapter 6.1. As recommended in the demographic literature (see Chapter 4.1.2.), different types of information were used to define these assumptions: time-series data, academic publications and population projections which were published during the past decade.

Time-series data on past demographic trends in Germany could be obtained from the Federal Statistical Office. Table 5 gives an overview of the data sources used for each demographic component.[328] As can be seen, time series cover between thirty and fifty years. Most of the data distinguish by age, sex and citizenship, so that it is possible to analyse past demographic trends in detail for different population groups.

In addition to demographic data, academic publications were consulted. These publications provided insights into which factors have influenced fertility, mortality, migration and naturalization trends in the past. Some publications also

[328] Apart from the data mentioned in Table 5, additional statistics on the demographic behaviour of foreign residents could be obtained from the Federal Statistical Office. These statistics are based on the AZR. They include population data for the years 1998 to 2010 as well as data on cases of death among the foreign population for the years 2005 to 2009. Longer time-series were not available. Long-term analyses of demographic trends were thus not possible with these data and they were used for comparative purposes only.

provided hypotheses as to how these demographic factors might develop in the future. The literature that was consulted is mentioned in the individual chapters on demographic assumptions (Chapter 6.1.).

Table 5: Data sources used for demographic assumptions, 2011-2030

Demographic component	Data source	Time period covered by data
Population size and structure	Population statistics[329]	1970 – 2010
Fertility	Birth statistics[330]	1972 – 2010
Mortality	Statistics on deaths[331]	1980 – 2010
Migration	Migration statistics[332]	1962 – 2010
Citizenship acquisition at birth	Birth statistics	1972 – 2010
Changes of citizenship	Naturalization statistics[333]	1974 – 2010

Source: Data provided by the Federal Statistical Office.
Note: Data before 1990 refer to the former West German states only. Older data than those mentioned in the table are partly available, but they do not distinguish by citizenship and/or age.

Finally, population projections that were published in the past years by statistical offices and demographic researchers were consulted, including both single state and multistate projections.[334] Some multistate projections, notably by Münz and

[329] *Statistisches Bundesamt*, Fortschreibung, 2008.
[330] *Statistisches Bundesamt*, Geburten, 2010, p. 3.
[331] *Statistisches Bundesamt*, Sterbefälle, 2010, p. 3.
[332] *Statistisches Bundesamt*, Wanderungsstatistik, 2008, p. 3.
[333] Complete data on cases of naturalization in Germany are only available since the year 2000. Before this year, data are partly incomplete. The naturalization data before 2000 and after 2000 are also not directly comparable due to a change in law: Before 1999, ethnic Germans resettlers who acquired German citizenship were counted in the naturalization statistics; since 2000, these cases are not included in the statistics any more (*Statistisches Bundesamt*, Einbürgerungsstatistik, 2012, p. 6). In order to increase the comparability of the data, the number of naturalizations by ethnic Germans was deducted from the annual naturalization statistics of the years 1974-1999. By means of this procedure, sets of naturalization statistics could be obtained for each year between 1974 and 2010 that only cover the naturalization of foreign migrants and exclude ethnic Germans. For the years 2000 to 2010, the Statistical Office of Germany also provided data which exclude cases of naturalization that occurred abroad. For previous years, such separate statistics do not exist.
[334] In particular, the following projections were used: *Statistisches Bundesamt*, Bevölkerung Deutschlands, 2009; *Eurostat*, Online database, 2012; *Bundesministerium des Innern*,

Ulrich, project the population by citizenship. Other multistate projections, for instance by Lanzieri, also project the German and foreign population separately, but define the foreign population by place of birth or other indicators rather than by citizenship. Comparing these projections helped to gain an overview of the demographic trends which demographers expect to develop during the coming years. Since some of the projections were published several years ago, it was possible to compare assumptions with actual demographic trends and to identify which demographic components were particularly prone to be under- or overestimated.

The insights gained from consulting past demographic trends, academic literature and existing demographic projections were combined to generate demographic assumptions for the multistate projections. One or two assumptions were defined for each demographic component, reflecting the developments that appear most likely given the available information.

4.2. Policy scenarios

4.2.1. Method

The influence of legal changes on the future development of the electorate is estimated with the help of policy scenarios. Policy scenarios are based on assumptions about how laws and policies might change in the future. After identifying possible legal developments, their impact is assessed. Thereby, policy scenarios are tests for different policy options. They are "'practice runs' of possible future situations which indicate the likely effect of decisions".[335] By comparing policy scenarios that represent different potential legal reforms, a range of possible outcomes can be estimated and evaluated.

Modellrechnungen, 2000; *Münz, R./Seifert, W./Ulrich, R.*, Zuwanderung, 1999; *Ulrich, R.*, Bevölkerungsstruktur, 2001; *Birg, H./Flöthmann, E.-J.*, Bevölkerungsprojektionen, 1993; *Birg, H./Flöthmann, E.-J.*, Projektionsrechnungen, 2001; *Enquete-Kommission 'Demographischer Wandel'*, Zwischenbericht, 1998; *Lutz, W./Scherbov, S.*, Bevölkerungsprognosen, 1998; *Lanzieri, G.*, Projections, 2011.

335 *van Notten, P.*, Scenario development, 2006, p. 75; see also *Therond, O., et al.*, Methodology, 2009, p. 620 f.

The implementation of policy scenarios involves a two step procedure: First, assumptions about possible future legal developments have to be defined. Börjeson and colleagues distinguish several types of scenarios, depending on whether the underlying assumptions are predictive, explorative or normative in character. Normative scenarios describe developments and their consequences that are considered desirable or preferable. Predictive scenarios, by contrast, describe developments that are likely to happen in the future, but that are not necessarily desirable. Explorative scenarios, finally, assess the consequences of developments that are considered possible, but not necessarily likely, to happen. Among explorative scenarios, Börjeson and colleagues differentiate between two subtypes: *External* explorative scenarios focus on factors that are not under the control of concerned actors. *Strategic* explorative scenarios, by contrast, illustrate the consequences of actions that are under the control of relevant actors.[336] Börjeson and colleagues elaborate:

> "The aim of strategic scenarios is to describe a range of possible consequences of strategic decisions. [...] Different policies are typically tested and their impact on the target variables is studied. The strategic scenarios are not only relevant to decision makers, they are also useful as inspiration for interested parties, such as policy analysts or research groups."[337]

The policy scenarios which are defined and assessed in this study are strategic explorative scenarios since they illustrate the consequences of a spectrum of legal options that are available to policy makers. Possible future changes of laws were identified by considering both academic literature and parliamentary debates on the citizenship and the age criteria. As was stated before, these two electoral criteria exclude the largest number of persons from the franchise today and are likely to remain as important in the future. All policy scenarios that were selected and calculated in this study therefore deal with these two electoral

---

336 *Börjeson, L., et al.*, Scenario types, 2006, pp. 725-730; see also *Therond, O., et al.*, Methodology, 2009, p. 621.

337 *Börjeson, L., et al.*, Scenario types, 2006, p. 728.

criteria. Reform proposals that have been discussed by academics and have also been tabled in Bundestag or Bundesrat by political parties were considered as policy options that may possibly be implemented in the future, even if their adoption is not necessarily likely. Each policy scenario used in this study assumes that one or multiple policy options are adopted and enacted in the base-year of the projection, 2010, and remain in force throughout the projection period. Ten policy scenarios were defined in this manner, each reflecting different changes of either the age criterion or the citizenship criterion or of both criteria.

While the policy scenarios selected for this study show the effects of possible legal developments, they are not intended to be normative in character. A range of political science and legal studies have already commented on the normative desirability of different policy options. While this study builds on these debates, it will not add further arguments in favour or against different reform proposals since this would be beyond the scope of this study. The scenarios are also not intended to be predictive in character. In order to predict which policy scenarios are most likely to be implemented, party programmes and coalition documents, required majorities and the existence of potential veto players would have to be analysed. Again, such an endeavour is beyond the scope of this study. Instead, it is the aim here to explore and quantify the consequences of different policy choices which may possibly, but not necessarily, be adopted by policy makers and to show their consequences, since this has not yet been done in the academic literature.

After having defined different policy scenarios, their consequences can be estimated. Alcamo distinguishes two ways in which scenarios can be carried out. On the one hand, scenarios can be qualitative in character. Such scenarios describe the consequences of assumed developments verbally, often in the form of so-called 'storylines'. Alcamo stresses that qualitative scenarios have the advantage of constituting "an understandable and interesting way of communicating information about the future".[338] Nonetheless, they cannot satisfy potential needs for numerical assessment of consequences. On the other

[338] *Alcamo, J.*, SAS approach, 2009, p. 124.

hand, the effect of scenarios can be calculated. Such a quantitative assessment describes the consequences of scenarios in numerical terms.[339]

This study analyzes the consequences of different policy changes on the development of the electorate in quantitative terms. Policy scenarios are introduced into the demographic population projections either by changing individual projection parameters or by re-aggregating projection results. The choice between these two options depends on the requirements of each scenario. For instance, changes in naturalization policies are modelled by changing the naturalization rates on which the demographic projections are based. The effects of changes in the minimum voting age, by contrast, can be calculated by re-aggregating projection results, i.e. by counting newly enfranchised population members as members of the electorate.

In order to illustrate the effects of different reform options, two types of policy scenarios were calculated in this study. At first, the effect of each potential reform is calculated individually (single scenarios). After that, individual reforms are combined into mixed scenarios. These mixed scenarios show how the size and composition of the electorate would change if several of the proposed policy changes would be enacted at the same time.

4.2.2. Uncertainty

The calculation of policy scenarios results in very precise quantitative results. This precision may be misleading. Alcamo stresses that "the exactness of their numbers gives a false sense of knowing more about the future than we actually do".[340] Therefore, it is important to stress that if one or several of the different policy reforms were to be enacted, the proportion of eligible voters and the median age of the electorate is not likely to develop exactly as calculated. The de facto development of the electorate depends on demographic developments and potentially on third factors such as changes in borders as well. Therefore the

[339] *Alcamo, J.*, SAS approach, 2009, p. 124. He also describes an approach that combines both quantitative and qualitative elements (see *Alcamo, J.*, SAS approach, 2009, p. 125 f.). See also *Kosow, H./Gaßner, R.*, Scenario analysis, 2008, p. 33 f.

[340] *Alcamo, J.*, SAS approach, 2009, p. 125; see also *Therond, O., et al.*, Methodology, 2009, p. 622.

de facto effect of legal changes may differ from the results of the policy scenarios calculated here.

While the policy scenario calculations should be treated with caution, they do provide valuable information on the extent to which various policy choices would influence the development of the electorate. When comparing the results of different policy scenarios, the legal options that would have the strongest effect on the proportion of eligible voters and the median age of the electorate can be identified. These insights hold true irrespective of the precise numerical results of each scenario.

4.2.3. Data

In order to choose and define policy scenarios, two types of sources were consulted: Academic literature was reviewed to gain an overview of different reform proposals which have been discussed by legal, political and social science scholars. Relevant literature was identified via key-word based research in literature catalogues and e-journal libraries. After that, an analysis of bills and motions tabled in Bundestag and Bundesrat revealed which of these reform proposals have been taken up by policy makers. By means of a keyword-based search in the Parliamentary Material Information System (*Dokumentations- und Informationssystem für Parlamentarische Vorgänge, DIP*), bills and motions which have aimed at changing or abolishing the age criterion or the citizenship criterion or which aimed at reforming naturalization procedures could be identified.[341] The online research was completed in February 2012. Later legal developments could not be taken into account.

A special focus was put on bills and motions that were tabled in Bundestag and Bundesrat since 2002. The year 2002 is of particular interest, since the 'Enquete-Commission on Demographic Change' presented its final report then. The commission – composed of academic experts and parliamentarians from all

[341] The Parliamentary Material Information System can be accessed online: http://dipbt.bundestag.de/dip21.web/bt (in German). For the keyword-based research, the following keywords were used: *Einbürgerung, Kinderwahlrecht, Staatsangehörigkeitsgesetz, Staatsangehörigkeitrecht, Wahlalter, Wahlberechtigte, Wahlberechtigung, Wahlgesetz* and *Wahlrecht*.

major parties – had been appointed by the Bundestag in 1992 to analyse the effects of demographic change on the German economy and society. While the main focus of the final report lay on employment, integration, health and the pension system, the authors also dedicated different sections to political rights. They briefly discuss the lack of voting rights of children and adolescents as well as of foreign residents and propose policy options to include these population groups into the electorate. After its publication, the report put the demographic change back on the agenda of the Bundestag and led to controversial debates on topics such as the ageing of the population, intergenerational relationships and the integration of foreign residents.[342]

4.3. Software and indicators

The population projections and policy scenarios of this study were calculated with the PDE (Population – Development – Environment) population projection software. This software is available free of charge.[343] It was developed by the International Institute for Applied Systems Analysis (IIASA) in Vienna and has been used in a number of dissertations and journal articles during the past years.[344]

The PDE population projection software allows the user to enter base-year data and demographic assumptions for each projection year manually or by uploading data which have been prepared on Excel-spreadsheets. The program also allows the user to modify the uploaded data by using interpolation and copy and paste functions, by applying proportional changes to age-, sex- and citizenship-specific rates or by manually altering single data points on graphical visualizations.[345] The projection results for each year are presented in the form of tables, population pyramids and stacked area curves and can be exported for

342 See *Deutscher Bundestag*, Bericht, 2002, pp. 23196-23209.

343 The program is available for download at: http://www.iiasa.ac.at/Research/POP/pub/software.html (last accessed: 14.04.2014).

344 See for instance *Kaufmann, E./Goujon, A./Skirbekk, V.*, Political affiliation, 2012; *Ziegler, U.*, Dementia, 2010; *Goujon, A., et al.*, New times, 2007; *Goujon, A.*, Education, 2003.

345 See *Dippolt, M./Goujon, A./Wils, A.*, User's manual, 1998, p. 11 f.; *Goujon, A.*, Education, 2003, p. 46.

further use to the Excel programme. They contain information about the number of persons who are alive at the end of each projection year and distinguish by age, sex and other characteristics (here: citizenship).

By aggregating these data, the number of individuals who fulfil the age and citizenship requirement and are therefore entitled to vote in Bundestag elections can be determined. The proportion of eligible voters among the total population can be calculated from these population data for each projection year. The following formula is used for this purpose:

$$\text{Proportion of electors} = \frac{\text{ResDem}}{\text{Res}} \text{ x } 100$$

with ResDem being the number of residents who are members of the demos and Res being the overall number of residents of the country.

The future development of the age structure of the electorate is quantified by calculating the median age of the electorate for each projection year, i.e. "the age at which exactly half the population is older and half is younger".[346] It is estimated as follows:

$$\text{Median age of the electorate} = \text{I}_{Md} + \frac{\frac{N}{2} - \sum f_x}{f_{Md}}$$

with I_{Md} being the lower limit of the age group which divides the electorate into two equal halves (or, in other words, containing the N/2nd item); N the sum of all members of the electorate; $\sum f_x$ the number of electors in all age groups preceding the age group containing the N/2th item; and f_{Md} the number of electors in the age group containing the N/2th item.[347] The following example

[346] *Haupt, A./Kane, T. T.*, Handbook, 2004, p. 6.

[347] The formula has been taken and adjusted from *Shryock, H. S./Siegel, J. S.*, Demography 1, 1971, p. 233. Other indicators have been proposed and used to estimate changing age structures of an electorate. Some studies for instance measure the proportion of 'younger' 'middle-aged' and 'older' persons among the electorate (see for instance *Menning, S.*, Wahlverhalten, 2009; *Wilson, G.*, Ageing electorate, 1993, p. 95). This type of measurement has the disadvantage that age limits have to be defined. Such definitions are always arbitrary to a certain extent (see also *Shryock, H. S./Siegel, J. S.*, Demography 1, 1971, p. 234). The median age indicator avoids the requirement of age definitions by quantifying changes in the age structure in one single number. The average age (also referred to as arithmetic mean) of the electorate could also be calculated.

may illustrate the the use of the formula: Suppose an electorate includes 72.934.000 persons, the age interval 48 to 49 years divides the electoral into two halves, 35.716.000 electors would be aged 18 to 48, and 985.000 electors would be aged 48 to 49 in a given year. Then the median age would be calculated as follows:

$$\text{Median age of the electorate} = 48 + \frac{\frac{72.934.000}{2} - 35.716.000}{985.000}$$
$$= 48 + 0.7624$$
$$= 48.76$$

Apart from these two principal indicators, additional indicators such as the absolute number of eligible voters in Germany or the size of different citizenship or age groups are occasionally shown in the results Chapters 5.2., 6.3. and 7.3. in order to visualize individual projection outcomes.

The average age indicator however is more easily influenced by data points which are extreme outliers than the median age (see also *Shryock, H. S./Siegel, J. S.*, Demography 1, 1971, p. 233).

Chapter 5. Base-year data projection

The base-year projection shows how the size and age structure of the electorate in Germany would develop if demographic trends of the base-year 2010 and the current restrictions defined in electoral law would remain constant throughout the projection period. The legal restrictions which determined membership in the electorate in 2009/10 can be reviewed in Table 2 in Chapter 2.3.2. The demographic conditions in 2010 will be briefly recapitulated in the following. The influence of these demographic and legal conditions on the future development of the electorate will be described in the result section at the end of the chapter.

5.1. Base-year demographic data

At the turn of the year 2009/2010, 81.4 million persons were living in Germany. Most of these persons were German citizens (74.7 million persons or 91.7% of the total population, see Figure 39).

A minority of these German citizens – around 414.000 persons aged 0 to 19 – were ius soli-citizens (around 0.6% of the German population and around 0.5% of the total population). In addition, 6.8 millions foreign residents were living in Germany in 2010 (8.3% of the total population). 62.2 million adult German citizens formed the electorate (age groups 18 and older). This number includes the two oldest cohorts of ius soli-citizens aged 18 and 19 in 2010, around 7.100 individuals. The demos of Germany comprised 76% of the resident population of Germany in 2010. The median age of the electorate was around 49.8 years.

Figure 39: Population of Germany by age, sex and citizenship, 2009/2010

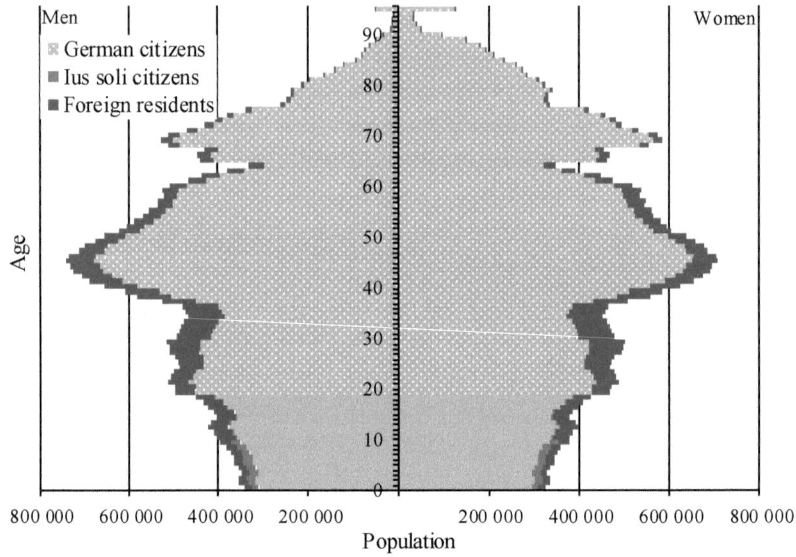

Source: Own illustration based on Population Statistics of 2009/2010, obtained from Federal Statistical Office.

Figure 40: Age-specific fertility rates of German and foreign women, 2010

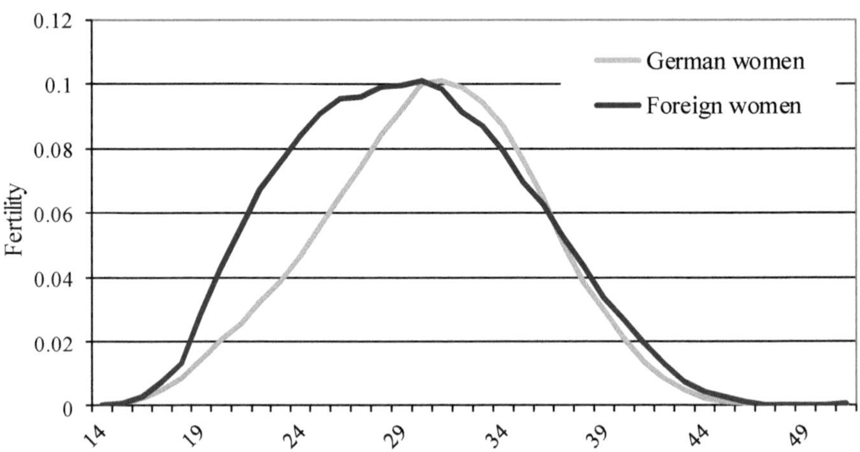

Source: Own calculations based on Population Statistics and Birth Statistics of 2010, obtained from the Federal Statistical Office.

Women with German citizenship (including ius soli-citizens) gave birth to around 564.000 children in 2010 and about 113.000 children were born to foreign women in Germany. These numbers correspond to total fertility rates of 1.36 (German women) and 1.66 (foreign women). Foreign women gave birth at slightly younger age than German women: Age-specific fertility increased faster and peaked at age 30 among foreign women whereas the age-specific fertility curve of German women reached the highest value at age 31 (see Figure 40).

Figure 41: Age-specific mortality rates of German men and women, 2010

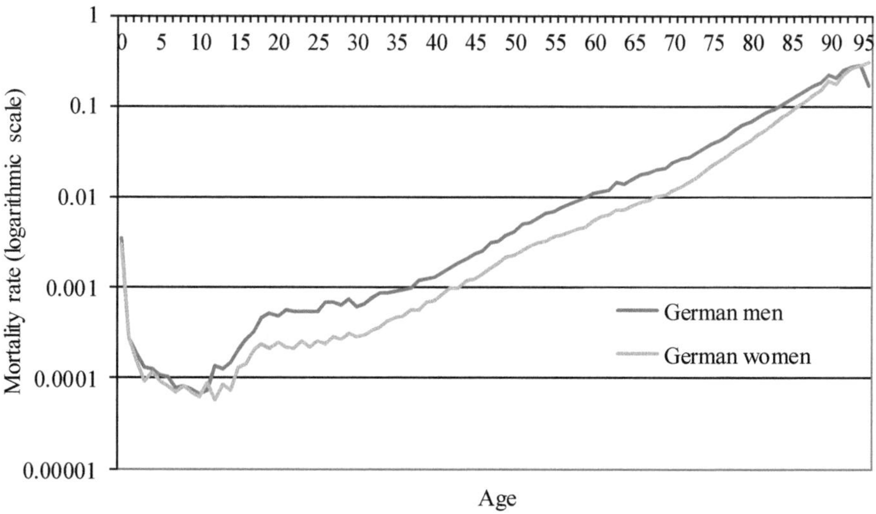

Source: Own calculations based on Population Statistics and Death Statistics of 2010, obtained from the Federal Statistical Office.

German boys (including ius soli-citizens) who were born in 2010 have a life expectancy of 78 years, provided that the mortality rates displayed by the German population in that year remain stable throughout their lives. German girls born in 2010 can expect to live five years longer and reach 83 years of age. Figure 41 shows the age-specific mortality rates of German men and women in 2010 in log scale. Mortality rates decrease very rapidly after birth and remain at low levels until around age 30. Starting from this age, mortality rates rise and

are highest in the oldest age groups. Mortality of women is lower than that of men across almost all ages, explaining their higher life expectancy.
Foreign residents in Germany had a higher life expectancy than German citizens in 2010. Modelled mortality rates (see Chapter 4.1.3.1.) suggest that boys with foreign citizenship who were born in 2010 have a life expectancy of 79 years, girls of 85 years. Again, the age-specific mortality rates of foreign women were lower than those of men across most age groups (see Figure 42).

Figure 42: Age-specific mortality rates of foreign men and women, 2010

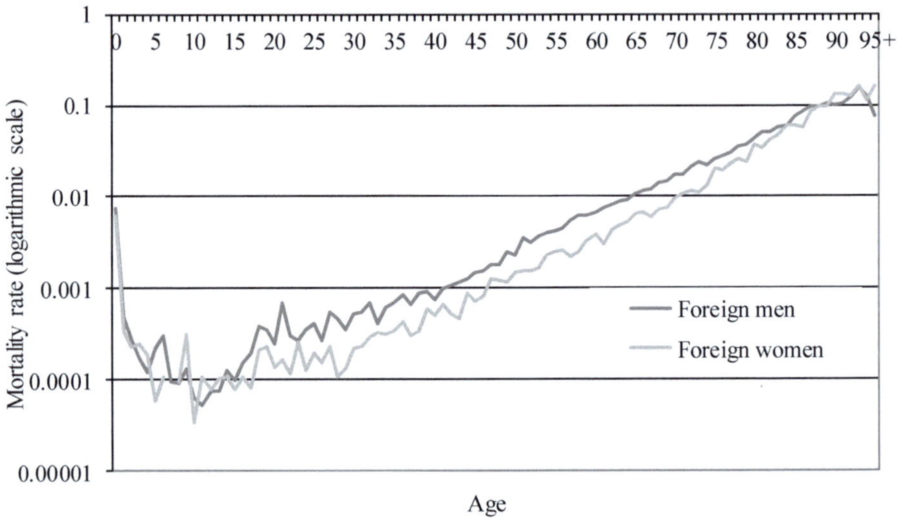

Source: Own calculations based on Population Statistics and Death Statistics of 2010, obtain from the Federal Statistical Office.

Around 114.800 German citizens moved to Germany in 2010 and 141.000 Germans moved away. As the black line in Figure 43 shows, this resulted in negative net migration numbers across nearly all age groups. Only among the youngest two age groups and the age groups 17 to 20 did the number of immigrants surpass the number of emigrants.

Figure 43: Age-specific migration numbers of German citizens, 2010

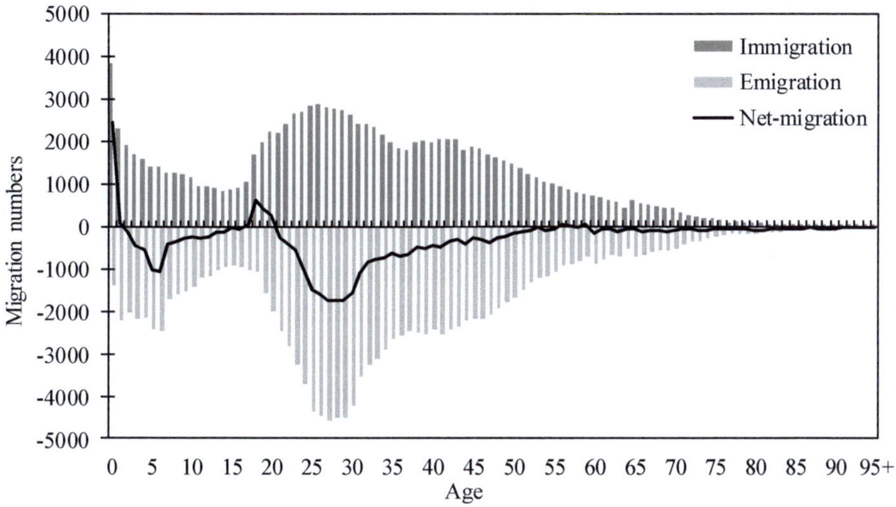

Source: Own illustration based on Migration Statistics of 2010, obtained from the Federal Statistical Office.

Figure 44: Age-specific migration numbers of foreign residents, 2010

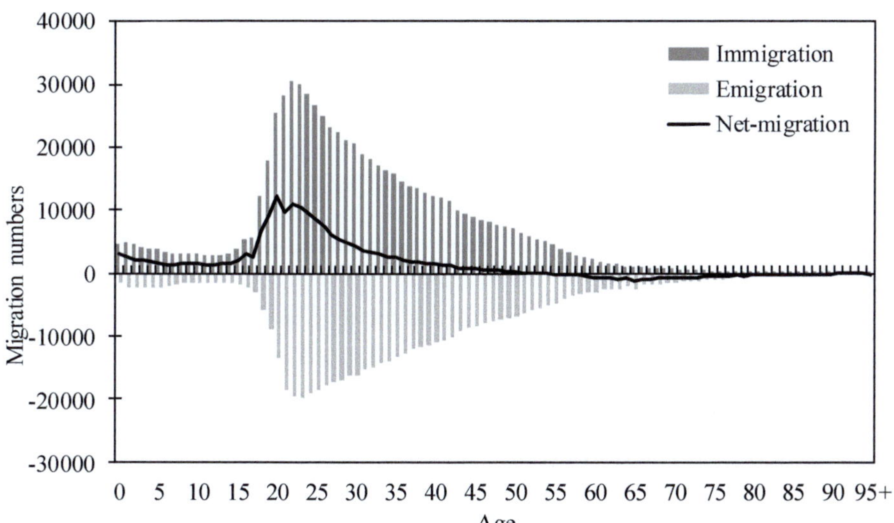

Source: Own illustration based on Migration Statistics of 2010, obtained from the Federal Statistical Office.

In contrast to this, the net migration balance of foreign residents was positive in 2010. Around 683.500 persons immigrated to Germany while around 530.000 moved away. Figure 44 shows that immigration and emigration numbers among foreign citizens were especially high in young adult ages (ages 19-30).

Among the children who were born to foreign mothers in 2010 or immigrated to Germany during this year, around 43% acquired German citizenship either because they had a German father or because they were naturalized during the first year of their life. An additional 25% of these children acquired German citizenship at birth on the basis of the ius soli-regulation. The remaining 32% of the children acquired the foreign citizenship(s) of their parents at birth (Figure 45). Children born to German mothers – including ius soli-citizens – all acquired the German citizenship via the ius sanguinis principle.

Figure 45: Citizenship acquired by children born to foreign women (in %), 2010

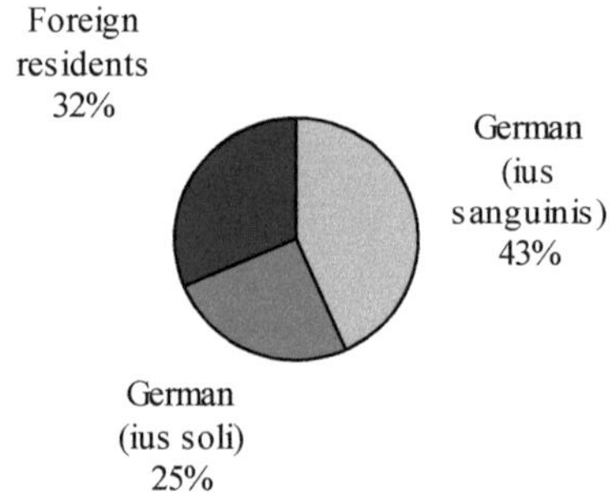

Source: Own calculation based on Birth Statistics and Naturalization Statistics of 2010, obtained from the Federal Statistical Office.

Nearly 99.000 foreign residents or 1.4% of the total foreign population living in Germany acquired German citizenship in 2010 via naturalization. As can be seen in Figure 46, especially young men and women between ages 15 and 23 naturalized in Germany. Children and middle-aged foreign residents naturalized somewhat less often and the lowest naturalization rates were registered among older foreign residents living in Germany. Women were somewhat more likely to naturalize than foreign men.

Figure 46: Age-specific naturalization rates of foreign men and women, 2010

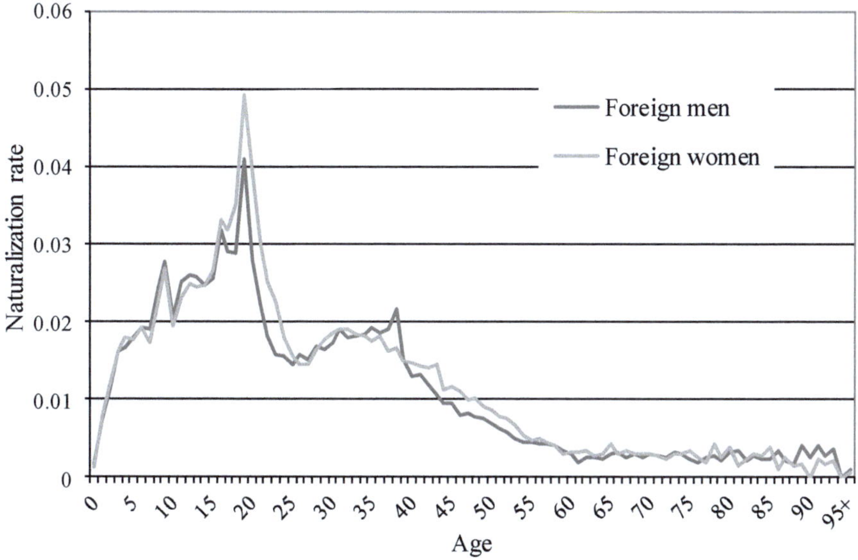

Source: Own illustration based on Naturalization Statistics and Population Statistics of 2010, obtained from the Federal Statistical Office.

5.2. Base-year projection results

The population pyramids in Figure 47 reveal how the structure of the population and the electorate in Germany would change between 2010 and 2030 if the demographic behaviour of the population were to remain stable during the entire period and if the legal definition of the electorate would not change. The horizontal bars that compose the pyramids show the size of individual age groups and the differently coloured sections of each bar represent different citizenship groups (light grey: German majority population, mid-grey: ius soli-population, dark grey: foreign population). Germans aged 18 and older constitute the German electorate. The left side of the pyramids represent the male part of the population of Germany. The female population is located on the right.

Figure 47: Projected population of Germany by age, sex and citizenship, 2010 and 2030

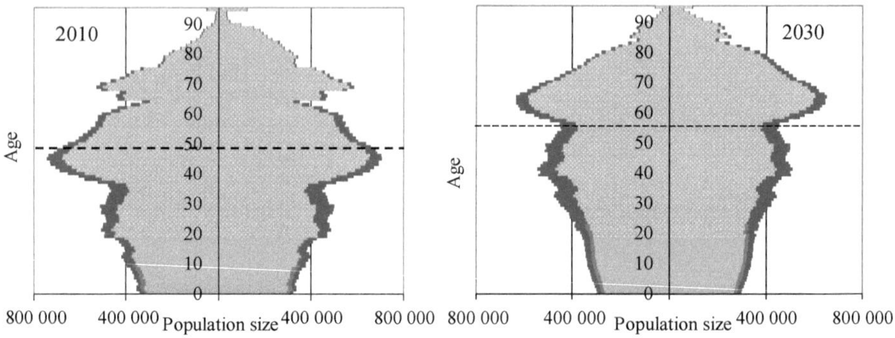

Source: Own calculations based on demographic data provided by the Federal Statistical Office.

As can be seen in the figures, the youngest cohorts born during the projection years are small due to the low fertility rates especially among German women. The number of births each year would be so low that they would be surpassed by the number of deaths. This birth gap could not be closed by migration, even though overall net migration numbers would be positive in each projection year. The population living in Germany would therefore decline between 2010 and 2030 from 81.4 million persons to 76.5 million persons.

Not all population groups would be affected by this decline to the same extent: The foreign population in Germany would in fact increase in size from 6.8 million persons in 2010 (8.3% of the total population) to 7.9 million persons in 2030 (10.3% of the total population). In 2030, one in ten residents of Germany would therefore not be able to participate in Bundestag elections due to lack of German citizenship. Children of foreign citizenship would of course be doubly excluded: They would not be entitled to vote both because of their young age and their lack of citizenship.

The population of underage German citizens would decrease in size from 12.5 million persons (15.3% of the total population) to 11.1 million persons during the projection period (14.5% of the total population). One in seven residents of Germany would be excluded from Bundestag elections in the last projection year on the basis of the minimum voting age criterion. Less than 0.5% of all German children and adolescents would be ius soli-citizens in each projection year.

Figure 48: Projected relative size of different population groups in Germany, 2010-2030 (in %)

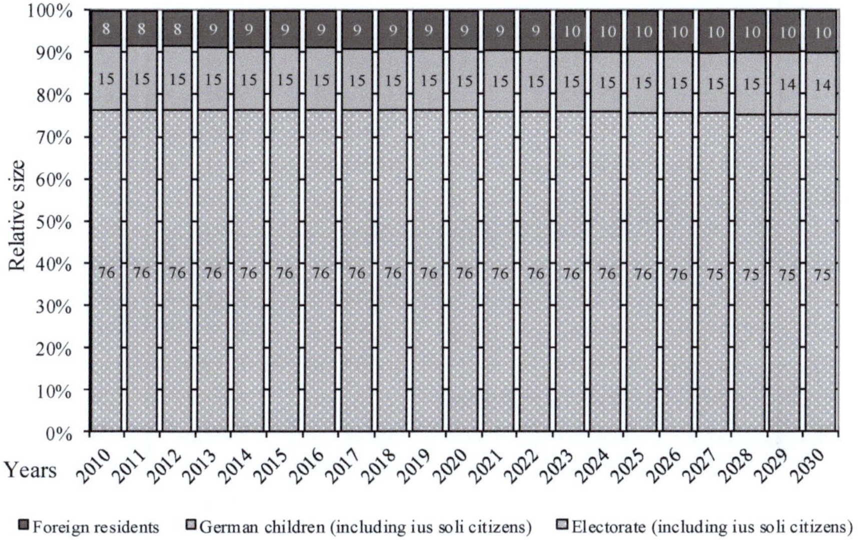

Source: Own calculations based on demographic data provided by the Federal Statistical Office.

The number of eligible voters (citizens aged 18 and older) would also decline during the projection period: In 2010, the electorate encompassed 62.2 million persons (76.4% of the total population). By 2030, it would include only 57.6 million persons (around 75.2% of the total population). 152.000 eligible voters would belong to the ius soli-population in the last projection year.

Figure 48 and Table 6 summarize these developments. Table 6 shows the total number of persons in each of the main population groups who would live in Germany in each projection year. Figure 48 visualizes the proportion they contribute to the total population size. Overall, the changes in the proportion of the different population groups are small in character.

Table 6: Projected number of German children, eligible voters and foreign residents living in Germany each year, 2010-2030 (in 1,000)

Years	German children (aged 0-18)		Eligible voters (aged 18 and older)		Foreign residents (all ages)	Total Population
	Ius soli-citizens	Other citizens	Ius soli-citizens	Other citizens		
	in 1,000					
2010	407,1	12074,9	7,1	62182,2	6776,3	81447,6
2011	432,1	11949,1	11,2	62131,2	6842,6	81366,2
2012	456,9	11836,4	15,3	62052,2	6907,7	81268,6
2013	481,2	11748,9	19,8	61932,3	6971,7	81154,0
2014	505,1	11665,9	21,2	61794,1	7034,9	81021,2
2015	528,3	11557,8	22,7	61668,7	7097,1	80874,5
2016	550,7	11434,4	24,6	61544,1	7158,2	80711,9
2017	572,6	11330,5	26,7	61382,7	7218,1	80530,6
2018	593,9	11237,2	29,0	61193,2	7277,1	80330,5
2019	580,8	11157,8	65,5	60970,8	7334,9	80109,9
2020	570,5	11102,2	98,6	60705,9	7391,8	79869,0
2021	561,3	11056,1	130,2	60415,0	7447,6	79610,2
2022	553,1	11014,8	160,5	60104,6	7501,9	79334,8
2023	545,1	10966,0	190,4	59786,6	7554,6	79042,6
2024	534,1	10927,6	189,3	59473,1	7608,9	78733,0
2025	523,9	10891,9	189,7	59138,8	7661,1	78405,5
2026	517,0	10834,5	187,8	58809,9	7711,1	78060,3
2027	515,1	10767,0	181,3	58477,9	7758,9	77700,3
2028	514,4	10711,3	173,3	58122,8	7804,7	77326,5
2029	513,2	10635,8	162,3	57780,0	7848,9	76940,3
2030	511,9	10556,7	152,3	57431,0	7890,9	76542,7

Source: Own calculations based on demographic data provided by the Federal Statistical Office.

The electorate would not only decline, it would also age if current demographic conditions and electoral law were to persist in the future. The median age of the electorate was 49.8 years in 2010. Until 2030, it would rise to 55.2 years (Figure 49). The increase of this indicator would be triggered by a shift in the age structure of the electorate: The numerically strong cohorts of the baby boom were aged 40 to 50 in 2010. Until 2030, these cohorts would grow older and reach the age groups 60 to 70, thus giving more quantitative weight to the older age groups among the electorate (see population pyramids in Figure 47). The cohorts that follow the baby boom generation are too small to counterbalance this trend.

Figure 49: Projected development of the median age of the electorate, 2010-2030

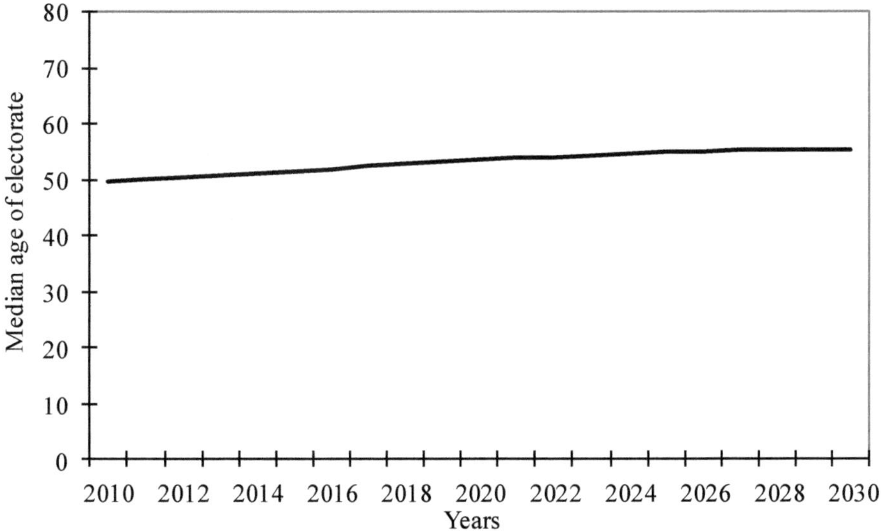

Source: Own calculations based on demographic data provided by the Federal Statistical Office.

The projection results appear to confirm the two expectations which have been raised and debated in recent years. First, many authors expect that the native German population will decline in the future while the size of the foreign population will increase. They deduce from these expectations that the proportion of eligible voters should decrease in the future. Second, other researchers expect that the electorate will age. According to the stable population scenario, these expectations are correct: The proportion of disenfranchised foreign residents indeed increases until 2030, the proportion of electors among the total population declines and the median age of the electorate increases during the projection period.

Nonetheless, the base line projection assumes that the prevailing demographic conditions in Germany will remain stable in the future and that the electoral law will not be changed. These assumptions are unlikely to occur in reality. During the past century, demographic behaviour has been subject to frequent changes and none of the demographic factors included here – fertility, mortality, migration or naturalization – has remained stable over the course of several decades. It has also been shown in previous chapters that the definition of membership in the German demos has frequently been changed during the past decades. From this perspective, further changes in law may not be ruled out. The base-year scenario calculated here should therefore be used as a reference scenario only. It illustrates the mid-term effects of current demographic behaviours and current legal definitions on the electorate and can be used as a yardstick to measure the effect of other scenarios. In the two following chapters, a number of such alternative demographic and policy scenarios will be presented. The assumptions that lie behind these scenarios will be discussed first. After that, the results of the different demographic projections and policy scenarios will be presented.

Chapter 6. Demographic projections: The influence of demographic trends on the development of the electorate

6.1. Demographic assumptions

In the following, the assumptions which are used for the demographic population projections are presented. The assumptions define how fertility, mortality, migration and naturalization trends may develop in the future, both among the German and the foreign population. The assumptions are then combined into scenarios, each depicting a distinct set of assumptions on future fertility, mortality and migration trends as well as changes of citizenship. The results of the scenario calculations are presented at the end of this chapter.

When defining the assumptions, one challenge had to be dealt with. While this study aims at projecting the ius soli-population as a distinct population group, separate assumptions on the demographic behaviour of ius soli-citizens could not be defined. As was stated in Chapter 4, data on the demographic behaviour of ius soli-citizens are not available. Cases of birth, death and migration that occur among this population group are incorporated in the same statistics as demographic events occurring to the German majority population. It is not possible to disentangle the statistics for these two population groups.

In the following, only one set of fertility, mortality and migration assumptions is therefore defined for Germans and these assumptions are applied both to the ius soli-population and to the German majority population. This approach implicitly assumes that the demographic behaviour of both population groups is the same. Given that ius soli-citizens were born and socialised in Germany, this assumption is reasonable. Even if the demographic behaviour of the two population groups should differ, the assumption of similar behaviour should not distort the projection results in a noticeable way. This was confirmed with the help of sensitivity projections. Results cannot be shown here, but are available upon request. Ius soli-citizens form a very small part of the population in

Germany so that even if their demographic rates are over- or underestimated by equating them with those of the German majority population, the impact on the overall projection results is very small.

6.1.1. Fertility assumptions

6.1.1.1. German citizens

After the end of the baby boom in the 1960s, fertility levels in Germany declined rapidly. Between 1966 and 1976, the total fertility rate (TFR) of German women dropped nearly by half from around 2.5 to 1.36. Since then, it has remained relatively stable at levels between 1.25 and 1.4.[348] These fertility levels lie within a range that has been termed "very low" (values below 1.5) and "lowest-low" (values below 1.3) in the demographic literature.[349]

From a 'mechanical' perspective, the drop of the TFR since the late 1960s and the subsequent persistence at low levels has been caused by a decline in the number of children born per woman and a postponement of childbearing to higher ages. A range of factors have been discussed to explain these processes, among them changes in values, improvements in contraception and the difficulty of couples to reconcile professional and private obligations. While these and other social, economic, cultural and ideational factors are thought to have contributed to the decline in fertility, no consensus has yet emerged about the exact contribution of each.[350]

Since the onset of the fertility decline in the late 1960s, demographers have also discussed whether low fertility is a temporary or a permanent phenomenon and whether, when and to what extent TFR values might increase again. When fertility rates first started to decline, many demographers assumed that this would not be a long-term process but that they would eventually stop decreasing. Some demographers proposed that the replacement level of 2.1 children per woman would be such a lower limit of fertility. Others suggested

---

[348] Only the period around German reunification is an exception, see Chapter 3.3.1.1.

[349] See *Frejka, T./Sobotka, T.*, Fertility, 2008, p. 17; *Kohler, H.-P./Billari, F. C./Ortega, J. A.*, Lowest-low fertility, 2002, p. 642.

[350] See *Bongaarts, J.*, Fertility transition, 2002, p. 436.

that the TFR might decline to lower levels such as 1.5, but increase again afterwards.[351] In reality, these expectations have proven to be wrong. The TFR in Germany and other countries dropped to lower levels than anticipated and has not substantially increased again over the last decades. Nonetheless, the question whether fertility rates might increase again in the future or if low fertility is a permanent characteristic of industrialized societies is ongoing today. It is "one of the most controversial issues in contemporary demography".[352]

Some demographers argue that the TFR in Germany and other low-fertility countries is likely to increase again in the near future. They point out that the low levels of fertility of the past decades are partly the result of a postponement process. Women have born children at increasingly higher ages during past years, so that in any given year some births were not realized that would have occurred if age-specific fertility patterns had remained stable. This postponement process eventually has to end, since there is a biological age limit to fertility beyond which childbearing cannot be realized. Once the postponement process slows down and then stops, the tempo effect will disappear. Demographers such as Bongaarts stress that fertility rates should rise again at this point.[353] Exactly until which age women can postpone childbearing and when an increase in fertility rates can thus be expected, however, is not clear. McDonald for instance sees no indication that the tempo effect will disappear anytime soon in low-fertility countries and has somewhat sceptically stated that "waiting for tempo is beginning to look like waiting for Godot".[354] Goldstein and colleagues, by contrast, have suggested that the recent slight fertility increases in industrialized countries are a sign that the postponement process is losing its momentum.[355] While demographers disagree about the end

---

351 See *Kohler, H.-P./Billari, F. C./Ortega, J. A.*, Lowest-low fertility, 2002, p. 641 and footnote 1 on p. 672; *Bongaarts, J.*, Fertility transition, 2002, p. 419; *Bretz, M.*, Bevölkerungs-vorausberechnungen, 2001, p. 4 f. For brief information on the replacement level of 2.1., see Chapter 3.2.

352 *Bongaarts, J.*, Fertility, 2001, p. 276.

353 *Bongaarts, J.*, Fertility, 2001, p. 278. See also *Frejka, T./Sobotka, T.*, Fertility, 2008, p. 25 f.

354 *McDonald, P.*, Low fertility, 2006, p. 487.

355 *Goldstein, J. R./Sobotka, T./Jasilioniene, A.*, 'Lowest-low' fertility, 2009, p. 24. See also *Sobotka, T.*, Lowest-low fertility, 2004, p. 196. Kohler and colleagues discuss until which age

of postponement processes, they agree that the TFR is not likely to rise back to the replacement level of 2.1 children per women once the tempo effect disappears. Instead, they assume that the resulting fertility increase will be of a moderate nature only.[356]

Demographers who assume that fertility rates might increase in the future also invoke fertility preferences to justify their expectation. From a bio-evolutionary perspective, Foster argues that humans are genetically and biologically predisposed to nurture, and that this predisposition is often reinforced by exposure to infants or social pressure. She stresses that due to these inherited behavioural predispositions and stimuli most women will want to have at least one child.[357] A survey conducted in 2004 in fact revealed that women in West Germany on average want to bear 1.73 children (East Germany: 1.78), a value which is higher than TFR values that have been measured in recent decades.[358] Some fertility experts argue that the gap between fertility preferences and the measured period TFR is a sign that obstacles currently prevent women from fulfilling their fertility intentions. Such obstacles might for instance be the difficulty of combining professional and private obligations or a lack of financial stability. These demographers argue that an upturn in the future TFR could be achieved if obstacles were removed and if women would be supported in bearing the number of children they prefer. In this context, the role of public policies has been discussed. While conclusive evidence on the effect of policies on fertility is so far lacking, recent studies suggest that comprehensive family policy packages may have a small impact on the timing of childbearing, provided that they remain in place over long periods of time. Policies that facilitate the reconciliation of work and family obligations and combat gender

---

childbearing can be postponed: *Kohler, H.-P./Billari, F. C./Ortega, J. A.*, Lowest-low fertility, 2002, p. 668.

356 See for instance *Alders, M./Keilman, N./Cruijsen, H.*, Assumptions, 2007, p. 63; *Sobotka, T.*, Lowest-low fertility, 2004, pp. 207 and 213; *Bongaarts, J.*, Fertility transition, 2002, p. 439; *Lesthaeghe, R./Willems, P.*, Low fertility, 1999, p. 221; *Avramov, D./Cliquet, R.*, Economy of time, 2003, p. 388.

357 *Foster, C.*, Limits, 2000. For a similar expectation see *Frejka, T., et al.*, Summary, 2008, p. 7.

358 Men prefer to have an average number of 1.59 children (West Germany)/1.46 (East Germany). See *Dorbritz, J.*, Germany, 2008, p. 583.

discrimination appear to be most influential. By contrast, policies do not appear to have an effect on the average number of children born per woman.[359]

Demographers have also suggested that favourable economic developments might push fertility upward in the future, provided that they foster the early economic and financial independence of young adults. Early independence might allow couples to fulfil fertility intentions at an earlier age and to have a higher number of children. Finally, Preston discusses the role of values and stresses that fertility rates may increase in the future if individuals put a stronger value again on parenthood and childbearing.[360]

Other researchers are more sceptical about whether fertility rates will rise again in the near future. They argue that many of the factors which have provoked the fertility decline in the past – the challenge of combining work and family obligations and the high costs of raising children, among others – will not disappear and therefore continue to influence fertility levels.[361] The difficulty of reconciling family and professional life may in fact become even more influential in the future, since cohorts of young women who are currently entering childbearing ages have on average higher educational attainments than their mothers and might consequently have higher career aspirations.[362] Unfavourable economic conditions, high youth unemployment rates, precarious working conditions, an increasing preference for personal independence and the strive for self-fulfilment are further factors that might contribute to keep fertility at low levels. Lutz and Skirbekk even hypothesize that these factors will not only keep fertility at currently low levels. Instead, "the match of high aspirations and pessimism about the economic future will result in even lower fertility".[363]

---

[359] See *Gauthier, A. H.*, Impact, 2007; *McDonald, P.*, Low fertility, 2006, pp. 500-505; *Avramov, D./Cliquet, R.*, Economy of time, 2003, p. 383 f.; *Wingen, M.*, Plädoyer, 2002; *Bertram, H., et al.*, Familienpolitik, 2012.

[360] *Preston, S. H.*, Values, 1986, p. 191; see also *Kohler, H.-P./Billari, F. C./Ortega, J. A.*, Lowest-low fertility, 2002, p. 671.

[361] See *Keyfitz, N.*, Knowledge, 1982, p. 733; *Westoff, C. F.*, Fertility decline, 1983, p. 101; *Birg, H.*, Bevölkerungsentwicklung, 2000, p. 43.

[362] See *Enquete-Kommission 'Demographischer Wandel'*, Zwischenbericht, 1998, p. 66.

[363] *Lutz, W./Skirbekk, V.*, Policies, 2005, p. 702. Goldstein and colleagues, by contrast, expect that drops in fertility due to the economic crisis of recent years should be temporary only, if they occur at all (*Goldstein, J. R./Sobotka, T./Jasilioniene, A.*, 'Lowest-low' fertility, 2009, p. 25). See

Demographers who do not expect fertility rates to increase in the near future are also sceptical about the value of surveys which indicate that fertility preferences are currently higher than fertility rates. Gauthier for instance critically discusses whether surveys which ask for the desired number of children indeed provide information on the genuine personal fertility preferences of the interviewees or whether they rather reflect what interviewees perceive to be the number of children that people 'in general' should have.[364] Other researchers have pointed out that even if fertility preferences which are measured in surveys are higher than actual fertility rates, the proportion of young adults in Germany who declare that they do not want to have children is rising. Already today, the proportion of women who remain childless is very high in international comparison: Among women born in 1967 in West Germany, every fourth does not have children.[365] Dorbritz suggests that if this trend continues, policies might not be successful in closing the gap between measured fertility preferences and fertility outcomes in the future:

> "With the fall in desired fertility, a barrier could have been formed in Germany which may even prevent fertility from increasing in the long term."[366]

Demographers who are sceptical about future increases in fertility have also discussed the role of fertility postponement. Kohler and colleagues question whether an end of fertility postponement will lead to an increase in the TFR. They argue that once women postpone fertility to higher ages, less time remains to have children, since infertility and the risk of fetal loss increase with the age of the mother. Not all postponed births may thus be recuperated. A lack of a suitable partner may also result in involuntary childlessness if childbearing is

also discussions of future fertility developments in *Presser, H. B.*, Gender perspective, 2001, p. 180; *Dorbritz, J.*, Demographisches Wissen, 2004, p. 354 f.

364 *Gauthier, A. H.*, Impact, 2007, p. 328.

365 See *Bujard, M., et al.*, Kinder, 2012, p. 52.

366 *Dorbritz, J.*, Germany, 2008, p. 593; see also *Dorbritz, J.*, Demographisches Wissen, 2004, p. 356. For a debate on the influence of socialisation on fertility preferences see *Lutz, W./Skirbekk, V.*, Policies, 2005, p. 702 f.

postponed to higher ages.[367] All of these factors may prevent the TFR from rising even after the postponement process has stopped.

So far, the TFR in Germany has remained at low levels even though a slight upturn was registered in recent years. Whether this upturn is of a temporary nature or the onset of a long-term trend is not yet clear. Population projections that were published in recent years have attempted to reflect this uncertainty by including several fertility assumptions in their scenarios. The Federal Statistical Office of Germany for instance has considered likely a moderate increase of the TFR to a level of 1.6 in 2025, a constant level of 1.4 and a further decrease of the TFR to 1.2 until 2060. Birg and Flöthmann work with two assumptions, one hypothesising that the TFR will increase to 1.64 until 2040, the other assuming that it will remain constant at a level of 1.4.[368] Other projections assume that the TFR will remain constant at a level of 1.3 to 1.4.[369]

In order to account for the multitude of economic, social, cultural and ideational factors that may influence fertility preferences and behaviours in the future, the following two different assumptions are defined here. These assumptions are applied to ius soli-citizens and the German majority population when calculating the projections.

<u>Fertility of Germans 1, 2011-2030 **(FG1)**: Increase in fertility.</u> The first fertility assumption hypothesizes that the TFR of German women will slightly increase until 2030 at the same pace as that observed during recent years. This assumption is based on the expectation that the end of the tempo effect will put an upward pressure on fertility. Public policies that remove obstacles to childbearing, favourable economic conditions or a resurgence of family-friendly norms and values may also contribute to a rise in fertility. The TFR values for each projection year were obtained by extrapolating the recent rise in the TFR observed since 1994 into the future. The age-specific fertility patterns were assumed to remain stable in this scenario – i.e. no further postponement of

---

[367] *Kohler, H.-P./Billari, F. C./Ortega, J. A.*, Lowest-low fertility, 2002, pp. 646 and 668; *Beier, H. M., et al.*, Fertilität, 2012.

[368] *Statistisches Bundesamt*, Bevölkerung Deutschlands, 2009, p. 27; *Birg, H./Flöthmann, E.-J.*, Projektionsrechnungen, 2001, p. 17 f.

[369] See *Münz, R./Seifert, W./Ulrich, R.*, Zuwanderung, 1999, p. 167; *Ulrich, R.*, Bevölkerungsstruktur, 2001, p. 15; *Bundesministerium des Innern*, Modellrechnungen, 2000, p. 15.

fertility is assumed to take place – so that women aged 31 have the highest age-specific fertility rate in each projection year. Following these assumptions, the TFR would increase by a value of 0.16 from 1.36 in 2010 to 1.52 in 2030.

Figure 50: Fertility assumptions for German women (FG1 and FG2), 2011-2030

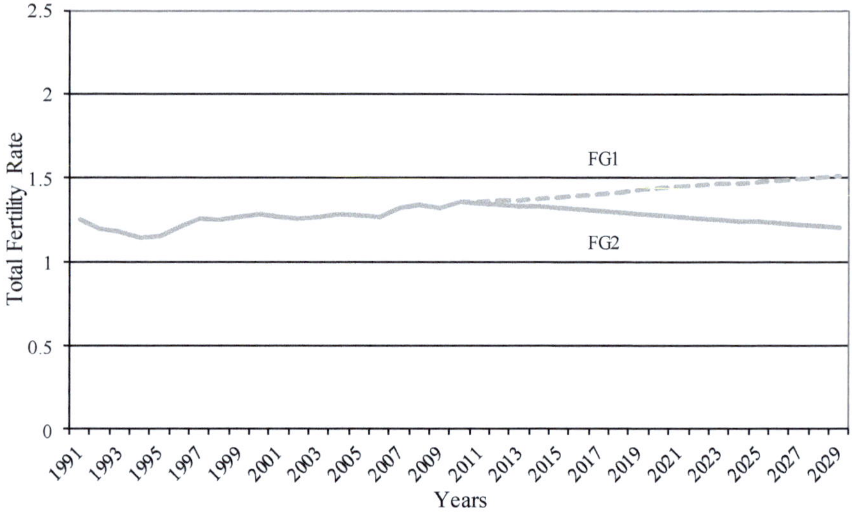

Source: Own illustration. Data for the years 1991-2010 based on Birth Statistics and Population Statistics obtained from the Federal Statistical Office.

Fertility of Germans 2, 2011-2030 **(FG2)**: Decrease in fertility. In contrast to this, the second fertility assumption reflects the expectation that the reconciliation of family and work will remain difficult in the future, that the financial or employment conditions of young adults might deteriorate and that fertility preferences might continue to decline. To reflect the strand of the academic literature which has stressed the importance of these factors, it was assumed that the TFR will take the opposite course as in the FG1 assumption and decrease by a value of 0.16 from 1.36 in 2010 to 1.20 in 2030. Again, it was assumed that age-specific fertility patterns will not change further in the future, i.e. that the decline in fertility will occur even in the absence of further postponement processes.

6.1.1.2. Foreign residents

Foreign women have had a higher TFR than German women since 1972, the year in which fertility statistics started to distinguish by the citizenship of mothers. During past decades, the fertility gap has started to close, but in 2010 the TFR of foreign women was still around 0.2 points higher than that of German women. Age-specific fertility patterns have also approached but not yet converged with those of German women.[370]

The gradual approximation of fertility behaviours during the last decades has been attributed to changes in norms and values. Demographers have argued that foreign residents gradually adopt the childbearing norms, values and behaviours of the German population the longer they stay in Germany. During the last decades, fertility rates have also decreased in many countries of origin. Almost all countries in Europe had TFR values below the replacement level of 2.1 children per woman in 2010. Turkey had a TFR of 2.1 and Asia and the Americas had an average TFR of 2.2. Only African countries maintain high fertility levels. The average TFR for this continent stood at 4.7 in 2010, but it has been declining as well.[371] In contrast to the guest worker and family migration of the 1960s and 1970s, most foreign residents who have moved to Germany in recent years thus do not come from high-fertility countries any more and immigration does not push the fertility rate of foreign women upward to the same extent as it has done in the past.[372]

Most demographers assume that the TFR of foreign women will continue to approach the German TFR in the future. Foreigners already living in Germany are expected to further adapt to German fertility behaviours over time. In addition, it is assumed that fertility rates will continue to decline or remain at low levels in countries of origin such as Turkey, so that immigrants who move to Germany in the future will on average have lower fertility preferences than in the past. Pötzsch also suggests that many young immigrants may come to

---

370 See Chapter 3.3.1.2.

371 Information on TFR data is taken from *Population Reference Bureau*, World population, 2010 and *Schmid, S./Borchers, K.*, Migration, 2010, p. 41.

372 See *Schmid, S./Kohls, M.*, Generatives Verhalten, 2011, pp. 171 and 175; *Pötzsch, O.*, Geburtenentwicklung, 2010, p. 38 f.; *Münz, R./Seifert, W./Ulrich, R.*, Zuwanderung, 1999, p. 70.

Germany for limited periods of time in order to work. For these women, family formation and childbearing might not be a priority.[373]

A few demographers suggest that differences in fertility may persist in the future. Coleman for instance suggests that a convergence of the fertility rates of foreign women with those of natives may not necessarily occur, for instance if foreigners remain distinct subpopulations in their countries of residence:

> "Fertility differences may persist if immigrant groups do not achieve socioeconomic equality, if they retain strong attachment to religious or other elements of foreign culture, and if they continue to be numerically and culturally reinforced by large-scale migration [...]. Their minority status per se may make some groups resistant to change."[374]

The majority of demographers who make explicit assumptions about future fertility trends however assume that the gradual approximation of foreign fertility levels to those of Germans will continue.[375]

Fertility of foreign residents, 2011-2030 **(FF)**: Convergence. In line with the expectation of most demographers, it is assumed here that the fertility behaviour of foreign women will continue to approach that of German women and eventually converge. The appropriate TFR values were obtained by first extrapolating the decline in the TFR of foreign women, observed during the past two decades, into the future. It was assumed that once the extrapolated fertility trend of foreign women reaches the projected fertility level of German women –

---

373 See *Pötzsch, O.*, Geburtenentwicklung, 2010, p. 38 f.; *Münz, R./Seifert, W./Ulrich, R.*, Zuwanderung, 1999, p. 168.

374 *Coleman, D.*, Immigration, 2006, p. 410.

375 A further approximation or even convergence of fertility rates is assumed by *Statistisches Bundesamt*, Bevölkerung Deutschlands, 2009, p. 24; *Enquete-Kommission 'Demographischer Wandel'*, Zwischenbericht, 1998, p. 66 and *Birg, H./Flöthmann, E.-J.*, Projektionsrechnungen, 2001, pp. 17-19. *Münz, R./Seifert, W./Ulrich, R.*, Zuwanderung, 1999, p. 168 and *Ulrich, R.*, Bevölkerungsstruktur, 2001, p. 14 f. make separate fertility assumptions for different groups of foreign residents. They assume a further decline of fertility rates of Turkish women, but assume that the fertility of foreign women from other countries which is already at a very low level will remain constant. The projection in *Bundesministerium des Innern*, Modellrechnungen, 2000, p. 16 is the only outlier since it assumes that the fertility of all foreign women will remain constant at the long-term average value of 1.5 children per woman. This assumption is not explicitly justified by the authors.

in 2017 under the FG1 assumption and in 2023 under the FG2 assumption – foreign women will have the same fertility rates as German women for the rest of the projection period. It was further assumed that the age-specific fertility rates of foreign women will also converge with those of German women by 2017 and 2023, respectively.

Figure 51: Fertility assumptions for foreign women (FF), 2011-2030

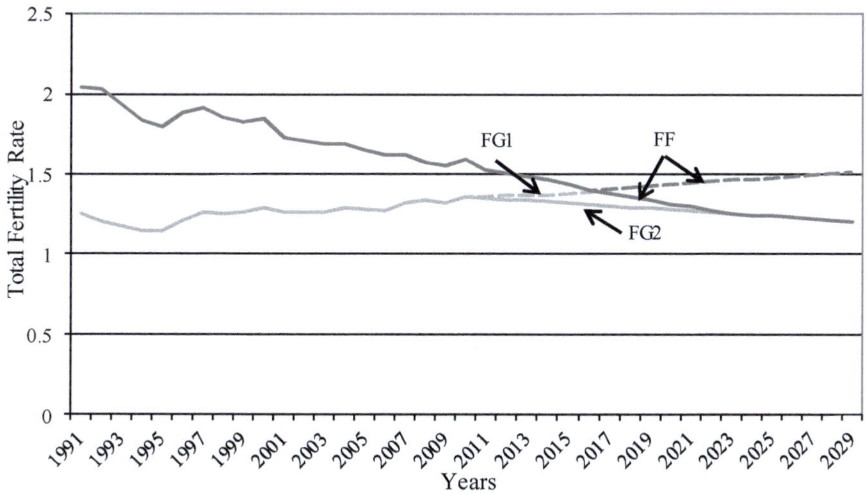

Source: Own illustration. Data for the years 1991-2010 based on Birth Statistics and Population Statistics obtained from the Federal Statistical Office.

6.1.2. Mortality assumptions

6.1.2.1. German citizens

Since the beginning of the 20th century, life expectancy at birth of German men and women has nearly doubled. This development is not limited to Germany, but has been recorded in other industrialized countries as well. The increase in life expectancy has been of a remarkably constant, nearly linear nature. In a study on the development of record life expectancies across different countries, Oeppen and Vaupel note that the increase since 1840 has been so steady that it is possibly "the most remarkable regularity of mass endeavour ever observed".[376] It has been the result of decreases in the mortality of infants, children and women during or after childbirth. Since the 1950s, advances in medical diagnoses and treatment as well as life style changes have also reduced mortality at middle and older ages.[377]

While mortality experts largely agree on explanations for past developments, the question of how human mortality will develop in the future is highly contested. Some demographers have assume that there is a limit to human life expectancy due to genetic and biological predispositions of the human body. Various maximum life expectancies were proposed: In the 1920s, Louis Dublin argued that 65 years would constitute the ultimate limit to average life expectancy.[378] In 1980 and later in the 1990s, James Fries, Jay Olshansky and colleagues considered 85 years to be the maximum average life expectancy that populations may reach.[379] It was assumed that once this innate maximum human life expectancy was reached, the mortality of human populations would not decline further and life expectancy would remain constant. While individual persons might live beyond the maximum average life expectancy, it was assumed that the majority of persons would not surpass this limit.

Mortality developments during the last decades have broken these alleged limits to life expectancy. Men and especially women have become older than was thought to be possible. Even the age limit of 85 years has been broken in a number of countries, for example by female populations of Hong Kong, Japan and San Marino.[380]

The question how old human beings can on average become therefore remains one of the most strongly disputed topics in demography. Two opposing perspectives are currently discussed in the literature.[381] Some researchers such as

---

376 *Oeppen, J./Vaupel, J.*, Broken limits, 2002, p. 1029.

377 See *Luy, M.*, Sterblichkeitsentwicklung, 2004, p. 10; see also Chapter 3.3.2.1.

378 See *Oeppen, J./Vaupel, J.*, Broken limits, 2002, p. 1029.

379 See *Vaupel, J.*, Biodemography, 2004, p. 48; *Manton, K. G./Stallard, E./Tolley, H. D.*, Limits, 1991, p. 603; *Olshansky, S. J./Carnes, B. A./Cassel, C.*, Methuselah, 1990, p. 638.

380 See *Bongaarts, J.*, How long, 2006, p. 607; *Alders, M./Keilman, N./Cruijsen, H.*, Assumptions, 2007, p. 63; *Population Reference Bureau*, World population, 2010.

381 See *Bongaarts, J.*, How long, 2006, p. 605.

Olshansky, Carnes and Cassel maintain that there is a limit to how old human beings can become. They insist that increases in longevity cannot continue without limits due to biomechanical, biochemical and biodemographic constraints of the human body. They also point out that factors such as the increasing prevalence of obesity and diabetes in industrialized countries or outbreaks of infectious diseases could have a depressing effect on life expectancy in the future. Furthermore, they argue that mortality among children and middle aged persons in industrialized countries is so low already that it cannot decline much further. In order for life expectancy to increase to the same degree as observed in the past, mortality at older ages would have to decline substantially.[382] Olshansky and colleagues consider such a strong decline of mortality at older ages unlikely. They argue that unless major medical breakthroughs fundamentally alter the aging process of human beings, the maximum average human life expectancy should remain at a level far below 100 years:

> "There are no life-style changes, surgical procedures, vitamins, antioxidants, hormones, or techniques of genetic engineering available today with the capacity to repeat the gains in life expectancy that were achieved during the 20th century."[383]

In contrast to this approach, other researchers assume that the genetically determined limit to human life expectancy has not yet been reached, if it exists at all, and that life expectancy will continue to grow for the foreseeable future. Factors such as developments in preventive and curative medical treatments, increasing awareness of the importance of good nutrition and a healthy life style, declining numbers of deaths related to traffic accidents or accidents at the work place have contributed to the decrease in mortality at middle and old ages in the

---

382 *Olshansky, S. J./Carnes, B. A./Désesquelles, A.*, Prospects, 2001, p. 1491 f.; *Olshansky, S. J./Carnes, B. A.*, Future, 2009; *Olshansky, S. J./Carnes, B. A./Brody, J.*, Life span, 2002, p. 507. Regarding the observation that mortality among infants and children is so low already that it cannot decline much further also see *Bongaarts, J.*, Long-range trends, 2005, p. 23 and *Bongaarts, J.*, How long, 2006, p. 623.

383 *Olshansky, S. J./Carnes, B. A./Désesquelles, A.*, Prospects, 2001, p. 1492.

past years. Demographers such as Vaupel and Bongaarts expect that they will remain important in the near future.[384] Bongaarts argues that

> "there is no reason to believe that advances in biotechnology, preventive and curative medicine, and drug treatment will be less effective in reducing senescent mortality in the future than in the past. In fact, an acceleration of improvements cannot be ruled out".[385]

So far, mortality rates continue to decline steadily in Germany and other industrialized countries and show no sign of slowing down. This appears to confirm the second group of researchers who are optimistic about future gains in longevity. Most recent population projections published by demographers or statistical offices such as the Federal Statistical Office of Germany and Eurostat have assented to the view that in the absence of future wars, epidemics or environmental disasters, a further decline in mortality and increase in longevity are to be expected. Some researchers and institutes however assume that the pace of mortality decline will slow down, so that life expectancy will increase somewhat slower than in past decades.[386] Hence, the main focus of the academic discussion "has shifted from the limits to life expectancy to the size of future increases in life expectancy".[387] In order to reflect the uncertainty about the size of future mortality reductions, two different assumptions are used in this study. They are used both for the ius soli-population and for the German majority population.

Mortality of Germans 1, 2011-2030 **(MG1)**: Linear increase in life expectancy. The first mortality assumption presumes that life expectancy at birth will

---

[384] See *Vaupel, J.*, Biodemography, 2004, p. 57; *Manton, K. G./Stallard, E./Tolley, H. D.*, Limits, 1991, p. 631; *Birg, H.*, Life expectancy, 2000, p. 195.

[385] *Bongaarts, J.*, How long, 2006, p. 623.

[386] See *Statistisches Bundesamt*, Bevölkerung Deutschlands, 2009, p. 29 f.; *Bundesministerium des Innern*, Modellrechnungen, 2000, p. 7; *Ulrich, R.*, Bevölkerungsstruktur, 2001, p. 15; *Lanzieri, G.*, Europop, 2009, p. 12 f.; *Birg, H./Flöthmann, E.-J.*, Projektionsrechnungen, 2001, p. 63. Some of these projections do not distinguish by citizenship and therefore these studies do not define separate mortality assumptions for the German population. Instead, they define one set of assumption that is applied to the entire resident population of Germany. In contrast to other projections, Münz and colleagues assume that there is a limit to life expectancy: *Münz, R./Seifert, W./Ulrich, R.*, Zuwanderung, 1999, p. 168.

[387] *Bongaarts, J.*, How long, 2006, p. 608.

continue to grow until 2030 at the same pace as observed in the past. This assumption is based on the above-mentioned expectation by Vaupel, Bongaarts and other demographers that future gains in longevity are likely. It also reflects the observation that the increase in life expectancy in Germany so far shows no sign of slowing down. Following the assumption of further linear increase, life expectancy of German men at birth would rise from 77.7 years in 2010 to 83.3 years in 2030. Life expectancy of German women would increase from 82.6 years in 2010 to 86.9 years in 2030. These values were obtained by extrapolating the trend of rising life expectancy at birth between 1980[388] and 2010 to the period 2011 to 2030.

Figure 52: Mortality assumptions for German men and women (MG1 and MG2), 2011-2030

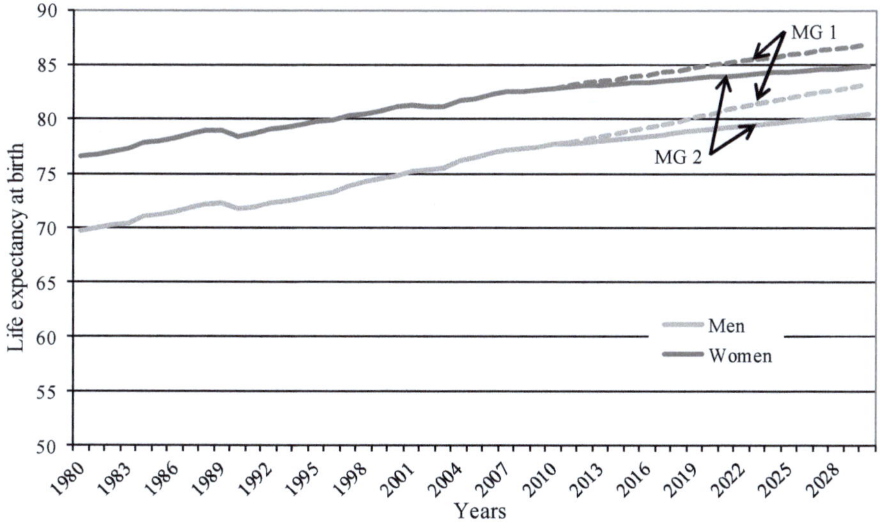

Source: Own illustration. Data for the years 1980-2010 based on Death Statistics and Population Statistics obtained from the Federal Statistical Office.
Note: Data before 1990 refer to the former West German states only.

Age-specific mortality rates for individual projection years were generated by proportionately reducing the base-year mortality rates with the help of editing

388 1980 was the first year for which death statistics could be obtained on the German population only, thus excluding cases of death among foreign residents in Germany.

options in the PDE population projection software until the life expectancy values for each projection year were reached. This procedure ensures that presumed future gains in life expectancy will especially occur at older ages. In addition, this procedure ensures that life expectancy values of German men at birth continue to catch up with those of German women. This is in line with expectations stated in the demographic literature.[389]

Mortality of Germans 2, 2011-2030 **(MG2)**: Slower increase in life expectancy. The second mortality assumption is based on the more sceptical expectation that mortality rates might continue to decline in the future, but are likely to do so at a slower pace than in the past. To reflect this strand of the academic literature, it was assumed that life expectancy at birth will increase half as much as under assumption MG1 during the projection period. Following this assumption, life expectancy at birth of men would increase from 77.7 years (2010) to 80.5 years (2030) and life expectancy of women from 82.6 years (2010) to 84.9 years (2030). Again, the gap in life expectancy between men and women would decrease during the projection period and the reduction in mortality would affect older age groups more strongly than younger age groups.

6.1.2.2. Foreign residents

It was already discussed in Chapter 4.1.3.1. that reliable data on the mortality of foreign residents in Germany do not exist. Therefore, it is difficult to estimate past and current mortality developments for this population group. Predicting future developments of mortality is an even more challenging endeavour. Since reliable data on past mortality developments are not available, trend extrapolations are not possible. Therefore, only two sources of input remained which could be consulted to define assumptions on future mortality trends: demographic studies and previously published population projections.

In recent years, a number of studies have analysed the mortality of foreign residents by using various datasets (e.g. German pension data or data from health insurances). Overall, these studies have come to the conclusion that mortality rates of foreign residents in Germany are higher during childhood but

389 See *Enquete-Kommission 'Demographischer Wandel'*, Zwischenbericht, 1998, p. 83.

lower in adult and older age groups than those of Germans. A number of different hypotheses have been discussed to explain this mortality advantage, the most important being the 'healthy migrant effect' and the 'salmon bias effect'. Both of these hypothesised effects postulate that persons with a migration background are a positively selected group in terms of health and that lower mortality rates are therefore to be expected.[390]

Some researchers have argued that the mortality advantage of foreign residents should diminish over time, especially due to their lower average socio-economic status. Recent research findings by Kohls, Kibele and colleagues confirm this hypothesis. Their findings suggest that the mortality rates of foreign residents have started to approach those of Germans. The mortality rates of older male foreign residents even appear to be already slightly higher than those of their German peers.[391]

Mortality of foreign residents, 2011-2030 **(MF)**: Convergence. Based on these recent research findings, it is assumed in this study that the mortality rates of foreign residents will approach those of Germans over the course of the projection period and converge by 2030. Life expectancy of foreign men at birth would consequently reach 80.5 years or 83.3 years in 2030, depending on which mortality assumption is chosen for the German population (MG1 or MG2). Life expectancy of foreign women would reach 84.9 or 86.9 years, again depending on which mortality assumption is chosen for the German population. Figure 53 shows the mortality assumptions of foreign men as an example.

The convergence assumption is in line with other population projections which were published during the last years. Most projections have assumed that a convergence of mortality rates will take place over time.[392] Other studies even

---

390 See Chapter 3.3.2.2.

391 *Kohls, M.*, Healthy-migrant-effect, 2008, p. 40; *Kohls, M.*, Mortalität, 2008, p. 44; *Kohls, M.*, Morbidität, 2011, p. 214; *Kibele, E./Scholz, R./Shkolnikov, V. M.*, Migrant mortality, 2008, p. 392.

392 See *Birg, H./Flöthmann, E.-J.*, Projektionsrechnungen, 2001, p. 63; *Enquete-Kommission 'Demographischer Wandel'*, Zwischenbericht, 1998, p. 83; *Bundesministerium des Innern*, Modellrechnungen, 2000, p. 16 f.; *Ulrich, R.*, Bevölkerungsstruktur, 2001, p. 15. Some studies do not explicitly assume a convergence of mortality. Instead, they assume constant mortality levels among the foreign population and declining mortality rates among Germans during the projection period. This however also amounts to an approach of rates over time.

assume that a convergence has already occurred.[393] The latter assumption was not followed here, since recent studies mentioned above find that mortality differences between the German and the foreign population persist at least in some age groups.

Figure 53: Mortality assumptions for foreign men (MF), 2011-2030

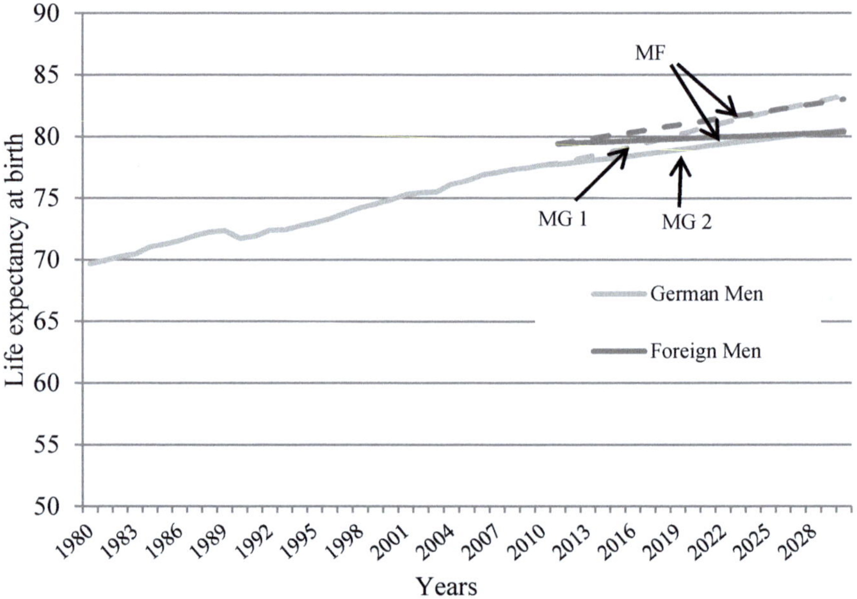

Source: Own illustration. Data for the years 1980-2010 based on Death Statistics and Population Statistics obtained from the Federal Statistical Office.
Note: Data before 1990 refer to the former West German states only.

Due to the lack of reliable data, the convergence assumption is somewhat speculative. Nonetheless, in the light of available research findings it appears to be the most plausible one. Sensitivity analyses (not shown here) have revealed that if other mortality trends would have been assumed for the projection period, e.g. a persistence of foreign residents' mortality advantages over time, the results of the population projections in terms of the proportion of eligible voters

[393] See for instance *Lanzieri, G.*, Projections, 2011, p. 11. The assumption of convergence is not made explicit. Instead, Lanzieri uses one set of mortality assumptions for the foreign and the German population and thus implicitly assumes a convergence as well.

and the median age of the electorate would differ only marginally. The convergence assumption taken here therefore does not appear to influence projection results to a strong degree.

6.1.3. Migration assumptions

6.1.3.1. German citizens

Migration of Germans has contributed to overall population growth during the past decades. Between 1954 and German reunification in 1990, 8.3 million cases of immigration were registered, while 3.3 million Germans left the country. The German population thus increased by around 5 million persons through migration during this period. Since 1990, 3.9 million German immigrants and 2.6 million emigrants moved across Germany's external borders. The population thus increased by another 1.3 million persons through migration during the last twenty years. Ethnic Germans and citizens from the GDR have been the quantitatively most important immigrant groups over time. The contribution of these two groups to overall immigration numbers is visualized in Figure 54. It shows the absolute number of German immigrants per year. The light grey parts of the bars show the number of ethnic Germans among these immigrants. The contribution of GDR citizens to overall immigration numbers is visualized in the dark grey parts of bars. The black section of the bars is made up by all other groups of German immigrants. As can be seen, citizens from the former GDR strongly contributed to immigration flows during the 1950s and early 1960s until the construction of the Berlin Wall. 3.5 million immigrants moved to (West) Germany during these years, 2.6 million of which came from the GDR. GDR citizens also migrated to Germany in large numbers between 1988 and 1990. Among the 1.8 million immigrants who moved to Germany during these three years, 0.8 million came from the (former) GDR. During the rest of the period, i.e. the 1960s, 1970s and the early 1980s, travel restrictions curtailed most migration by GDR citizens. Since 1991, migration between the new and the old Länder is classified as internal German migration and is no longer counted in the international migration statistics.

Figure 54: Different groups of German immigrants, 1954-2010

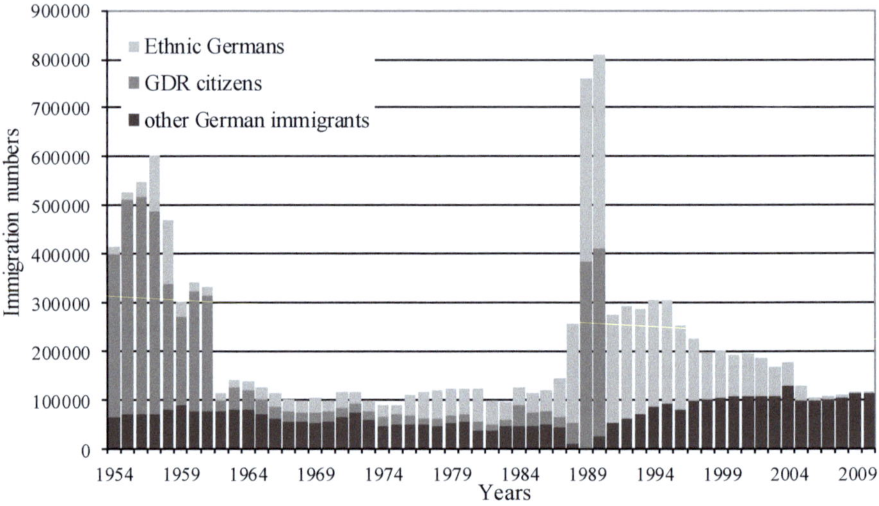

Source: Own calculations based on Migration Statistics of 1954-2010 provided by the Federal Statistical Office. Statistics on the number of ethnic German immigrants were obtained from the Federation of Expellees (*Bund der Vertriebenen*), from the Federal Office of Administration (*Bundesverwaltungsamt*) and from the following publications: *Bundesamt für Migration und Flüchtlinge*, Migrationsbericht 2008, 2010; *Bundesamt für Migration und Flüchtlinge*, Migrationsbericht 2010, 2011.

Note: Data before 1990 refer to the former West German states only, i.e. including migration to and from the German Democratic Republic.

Ethnic Germans also made up large numbers of all registered immigrants especially between the late 1980s and throughout the 1990s. During these years, travel and migration to and from Central and Eastern European countries became possible and many ethnic Germans who lived in that region took advantage of their right to migrate to Germany and acquire German citizenship. Between 1989 and 1999, 2.4 million of the 3.9 million German immigrants had an ethnic German background.[394]

---

394 Ethnic Germans also migrated to Germany in earlier decades, even though in smaller numbers. Data on ethnic Germans for the years 1954 to 1992 which are visualized in Figure 54 have to be treated with caution. Exact data on the contribution which ethnic Germans made to the migration statistics of German citizens are only available from 1993. Before this date, it is not clear if all ethnic German immigrants were registered in the migration statistics as Germans or as foreigners. Ette and Sauer estimate that most of the immigrants before 1993 were registered as

Both GDR citizens and ethnic Germans also contributed to emigration numbers during the past decades. The exact contribution of these two groups to the emigration statistics can however not be quantified, since separate data on different emigrant groups are not available.[395]

While GDR citizens and ethnic Germans were the most important immigrant groups in the past, they will not drive migration trends in the future. As was already stated, migration between the old and new Länder is captured in the statistics of internal migration since 1991 and therefore does not play a role any more in studies of international migration trends. Migration by ethnic Germans, on the other hand, has strongly declined during the last years. In 2010, only 2054 ethnic Germans moved to Germany, the lowest number since 1954. This decline is partly due to legal changes enacted since the early 1990s which restrict the immigration of ethnic Germans.[396] In addition, it has been argued that most persons who are willing and entitled to move to Germany as ethnic Germans have probably done so over the last decades. Migration experts agree in their expectation that the immigration of ethnic Germans to Germany will become insignificant in the future.[397]

When formulating migration assumptions for the next two decades, it would therefore be misleading to simply extrapolate past trends which include migration by GDR citizens and ethnic Germans. Instead, it is more instructive to exclude these two groups of immigrants from the analysis and only trace and extrapolate other types of German immigration. Such other types of migration include return immigration by Germans who have lived abroad for some time and immigration by children who were born abroad.[398] Figure 55 shows the annual number of these types of immigration since 1954 if ethnic Germans and

---

Germans in the statistics. In that case, the data should be reliable (*Ette, A./Sauer, L.*, Auswanderung, 2010, p. 57).

395 See *Ulrich, R.*, Bevölkerungsstruktur, 2001, p. 17.

396 See also Chapter 3.3.3.1.

397 See for instance *Münz, R./Seifert, W./Ulrich, R.*, Zuwanderung, 1999, p. 34; *Alders, M./Keilman, N./Cruijsen, H.*, Assumptions, 2007, p. 60; *Bijak, J./Kupiszewski, M./Kicinger, A.*, Migration scenarios, 2004, p. 22.

398 See *Sauer, L./Ette, A.*, Auswanderung, 2007, p. 30.

GDR citizens are excluded.[399] The figure also shows emigration numbers for these years. For these numbers, a similar differentiation into ethnic Germans, GDR citizens and other cases of migration is not possible. The emigration numbers in Figure 55 may therefore include emigration moves by ethnic Germans and former GDR citizens. If these emigration cases were also deduced from the statistics, the emigration numbers would likely be lower than shown here. The net migration numbers shown in Figure 55 might consequently be somewhat more balanced.[400]

Figure 55: Migration trends of German citizens (immigration numbers excluding ethnic Germans and GDR citizens), 1954-2010

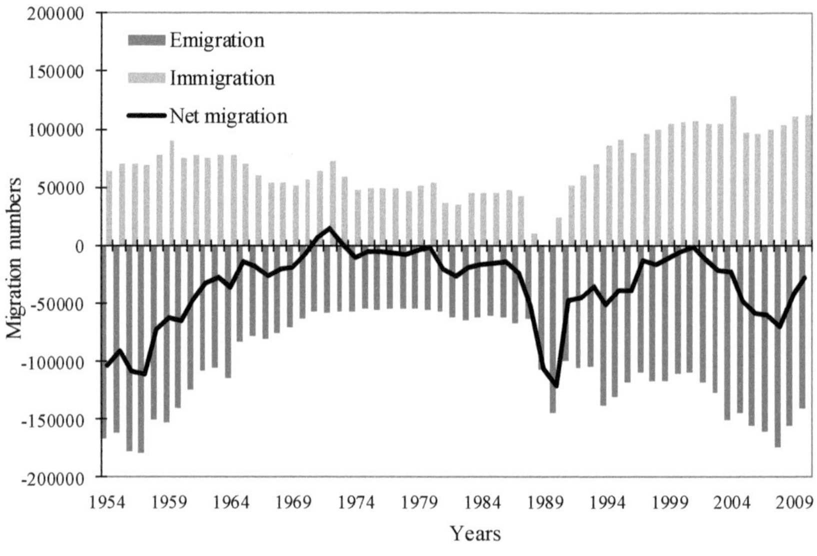

Source: Own calculations based on Migration Statistics of 1954-2010 provided by the Federal Statistical Office and statistics on the number of ethnic German immigrants, obtained from the Federation of Expellees (*Bund der Vertriebenen*), from the Federal Office of Administration (*Bundesverwaltungsamt*) and from the following publications: *Bundesamt für Migration und Flüchtlinge*, Migrationsbericht 2008, 2010; *Bundesamt für Migration und Flüchtlinge*, Migrationsbericht 2010, 2011.

Note: Data before 1990 refer to the former West German states only.

---

[399] The number of migration cases which occurred for these reasons in the past is also visible in Figure 55 under the denotation 'other German immigrants'. From the year 2000, these immigration numbers include migration cases by ius soli-citizens.

[400] See also *Ulrich, R.*, Bevölkerungsstruktur, 2001, p. 17.

As can be seen in the figure, once ethnic Germans and GDR citizens are deducted from the immigration statistics, the net migration balance of Germans turns negative for almost all years between 1954 and 2010. Only the short period between 1971 and 1973 is an exception. The lowest net migration numbers were recorded during the mid-1950s and around the time of German reunification. During the last decade, net migration was almost balanced in the years 2000 and 2001 and then decreased until 2008. In that year, the number of emigrants surpassed the number of immigrants by around 70.000 persons. During the last two years shown in the figure, net migration numbers have become more balanced again. In 2010, the net migration value was roughly -28.000. Overall, it appears that the propensity of Germans to emigrate has been higher than their propensity to (re-)migrate to Germany for nearly the entire last sixty years. This trend was concealed by the high immigration numbers of ethnic Germans and citizens from the GDR.

Given that ethnic Germans are very unlikely to become an important immigrant group again, future trends in migration will depend on how many Germans will decide to move abroad for purposes of work, study, family unification or retirement, and on how many Germans will return and possibly bring along children who were born abroad. The development of these types of migration, in turn, will depend on a variety of economic, political and social factors. It will for instance depend on the extent to which universities encourage German students to pass part of their academic education abroad, the economic and labour market conditions in Germany and in foreign countries and the living conditions in countries which have become destinations for German retirees.[401]

Migration of Germans, 2011-2030 **(MiG)**: Negative net migration numbers. Given that the number of Germans who emigrate from Germany has almost constantly been higher during the past sixty years than the number of immigrants, it is assumed here that net migration numbers will remain negative during the next twenty years. The number of German emigrants is expected to

[401] For a detailed discussion of the international migration of German citizens, see *Ette, A./Sauer, L.*, Auswanderung, 2010.

surpass the number of German immigrants by 32.000 persons each year. This number corresponds to the annual average number since the early 1990s.

Figure 56: Migration assumptions for German citizens (MiG), 2011-2030

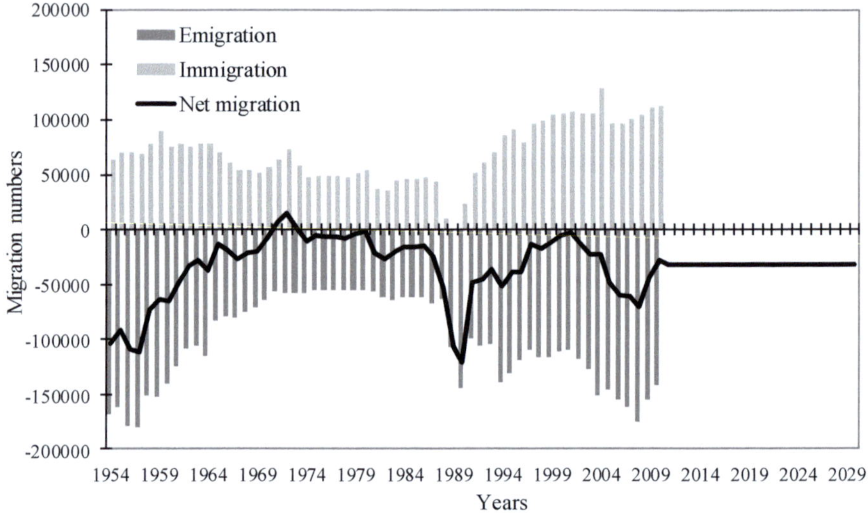

Source: Own illustration. Data for the years 1954-2010 based on Migration Statistics, obtained from the Federal Statistical Office.

Note: Until 1990, data refer to immigration and emigration to and from the former West German states only.

Further, it is assumed that the proportion of men among German migrants will be slightly higher than the proportion of women (55% vs. 45%). Again, this corresponds to the ratio that has been observed in past years. The age pattern is also supposed to show the same characteristics as in the past, so that children and young adults contribute most strongly to migration numbers. Finally, it is assumed that ius soli-Germans and the German majority population contribute to the future net migration number of -32.000 per year equally in proportion to their population size.

The assumptions taken here correspond to assumptions taken by Münz, Seifert and Ulrich in a multistate population projection published in 1999 but differ from those of other researchers. A multistate projection published by the Enquete Commission on Demographic Change in 1996 for instance assumes that net migration values of the German population will lie between +10.000 and +30.000 during the projection period (1996-2050). This assumption was not followed here. As stated above, if ethnic Germans and GDR citizens are deduced from the immigration statistics, net migration numbers would have been negative for nearly the entire past sixty years. On the basis of these past trends, it was not considered likely that net migration numbers will be positive throughout the next two decades.

Projections published by Ulrich and by the Federal Ministry of the Interior in 2000 are more similar to the assumptions taken in this study. They argue that the immigration of ethnic Germans will decline in the future. Consequently, they expect that the positive net migration numbers of Germans which were observed at the time of these publications should also decrease and reach zero or turn negative. The drop in the number of ethnic Germans coming to Germany during the last ten years was however stronger than anticipated by these two studies and net migration values turned negative earlier than expected.[402]

The most recent population projection of the Federal Statistical Office assumes that immigration and emigration numbers of Germans will be balanced in the future. The authors of the study justify this assumption by stating that the number of young adults, who are most prone to migrate, will decrease in the future and that fewer individuals should therefore emigrate than in the past. This assumption was not followed here, since the future development of migration will not depend on the shift in the German age structure alone. While the number of young adults might be declining, they are more likely today to spend part of their educational career abroad than in the past. Study programs such as Erasmus encourage students to study at foreign universities and other European programs facilitate the exchange of young workers or employees as well as of pupils. If these programs continue or even expand in the future, the number of Germans who temporarily or permanently move abroad may remain stable or even increase even though the absolute number of young adults in Germany may

---

[402] See *Münz, R./Seifert, W./Ulrich, R.*, Zuwanderung, 1999, p. 165; *Enquete-Kommission 'Demographischer Wandel'*, Zwischenbericht, 1998, p. 134; *Ulrich, R.*, Bevölkerungsstruktur, 2001, pp. 17 f. and 26; *Bundesministerium des Innern*, Modellrechnungen, 2000, pp. 8 and 18 f.

decline. In addition, even if the migration numbers of young adults should decline, other age groups, such as retired persons, have in recent years become more likely to emigrate from Germany. These new emigration trends may counterbalance potential declines in the emigration behaviour of young adults in the future.[403]

6.1.3.2. Foreign residents

Demographers generally describe migration of foreigners as the demographic factor that is most difficult to project. The difficulty of predicting future migration trends is especially due to two reasons: First, migration processes to and from foreign countries can be very volatile because they are influenced by a variety of factors such as migration policies, political and economic developments in countries of origin and destination, by social factors and ecological developments.[404] Second, data on international migration statistics are not always of the best quality. Immigration data for instance generally do not capture illegal immigration. Emigration statistics underestimate the true size of migration flows if emigrants do not notify the state administration that they will move abroad.[405] If past migration data are distorted by these factors, they may only provide limited insights into how migration trends may develop in the future.

In order to meet these challenges, researchers from different academic fields have developed a number of migration theories. These theories seek to explain migration behaviours that were observed in the past and attempt to deduce from these findings how migration numbers might develop in the future. Building on work by Zlotnik and Kupiszewski, Bijak distinguishes between economic, sociological, geographical and unifying theories of migration.[406]

---

[403] See *Statistisches Bundesamt*, Bevölkerung Deutschlands, 2009, p. 32. As regards migration trends among students and among retired persons, see *Sauer, L./Ette, A.*, Auswanderung, 2007, pp. 48 f. and 66.

[404] See *Alders, M./Keilman, N./Cruijsen, H.*, Assumptions, 2007, p. 48; *de Beer, J.*, Uncertainty, 1995, p. 18; *Sobotka, T.*, Rising importance, 2008, p. 226; *Bijak, J./Kupiszewski, M./Kicinger, A.*, Migration scenarios, 2004, p. 59.

[405] See Chapter 4.1.3.1. for more detail.

[406] *Bijak, J.*, Forecasting, 2006, pp. 1-15; see also *Bijak, J./Kupiszewski, M./Kicinger, A.*, Migration scenarios, 2004.

Economic theories are most powerful in explaining labour migration. They take either a macro-, meso- or a micro perspective, thus explaining migration either from the perspective of an individual, a family or ethnic community, or by focusing on disparities between regions or states. Depending on the focus that is chosen, economic theories assume that migration occurs because of disequilibria in wage rates between countries, because post-industrial destination countries have an intrinsic demand for foreign workers who take up low-paid, unstable and unskilled jobs, because the benefits that migrants reap from migration outweigh the costs or because families send some of their members to work in other countries in order to diversify the sources of household income.[407] Finally, world systems theory argues that migration is essentially a result of the spread of capitalist economic relations across the world. Multinational firms enter peripheral world regions that are mainly based on agriculture in order to look for new markets, labour and commodities. As capital and foreign investment flow into these regions and capital-intensive production methods are introduced, parts of the native population are uprooted and lose their traditional means of subsistence. These groups of the population are mobile and prone to migrate. World systems theory suggests that migration processes are especially likely to develop between countries that have cultural, linguistic or administrative links, generated for example by a colonial past.[408]

Sociological approaches take a somewhat broader perspective on migration by also considering sociological and political factors. One of the most influential approaches is Lee's concept of push and pull factors. According to Lee, migration takes place if certain push factors in the countries of origin compel persons to leave and/or if pull factors in countries of destination attract immigrants to move there. Push factors include wars and conflicts, environmental catastrophes, but also unemployment and social discrimination. Examples for pull factors in the destination areas are favourable economic conditions, high wage levels and political stability. Apart from push and pull

---

[407] See *Bijak, J.*, Forecasting, 2006, pp. 8-13; *Borchers, K.*, Datenlage, 2008, pp. 10-13; *Massey, D. S., et al.*, Theories, 1993, pp. 434-444.

[408] See *Massey, D. S.*, Synthenic theory 2002, p. 143; *Bijak, J.*, Forecasting, 2006, p. 10.

factors, Lee also assumes that intervening factors such as migration policies may influence migration trends.[409]

Other sociological theories do not focus on the start of migration flows, but on their persistence over time. They assume that migration flows can continue over long periods of time if social networks of family members and friends or non-governmental organizations develop in countries of destination which help migrants to lower the costs and risks of migration. Other theories suggest that migration flows continue if a 'migration culture' arises in countries of destination. In this case, young persons may be expected to contribute to the income of their households by seeking work abroad.[410]

Finally, geographic theories focus on spatial aspects of migration. These theories suggest that migration between two regions is influenced by their geographical distance, population sizes and population growth, transport options or their stages of economic development.[411]

Overall, the number of migration theories that have been proposed, debated and developed during the past decades is large. In terms of their applicability for projections, however, the different theories have one drawback: The theories help to explain certain types of migration (e.g. work migration or family migration) or different stages of the migration process (e.g. the onset or persistence of migration flows), but do not explain overall migration to and from a specific country. During recent years, a number of attempts have been made to synthesize the insights derived from different migration theories into a 'grand' theory of migration (so-called 'unifying theories of migration'). Nonetheless, these theories explain migration flows in very abstract terms which are difficult to operationalize in order to derive quantifiable migration assumptions for specific countries.[412]

Even if they are not directly quantifiable, the theories presented above are important for assumptions on future migration as they indicate a range of factors

---

409 See *Bijak, J./Kupiszewski, M./Kicinger, A.*, Migration scenarios, 2004, p. 10.

410 See *Borchers, K.*, Datenlage, 2008, pp. 14-16; *Massey, D. S., et al.*, Theories, 1993, pp. 448-454; *Bijak, J./Kupiszewski, M./Kicinger, A.*, Migration scenarios, 2004, p. 10 f.

411 See *Bijak, J.*, Forecasting, 2006, p. 13 ff.

412 See *de Beer, J.*, Conceptual framework, 1995, p. 333; *Bijak, J.*, Forecasting, 2006, p. 15 f.; *Borchers, K.*, Datenlage, 2008, p. 10; *Massey, D. S.*, Synthenic theory, 2002.

which may trigger or sustain migration processes.[413] These are economic factors such as wage or unemployment rates, demographic factors such as population size or density, political factors such as wars or armed conflicts, social factors such as the presence of social networks, ecological factors such as environmental catastrophes as well as infrastructural factors such as the quality of the education system. All of them work both at the level of the countries of origin and the countries of destination. The spatial difference between countries and cultural similarities such as a shared language may also matter. When considering these factors there appear to be good reasons to assume that Germany will remain an important destination country for foreign migrants in the near future:

From an economic perspective, Germany is likely to remain an attractive destination for migrants from member states of the European Union and beyond. Within the EU, the German economy currently appears to be among the most robust. While the ongoing sovereign-debt crisis in Europe has stopped economic growth in many countries and caused unemployment and poverty rates to rise, the German economy has so far been less strongly affected by these developments. If Germany keeps this strong economic position and if unemployment rates remain high in other European countries, an increasing number of migrants from other EU countries may move to Germany to look for work. Due to the liberty of movement and settlement within the EU, this type of work immigration from other EU countries can generally not be restricted.[414] Statistics of the year indicate that work-related intra-EU migration towards Germany has already increased: The number of immigrants from countries such as Spain or Greece, which were particularly hit by the crisis and have high rates of unemployment among young adults, have risen.[415] Whether this is only a short term trend or whether it will persist in the future, however, is unclear. It is also difficult to estimate whether migrants from other EU member states will stay in Germany for a limited period of time only or whether they will settle

---

413 See *Borchers, K.*, Datenlage, 2008, p. 16 ff.; *Bijak, J./Kupiszewski, M./Kicinger, A.*, Migration scenarios, 2004, p. 13.

414 See *Verwiebe, R.*, Wanderungsgründe, 2005, p. 130.

415 See *Bundesamt für Migration und Flüchtlinge*, Migrationsbericht 2010, 2011, p. 44.

down for a longer term. These questions are likely to depend on how the German economy will develop in comparison to other European countries.

Taking a wider geographic perspective, large socio-economic differences persist between the member states of the EU and its neighbouring regions, particularly Northern and Sub-Saharan Africa. Many countries in these regions have growing populations with a young age structure, creating a strong demand for jobs. At the same time, unemployment and poverty levels are still higher than in Western Europe, even though the economies of some African countries have grown in past years. The gap between labour demand and supply as well as the economic gap between the two continents might lead to an increasing migration pressure in the near future.[416] Avramov and Cliquet argue:

> "Developing countries have a huge stock of potential emigrants because of the combination of their population and development imbalances and the lack of democracy and good governance in many countries, leading both to economic and political migration push factors. [...] It can be expected that the vacuum of the younger active age groups created by below-replacement fertility in developed countries may be filled up by legal and/or illegal immigration."[417]

Researchers also stress that developing countries in Africa and elsewhere have an interest in promoting emigration as a means to reduce unemployment and population pressure and in order to increase remittances – financial contributions sent by migrants from countries of residence to their countries of origin. Because of these beneficial impacts, authors such as Portes and de Wind suggest that countries of origin will not completely regulate and channel emigration from their territories in the future.[418]

While there appears to be a strong migration pressure especially in many African countries, it is not clear whether Germany will be their prime

---

[416] See *Schmid, S./Borchers, K.*, Migration, 2010, pp. 63 and 182; *Castles, S.*, Migration policies, 2004, p. 211; *Coleman, D.*, Immigration, 2006, p. 411; *Portes, A./DeWind, J.*, Dialogue, 2007, p. 6.

[417] *Avramov, D./Cliquet, R.*, Economy of time, 2003, p. 380.

[418] See *Portes, A./DeWind, J.*, Dialogue, 2007, p. 6; *Castles, S.*, Factors, 2007, p. 37.

destination. Schmid and Borchers argue that most migrants move from one African country to another rather than leaving the continent. If they do, countries in Southern Europe – Italy, Spain and France – have so far been more important destinations than Germany. The authors suggest that due to these existing migration links, southern European countries are likely to be the most important destination countries if migration flows from Africa should increase in the future.[419]

Nonetheless, Germany may become more attractive for migrants from developing countries not only because of its relative economic stability and prosperity, but also because of its demographic situation. As described in previous chapters, the population in Germany is declining and ageing. The numerically strong cohorts born during the baby boom period will reach retirement age in the coming years. The cohorts that will enter the labour force during the same period of time are too small to quantitatively replace them. Companies and industries in some economic areas or geographical regions may therefore encounter greater difficulties in hiring qualified personnel. Some researchers argue that if such a gap between labour demand and supply arises in the future, it might create a new demand for international immigration.[420]

Not all researchers, however, share this expectation. Some have pointed out that an increasing demand for labour may also be met by activating and integrating long-term unemployed persons, older persons or stay-home mothers into the workforce. Others have stressed that even if a demand for foreign workers arises in the future, it is not clear to what extent this could be met by migrants from developing countries. For one, many European countries face similar demographic prospects as Germany and even though unemployment rates are currently high especially in Southern Europe, this might change in the future.[421] Germany might then have to compete with other countries for migrant workers. In addition, the German economy mostly requires skilled workers and employees, so that mainly well educated individuals from developing countries

---

[419] *Schmid, S./Borchers, K.*, Migration, 2010, pp. 118-144, see especially p. 143.
[420] See *Schmid, S./Borchers, K.*, Migration, 2010, p. 81.
[421] See *Malacic, J.*, Migration trends, 2002, p. 124 on Eastern Europe.

would be interesting for German employers. Development organizations warn however that large-scale immigration of highly skilled workers should not be encouraged since it might result in a 'brain drain' that would entail negative consequences for the socio-economic development of sending countries. Other researchers have cautioned that large-scale immigration might trigger social tensions, especially if new groups of residents are not fully integrated in the German society. The question whether immigration of foreign workers is an adequate means of dealing with shortages of labour is therefore highly controversial.[422]

In addition to work migration, Germany will also continue to accommodate refugees and asylum seekers in the future. Most politically motivated migration is likely to come from countries outside of Europe, since Germany is geographically surrounded by countries with stable political systems. Social tensions only continue to exist in the Balkan area and the easternmost zones of Europe.[423] This is reflected in current asylum statistics. In 2012, the largest numbers of asylum seekers have come from Serbia, Macedonia and Russia, in addition to Asian countries such as Afghanistan, Iraq, Syria, Iran and Pakistan.[424] The future number of asylum seekers and refugees will depend on how the political situation in these countries of origin will develop. In addition, it will depend on whether new political or ethnic conflicts will break out in other regions of the world and on the extent to which refugees and asylum seekers will apply for asylum in Germany.

Future migration flows will be also shaped by international, European and German migration laws. International treaties for instance matter for the migration of refugees and asylum seekers. Legislative acts of the EU stipulate the freedom of movement of EU citizens and regulate asylum procedures and family reunification. Migration that occurs for educational or economic reasons

---

422 See *Avramov, D./Cliquet, R.*, Economy of time, 2003, p. 382 f.

423 See *Bijak, J./Kupiszewski, M./Kicinger, A.*, Migration scenarios, 2004, p. 15 f.

424 See *Bundesamt für Migration und Flüchtlinge*, Aktuelle Zahlen, 2012, p. 6. Also see *Münz, R./Ulrich, R.*, Wachstum, 1997, p. 36.

is still largely regulated by German laws.[425] If these treaties and laws should change in the future, this might create new legal options for migration or, by contrast, restrict existing options. Whether changes in migration law are enacted is difficult to predict. Apart from economic and demographic requirements in Germany, developments in law may depend on future election results and on trends in public opinion towards migration and integration. Even if migration policies are changed, they may not necessarily be effective in curtailing or encouraging migration flows. Some foreign migrants might enter the country illegally, irrespective of how migration law develops, and other migrant groups may not move to Germany in as large numbers as might be expected.[426]

Independently of economic or political developments in Germany and elsewhere, migration to Germany is also likely to continue in the near future due to existing migrant networks that have developed during the last decades. The first guest workers moved to Germany in the 1950s. During the decades that have passed since then, closely knit family networks and ethnic communities were formed which link foreign residents in Germany to families, villages and communities in countries of origin. Through these links, new families are founded and information about existing employment opportunities in Germany is passed on. Foreign residents in Germany have also created associations and organizations to help newcomers and to facilitate their socio-economic integration in Germany. These links and institutions may perpetuate migration flows, a process which is referred to as 'chain migration'.[427] During the last years, the quantitatively largest groups of long-term foreign residents in Germany came from Poland, Turkey, Romania, Bulgaria and Serbia.[428] The potential for future chain migration should be high among these groups of foreign residents.

---

[425] See *Joppke, C.*, Immigration challenges, 1998, p. 11; *Müller-Graff, P.-C./Kainer, F.*, Visapolitik, 2009; *Münch, U.*, Asylpolitik, 1993; *Cicekli, B.*, Turkish migrants, 1999; *Groenendijk, K./Guild, E./Barzilay, R.*, Legal status, 2000; *Kostakopoulou, T.*, Third-country nationals, 2002.

[426] See *de Beer, J.*, Conceptual framework, 1995, p. 335; *Bijak, J./Kupiszewski, M./Kicinger, A.*, Migration scenarios, 2004, p. 17; *Castles, S.*, Factors, 2007, p. 37; *Sassen, S.*, Transnationalizing, 1998, p. 62.

[427] See *Coleman, D.*, Immigration, 2006, p. 412; *Ulrich, R.*, Bevölkerungsstruktur, 2001, p. 22.

[428] See *Bundesamt für Migration und Flüchtlinge*, Migrationsbericht 2010, 2011, pp. 28 and 38.

Migration for the purposes of education may also contribute to keep migration numbers up in the future. Students who move to Germany to study at universities or receive other types of education have in fact been among the most important immigrant groups during the past decades. Between 1993 and 2010, the number of foreign students in Germany (so-called '*Bildungsausländer*') has more than doubled. A further increase in the number of foreign students is likely, given that universities in Germany and other countries encourage students to receive part of their academic education abroad.[429] European and international exchange programs such as Erasmus facilitate these temporary stays abroad and support students financially and administratively.

Finally, ecological factors may trigger migration flows in the future. The process of global warming is likely to affect regions in Africa and this may lead to higher immigration to Germany. This expectation is held by the Federal Statistical Office who argue in their latest projection that

> "the effects of the global climate warming, which according to previous estimates will be milder in Central Europe than in other parts of the world, could reinforce immigration by increasing the 'migration pressure' in regions of origin".[430]

Overall, the relatively strong economy, political stability, long migration history and declining population size of Germany suggest that this country may remain an attractive destination for foreign migration in the future and that there may also be a growing demand for qualified foreign workers. These considerations imply that net migration levels should at least remain around current levels or even increase in the future. Nonetheless, it is important to stress that future levels of migration do not only depend on economic, demographic, political, social, ecological and infrastructural developments in Germany and in countries

---

[429] For numbers on foreign students in Germany, see *Bundesamt für Migration und Flüchtlinge*, Migrationsbericht 2010, 2011, p. 56.

[430] *Statistisches Bundesamt*, Bevölkerung Deutschlands, 2009, p. 34. In German, the quote reads: „die Auswirkungen der globalen Klimaerwärmung, die in Mitteleuropa nach bisherigen Schätzungen milder ausfallen würden als in den anderen Erdteilen, könnten eine Zuwanderung durch die Erhöhung des „Wanderungsdrucks" in den Herkunftsregionen verstärken".

of origin. Instead, further migration trends also depend on whether other countries of destination – the USA, Canada and Australia, but potentially also emerging economic powers such as China, India and Brazil – will be more attractive than Germany for migrants around the world. The complex array of factors that might influence foreign migration in the future makes it difficult to define future immigration and emigration trends from Germany. Due to this uncertainty, two different migration assumptions were defined for the projections.

Figure 57: Migration assumptions for foreign residents (MiF1 and MiF2), 2011-2030

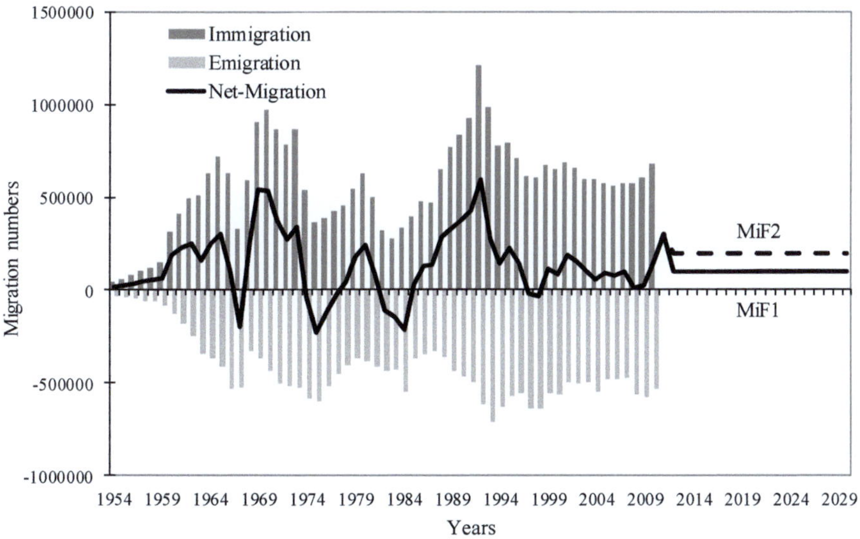

Source: Own illustration. Data for the years 1954-2010 based on Migration Statistics, obtained from the Federal Statistical Office.

Note: Until 1990, data refer to immigration and emigration to and from the former West German states only.

<u>Migration of foreign residents 1, 2011-2030 **(MiF1)**: Low positive net migration.</u> In the low migration scenario, it is assumed that future net migration numbers of foreigners will reach a level of +100.000 per year. This value is slightly higher than the average net migration level observed during the past decade. The assumption reflects the expectation that future immigration flows to

Germany might continue to be predominantly of short term character and thereby lead to relatively balanced immigration and emigration numbers. Future migration to Germany might especially be of short-term character if immigrants continue to be predominantly seasonal workers, students or asylum seekers who remain in Germany for limited periods of time only. Net migration numbers would also remain low if other countries became important destinations for migrants or if immigration law in Germany will become more restrictive in the future.

Migration of foreign residents 2, 2011-2030 **(MiF2)**: High positive net migration. The second migration scenario reflects the possibility that migration flows may increase in the future due to economic, political, demographic or ecological developments in Germany or in sending countries. It also reflects the possibility that migration will be of a longer-term character and that immigration numbers will therefore outweigh emigration numbers more strongly than currently observed. Under these conditions, it is assumed that the net migration of foreigners will reach an annual level of +200.000 persons in the future. This value corresponds to the average net migration values reached during the guest worker period (1955 – 1973), a past period of time which was characterized by high immigration.

Under both of the assumptions, it is expected that the proportion of men among migrants will be somewhat higher than that of women and that most migrants will be young adults. Both of these expectations reflect past trends observed in Germany.[431] Both assumptions also suggest that net migration values will remain stable throughout the projection period. It is acknowledged that in reality migration trends are likely to fluctuate from year to year. Such fluctuations are however difficult to capture in migration assumptions. The migration trends suggested here have to be understood as averages around which net migration numbers may oscillate.

The future levels of net migration assumed here – between +100.000 and +200.000 – are somewhat lower than the range covered by assumptions in other works. Population projections by Münz and colleagues, Ulrich and the Federal

---

[431] Compare Chapter 3.3.3.2.

Ministry of the Interior, for instance, all include a higher migration assumption which hypothesizes that net migration might reach and remain at a level of around +300.000 per year.[432] Such high migration numbers were not chosen for this projection since they do not appear plausible: The long-term annual average net-migration figure for the period 1954 to 2010 was +136.000 and the short-term net migration value of the last ten years (2001-2010) was around +100.000. Net migration values of +300.000 were only reached in few years during the past decades, for instance during the early 1970s or in the late 1980s/early 1990s. These years were characterized by the massive recruitment of guest workers and the strong influx of migrants in the context of the end of the Cold War, respectively. The assumption that an annual average net migration level of +300.000 persons could be maintained during the entire projection period suggests that the net-migration numbers reached in the peak years of guest-worker migration or in exceptionally turbulent political times would become normality. It would mean that Germany would experience a net migration level that is more than twice as high as the long-term trend and even three times higher than the net migration numbers of the last years. Even in the light of the previous argument that Germany may remain an attractive destination country in the future, such an assumed net migration number of +300.000 per year appears to be unrealistic. In their latest population projection of 2009, the Federal Statistical Office has followed similar considerations and has limited net migration assumptions to two scenarios of +100.000 and +200.000. The accompanying press brochure states that these assumptions are intended to reflect longer average migration trends and that "the exorbitantly high immigration of the early 1990s is an exceptional development and no longer considered [for the definition of migration assumptions]".[433]

---

[432] *Münz, R./Seifert, W./Ulrich, R.*, Zuwanderung, 1999, p. 163; *Ulrich, R.*, Bevölkerungsstruktur, 2001, p. 27; *Bundesministerium des Innern*, Modellrechnungen, 2000, p. 21; *Enquete-Kommission 'Demographischer Wandel'*, Zwischenbericht, 1998, p. 134; *Lutz, W./Scherbov, S.*, Bevölkerungsprognosen, 1998, p. 91. Birg and Flöthmann use lower migration assumptions. Similar to this study, their highest migration assumption assumes an annual net saldo of around +200.000 (*Birg, H./Flöthmann, E.-J.*, Projektionsrechnungen, 2001, p. 64).

[433] *Statistisches Bundesamt*, Bevölkerung Deutschlands, 2009, p. 32. In the German original, the quote reads: „Die exorbitant hohe Zuwanderung Anfang der 1990er Jahre wird als eine

6.1.4. Assumptions on citizenship acquisition at birth

6.1.4.1. Children born to German citizens (majority population)

As was stated in Chapter 2.3.3., children who are born in Germany can acquire German citizenship on the basis of two principles: ius sanguinis and ius soli. The ius sanguinis principle stipulates that all children born to a German parent become German citizens at birth. Children who are born in Germany to two foreign parents acquire the German citizenship at birth if at least one of the parents fulfils particular requirements in terms of residence permit and residence duration (ius soli).

Citizenship acquisition of children born by German women, 2011-2030 **(CAG)**: German citizenship. It was assumed here that current citizenship law will not be changed and that all children born to German mothers during the projection period will also be German citizens.

6.1.4.2. Children born to ius soli-citizens

Children born to ius soli-Germans also acquire German citizenship at birth on the basis of the ius sanguinis principle.

Citizenship acquisition of children born by ius soli-Germans, 2011-2030 **(CAI)**: German citizenship. Again, it was assumed that citizenship law will not be changed in this respect and that all children born to women with ius soli-citizenship during the next two decades will become German citizens at birth.

6.1.4.3. Children born to foreign residents

Among children born to foreign mothers in 2010, 44.5% acquired German citizenship because their father is a German citizen (ius sanguinis) and 26.0% acquired German citizenship because one or both parents had a right of permanent residence and had lived in Germany for at least eight years at the

---

Sonderentwicklung nicht mehr berücksichtigt.“ Note that since the population projection of the Federal Statistical Office does not distinguish between German citizens and foreign residents, the net migration figures apply to the entire population of Germany. The creators of the projection however assume that immigration numbers and emigration numbers of German citizens will balance each other during later years of the projection period. In these later years, the assumed positive net migration numbers therefore reflects a migration surplus of foreign residents only.

time of the child's birth (ius soli). The remaining 29.5% of all children acquired a foreign citizenship at birth only.[434]

The future proportion of children born to foreign mothers who acquire German citizenship qua ius sanguinis or ius soli will be influenced by a variety of different factors. The proportion of ius sanguinis cases will depend especially on the future marriage and partnership formation behaviour of foreign women in Germany, but also on future migration and naturalization trends. The higher the proportion of foreign women who have children with a native German citizen or a naturalized citizen, the higher will be the proportion of children who acquire German citizenship at birth qua ius sanguinis. Conversely, the higher the proportion of women who have children with a foreign resident from their own country of origin or from a third country, the lower the proportion of births in which the ius sanguinis principle applies. The proportion of children who acquire German citizenship qua ius soli will depend on the proportion of foreign residents in Germany who possess a right of permanent residence and have lived in Germany for at least eight years. This development, in turn, will especially depend on future migration trends.

The sheer number of factors which may have an influence makes it difficult to predict future citizenship acquisition trends with precision. Academic debates about possible future trends are also sparse. Some multistate population projections even disregard the question of citizenship acquisition at birth and do not formulate explicit assumptions on the topic. Münz and colleagues as well as Ulrich for instance mention that children who are born to foreign parents may acquire German citizenship qua ius soli and that some German children have a foreign parent. In their projection model, they however only include explicit assumptions on the future proportion of children who acquire the German citizenship qua ius soli. They do not present assumptions on the proportion of children who will acquire German citizenship qua ius sanguinis.[435] Similarly, the

---

[434] See Chapter 3.3.4.2.

[435] *Ulrich, R.*, Bevölkerungsstruktur, 2001, pp. 4 f. and 27; *Münz, R./Seifert, W./Ulrich, R.*, Zuwanderung, 1999, pp. 68 and 166 f. Note that these two studies look at the proportion of ius soli-children among all children born to two foreign parents, while in the present study the proportion of ius soli-children is defined with reference to all children born to foreign mothers.

Enquete Commission on Demographic Change and the Federal Ministry of the Interior do not formulate explicit assumptions in their projections about the proportion of children born to foreign mothers who acquire German citizenship because they have a German father.[436]

The limited or even total lack of discussion on citizenship acquisition at birth is surprising, since it is an important factor that may influence future developments of the foreign and the German population. Brubaker already commented on the relative lack of academic attention on the topic in 1992. His estimation of the importance of citizenship ascription at birth, as he refers to it, remains true today:

> "It is not enough to consider the voluntary acquisition of citizenship by naturalization or individual declaration. We must also consider the attribution of citizenship by the state. [...] Working invisibly and automatically, independently of the will – and sometimes even the knowledge – of the persons concerned, the rules governing the ascription of citizenship have been all but ignored by the meagre literature on immigration and citizenship. Yet they are more important than naturalization rules in shaping patterns of civic incorporation [...]. Ascription constitutes and perpetually reconstitutes the citizenry; naturalization reshapes it at the margins."[437]

<u>Citizenship acquisition of children born by foreign women, 2011-2030 **(CAF)**: German or foreign citizenship.</u> Due to the lack of academic studies on citizenship acquisition at birth, the assumptions for this study were made solely on the basis of trend extrapolations. It was hypothesized that 45% of all children born to foreign mothers during the projection period will acquire German citizenship qua ius sanguinis, i.e. because they have a German father who may either be a native German or a naturalized citizen. The proportion of ius sanguinis cases has approached this value in recent years, after a sharp increase

[436] *Enquete-Kommission 'Demographischer Wandel'*, Zwischenbericht, 1998, p. 132 ff.; *Bundesministerium des Innern*, Modellrechnungen, 2000, pp. 22-25.

[437] *Brubaker, W. R.*, Citizenship, 1994, p. 80 f.

in the years 2000 to 2004 (see Figure 58). It was assumed that a further 30% of the children born to foreign mothers in each projection year will acquire German citizenship on the basis of the ius soli-principle. This proportion corresponds to the average of the last eleven years which have passed since the introduction of the ius soli-principle into German citizenship law. The remaining 25% of children born to foreign mothers in each projection year are assumed to only acquire a foreign citizenship at birth.

Figure 58: Assumptions about citizenship acquired at birth by children born to foreign mothers (CAF), 2011-2030

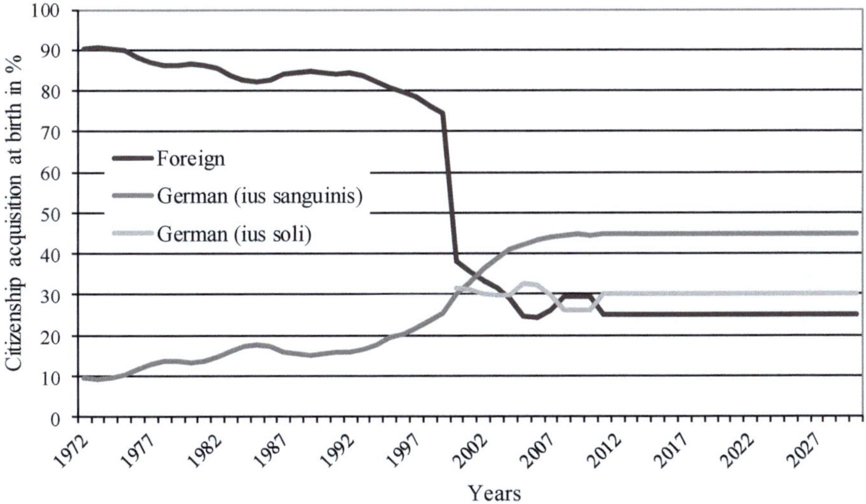

Source: Own illustration. Data for the years 1972-2010 based on Birth Statistics, obtained from the Federal Statistical Office.
Note: Before 1990, data refer to the former West German states only.

6.1.5. Assumptions on citizenship changes during the life course

6.1.5.1. German citizens (majority population)

German citizens who live in Germany can under certain conditions revoke their citizenship or be deprived of it. It is not clear how many Germans lose their citizenship each year, since comprehensive statistics on this issue do not exist. Individual estimations which are available suggest that the number is likely to be very small. Between 2002 and 2005, for instance, only around 84 Germans appear to have been deprived of their citizenship.[438]

Probably due to the small number of cases and the lack of a comprehensive statistics, the question how and why Germans lose their citizenship each year is hardly ever discussed in the academic literature. Where this topic is mentioned at all, researchers tend to discuss the main relevant regulations of the citizenship law but rarely discuss how they may affect citizens in practice. No population projection is known to the author of this work in which rates of citizenship loss have ever been discussed or form part of the set of assumptions. Overall, then, very little information is available on which assumptions for this study could be based.

Changes of citizenship among Germans, 2011-2030 **(CCG)**: No changes of citizenship. Since the few available data points suggest that the number of Germans who lose their citizenship each year is very small, it is assumed here for the sake of simplicity that no German citizen who is resident in Germany will lose his/her citizenship during the projection period.

6.1.5.2. Ius soli-citizens

The first cohorts of ius soli-citizens born between 1990 and 1994 have reached the age of 18 years since 2008 and have entered the transitory period during which they have to opt between their German and their foreign citizenship. In 2013, the first of these cohorts will turn 23 years old. Only after this point in time will comprehensive statistics about their choice become available. At the moment, only preliminary data and anecdotal information can be consulted. These sources indicate that almost all ius soli-citizens who have already made a decision have either kept their German citizenship and revoked their foreign citizenship or have been entitled to retain both citizenships.[439] These members of the first ius soli-cohorts retain the German citizenship and the right to vote beyond their 23rd birthday.

---

[438] Compare Chapter 3.3.5.1.

[439] See *Göbel-Zimmermann, R./Eichhorn, A.*, Entwicklungen I, 2010, p. 296; *Weinmann, M./Becher, I./Babka von Gostomski, C.*, Einbürgerungsverhalten, 2012, p. 8.

On the basis of these preliminary data, it might be assumed that all or almost all ius soli-citizens will keep the German citizenship in the future. Nonetheless, researchers currently discuss a number of reasons for why this conclusion might be too hasty: First, the ius soli-citizens who have already opted for the German citizenship are likely those that were most certain about their choice. Ius soli-citizens who have so far postponed their decision might waver more about which citizenship to keep. Some ius soli-citizens may also have decided to keep their foreign citizenship, but may not inform the citizenship authorities of this choice until the end of the transition period.[440] Once these individuals will inform the German administrative bodies about their choice at the end of the period, the proportion of those who opt for the foreign citizenship might increase.

Second, Marie Böhmer, Minister of State for Migration, Refugees and Integration, has reported that many ius soli-citizens have difficulties in understanding the complex requirements and procedures defined in citizenship law. Some ius soli-citizens apparently assume that it is enough to wait for the expiration of the foreign passport in order to revoke their foreign citizenship. Others do not even seem to know whether they have a second citizenship apart from their German one and consequently do not know whether they have to opt between their citizenships. Finally, some ius soli-citizens who hold the citizenship of another EU country in addition to their German one appear to believe that they can retain both of their citizenships automatically.[441] Due to misconceptions such as these, some individuals may fail to comply with administrative rules and inadvertently lose the German citizenship upon their 23rd birthday. Such cases will only become apparent in the statistics in 2013 when the five-year consideration period has passed for the first ius soli-cohort.

It has also been suggested that the proportion of ius soli-citizens who opt for the German citizenship may be higher among the cohorts of 1990 to 1999 than

[440] See *Lämmermann, F.*, Ius soli, 2011, p. 3; *Weinmann, M./Becher, I./Babka von Gostomski, C.*, Einbürgerungsverhalten, 2012, p. 8 f.

[441] *Beauftragte der Bundesregierung für Migration, Flüchtlinge und Integration*, Migrationsbericht, 2010, p. 458 f.; *Weinmann, M./Becher, I./Babka von Gostomski, C.*, Einbürgerungsverhalten, 2012, p. 9 f.; *Lämmermann, F.*, Ius soli, 2011, p. 3.

among cohorts born in 2000 and after. The cohorts born in the 1990s could only acquire German citizenship if their parents made use of the transitional clause in the Citizenship Act of 2000 and applied for German citizenship in lieu of their children. It may be assumed that parents who used this option may also be supportive if their children decide to keep the German citizenship beyond their 23rd birthday.[442] In contrast to this, ius soli-cohorts born in 2000 or later have automatically acquired the German citizenship if one or both of their parents fulfilled the necessary conditions. Their parents may not be as understanding if their children prefer to keep the German citizenship. Masing expects conflicts of identity to arise:

> "The children who have just reached majority age are closely integrated in their families of origin, are emotionally and financially dependent on them and still have insecure career prospects. In this situation they are expected to consciously decide to distance themselves politically from their parents' homeland. This does not only presuppose a very stable personality, but can also become a crucial test for the family."[443]

Young adults who have to choose between their citizenships in such a context might be more likely to opt for their foreign citizenship than children whose parents have already shown their support by applying for the German citizenship on their behalf. If this hypothesis is correct, then the proportion of ius soli-citizens who retain the German citizenship might be lower among ius soli-children born in 2000 and later years than among earlier cohorts.

Nonetheless, even if the proportion of ius soli-citizens who retain their German citizenship may be lower than statistics currently suggest, most researchers still expect that a large majority will remain German after their 23rd birthday. Many

---

442 See *Lämmermann, F.*, Ius soli, 2011, p. 2.

443 *Masing, J.*, Wandel, 2001, p. 38. In the original German text, the quote reads: „Die gerade volljährig gewordenen sind eng in ihre Herkunftsfamilien eingebunden, von ihnen emotional wie finanziell abhängig und haben weiterhin ungesicherte Berufsperspektiven. Gerade in dieser Situation nun versucht man ihnen die bewußte Entscheidung abzuringen, sich politisch von der Heimat ihrer Eltern zu verabschieden. Dies setzt nicht nur eine sehr gefestigte Persönlichkeitsstruktur voraus, sondern kann auch für die Familie zu einer Zerreißprobe werden."

ius soli-citizens will be entitled to keep both of their citizenships beyond their 23rd birthday if they apply for it in time, e.g. ius soli-citizens who are also citizens of other EU countries or refugees. Ius soli-citizens who opt between their citizenships on the basis of practical and instrumental considerations may choose the German citizenship since it is likely to be more valuable in their everyday life than their foreign citizenship. Finally, some ius soli-citizens may also choose the German citizenship if they feel more connected to Germany than to their parents' country of origin.[444]

Changes of citizenship among ius soli-citizens, 2011-2030 **(CCI)**: Majority retains German citizenship. It is assumed here that all ius soli-citizens will opt between their citizenships at age 23. In light of the above arguments, it is considered plausible that most but not all ius soli-citizens will remain German citizens at this point. The annual proportion of ius soli-citizens who retain the German citizenship because they opt for it or because they are entitled to keep both citizenships is assumed to be 90%. The remaining 10% of all annual ius soli-cases are consequently assumed to lose the German citizenship at age 23, either because they opt for their foreign citizenship or because they do not comply with required procedures or deadlines.

These assumptions differ somewhat from those made in other projections. In 2000, the Federal Ministry of the Interior assumed in a projection that around 80% of all ius soli-citizens will retain German citizenship.[445] In the light of preliminary data on the decision-making behaviour of ius soli-citizens referred to above, this assumed proportion appears to be too low. Münz, Seifert and Ulrich, by contrast, assume that all ius soli-citizens will eventually decide to retain the German citizenship.[446] This assumption was also not followed here, given that at least some ius soli-citizens may lose the German citizenship by choice, by inactivity or by non-compliance with legal requirements.

---

444 See *Lämmermann, F.*, Ius soli, 2011, p. 2 f.; *Weinmann, M./Becher, I./Babka von Gostomski, C.*, Einbürgerungsverhalten, 2012, p. 9.

445 *Bundesministerium des Innern*, Modellrechnungen, 2000, p. 24.

446 *Münz, R./Seifert, W./Ulrich, R.*, Zuwanderung, 1999, p. 16; *Ulrich, R.*, Bevölkerungsstruktur, 2001, p. 28.

6.1.5.3. Foreign residents

The naturalization rate in Germany has undergone substantial changes during the past decades. Until the 1980s it fluctuated around a level of 0.4%. Then it increased nearly six fold during the 1990s and reached its peak in the year 2000, when 2.3% of all foreign residents in Germany acquired German citizenship. Since then, the naturalization rate has almost continuously declined again until 2008. Only in 2009 and 2010 has it increased again to reach a level of 1.4%.

Scholars who have discussed these trends agree more on why the naturalization rate rose before 2000 than on why it declined thereafter. Various social scientists have for instance argued that German citizenship law was very restrictive until the 1980s and only allowed naturalization once requirements on residence duration, language skills, social integration and other factors were met. Even then, foreign residents did not have a right to acquire German citizenship but depended on the approval of naturalization offices. The low naturalization rates of the 1970s and 1980s are attributed to these strict regulations, among other factors. During the 1990s, these requirements were successively lowered and naturalization law received a large degree of public and media attention. The increase of naturalization rates during the 1990s is especially explained by these legal reforms and publicity of the topic.[447]

A further major citizenship reform was enacted in the year 2000. One of its main goals was to encourage foreign residents to apply for citizenship. Some naturalization requirements were lowered, for instance the required duration of legal residence in Germany. Many migration and integration researchers predicted that naturalization rates would rise after the enactment of the reform. Wüst for instance hypothesised:

> "It is obvious that the new naturalization law will result in […] a rise in naturalizations of non-resettlers [i.e. foreign residents who do not have an ethnic German background]."[448]

---

[447] See Chapter 3.3.5.3.

[448] *Wüst, A.*, New citizens, 2000, p. 561. See also *Hagedorn, H.*, Einbürgerung, 2001, p. 127; *Diehl, C./Blohm, M.*, Apathy, 2001, p. 409.

The decline in naturalization rates after 2000 proved these expectations wrong. Researchers have proposed and debated different reasons to explain the unexpected decline in the naturalization rate after the reform. Among other factors, new requirements that were introduced by the reform in 2000 and other reforms thereafter have been considered as well as the special legal situation of Turkish residents in Germany. The drop in the naturalization rate has also been attributed to a saturation effect among foreign residents in Germany.[449]

In addition, social scientists continue to debate the costs and benefits of naturalizing in Germany as well as the potential influence of public naturalization campaigns and media coverage on the naturalization behaviour of foreign residents. As regards the costs of naturalizing, researchers distinguish between financial, economic, social and emotional costs. Researchers argue that these costs are particularly high for naturalization applicants who are obliged to revoke their previous citizenship. The revocation of the previous citizenship entails financial costs for the necessary administrative procedures and it may entail the loss of economic rights, e.g. to inherit or possess property in the country of origin. Emotional and social costs might be high for naturalization applicants who do not feel accepted by the German host society as well as for persons who remain strongly attached to their country of origin. These individuals might interpret the revocation of their old citizenship as a sign of rejection of their roots and heritage. Families and friends may also interpret this step in such a way which may lead to intra-familial conflicts.[450] The German naturalization law today includes many exceptions in which the retention of the previous citizenship is allowed, so that these costs of naturalization can be avoided in many cases. Nonetheless, studies show that many foreign residents do not seem to be aware whether these exceptions apply in their case.[451] Some researchers conclude from this that as long as the retention of the previous citizenship is not generally tolerated in Germany and the perceived costs of

---

[449] See Chapter 3.3.5.3. for more details on these points.

[450] See *Diehl, C./Blohm, M.*, Entscheidung, 2008, p. 445; *Diehl, C./Blohm, M.*, Rights, 2003, p. 140 f.; *Cyrus, N./Vogel, D.*, Förderung, 2008, p. 21; *Weinmann, M./Becher, I./Babka von Gostomski, C.*, Einbürgerungsverhalten, 2012, p. 8.

[451] See *Anil, M.*, Citizenship law, 2006, p. 450; *Böcker, A./Thränhardt, D.*, Multiple citizenship, 2006, p. 91; *Worbs, S.*, Einbürgerung, 2008, p. 41.

naturalization remain high, naturalization rates will stay at lower levels than in many other European countries.

Apart from the costs of naturalizing, the academic debate has focused on the benefits which individual groups of foreign residents receive from naturalizing in Germany. At least for some groups of long-term foreign residents, benefits are assumed to be small. Long-term foreign residents today already enjoy many economic, social, civic and even political rights in Germany. This is particularly true for foreign residents who are citizens of another EU member state. EU citizens for instance enjoy the freedom of movement, have the right to work in nearly all types of jobs, may not be discriminated in terms of their nationality and enjoy the right to vote in municipal elections and elections to the European parliament in Germany. The acquisition of the German citizenship would entail only few additional rights for them, among them the right to vote in Bundestag elections. The large range of rights that EU citizens already enjoy in Germany is held responsible for the fact that their naturalization propensity is low. Similar explanations are used to account for the low naturalization rate of foreign residents who are citizens of economically strong and politically stable third countries.[452] Foreign residents who plan to re-migrate to their countries of origin after a temporary stay in Germany may also see little benefit in acquiring the German citizenship. Refugees and asylum seekers as well as long-term foreign residents from poorer or politically instable countries, by contrast, naturalize at higher rates. It has been suggested that they have relatively more to gain from becoming German citizens: the unlimited right to live in an economically and politically stable country as well as the German passport which facilitates travel to many other countries are just two examples.[453]

Finally, some researchers have stressed the importance of information campaigns and media coverage on naturalization rules and procedures. Böcker and Thränhardt for instance argue that that the degree to which foreigners make

---

[452] See *Weinmann, M./Becher, I./Babka von Gostomski, C.*, Einbürgerungsverhalten, 2012; *Diehl, C./Blohm, M.*, Rights, 2003, pp. 141-143; *Thränhardt, D.*, Einbürgerung, 2008, pp. 32-35; *Böcker, A./Thränhardt, D.*, Multiple citizenship, 2006, p. 89; *Steinhardt, M. F.*, Aktuelle Trends, 2007, p. 547 f.

[453] See *Böcker, A./Thränhardt, D.*, Multiple citizenship, 2006, p. 89.

use of their naturalization rights may be influenced by whether they are informed and encouraged to do so.[454] A conclusive answer as to which of these factors are most influential in driving naturalization trends has not yet been agreed upon and the debate on why the naturalization rate declined during the last decade is ongoing. Social scientists discuss equally controversially whether a further increase in the naturalization rate may be expected in the next years, or whether the naturalization rate might continue to decline.

In order to account for this uncertainty, two different assumptions were formulated for the population projection. The assumptions are defined as long-term averages, around which de facto developments may fluctuate. Both assumptions disregard the effect that future changes in citizenship law may have, since the effects of such reforms will be explored in greater detail in the following chapter on policy scenarios (see Chapter 7.1.2.).

<u>Changes of citizenship among foreign residents 1, 2011-2030 **(CCF1)**: Low average naturalization rates.</u> The first naturalization assumption reflects the hypothesis that fewer foreign residents may be interested in acquiring German citizenship in the future. This may be the case if more persons from EU member states or prosperous third countries will live in Germany in the future or if a larger proportion of foreign residents will plan to stay in Germany for a temporary period of time only. Potential future enlargements of the EU, which would lead to an extension of the favourable EU citizen status to larger numbers of foreign residents in Germany, might also play a role here.[455]

Nonetheless, even if the naturalization rate will further decline in the future, it is considered unlikely that it will drop back to the very low levels observed during the 1970s and 1980s. During these decades, naturalization requirements were relatively strict and naturalization offices had to approve each case of naturalization discretionarily. Today, naturalization is easier and has become a right once certain conditions are met. Therefore, while it is considered possible that the naturalization rate will further decline in the future, it is not considered likely that it will drop back to a level of 0.4% as in the 1970s and 1980s. Instead,

---

[454] *Böcker, A./Thränhardt, D.*, Multiple citizenship, 2006, p. 91.

[455] See *Thränhardt, D.*, Einbürgerung, 2008, p. 41.

it was assumed here that an average lower level of 1.0 % may be reached in the future.

Figure 59: Assumptions about changes in citizenship among foreign residents (CCF1 and CCF2), 2011-2030

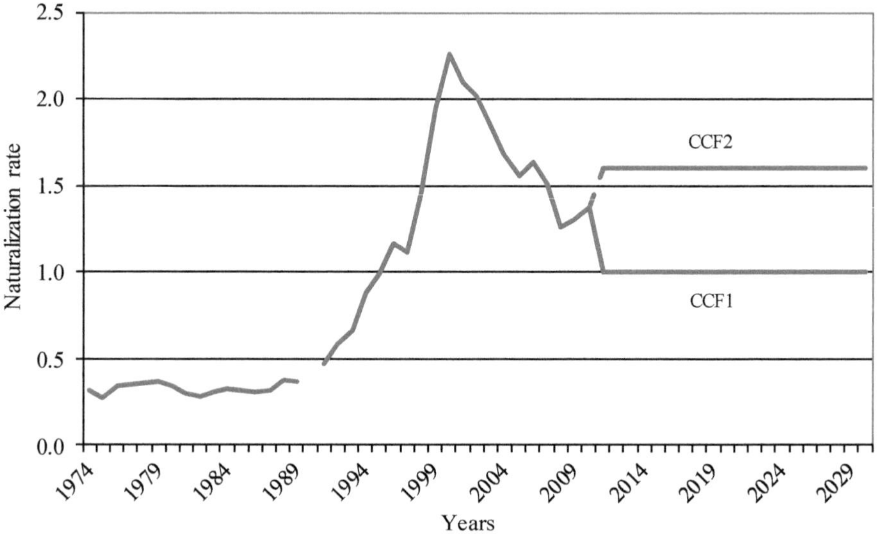

Source: Own illustration. Data for the years 1974-2010 based on Naturalization Statistics, obtained from the Federal Statistical Office.

Note: Before 1991, data refer to the former West German states only. Value for 1990 was not calculated due to nominator-denominator mismatch: Population data of this year refer to the reunified Germany, while naturalization data refer to West Germany only.

Changes of citizenship among foreign residents 2, 2011-2030 **(CCF2)**: High average naturalization rates. The second naturalization assumption hypothesises that an average proportion of 1.6% of the foreign population in Germany will naturalize annually during the projection period. This proportion is higher than the most recent rate observed in 2010 (1.4%), but similar to levels reached in 2004 and 2006. The assumption reflects the possibility that a higher proportion of foreign residents will be both willing and able to acquire German citizenship in future years. This may for instance be the case if more people from economically weak or instable countries will live in Germany in the future or if more foreign migrants decide to permanently settle down in Germany. The

naturalization assumption also reflects the possibility that a larger number of foreign residents who fulfil the naturalization requirements but were so far hesitant to make use of their right might be encouraged to do so via public naturalization campaigns.
For both assumptions, it is hypothesised that the naturalization rate will be higher among children, adolescents and young adults than among older foreign residents. This was the pattern observed during past years. It is also assumed that the proportion of men and women among naturalized persons will be as balanced as during the past years.

6.2. Overview of scenarios

The different assumptions which were defined in the previous sections on fertility, mortality and migration trends as well as acquisition and changes of citizenship are summarized in Table 7. Either one or two assumptions were defined per demographic indicator. Where two assumptions were made, these are highlighted in bold in the table. This concerns the following indicators: fertility of Germans, including ius soli-citizens (FG1 and FG2), mortality of Germans, including ius soli-citizens (MG1 and MG2), net migration numbers of foreign residents (MiF1 and MiF2) and changes of citizenship among foreign residents (CCF1 and CCF2). These assumptions can be combined to 16 different scenarios. The possible variations are presented in Table 8. Scenario no. 2 for instance combines the assumption that the fertility of Germans (including ius soli-citizens) will increase until 2030 (FG1), that the mortality rates of German citizens (including ius soli-citizens) will decrease only slowly (MG2) and that net migration numbers and the naturalization rate of foreign residents will both remain low (MiF1 and CCF1).

Table 7: Overview of demographic assumptions, 2011-2030

Demographic indicator	Citizenship group	Abbreviation	Assumptions
Fertility	German citizens (incl. ius soli-citizens)	**FG1**	Increase in fertility: TFR will increase from 1.36 (2010) to 1.52 (2030)
		FG2	Decrease in fertility: TFR will decrease from 1.36 (2010) to 1.20 (2030)
	Foreign residents	FF	Convergence: TFR will continue to decrease and converge with TFR of German women in 2017 (in case of FG1) or in 2023 (in case of FG2)
Mortality	German citizens (incl. ius soli-citizens)	**MG1**	Linear increase in life expectancy: Life expectancy will increase from 77.7 years in 2010 to 83.3 years in 2030 (men), and from 82.6 years in 2010 to 86.9 years in 2030 (women)
		MG2	Slower increase in life expectancy: Life expectancy will increase from 77.7 years in 2010 to 80.5 years in 2030 (men), and from 82.6 years in 2010 to 84.9 years in 2030 (women)
	Foreign residents	MF	Convergence: Mortality rates will approach those of German men and women and converge with them in 2030
Net- migration	German citizens (incl. ius soli-citizens)	MiG	Negative net migration numbers: The number of German emigrants will surpass the number of immigrants by 32.000 per projection year
	Foreign residents	**MiF1**	Low positive net migration numbers: The number of foreign immigrants will surpass the number of emigrants by 100.000 per projection year
		MiF2	High positive net migration numbers: The number of foreign immigrants will surpass the number of emigrants by 200.000 per projection year

Continuation of Table 7

Demographic indicator	Citizenship group	Abbreviation	Assumptions
Citizenship acquired by children of…	German women (excl. ius soli-citizens)	CAG	German citizenship: All children born by German mothers acquire German citizenship at birth
	Ius soli-citizens	CAI	German citizenship: All children born by ius soli-citizens acquire German citizenship at birth
	Foreign women	CAF	German or foreign citizenship: 45% of all children born by foreign mothers acquire German citizenship qua ius sanguinis, 30% acquire German citizenship qua ius soli, 25% acquire a foreign citizenship
Changes of citizenship	German citizens (excl. ius soli-citizens)	CCG	No changes of citizenship: No German citizen will lose the German citizenship while living in Germany
	Ius soli-citizens	CCI	Majority retains German citizenship: 90% of all ius soli-citizens will retain their German citizenship beyond the 23rd birthday, 10% will lose it
	Foreign residents	**CCF1**	Low average naturalization rates: 1.0% of all foreign residents will acquire German citizenship in each projection year
		CCF2	High average naturalization rates: 1.6% of all foreign residents will acquire German citizenship in each projection year

Source: Own illustration

Table 8: Overview: Combining demographic assumptions into scenarios

		FG1		FG2	
		MG1	**MG2**	**MG1**	**MG2**
MiF1	**CCF1**	Sc. 1	Sc. 2	Sc. 3	Sc. 4
	CCF2	Sc. 5	Sc. 6	Sc. 7	Sc. 8
MiF2	**CCF1**	Sc. 9	Sc. 10	Sc. 11	Sc. 12
	CCF2	Sc. 13	Sc. 14	Sc. 15	Sc. 16

Source: Own illustration

Only one assumption each was defined on fertility and mortality of foreign residents, migration trends among German citizens (including ius soli-citizens), citizenship acquisitions at birth and changes of citizenship among German citizens (majority population) and ius soli-citizens. These individual assumptions were used in all 16 demographic scenarios. In other words, all 16 scenarios in Table 8 are based on the assumption that the fertility of foreign women and the mortality of foreign residents will converge with those of Germans (FF and MF), that all children born to German mothers will acquire German citizenship at birth (CAG and CAI), that 75% of all children born to foreign mothers will acquire German citizenship at birth via ius soli or ius sanguinis (CAF), that net migration numbers of German citizens will remain at a level of around -32.000 throughout the projection period (MiG), that no German citizens will lose or revoke the citizenship as long as they live in Germany (CCG) and that 90% of all ius soli-citizens will opt for the German citizenship (CCI). The 16 scenarios, thus defined, form the input of the demographic population projections. In the following, the results of these projections will be presented.

6.3. Projection results

The demographic projections provide information on how demographic trends will change the population in Germany, provided that the underlying assumptions are accepted as plausible. In addition, the projections reveal how many German citizens of minor age, foreign residents and eligible voters will live in Germany in the future. From these data, the proportion of eligible voters and the median age of the electorate can be calculated for each projection year and each scenario. The projection results also suggest which demographic factors will have the biggest influence on the development of each specific population group and indicator.

6.3.1. The total resident population of Germany

The population of Germany declines in size until 2030 in all 16 scenarios calculated here. This projection result is visualized in Figure 60. Each grey line in the figure visualizes the result of one of the 16 scenarios and shows the total number of residents (i.e. including German citizens, ius soli-citizens, foreign residents) living in Germany in each projection year. Each of the grey lines is marked by the respective scenario number. This number allows the reader to link each displayed development to the respective set of underlying assumptions that are shown in Table 8 in Chapter 6.2.

Depending on the set of assumptions that is chosen, the total population of Germany will decrease from 81.4 million persons in 2010 to between 80.7 million persons and 75.7 million persons in 2030. These results are similar to those obtained by previously published population projections.[456]

---

[456] See for instance *Statistisches Bundesamt*, Bevölkerung Deutschlands, 2009, p. 46; *Bundesministerium des Innern*, Modellrechnungen, 2000, p. 42; *Birg, H./Flöthmann, E.-J.*, Projektionsrechnungen, 2001, p. 115; *Enquete-Kommission 'Demographischer Wandel'*, Zwischenbericht, 1998, p. 128; *Eurostat*, Online database, 2012; *Lutz, W./Scherbov, S.*, Bevölkerungsprognosen, 1998, p. 93.

Figure 60: Projected size of the population living in Germany, 2010-2030

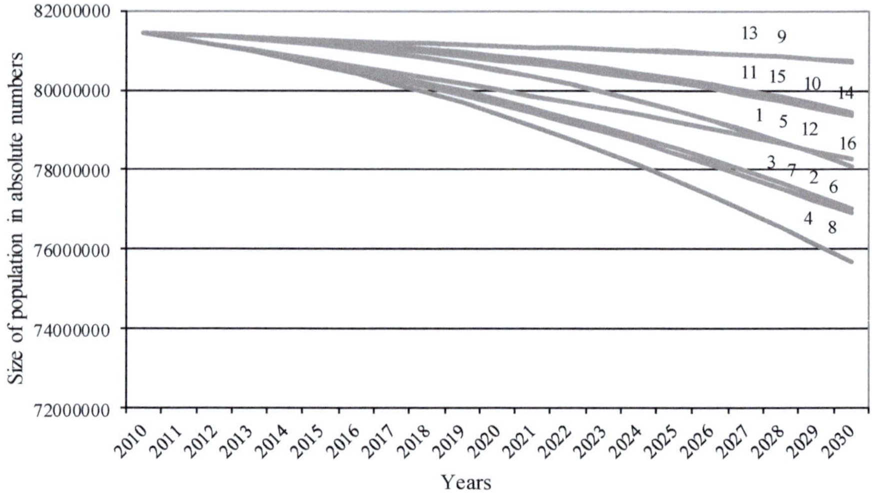

Source: Own calculations based on demographic data provided by the Federal Statistical Office.

Figure 60 shows that the population will decline in size most strongly in scenarios 4 and 8. These scenarios are based on the assumption that fertility in Germany will decline in the future (FG2), that life expectancy will increase slowly (MG2) and that net migration numbers of foreigners will be positive but remain at rather low levels (+100.000; MiF1). The effects of these trends on the age structure of the population are visualized in Figure 61.

The figure contrasts the population of Germany in 2010 with the population in 2030 under the assumptions of scenarios 4 and 8. Due to the decline in fertility rates, an increasingly smaller number of children would be born each projection year by German and foreign women. The base of the population pyramid in Figure 61 is therefore further hollowed out in 2030. At the same time, the number of persons who reach very old ages would modestly increase due to the rather slow increase in life expectancy.

Figure 61: Projected population of Germany by age, sex and citizenship, 2010 and 2030 (scenarios 4 and 8)

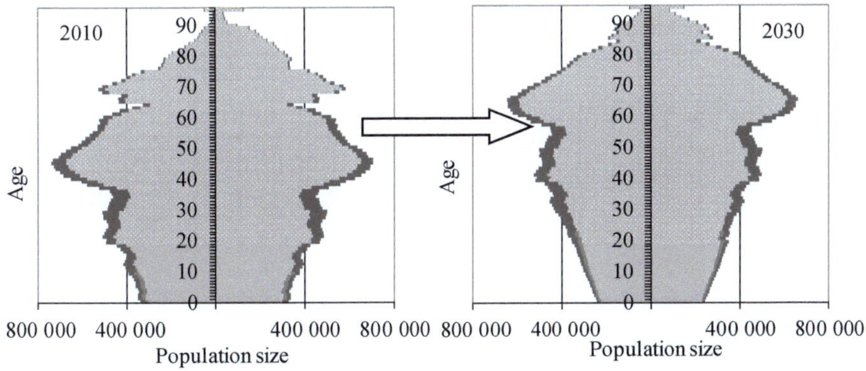

Source: Own calculations based on demographic data provided by the Federal Statistical Office.

The population of Germany would decline least strongly in size in scenarios 9 and 13 (see Figure 60). In these scenarios it was assumed that fertility rates increase in the coming years (FG1), that life expectancy continues to rise in a linear manner (MG1) and that net migration numbers of foreigners will be high (+200.000; MiF2). Again, the effects of these assumptions on the population structure are displayed in the form of population pyramids in Figure 62. As can be seen, the assumed increase in fertility would keep the base of the population pyramid from decreasing further in size. In addition, a somewhat larger number of persons would reach the oldest age groups than in scenarios 4 and 8 due to the stronger decrease in mortality rates.

The other scenarios which combine these fertility, mortality and migration assumptions in different ways lie somewhere between these four scenarios (see Figure 60). The future development of the naturalization rate of foreign residents is of little influence for the development of the overall population size, since naturalization changes the composition of the population by citizenship, but does not lead to population increase or decline as such. Therefore, scenarios that only differ with regard to the naturalization assumption (e.g. scenarios 9 and 13 or scenarios 4 and 8) lead to very similar results as regards the future population size of Germany.[457]

Figure 62: Projected population of Germany by age, sex and citizenship, 2010 and 2030 (scenarios 9 and 13)

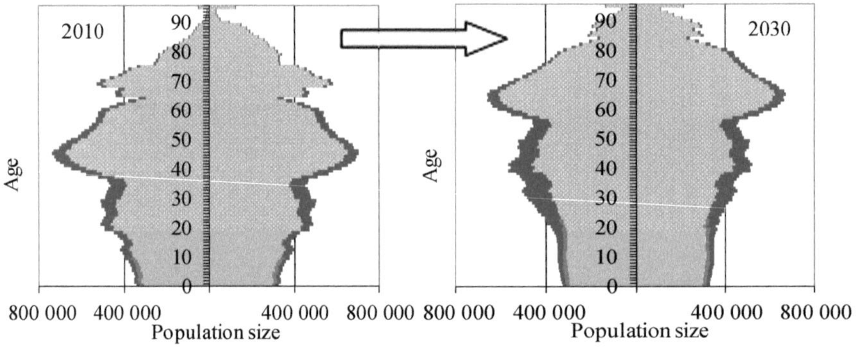

Source: Own calculations based on demographic data provided by the Federal Statistical Office.

In total the projection results suggest that the size of the resident population of Germany will decline in the next two decades, irrespective of which fertility, mortality and migration assumptions are chosen. The projection results also reveal that the median age of the population will increase irrespective of which assumptions are chosen. Figure 63 shows that the median age will increase from 44.1 years (2010) to between 47.8 and 50.3 years (2030) in all 16 scenarios. The biggest increase in the median age would occur under the assumptions taken in scenarios 3 and 7. In these scenarios, it was assumed that fertility rates decline (FG2) and migration numbers stay low (MiF1). Both trends would result in comparatively few younger members joining the population. In addition, it was assumed that life expectancy would increase linearly (MG1), so that a larger number of persons reaches high ages.

[457] There may be slight differences in projection results because the transition of population members from one citizenship group to another will subject them to different sets of demographic assumptions. The effects on the projection outcomes are however small.

Figure 63: Projected median age of the total population of Germany, 2010-2030

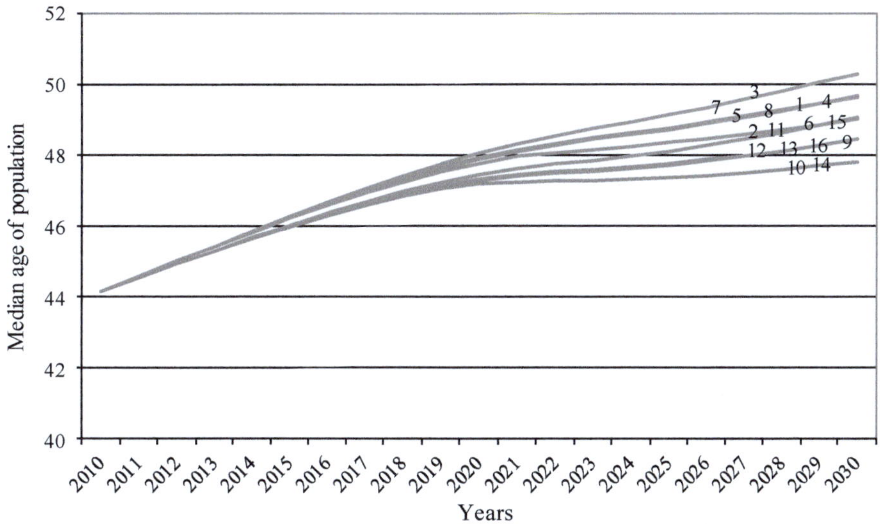

Source: Own calculations based on demographic data provided by the Federal Statistical Office.

The contrary development was assumed to take place in scenarios 10 and 14. In these scenarios, fertility rates were assumed to increase (FG1) and migration numbers were assumed to remain at a high level throughout the projection period (MiF2). Both developments would increase the number of young persons in the population. At the same time, life expectancy would increase slowly, so that comparatively fewer persons would reach very high ages (MG2). Even under these conditions, the median age would increase during the projection period, but less strongly than in the other scenarios.

6.3.2. *The population of underage German citizens*

The number of German children and adolescents aged 0 to 17 years (including ius soli-citizens) will decline until 2030 in each of the 16 scenarios calculated here. The detailed developments are displayed in Figure 64.

The figure reveals that the number of underage citizens will decrease from 12.5 million to around 11.8 million individuals until 2018 in all 16 demographic scenarios, irrespective of how different fertility, mortality and migration assumptions are combined. From 2018 onwards, four main trends can be identified. These trends differ in terms of the fertility and migration assumptions that were chosen. These two factors thus appear to have the strongest influence on the future number of German children and adolescents while mortality and naturalization trends do not seem to matter as much. As can be seen in Figure 64, the number of German children will decrease least strongly in scenarios 9, 10, 13 and 14. These scenarios assume that fertility rates increase until 2030 (FG1) and that foreign net migration numbers will be high (MiF2). In each of the four scenarios, the number of underage Germans declines to a maximum of 11.7 million in 2030. Conversely, in scenarios 3, 4, 7 and 8, the number of German children would decline most strongly to around 10.0 million individuals. These scenarios assume that fertility will decrease until 2030 (FG2) and that net migration among foreign residents will remain at low positive levels (MiF1).

Figure 64: Projected number of underage German citizens, 2010-2030

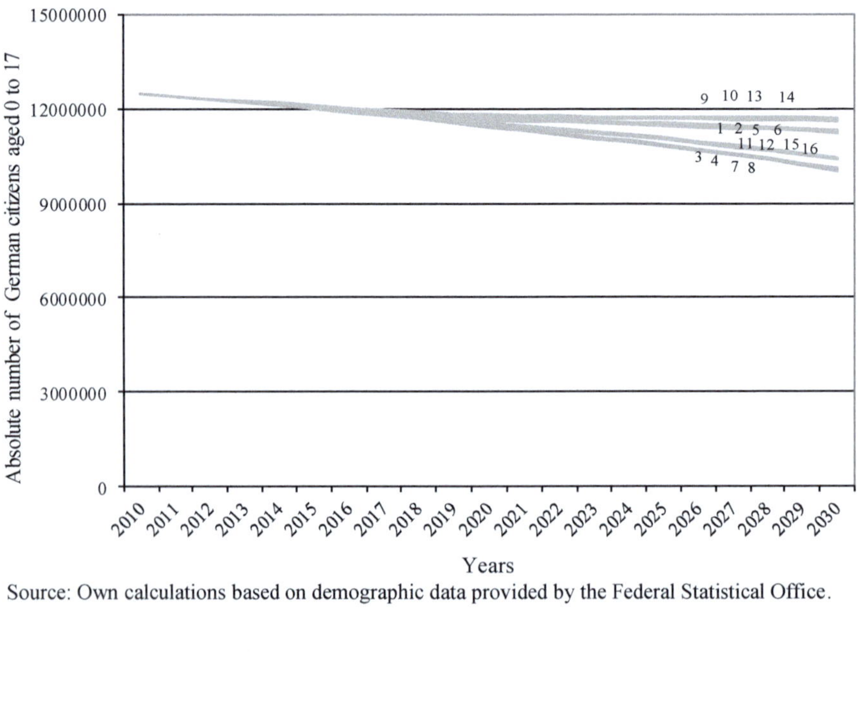

Source: Own calculations based on demographic data provided by the Federal Statistical Office.

The fact that the migration behaviour of foreigners influences how many German children will live in Germany in the future may appear surprising. The connection between the two is German citizenship law: As has been described in previous chapters, around 75% of all children born to foreign mothers today acquire German citizenship at birth, either qua the ius sanguinis principle or qua ius soli. If net migration numbers are high and especially young adult foreigners move to Germany, the number of children who are born in Germany to foreign mothers will increase in the projection model. Many of these children will acquire German citizenship at birth and thus increase the number of underage German citizens. As in the past, the acquisition of German citizenship via ius sanguinis will remain the more important mode of citizenship acquisition for children: Throughout the projection period and in all 16 scenarios, the proportion of ius soli-citizens among all German children never exceeds 5.5%. Ius soli-citizens thus remain a minority among the German population, irrespective of how fertility, migration or any of the other demographic factors considered here develop.

Figure 65: Projected proportion of underage German citizens among the total population, 2010-2030

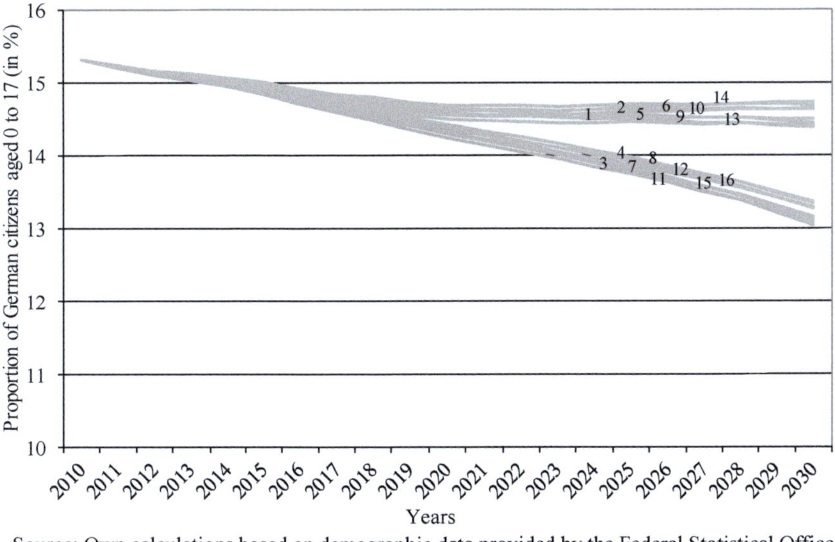

Source: Own calculations based on demographic data provided by the Federal Statistical Office.

The underage population of Germany will not only decline in absolute numbers, it will also decline as a proportion among the total resident population of Germany (Figure 65). In all sixteen scenarios calculated here, the proportion of underage children among the population will decrease from 15.3% in 2010 to around 14.8% in 2016. After this year, the development especially depends on the fertility assumptions that are taken. If fertility rates are assumed to increase in the future, as presupposed for instance in scenarios 1, 9 and 14, the proportion of children will remain at a level of around 14.4% to 14.7%. By contrast, if fertility rates decrease until 2030 as assumed for instance in scenarios 8, 11 and 16, fewer children are born and the proportion of underage citizens among the overall population will continue to decrease. By 2030, between 13.1% and 13.4% of the population would be of minor age and as such excluded from Bundestag elections.

6.3.3. The foreign population

While the number of underage German citizens will decline until 2030 in each of the 16 demographic scenarios calculated here, the number of foreign residents in Germany may increase, depending on which demographic scenario is considered.

Figure 66 shows the number of foreign residents of all age groups who are projected to live in Germany in each projection year and in each scenario. The 16 scenarios cluster in four groups. These clusters differ in terms of migration and naturalization assumptions. In other words, the development of the foreign population in Germany will essentially depend on future migration and naturalization trends, while fertility and mortality trends appear to have a small impact only. The foreign population in Germany increases most strongly in scenarios 9 to 12 which combine high net migration numbers (MiF2) with a low naturalization rate (CCF1). Under these assumptions, the foreign population would increase from around 6.8 million persons in 2010 to a maximum of 9.2 million persons in 2030. By contrast, the foreign population slightly declines in size in scenarios 5 to 8, which assume that migration numbers will be lower (MiF1) and that naturalization rates will increase (CCF2). Around 6.6 million foreign residents would live in Germany in 2030 in these scenarios. The other eight scenarios (1 to 4 and 13 to 16), which combine high net migration numbers with high naturalization rates and vice versa, lie in between these extremes.

Figure 66: Projected number of foreign residents (all age groups) in Germany, 2010-2030

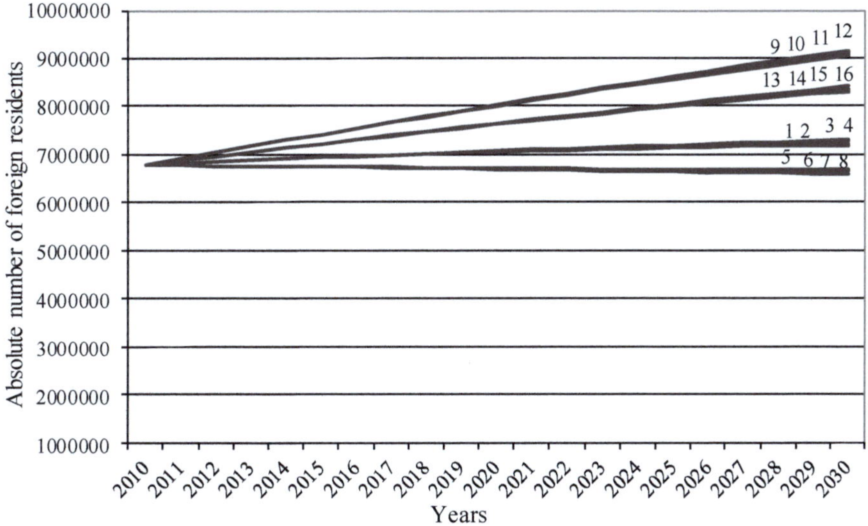

Source: Own calculations based on demographic data provided by the Federal Statistical Office.

Figure 67 visualizes the future development of the foreign population in relative numbers. As can be seen, the proportion of foreign residents among the total population of Germany increases in all 16 scenarios. Again, the increase is strongest in scenarios 9 to 12. If demographic trends would develop as suggested in these scenarios, around 11.5% of all residents in Germany would belong to the foreign population in 2030. In other words, nearly every ninth member of the population would be excluded from voting in Bundestag elections due to lack of citizenship. Foreign residents aged 0 to 17 would of course be excluded from voting not only because of their lack of German citizenship, but also due to their young age.

The smallest increase in the proportion of foreign residents would occur in scenarios 5 to 8 from 8.3% in 2010 to around 8.6% in 2030. Even though the absolute number of foreign residents in Germany would decrease in these scenarios, in relative terms their population size would grow because the German population will decline even faster in size. Overall, these results suggest that the proportion of foreign residents among the population of Germany is bound to increase in the future, irrespective of which combination of fertility, mortality, migration and naturalization assumptions are chosen. Between 8.6% and 11.5% of the total resident population of Germany are likely to be disenfranchised on the basis of the citizenship criterion in 2030.

Figure 67: Projected proportion of foreign residents among the total population, 2010-2030

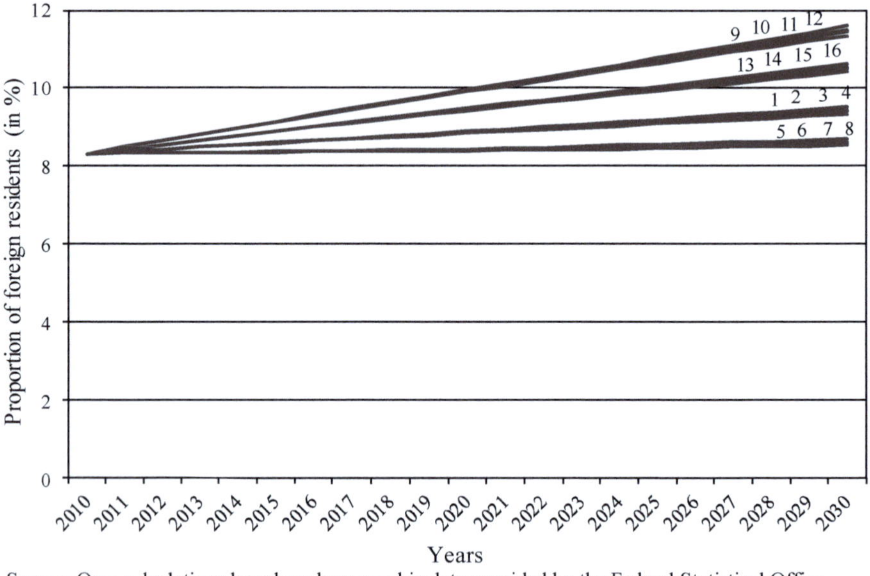

Source: Own calculations based on demographic data provided by the Federal Statistical Office.

6.3.4. The electorate

The absolute number of eligible voters will decline in each of the 16 scenarios calculated here. In 2010, 62.2 million persons in Germany were in possession of German citizenship and older than 18 years and were thus entitled to vote in

Bundestag elections. Depending on the set of assumptions chosen, this number will decline by two to four million persons during the projection period (Figure 68). In 2030, the electorate of Germany could thus comprise between 58.4 and 60.6 million electors. Only few of these electors would be ius soli-citizens. The proportion of this group of Germans among the electorate remains below 0.4% in all scenarios and in all projection years.

The projection results displayed in Figure 68 reveal that the future development of the electorate will be strongly influenced by mortality, migration and naturalization trends: If life expectancy in Germany increases linearly (MG1), if net migration numbers among foreign residents are high (MiF2) and if a larger proportion of foreign residents acquires German citizenship (CCF2) as in scenarios 15 and 13, the electorate will decrease least strongly in size.

Figure 68: Projected number of eligible voters, 2010-2030

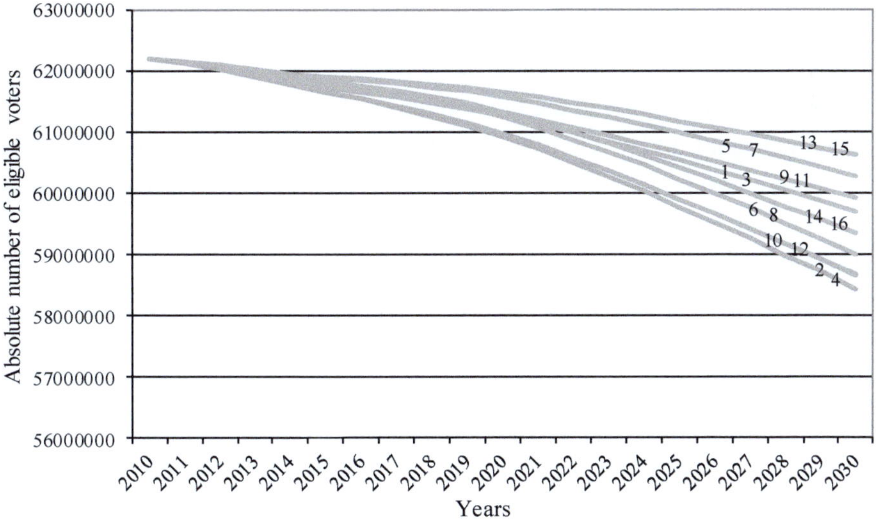

Source: Own calculations based on demographic data provided by the Federal Statistical Office.

At the other end of the spectrum, the number of electors could decrease to 58.4 million persons if longevity increases only modestly (MG2), migration numbers remain low (MiF1) and only a smaller proportion of foreign residents naturalizes (CCF1) as in scenarios 2 and 4. Fertility trends are of little importance for the future number of electors during the projection period: Increases or decreases in fertility rates influence the size of the electorate only with a delay of 18 years, when the newborn cohorts reach voting age. Hence, changes in fertility which begin in 2011 only influence the size of the electorate at the very end of the projection period. Demographic scenarios which differ only with regard to their fertility assumptions (e.g. scenarios 13 and 15) thus result in very similar developments of the electorate.

The development of the foreign population in Germany, the development of the underage German population and the development of the electorate all have an impact on the first indicator that is of interest in this study: the proportion of eligible voters among the total population. Figure 69 reveals how this indicator will develop over the next twenty years in each of the sixteen demographic scenarios.

In 2010, 76.4% of all persons living in Germany were in possession of the German citizenship and older than 18 years. Thus they fulfilled the two principal requirements to vote in Bundestag elections. Figure 69 shows that this proportion may increase in the future to up to 78.3% in 2030 (scenario 7). Such a development is likely if fertility rates decline (FG2) and net migration numbers of foreign residents remain low (MiF1), if mortality rates decline strongly (MG1) and naturalization rates are high (CCF2). The first two of these demographic trends would each lead to a decrease or stagnation of the number of disenfranchised persons in Germany – children and foreign residents – and thus push the proportion of electors upward. The latter two trends would lead to an increase in the number of electors: Stronger declines in mortality, as presupposed in this scenario, would increase the longevity of middle aged and older electors. High naturalization rates would lead to the inclusion of a larger number of foreign residents into the electorate. Both trends would also put an upward pressure on the proportion of electors. The opposite combination of demographic assumptions would lead to a decline in the proportion of eligible voters. If fertility rates increase in the future (FG1), if mortality rates decline only slowly (MG2), if foreign net migration numbers are high (MiF2) and if naturalization rates remain at a low level (CCF1) as in scenario 10, the proportion of eligible voters will decrease to 73.9% in 2030. Overall, Figure 69 suggests that both an increase and a decrease in the proportion of eligible voters are possible and that all demographic factors which were taken into consideration here – fertility, mortality, migration and changes of citizenship – may have an impact on future developments.

Figure 69: Projected proportion of eligible voters among the total population, 2010-2030

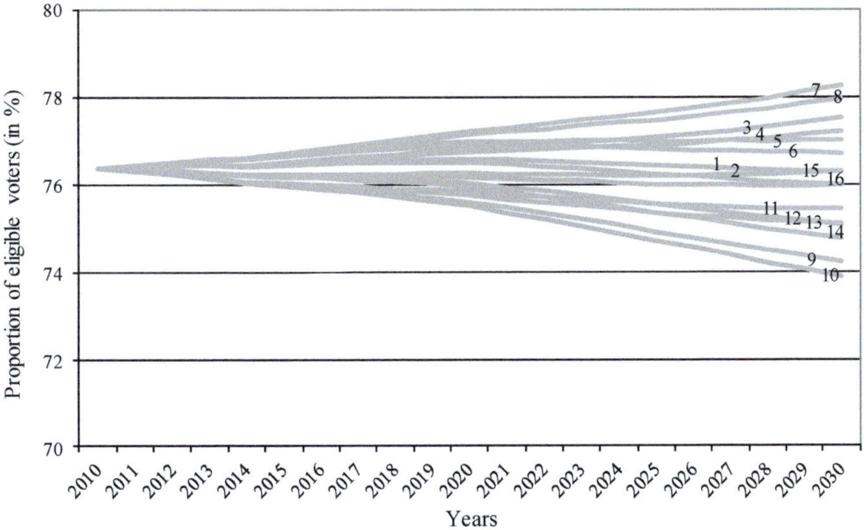

Source: Own calculations based on demographic data provided by the Federal Statistical Office.

In comparison to the proportion of eligible voters in Germany, the median age of the electorate appears to be much clearer to project. In all 16 projections that were calculated here, the median age increases in a fairly linear manner from 49.8 years in 2010 to between 56 and 57 years in 2030. This development occurs irrespective of which assumptions were defined for future fertility, mortality and migration trends as well as for future changes in citizenship. The reason for this clear trend is simple: Most persons who will form the German electorate over the next twenty years and thus shape the median age were already born in 2010. Some of these current or future electors may die or migrate during the projection period, but at least the approximate number of persons who will be eligible to vote in the future is known today. From the available data in 2010, it is for instance clear that the cohorts born during the baby boom period, who were around 40 to 50 years old in 2010, are quantitatively much stronger than any of the cohorts born afterwards. As the baby boom cohorts will slowly reach higher ages during the projection period, the median age will rise. Due to their quantitative weight, they will have a strong impact on the future development of the median age irrespective of how other population groups will develop.

Figure 70: Projected median age of the electorate, 2010-2030

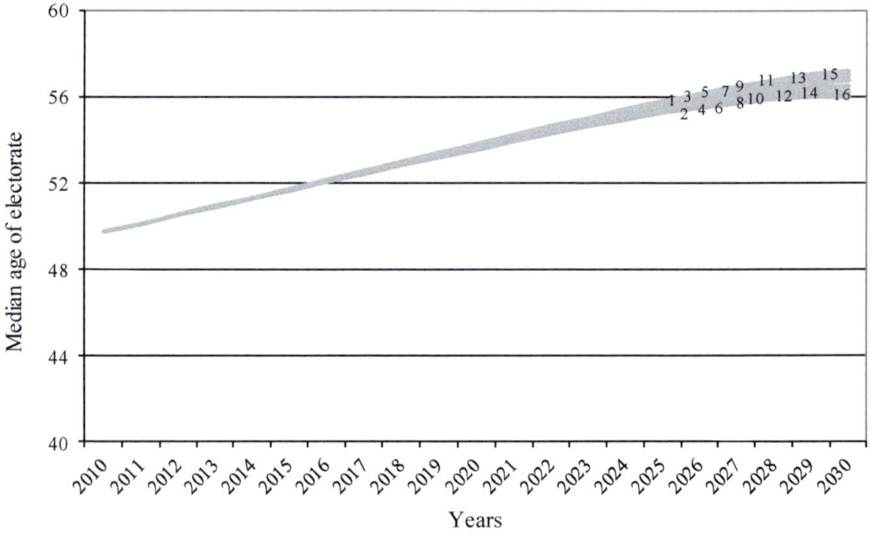

Source: Own calculations based on demographic data provided by the Federal Statistical Office.

6.3.5. *Summary of main findings*

In total, three insights can be gained from the projection results: First, a few core results were common to all sixteen demographic projections. Irrespective of which demographic assumptions on fertility, mortality, migration and naturalization were combined, the results always suggest that the total size of the population living in Germany will decline in the years to come; that the median age of the electorate will increase; that the proportion of foreign residents among the population will grow and that the proportion of children among the population will decline. The relative size of the two most important disenfranchised groups, children and foreign residents, thus develop in opposite directions, the latter of these groups becoming quantitatively stronger and the former group weaker. The future proportion of eligible voters is more uncertain. The results of the different scenarios imply that an increase is possible, but that a decrease may also occur. The development of this population group is uncertain because many different demographic factors - fertility, mortality, migration and changes of citizenship - may have an influence on its size.

Therefore, the second insight derived from the projections is that a large range of demographic factors are likely to have an influence on the future development of the electorate. As said, the future development of this population group appears to depend on the development of all four demographic components that were taken into consideration here. By contrast, the future size of the foreign population in Germany depends essentially on how migration and naturalization trends develop, while fertility and mortality trends do not lead to strong changes in results. The population of German children, by contrast, depends on future fertility rates and migration numbers, while mortality and naturalization trends have less of an impact. Hence, while not all demographic factors matter to the same degree for each population subgroup, the overall results suggest that changes in fertility, mortality, migration and citizenship all have to be considered when estimating potential future developments of the German electorate.

Third, the projection results attest to the importance of the academic and political debate on demography and democracy. Democratic theorists and social scientists have in recent years suggested that an increasing proportion of the population in Germany might be excluded from political participation in the future due to lack of citizenship and that the electorate might continue to age rapidly. The projections have revealed that these developments – especially the ageing of the electorate – are indeed very likely to occur. The projection results thus confirm that the debate about how the German demos will develop in the future, whether and how the political integration of foreign residents may be achieved and which consequences the ageing of the electorate may have is a highly relevant one. In the years to come questions such as these are likely to become ever more pertinent. The question whether changes in electoral law or citizenship law may be used to respond to these population trends and to shape the German demos is also likely to be high on the agenda. The next chapter will turn to legal changes which have recently been discussed in academia and politics and explore the possible effects that such reforms would have on the development of the electorate.

Chapter 7. Policy scenarios: The influence of legal changes on the development of the electorate

In the preceding chapters, the development of the German electorate was projected under the assumption that electoral law and citizenship law will remain unchanged in the future. In the following, this analysis will be extended by calculating how reforms of the Federal Election Act or the Citizenship Act would influence the development of the electorate.

Age and citizenship criteria currently exclude the largest number of persons from voting in Bundestag elections. 12.5 million underage citizens did not have the right to vote because of their young age in 2010 and 6.8 million foreign residents were excluded from the franchise because of their lack of citizenship. The demographic scenarios in the previous chapter revealed that between 6.6 and 9.2 million underage and adult foreign residents and between 10.0 and 11.7 million German children and adolescents may be excluded from the franchise in 2030. The age and citizenship criteria thus remain crucial in shaping the size and age structure of the German demos in the future.

Over the last two decades, both criteria have been subject to intensive debate in Germany. Academics as well as policy makers have proposed and controversially discussed a range of reform options. Most of these proposals aimed at abolishing or changing the age and citizenship criteria in order to make the demos of Germany more inclusive. To date, most of the proposals have been rejected and did not become law. There is as yet little information about the effect which the proposed reforms might have on the size and age composition of the electorate in the future if they were implemented.

In the following, different reform proposals which have been debated will be described. Proposals targeting the age criterion and proposals targeting the citizenship criterion will be discussed separately. In each of the two sections, a brief overview will be given of the arguments that have been exchanged in favour or against the diverse proposals by focusing on the academic debate and then by tracing debates in the Bundestag. In a second step, policy scenarios will be defined and calculated to quantify the effect of the different reform proposals on the electorate.

7.1. Policy assumptions

7.1.1. The age criterion

Across time and space, democracies have always limited membership in their demoi by defining a minimum age threshold. This threshold was often the age of majority, i.e. the age at which persons attain full legal responsibility. No democratic polity worldwide is known to the author that has ever entitled children to vote. Nonetheless, the age criterion has been contested, and it has been subject to numerous reforms. Germany is a case in point: After the foundation of the German Reich in 1871, the franchise was granted to men aged 25 years or older. After the end of the First World War, the voting age was lowered to 20 years, but then raised again to 21 years after the Second World War. The last change of the voting age for Bundestag elections occurred in 1970 when persons aged 18 to 20 were given the active right to vote. In some of the German Länder, the voting age for municipal and Landtag elections has since then been lowered further to 16 years.[458]

While the idea that the right to vote should only be acquired once a certain age is reached has persisted over time, it remains contested where exactly this age limit should be located. In recent years, debates have revolved around the question whether the current voting age of 18 years should be lowered or even be completely abolished.[459]

7.1.1.1. Academic debates

The question whether the right to vote should or should not be limited by age and whether the current voting age of 18 years is an appropriate age limit is of interdisciplinary concern. In recent years, it has been discussed by political scientists, lawyers, educationalists, sociologists, psychologists and philosophers

[458] See *Schmilowski, F.*, Demokratisierung, 2008, p. 89 f.
[459] See especially *Stiftung für die Rechte zukünftiger Generationen*, Wahlrecht, 2008 and *Palentien, C./Hurrelmann, K.*, Jugend, 1998.

alike, who have contributed different perspectives to the debate. Academics from these various fields largely agree that young citizens should be given more options to voice their concerns and interests in the political process. However, they differ as to how this goal may best be achieved. Some researchers, for instance the psychologist Rolf Oerter, the sociologist Klaus Hurrelmann or the legal scholar Hans Hattenhauer argue that the current voting age should be lowered or completely abolished.[460] Others such as the legal scholar Wolfgang Schreiber or the political scientist Eckhard Jesse by contrast argue that there are good reasons to maintain the current voting age and that children's and adolescents' views should be integrated into the political process via other modes of participation.[461] The critics and the supporters of the current voting age of 18 years have discussed the following arguments in recent debates:

Historical traditions: Schreiber has pointed out that democratic polities have always defined a minimum voting age and that it is therefore a historically substantiated criterion that should not be changed.[462] Other academics disagree and point out that the age criterion has in fact been amended several times during the last century and is therefore not as immutable as has been suggested. Merk and Willutzki have also pointed out that many eligibility criteria such as sex, property or race were once considered to be historically grown and therefore 'natural' criteria to restrict political participation but have been abolished. The fact that a minimum voting age has always been used in Germany and that it has been defined as 18 years for several decades does not mean that this cannot be changed, they argue.[463]

Voting age and age of majority: Jesse and Schreiber have also argued that full political rights should only be granted when reaching the age of majority, i.e. once members of the polity acquire full legal responsibility. Since full legal responsibility is currently reached at age 18, they argue that the right to vote should not be acquired before this point:

---

460 *Oerter, R.*, Wahlrecht, 2008, p. 207; *Hurrelmann, K.*, Wahlalter, 1998, p. 288; *Hattenhauer, H.*, Minderjährigenwahlrecht, 1998, p. 238.

461 See *Schreiber, W.*, Handbuch, 2002, p. 265 f.; *Jesse, E.*, Reformvorschläge, 2003, p. 9.

462 *Schreiber, W.*, Handbuch, 2002, pp. 258 and 263 ff. See also a summary of past debates in *Hattenhauer, H.*, Minderjährigenwahlrecht, 1998, p. 246 f.

463 *Merk, P.*, Wahlrecht, 1998, p. 268; *Willutzki, S.*, Wahlrecht, 2004, p. 4 f.

> "There is a strong interdependence between both age limits. Rights and duties belong together. […] Those who grant 16-year old persons the right to vote, but deny them full legal responsibility, devalue it."[464]

Krebs and Gründinger, by contrast, have pointed out that age of majority and voting rights have not always concurred. Between 1970 and 1972 the minimum voting age was defined as 18 years, while the age of majority was 21. Consequently, these critics do not share the view that the link between age of majority and the right to vote necessarily has to be maintained.[465]

Maturity: One of the most frequently mentioned reasons for maintaining the current voting age at 18 years is that children and adolescents below this age lack the maturity and knowledge to make reasoned decisions about political questions. Very young children even lack the physical abilities to cast a vote at the ballot box. Many academics, among them the democratic theorist Robert Dahl, argue that this lack of capacities justifies the disenfranchisement of underage citizens. They believe that the franchise would burden children and adolescents with responsibilities they cannot yet handle.[466]

Critics of the current voting age question the alleged immaturity of minors. The sociologists Hurrelmann and Tillmann for instance argue that 12- to 15-year-old children are cognitively developed enough to form opinions about social, ethical and political questions and that they match adults' capacity to reason and hypothesize.[467] Further, they point out that children and adolescents take on many responsibilities for their lives already, for instance at school, as media users and consumers. Within their families, they might have to cope with critical situations such as the unemployment of parents. In addition, internet and social

---

464 *Jesse, E.*, Reformvorschläge, 2003, p. 9. In the German original, the text reads: "Aber zwischen beiden Altersgrenzen besteht eine starke Abhängigkeit. Rechte und Pflichten gehören zusammen. […] Wer 16-Jährigen das Wahlrecht verleiht, ihnen aber die Volljährigkeit verweigert, entwertet es." See also *Schreiber, W.*, Handbuch, 2002, p. 264.

465 *Krebs, D.*, Amputierte Wahl, 2008, p. 273; *Gründinger, W.*, Wer wählt, 2008, p. 35.

466 *Dahl, R. A.*, Democracy, 1989, p. 127. *Schreiber, W.*, Handbuch, 2002, p. 264; *Berger, W.*, Partizipationsformen, 1998, p. 410 and *Oerter, R.*, Wahlrecht, 2008 also debate children`s competence for political participation.

467 *Hurrelmann, K.*, Wahlalter, 1998, p. 287; *Tillmann, F.*, Wähler, 2008, p. 133; see also *Berger, W.*, Partizipationsformen, 1998, p. 409.

networks provide them with a broad range of information on societal, economic and political developments.[468] These researchers suggest that at least teenagers have reached a degree of maturity that would allow them to become more involved in political questions. Their enfranchisement could even be beneficial for their development since it might encourage them to discuss political questions with parents and peers and might foster their sense of responsibility and self-confidence.[469]

Finally, some researchers have questioned whether maturity is a valid criterion to delimit membership in the demos in the first place. Merk for instance points out that adult electors do not have to prove their maturity in order to vote.[470] Gründinger adds that the concept of maturity has not even been properly defined. He stresses that this criterion should therefore not be applied to underage citizens:

> "The disenfranchisement of 14 million persons on the basis of a criterion which no one has defined and that does not even appear in the Basic Law is scarcely reconcilable with the imperative that elections be universal."[471]

Interest: In addition to not being mature enough, supporters of the current voting age have stated that many children and adolescents are not keen on acquiring the right to vote. The Deutsche Shell survey of 2006, for instance, shows that only around 25% of all interviewed adolescents were in favour of lowering of the

---

[468] See *Palentien, C./Hurrelmann, K.*, Veränderte Jugend, 1998, pp. 12-15; *Oerter, R.*, Wahlrecht, 2008, p. 197 f.; *Harring, M./Palentien, C./Rohlfs, C.*, Politische Orientierung, 2008, pp. 170-175.

[469] See *Weimann, M.*, Wahlrecht, 2008, p. 67; *Sohr, S./Boehnke, K./Stromberg, C.*, Politische Persönlichkeiten, 1998, p. 231.

[470] *Merk, P.*, Wahlrecht, 1998, p. 265. Adult citizens may only be disenfranchised if a legal guardian has been appointed to take care of all of their affairs, but not, for instance, in case of dementia (see Chapter 2.3.2.).

[471] *Gründinger, W.*, Wer wählt, 2008, p. 24. In the German original, the text reads: „Es ist schwerlich mit dem Gebot der Allgemeinheit der Wahl zu vereinbaren, fast 14 Millionen Menschen das Wahlrecht zu entziehen aufgrund eines Kriteriums, das niemand definiert hat und das auch gar nicht im Grundgesetz steht." For a discussion of the term ‚maturity' see *Tremmel, J.*, Ausprägung, 2008, p. 212 f.

voting age to 16 years.[472] Despite this lack of interest in the franchise, the sociologist Klaus Hurrelmann and colleagues stress that adolescents are generally highly interested in political questions and societal challenges such as unemployment and ecological deprivation, poverty and war. They interpret the discrepancy between high interest in political questions and low interest in voting rights as a sign of alienation. Surveys which they conducted with adolescents revealed that many young persons do not feel well represented by politicians and parties and that they do not trust them to find solutions to major societal challenges.[473] In order to counteract such feelings of alienation, some researchers suggest that a reform of the franchise might be required, even though many underage citizens do not demand it themselves.[474] In addition, Gründinger has pointed out that interest in the franchise is not a valid criterion when deciding about its distribution. Many adult electors refrain from voting and declare that they are not interested in political processes, but they nevertheless do not lose the right to vote.[475]

Tendency to vote for extremist parties: Supporters of the current minimum voting age have also expressed the concern that children and adolescents may have a stronger tendency to support extremist parties than adults. Electoral statistics indeed indicate that especially young male electors (aged 18 to 24) are more likely to prefer extremist parties than the average elector.[476] Palentien and colleagues interpret this as another sign of political alienation and exclusion among adolescents. They urge that this trend should be counteracted and believe that the political inclusion of adolescents may precisely reduce extremist tendencies.[477]

---

472 See *Harring, M./Palentien, C./Rohlfs, C.*, Politische Orientierung, 2008, p. 181. Also *Tillmann, F.*, Wähler, 2008, p. 129 f.; *Hoffmann-Lange, U./De Rijke, J.*, Wahlverhalten, 2008, p. 112.

473 *Palentien, C./Hurrelmann, K.*, Veränderte Jugend, 1998, pp. 16-19; *Hurrelmann, K.*, Wahlalter, 1998, p. 282 f.; see also *Harring, M./Palentien, C./Rohlfs, C.*, Politische Orientierung, 2008.

474 See *Oerter, R.*, Wahlrecht, 2008, p. 207; *Gründinger, W.*, Wer wählt, 2008, p. 33. More sceptical: *Hoffmann-Lange, U./De Rijke, J.*, Wahlverhalten, 2008, p. 112.

475 *Gründinger, W.*, Wer wählt, 2008, p. 32.

476 See *Hoffmann-Lange, U./De Rijke, J.*, Wahlverhalten, 2008, p. 101 f.; *Tillmann, F.*, Wähler, 2008, p. 127; *Palentien, C.*, Diskussion, 1998, p. 295.

477 *Palentien, C.*, Diskussion, 1998, p. 295 f.; *Harring, M./Palentien, C./Rohlfs, C.*, Politische Orientierung, 2008, p. 180.

Weimann criticizes that the political orientation of children should not be used to justify their disenfranchisement in the first place:

> "It is deeply undemocratic and therefore unconstitutional to exclude children so that they cannot vote for CDU, SPD, PDS, NPD, DKP"[478]

Lack of independence: Children and adolescents mostly live with their parents and are financially and legally dependent on them. Some commentators have suggested that this might make them easier to manipulate in their electoral choices and that the current minimum voting age should be maintained to prevent this. Other researchers such as Weimann and Merk acknowledge that children may indeed be more likely to be influenced in their electoral choices. Nonetheless, they stress that all electors, irrespective of their age, are to some extent influenced by family members, colleagues and friends.[479] They consider this a normal feature of democratic practice. They also consider it unlikely that many parents would influence their children in a very direct way if they were allowed to vote. If such direct manipulation would occur, they stress that this would constitute an illegal act which could be punished on the basis of existing criminal law.[480]

Representation of interests: Supporters of the existing voting age have also argued that a change of the minimum voting age is not necessary since members of the Bundestag represent the interests of all population members in Germany, including those of children and adolescents.[481] Critics of the current voting age find this argument unconvincing, since it might be used to justify the disenfranchisement of any population group. In addition, they question whether parliamentarians who are interested in being re-elected will really cater to the interests and needs of disenfranchised persons to the same degree as to those of

---

478 *Weimann, M.*, Wahlrecht, 2008, p. 66. In the German text, the quote reads: „Kinder ausschließen, damit diese nicht CDU, SPD, PDS, NPD, DKP usw. wählen, ist zutiefst undemokratisch und damit verfassungswidrig."

479 *Weimann, M.*, Wahlrecht, 2008, p. 67; *Merk, P.*, Wahlrecht, 1998, p. 266.

480 For a debate on this argument see *Gründinger, W.*, Wer wählt, 2008; *Palentien, C.*, Diskussion, 1998, p. 297.

481 This argument is mentioned by *Krebs, D.*, Amputierte Wahl, 2008, p. 270.

eligible voters.[482] Since the proportion of children among the population is bound to decline in the future and an increasing proportion of the adult population remains childless, they expect that the interests of children are likely to receive even less attention by policy makers in the future.[483]

Other researchers criticize this view as being too simplistic.[484] They argue that older electors may in fact share many interests of children and adolescents, for instance in terms of financial, social and ecological sustainability. Van Parijs stresses that while older electors might not experience the long-term consequences of environmental pollution and economic mismanagement to the same degree as children and adolescents, "they also have less to gain from the persistence of a way of consuming and producing that jeopardizes the welfare of mankind generations hence, and may therefore be, on average, more receptive to bad news about long-term damaging impacts […]".[485] Especially if older persons have children and grandchildren, they may support parties and policies that they perceive to be in the best interests of their younger family members. These commentators therefore suggest that an increase in the number of older electors does not necessarily imply that the interests of younger population members will not be represented any more.

Democratic principles: Finally, researchers have controversially debated whether the enfranchisement of children and adolescents is required by principles enshrined in the Basic Law. Art. 20(2) of the Basic Law states[486]:

---

482 See *Hinrichs, K.*, Enfranchising children, 2002, p, 39; *Merk, P.*, Wahlrecht, 1998, p. 271; *Gründinger, W.*, Wer wählt, 2008, p. 36.

483 See *Heußner, H. K.*, Stellvertreterwahlrecht, 2008, p. 242; *Gründinger, W.*, Wer wählt, 2008, p. 27 f.; *Hurrelmann, K.*, Wahlalter, 1998, p. 285 f.

484 See *Westle, B.*, Teilhabe, 2005, p. 14; *Stiftung für die Rechte zukünftiger Generationen*, Positionspapier, 2008, p. 360.

485 *van Parijs, P.*, Disenfranchisement, 1999, p. 323. See also *Krebs, D.*, Amputierte Wahl, 2008, p. 285 f.; *Goerres, A./Tiemann, G.*, Kinder, 2009, p. 58; *Glenn, N. D./Grimes, M.*, Aging, 1968, p. 573, footnote 37.

486 Art 20(2), GG. In German, the text reads: „Alle Staatsgewalt geht vom Volke aus. Sie wird vom Volke in Wahlen und Abstimmungen und durch besondere Organe der Gesetzgebung, der vollziehenden Gewalt und der Rechtsprechung ausgeübt."

> "All state authority is derived from the people. It shall be exercised by the people through elections and other votes and through specific legislative, executive and judicial bodies."

Critics of the current voting age argue that the term 'the people' in the first sentence of this article refers to all citizens of Germany, including children and adolescents of minor age, and that their enfranchisement is therefore required. They also stress that the disenfranchisement of minor citizens violates the principle that elections must be 'universal', as demanded by Article 38 of the Basic Law.[487]

Other researchers argue that all children will eventually be enfranchised when they attain the age of majority. Since their disenfranchisement is only of a temporary nature, they do not consider it to be a serious breach of the principle of universality. Moreover, since all citizens were disenfranchised during their childhood and youth, this practice concerns all members of the demos and is therefore not considered discriminatory.[488]

Overall, researchers of different academic fields remain deeply divided on the question whether children and adolescents need to be granted the right to vote. Academics who argue in favour of changing the current age restriction have proposed four different models:

First, some commentators, among them the psychologist Oerter, the social scientist Hurrelmann and the legal expert Willutzki, propose to lower the voting age. Oerter has suggested that adolescents might be granted the right to vote with 16 years, since they have reached a high degree of political knowledge and intellectual capacity at this age. 16- to 17-year old citizens are entitled to vote in some municipal and Landtag elections in Germany already and have shown capable of participating in political decision-making in these contexts.[489] Hurrelmann and Willutzki go further by suggesting 14 years as a new age limit. They stress that adolescents are able to act and judge independently at this age

[487] See *Willutzki, S.*, Wahlrecht, 2004, p. 2 f.; *Hinrichs, K.*, Enfranchising children, 2002, p. 51; *Gründinger, W.*, Wer wählt, 2008, p. 22 f.; *Krebs, D.*, Amputierte Wahl, 2008, p. 280 f.

[488] See *Westle, B.*, Teilhabe, 2005, p. 15; *Hinrichs, K.*, Enfranchising children, 2002, p. 53.

[489] *Oerter, R.*, Wahlrecht, 2008, p. 206. He also proposes some restrictions and conditions. See also *Palentien, C.*, Diskussion, 1998, p. 298.

and upon their 14th birthday they are considered mature enough to choose their religion and are held responsible for criminal acts.[490] Also other potential age limits to the franchise, e.g. 12 years, have been mentioned, but these have overall received less attention and support.[491]

Second, a number of researchers have argued that all age limits to the franchise are arbitrary and should therefore be completely abolished. This proposal is referred to as the 'children's right to vote'. Weimann and Tillmann are among its supporters.[492] They suggest that children should be granted the right to vote from birth and that they should be allowed to exercise this right as soon as they declare their wish to do so and personally register themselves in the electoral register. They stress that this would make elections truly universal in character. Other commentators are critical of this model. They argue that it would not be effective in increasing the voice of children in the political arena. Since most young children are physically and intellectually not able to participate in elections, their votes would be lost.[493]

Third, other researchers suggest that parents should vote in the place of their children until these have reached a legally determined age, e.g. 16 years, or until they declare that they want to exercise the franchise themselves. This model is referred to as the 'proxy vote' and is favoured for instance by the lawyer and politician Lore Peschel-Gutzeit and the legal scholar Hans Hattenhauer.[494] They suggest that families should have one vote per family member and that parents should allocate the children's votes between themselves. They would be obliged to use the children's votes by only taking each child's interests into consideration. Proponents of this model assume that most parents would not find it difficult to represent their children's interests at the ballot box, since they represent them in many other areas of life already, e.g. in financial or property

[490] *Hurrelmann, K.*, Wahlalter, 1998, p. 285; *Willutzki, S.*, Wahlrecht, 2004, p. 6.

[491] See *Willutzki, S.*, Wahlrecht, 2004, p. 6.

[492] *Weimann, M.*, Wahlrecht, 2008, p. 57; *Tillmann, F.*, Wähler, 2008, p. 133 f. See also *Stiftung für die Rechte zukünftiger Generationen*, Positionspapier, 2008, p. 361.

[493] See *Krebs, D.*, Amputierte Wahl, 2008, p. 276.

[494] *Peschel-Gutzeit, L. M.*, Wahlrecht, 2004, p. 10; *Hattenhauer, H.*, Minderjährigenwahlrecht, 1998, p. 238; see also *Merk, P.*, Wahlrecht, 1998, p. 266.

matters.[495] Other scholars are more sceptical. They caution that many parents might not differentiate between their own interests and those of their children and would simply cast their own and the child's vote for the same party. This would constitute an act of plural voting and violate the principle that all electors must have an equal influence on election outcomes. In addition, critics point out that the proxy vote model would violate the principle that elections must be direct and personal in character. They also caution that a number of practical problems might arise in the implementation of the model, for instance if parents disagree about the presumed political preferences of their child, if parents are of minor age themselves or if they are foreign citizens.[496]

Fourth, a final form of implementing the right to vote from birth is the so-called 'parents' right to vote'. Researchers who have proposed this model suggest that parents should be given one extra vote for each child without being obliged to use it in the child's best interests. The additional vote(s) might be granted to parents for as long as children of minor age are living in the same household, or, alternatively, throughout their lives. Supporters of the model speculate that this form of franchise might give policy makers a greater incentive to take the interest of families into account and might even encourage couples to have more children.[497] This model is the most controversial of all. Most researchers reject it, since it would breach the electoral principle of equality even more directly than the proxy vote model.[498]

Apart from these four models, van Parijs proposes and critically debates a plethora of other proposals to increase the political influence of children and adolescents in an overview article of 1999. The proposals include, among other suggestions, disenfranchising elderly electors, holding the median age of the

495 See *Gründinger, W.*, Wer wählt, 2008, pp. 29 and 39; *Heußner, H. K.*, Stellvertreterwahlrecht, 2008, pp. 232-236.

496 See *Schreiber, W.*, Handbuch, 2002, p. 265 f.; *Goerres, A./Tiemann, G.*, Kinder, 2009, p. 57; *Frankenberg, G.*, Stellungnahme, 2004, p. 2 ff.; *Hoffmann-Lange, U./De Rijke, J.*, Wahlverhalten, 2008, p. 103 f.; *van Parijs, P.*, Disenfranchisement, 1999, p. 324. Proponents of the proxy vote discuss and attempt to refute these objections, see *Hattenhauer, H.*, Minderjährigenwahlrecht, 1998, p. 256; *Heußner, H. K.*, Stellvertreterwahlrecht, 2008, p. 243 f.

497 See *van Parijs, P.*, Disenfranchisement, 1999, p. 312 and *Goerres, A./Tiemann, G.*, Kinder, 2009, p. 53 f. for a brief overview of the discussion.

498 See *Heußner, H. K.*, Stellvertreterwahlrecht, 2008, p. 229; *Willutzki, S.*, Wahlrecht, 2004, p. 4.

electorate constant by letting only persons of specific ages vote in annual elections or by giving younger electors several votes. None of these proposals have received much support from other scholars, at least in the German context.[499] A consensus on the necessity, the normative desirability and the constitutional possibility of lowering or even abolishing the voting age has not yet emerged. The proposal to enfranchise children and adolescents remains strongly contested among political scientists and legal experts.

7.1.1.2. Political debates

Members of the Bundestag have also discussed whether the voting age should be changed to give children and adolescents a greater say in political processes, but not all reform proposals that are debated among academics have found supporters among parliamentary groups (*Fraktionen*). Only the proxy vote model and the proposal to lower the voting age have been debated in the Bundestag. The arguments exchanged in the debates largely coincide with those brought forward in academic discussions. In the following, the main developments of the parliamentary debates will be summarized.

After the voting age had been lowered from 21 to 18 years in the early 1970s, it took five years before the age criterion was again taken up by Renate Hellwig, a member of the Christian-Democratic party (CDU) and at the time State Secretary for Social Questions, Health and the Environment in Rhineland-Palatinate. She suggested that the proxy vote model should be introduced in Germany. This idea did not receive much support from other politicians and parties. Hellwig restated her idea in 1980, but again failed to convince the leading parties of her proposal. Nonetheless, the proxy vote model was occasionally re-tabled during the following years. In 1986 and 1992, for instance, two members of the CDU proposed to reconsider its adoption in Germany and in 1993 the all-party children's commission of the Bundestag (*Kinderkommission des Deutschen Bundestages*) issued a statement to the same effect. The Federal Government, at the time a coalition of the CDU and the

[499] *van Parijs, P.*, Disenfranchisement, 1999; see also *Gründinger, W.*, Wer wählt, 2008, p. 24; *Merk, P.*, Wahlrecht, 1998, p. 266.

liberal party FDP, rejected the proxy vote model in 1997 by arguing that it would violate the principle of equality of elections.[500]

While the proxy vote model only found few supporters among members of the Bundestag until the early 1990s, proposals to lower the voting age received somewhat broader acclaim. The Left parliamentary group (PDS/Linke Liste) tabled several draft bills and resolution proposals during the 1990s which aimed at lowering the voting age in Bundestag elections to 16 years.[501] They justified these reform proposals with similar arguments as those exchanged in the academic literature, arguing for instance that 16- and 17-year-old adolescents are interested in political processes and mature enough to be granted full political rights. Furthermore, they pointed to demographic changes and argued that the franchise would help adolescents to protect their interests in an ageing population. The Green party (Bündnis 90/Die Grünen) also supported the idea of lowering the voting age during the mid-1990s.[502] Nonetheless, the coalition governments during these years – first a CDU/CSU and FDP coalition, from 1998 a coalition between the Social Democratic Party (SPD) and the Green Party – did not support the bills and all eventually failed. In 1997, the government justified its rejection by stating that the voting age should remain linked to the age of legal majority. The government also argued that many adolescents aged 16 to 17 are not interested in politics and that some are not mature enough to be given the right to vote.[503]

The debate about the voting age nonetheless continued in the years that followed. In 2002, the Enquete Commission on Demographic Change (*Enquête-Kommission „Demographischer Wandel"*) presented its final report after ten years of work. In this report, the commission members – representatives of academia and parliamentarians from all parliamentary groups – discussed the most important demographic trends in Germany and possible approaches to

---

[500] See *Hattenhauer, H.*, Minderjährigenwahlrecht, 1998, pp. 248-252; *van Parijs, P.*, Disenfranchisement, 1999, p. 311; BT-Drs. 13/7597 of 06.05.1997, p. 14.

[501] BT-Drs. 12/5127 of 15.06.1993, BT-Drs. 12/5128 of 15.06.1993, BT-Drs. 13/2375 of 20.09.1995, BT-Drs. 13/3519 of 17.01.1996, BT-Drs. 13/3520 of 17.01.1996, BT-Drs. 14/1126 of 09.06.1999.

[502] See *van Parijs, P.*, Disenfranchisement, 1999, p. 303.

[503] BT-Drs. 13/7597 of 06.05.1997, p. 15.

Table 9: Bills, resolution proposals and motions to change or abolish the minimum voting age, tabled during electoral terms 15 to 17

Electoral period	Document number	Title	Authors	Proposed change of the minimum voting age	Status of motion or bill
15	BT-Drs. 15/1544	Motion: Daring more democracy by introducing the right to vote from birth (*"Antrag: Mehr Demokratie wagen durch ein Wahlrecht von Geburt an"*)	Members of different parties	Introduce proxy vote model	Rejected
16	BT-Drs. 16/3543	Motion: Strengthening the participation of children and adolescents - increasing orientation towards children and adolescents through a new participatory culture (*"Antrag: Partizipation von Kindern und Jugend-lichen stärken - mehr Kinder- und Jugend-freundlichkeit durch eine neue Beteiligungskultur"*)	Bündnis 90/ Die Grünen	Lower the minimum voting age to 16 years	Rejected
	BT-Drs. 16/5780	Resolution proposal: Adolescents in Germany: Perspectives through access, participation and intergenerational justice ("*Entschließungsantrag: Jugendliche in Deutschland. Perspektiven durch Zugänge, Teilhabe und Generationengerechtigkeit*")	Bündnis 90/ Die Grünen	Lower the minimum voting age to 16 years	Rejected
	BT-Drs. 16/6647	Motion: Lower the active voting age for federal elections to 16 years (*"Antrag: Aktives Wahlalter bei Bundestagswahlen auf 16 Jahre absenken"*)	Bündnis 90/ Die Grünen	Lower the minimum voting age to 16 years	Rejected
	BT-Drs. 16/9868	Motion: Giving a voice to the future - For the right to vote from birth (*"Antrag: Der Zukunft eine Stimme geben - Für ein Wahlrecht von Geburt an"*)	Members of different parties	Introduce proxy vote model	No decision until the end of the legislative period

Continuation of Table 9

Electoral period	Document number	Title	Authors	Proposed change of the minimum voting age	Status of motion or bill
16	BT-Drs. 16/12344	Draft bill: Draft bill to amend the Basic Law (Article 38) (*"Gesetzesentwurf: Entwurf eines Gesetzes zur Änderung des Grundgesetzes (Artikel 38)"*)	Bündnis 90/ Die Grünen	Lower the minimum voting age to 16 years	Rejected
	BT-Drs. 16/12345	Draft bill: Draft bill to lower the voting age in the Federal Election Act and in the European Election Act (*"Gesetzesentwurf: Entwurf eines Gesetzes zur Herabsetzung des Wahlalters im Bundeswahlgesetz und im Europawahlgesetz"*)	Bündnis 90/ Die Grünen	Lower the minimum voting age to 16 years	Rejected
17	BT-Drs. 17/5896	Draft bill: Draft bill to change the Basic Law and to reform the electoral law (*"Gesetzesentwurf: Entwurf eines Gesetzes zur Änderung des Grundgesetzes und zur Reformierung des Wahlrechts"*)	Die Linke	Lower the minimum voting age to 16 years	Rejected

Legal documents obtained from Parliamentary Material Information System (in German: *Dokumentations- und Informationssystem; DIP*), accessible at: http://dipbt.bundestag.de/dip21.web/bt. See Annex 3.

meet the resulting challenges. While the main focus of the report lay on employment, integration, health and the pension system, its authors also dedicated a section to political rights. Similar to the academic debate, they noted that adolescents increasingly take on responsibilities in many areas of life and have clear political interests and expectations, but that they feel alienated from and not well represented by politicians. The authors of the report assumed that children's and adolescents` political influence will decline even further in the future, given the demographic outlook of Germany. They suggested that the adolescents' political rights might be extended by "directly conferring rights of political influence onto them, for instance by lowering the voting age".[504]

In the years that followed, several new bills were tabled in the Bundestag which aimed at lowering the voting age to 16 years. Table 9 provides a list with reform proposals which were issued during the last ten years, i.e. during the 15th, 16th and the ongoing 17th electoral term. Most bills and motions to lower the voting age were tabled by the parliamentary group Bündnis 90/Die Grünen. The left parliamentary group tabled one draft bill in 2009. The authors of the different motions justified their reform proposals by stating that 16- and 17- year old citizens are mature enough to gain more political influence, that the franchise would help them protect their specific interests in times of population ageing and that it would help to counter political alienation among this population group.[505] None of the bills and motions were enacted, since they failed to receive the necessary support from other parties.

The debate about the reform of the voting age reached its peak in 2003, when a group of 47 parliamentarians from all parliamentary groups – CDU/CSU, SPD, FDP and Bündnis 90/Die Grünen – tabled a motion on the proxy vote model. In this motion, entitled "Daring more democracy by introducing the right to vote from birth", the authors for the first time formally requested the government to propose a bill on the introduction of the right to vote from birth, vicariously exercised by parents for their underage children. Among its signatories were

[504] BT-Drs. 14/8800 of 28.03.2002, p. 41. In German, the full sentence reads: "Zu prüfen ist darüber hinaus eine direkte Übertragung von politischer Gestaltungsmacht an Jugendliche etwa durch eine Absenkung des Wahlalters."

[505] See for instance BT-Drs. 16/3543 of 22.11.2006, pp. 1 and 3.

Wolfgang Thierse (SPD), then president of the Bundestag, as well as the vice presidents Antje Vollmer (Bündnis 90/Die Grünen) and Hans-Jürgen Uhl (SPD). The endorsers of this reform justified their proposal by pointing to the aging of the population, the perceived need to give adolescents, children and families a stronger voice in the polity and by referring to the core democratic principle that elections should be universal in character.[506] In December 2004, five experts were consulted in a public hearing on the motion. Three of these experts supported it.[507] The other two experts declared that it would breach the principle of electoral equality, since it would de facto give parents plural votes. Therefore they advised the Bundestag against adopting the motion.[508] Eventually, the motion was rejected in 2005, after it had been discussed twice in the plenary session of the Bundestag. Doubts about its constitutionality as well as the practical implementation of the proxy vote model were among the main reasons mentioned for its rejection, but opponents of the reform also questioned whether parents would indeed consider children's interests when using their vote at the ballot box.[509] In 2008, a cross-party group of parliamentarians initiated a new attempt to introduce the proxy vote model in Germany by tabling another motion on the right to vote from birth, but failed to put it to a vote in the plenary session of the Bundestag before the end of the electoral term in 2009.[510]

A consensus on the need to change the voting age for Bundestag elections thus has not yet been reached. Parliamentary groups and individual members of the Bundestag continue to hold different views about whether a reform is necessary and constitutionally feasible. They also disagree about which model should be chosen, i.e. if the voting age should be lowered or if the age criterion should be completely abolished. One point however has been common to all bills and motions on the voting age which were tabled during the last years. They refer to the process of population ageing and argue that children and adolescents should

---

506 BT-Drs. 15/1544 of 11.09.2003, especially pp. 1 and 3.

507 See *Peschel-Gutzeit, L. M.*, Wahlrecht, 2004, p. 14; *Nees, A.*, Stellungnahme, 2004, p. 4; *Willutzki, S.*, Wahlrecht, 2004, p. 8.

508 See *Frankenberg, G.*, Stellungnahme, 2004, p. 4 f.; *Jesse, E.*, Stellungnahme, 2004, p. 2.

509 See BT-Drs. 15/4788 of 28.01.2005, p. 4.

510 See BT-Drs. 16/9868 of 27.06.2008.

gain more influence in the polity in order to protect their interests against a growing proportion of elderly electors.
Given this motivation of the bills, it is somewhat surprising researchers have so far not calculated the effect of the suggested reforms on the ageing process of the electorate. It is therefore not clear, for instance, whether a lowering of the voting age would slow down the increase of the median age of the electorate. Policy scenarios calculated in this chapter for the first time provide this type of information. Two different assumptions will be employed to measure the effect of the proposed reforms on the development of the electorate.
Voting Age Model, 2010-2030 **(VA)**: Minimum voting age is lowered to 16 years. The first assumption is based on the proposal to lower the voting age. It is assumed here that the voting age is lowered to 16 years, i.e. that all German citizens aged 16 and 17 will be entitled to vote in Bundestag elections. It is further assumed that the new voting age of 16 years will be maintained throughout the projection period, i.e. from 2010 to 2030.
Proxy Vote Model, 2010-2030 **(PV)**: Minimum voting age is completely abolished. The second assumption draws on the proposal to completely abolish the age requirement and to grant all German citizens the right to vote from birth. As described above, different suggestions have been made as to whether underage citizens should exercise the right to vote themselves or whether parents should vote on behalf of their children. Such questions about the de facto exercise of the franchise could not be modelled here. The assumption solely focuses on the de jure extension of the franchise to children and adolescents. It hypothesises that the voting age is completely abolished in 2010 and that no new age requirement is adopted until 2030. All German citizens are thus assumed to be members of the electorate during the entire projection period.

7.1.2. The citizenship criterion

Foreign residents in Germany have always been excluded from elections to the Bundestag. While the citizenship criterion has thus persisted over time, access to citizenship has changed. As was described in previous chapters, the Citizenship

Act has been subject to several reforms since the 1990s which overall facilitated naturalization. Policy makers thereby hoped to encourage foreign residents to apply for German citizenship. During the 1990s, the naturalization rate in fact increased and a large number of foreign residents acquired German citizenship and became members of the electorate.[511] Since the year 2000, however, the naturalization rate has declined again and is currently low in comparison to other European countries.[512] The debate about whether the foreign population of Germany should be included in the political community and which additional measures should be taken to reach this aim is therefore ongoing, both among scholars and members of Bundestag and Bundesrat.

7.1.2.1. Academic debates

Academics have discussed since the 1980s whether and how long-term foreign residents should be integrated into the demos.[513] Since then, a broad consensus has developed that Germany and other European countries should indeed integrate long-term foreign residents into their demoi, since this would allow them to better protect their interests. In addition, the enfranchisement of foreign residents would increase the congruence between resident population and the electorate and thereby raise the democratic legitimacy of political decisions and policies.[514]

Tomas Hammar proposed two strategies to achieve the political integration of long-term foreign residents, whom he refers to as 'denizens'. He termed these strategies 'naturalization model' and 'voting rights model'. The first strategy

---

511 See *Meier-Braun, K.-H.*, Einwanderungsland, 2006, p. 208.

512 See *Thränhardt, D.*, Einbürgerung, 2008, pp. 8-10; *Efler, M.*, Stellungnahme, 2008, p. 2.

513 See *Hammar, T.*, Dual citizenship, 1985; *Castles, S.*, Guests, 1985. Researchers generally agree that transient visitors, tourists and short-term guest workers should not be incorporated into the political community. Exactly when a foreign person stops being a visitor or short-term guest worker and becomes a long-term resident is however less clear. See later sections of this chapter for suggestions on this point. The question whether and how temporary migrants might be integrated in the polities in which they live has also raised debates during the past years (*Bauböck, R.*, History, 1998, p. 334; see also *Martiniello, M.*, Political participation, 2006, p. 98ff.). This debate is however beyond the scope of this study and will not be taken up in detail here.

514 See, for instance, *Bauböck, R.*, Preface, 1994, p. ix; *Koslowski, R.*, Migrants, 2000, p. 83.

aims at strongly facilitating and encouraging naturalization and to grant citizenship to descendants of immigrants:

> "Qualifying conditions [for naturalization] are reduced to a minimum. Application procedures are simplified, and campaigns are started to encourage denizens to apply for citizenship. Children born in the country, or children raised and educated there, obtain citizenship automatically or semi-automatically at the age of majority. Negotiations and agreements with countries of origin abolish or reduce obstacles to naturalization that follow from the domestic legislation of these sending countries. Naturalization is granted with no requirement that the previous citizenship shall be renounced – in other words, dual citizenship is accepted."[515]

The voting rights model would restore the congruence between demos and resident population by entitling long-term foreign residents to vote regardless of their citizenship:

> "Instead of changing its naturalization policy in accordance with the naturalization model, a state may grant full political rights to denizens with legal domicile in the country for a particular number of years. Full political rights should include voting rights [...] in all elections, including elections to the national Parliament, or else it would not completely replace the other alternative, naturalization."[516]

While Hammar presents these strategies as alternatives, he also stresses that they may be combined.[517] During recent years, academics have controversially discussed whether and which of these strategies should be used to integrate foreign residents into the German demos. In the following, the main arguments exchanged in the debate are briefly described. They are not always discussed

---

[515] *Hammar, T.*, Democracy, 1990, p. 196.
[516] *Hammar, T.*, Democracy, 1990, p. 198.
[517] *Hammar, T.*, Democracy, 1990, p. 199.

with reference to Germany only. Instead, many academic publications discuss the political incorporation of foreign residents in European countries in general.

Representation of interests: The first argument concerns the interests of foreign residents and German citizens. Thränhardt, Linden and Zinterer argue that policy makers are less likely to take foreigners' interests into consideration if these do not have the right to vote.[518] Some researchers even suggest that the lack of voting rights puts foreign residents in danger of being misused as scapegoats in the political process, leading to their marginalization or discrimination in other areas of public life.[519] These researchers stress that the inclusion of foreign residents into the demos might help them to protect their interests more forcefully. They acknowledge that foreign residents are already given some political rights in European countries, such as the right to demonstrate or the right to join unions and other pressure groups. Foreign residents are also represented by advisory boards (*Ausländerbeiräte*) in some cities across Europe. Nonetheless, the latter bodies tend to have consultative functions only. Authors such as Zinterer and Thränhardt therefore stress that they cannot be regarded as full substitutes for the franchise.[520]

Some commentators such as Castles are more sceptical and question whether the inclusion of foreign residents into the demos would indeed protect them from discrimination. They stress that the franchise alone is no guarantee for effective participation in the polity:

> "Formal enfranchisement does not in itself lead to political empowerment nor even fair participation in decision-making processes."[521]

---

[518] *Thränhardt, D.*, Allgemeines Wahlrecht, 1999, p. 21; *Linden, M.*, Interessensymmetrie, 2007, p. 92; *Zinterer, T.*, Interessenrepräsentation, 2007, p. 149.

[519] See *Massicotte, L./Blais, A./Yoshinaka, A.*, Rules of the game, 2004, p. 8; see also *Raskin, J. B.*, Legal aliens, 1993, p. 1442; *Thränhardt, D.*, Einbürgerung, 2008, p. 13.

[520] *Zinterer, T.*, Interessenrepräsentation, 2007, p. 149 ff.; *Thränhardt, D.*, Kommunales Wahlrecht, 2008, p. 4; see also *Martiniello, M.*, Political participation, 2006, p. 94 f.

[521] *Castles, S.*, Democracy, 1994, p. 13 f.; similar *Clarke, J./van Dam, E./Gooster, L.*, New Europeans, 1998, p. 46 f.

According to these researchers, enfranchisement may only be a first step towards incorporating foreign residents into the demos. They stress that it needs to be accompanied by other mechanisms to ensure that foreign residents may and do in fact make use of their rights.

Some researchers are critical of the naturalization model and the voting rights model. They stress that both models erode the principle that all electors should have equal political influence.[522] If foreigners would be allowed to become members of the German demos without having to revoke their previous citizenship, as suggested both by the voting rights model and the naturalization model, they might be entitled to vote in two countries, Germany and their country of origin. Most German citizens would not have the same opportunity to protect their interests and influence the political development of two countries. In order to avoid this disadvantage, Martin recommends that persons who enjoy the right to vote in two countries should exercise it in the country of ordinary residence only.[523]

Stability of the polity: The second argument takes a macro-perspective and focuses on the polity as a whole. Some political scientists assume that the long-term exclusion of foreign residents might lead to their political radicalization, particularly if they feel marginalized or discriminated. This would increase the danger of societal segregation and conflict.[524] Canefe for instance cautions:

> "In the long run, a democracy in which the desires, concerns and demands of an identifiable segment of the permanent population is not taken into account is prone to suffer from deep wounds within its civil society as well as in terms of the state-civil society relations. In order for a representative democracy to function, all constituent groups

---

[522] See *Martin, D.*, New rules, 2002, p. 57; *Gianni, M.*, Multiculturalism, 1998, p. 35; *Bauböck, R.*, Boundaries, 1994, p. 221.

[523] *Martin, D.*, New rules, 2002, p. 52 f. See also *Hammar, T.*, Dual citizenship, 1985, pp. 446-448; *Aleinikoff, T. A./Klusmeyer, D.*, Plural nationality, 2001, p. 82.

[524] See *Bauböck, R.*, Introduction, 2006, p. 12.

> should have access to the decision-making processes and public offices."[525]

Researchers who share these concerns argue that foreign residents should be integrated into the demos. By gaining the franchise, foreign residents would be able to defend their concerns and interests peacefully and as equals with other members of the electorate. Cyrus and Vogel as well as Wüst expect that this would strengthen their sense of community and identification with the German society. Foreign residents might also consider political decisions and policies as more legitimate if they would participate in elections and other forms of decision-making.[526]

Other commentators are more sceptical about whether a large-scale inclusion of foreign residents into the demos would strengthen the stability and democratic legitimacy of the polity. Political theorists such as Cohen stress that the stability of a democratic polity requires that members of the demos conceive themselves as forming a 'community of fate'. In other words, they should share similar values, strive for common interests and be prepared to make sacrifices in case of war.[527] Some commentators argue that foreign residents should only join the demos if they are fully integrated into society and share these feelings of commitment. If foreign residents were given the right to vote as suggested in the voting rights model or if they would be entitled to naturalize under very low requirements as suggested by the naturalization model, they might not (yet) identify with the demos. This, according to some participants in the debate, might be detrimental to for the overall degree of commitment and ownership of the demos towards the political system.[528]

Another concern that has been voiced in the literature is that foreign residents might freely move to their countries of origin after participating in an election in

---

525 *Canefe, N.*, Citizens, 1998, p. 539. Also see *Castles, S.*, Democracy, 1994, p. 20 f.; *Schnapper, D.*, European debate, 1997, p. 206.

526 *Cyrus, N./Vogel, D.*, Förderung, 2008, p. 19; *Wüst, A.*, Politische Repräsentation, 2006, p. 2. See also *Spiro, P.*, Dual nationality, 2002, p. 28.

527 *Cohen, J. L.*, Changing paradigms, 1999, p. 263. See also *Masing, J.*, Wandel, 2001, p. 59 f.; *Schreiber, W.*, Handbuch, 2002, p. 41 f.; *Betts, K.*, Democracy, 2002, p. 58.

528 See for instance debate in *Taylor, C.*, Democratic exclusion, 1998.

their host country, and thereby avoid its consequences. This might give them "an exit option that mononationals do not"[529] have. The latter concern is however not shared by all academics. Gusy, Ziegler and Davy have pointed out that German citizens enjoy the freedom of movement within the EU. They therefore share the right to move abroad in case they do not agree with political developments or election outcomes. Oeter adds that while foreign residents may have a legal right to move back to their countries of origin, in practice such a step might entail substantial financial, economic and emotional costs. Exit after elections might therefore be a theoretical, rather than a practically feasible option for many families of foreign origin.[530]

The meaning and role of citizenship: Researchers have also critically reflected on the historically grown link between citizenship and the franchise. The right to vote has always been the prerogative of German citizens and naturalization remained for a long time dependent on restrictive conditions.[531] Over the last two decades, many of the former requirements for naturalization have been eased. Nonetheless, core requirements remain. In principle, foreign residents are for instance still expected to revoke their previous citizenship upon naturalization, even though many exceptions exist today.[532] Many legal experts and political scientists have argued that this dependence of the franchise on citizenship as well as the rejection of dual citizenship upon naturalization do not accord well with new demographic realities. They stress that both legal traditions lead to the exclusion of a growing number of individuals.[533] In order to increase the congruence between resident population and demos, commentators such as Taylor stress that new approaches have to be tried and tested:

---

529 *Aleinikoff, T. A./Klusmeyer, D.*, Plural nationality, 2001, p. 82. See also *Faist, T./Gerdes, J./Rieple, B.*, Dual citizenship, 2007, p. 91 f.; *Taylor, C.*, Democratic exclusion, 1998, p. 149.

530 *Gusy, C./Ziegler, K.*, Volksbegriff, 1999, p. 244 f.; *Davy, U.*, Rechtliche Instrumente, 1999, p. 75; *Oeter, S.*, Allgemeines Wahlrecht, 1999, p. 41. See also *Hansen, R./Weil, P.*, Introduction, 2002, p. 8.

531 See *Masing, J.*, Wandel, 2001, p. 75; *Rittstieg, H.*, Dual citizenship, 1994, p. 61; *Hammar, T.*, Democracy, 1990, p. 61.

532 See Chapter 2.3.3. See also *Hagedorn, H.*, Einbürgerung, 2001.

533 See *Cinar, D.*, Aliens, 1994, p. 69; *Beckman, L.*, Citizenship, 2006, p. 162 f.

> "Democratic societies are going to have to engage in a constant process of self-reinvention in the coming century, redefining their common understandings to include new groups of people, and revising their traditional political cultures to accord varied identities both home-grown and newly arrived."[534]

The voting rights model and the naturalization model are considered as such potential strategies to react to the changing composition of the population. Researchers who support these models stress that they are already used in some democracies. New Zealand, Chile and Uruguay are often mentioned as countries where foreign residents may vote in parliamentary elections irrespective of their citizenship. New Zealand grants the active right to vote to all foreign residents who have lived on state territory for more than one year. In Chile, foreign residents enjoy the right to vote after five, in Uruguay after 15 years of residence.[535] Other countries facilitate the incorporation of foreign residents into the demos by accepting dual citizenship upon naturalization, for instance France, Sweden or the United Kingdom. Nonetheless, while these countries have higher naturalization rates than Germany it is difficult to identify whether this is due to the acceptance of dual citizenship or whether other factors also play a role.[536]

While many commentators argue that Germany should follow other countries in enfranchising long-term foreign residents or in further facilitating naturalization, this position is not shared by all. A number of scientists caution that the franchise is one of the most important, or 'noble' rights of a citizen. They stress that it should not be granted to foreign residents as proposed in the voting rights model, since this would deprive German citizenship of one of its most important

---

[534] *Taylor, C.*, Democratic exclusion, 1998, p. 149; see also *Beckman, L.*, Citizenship, 2006, p. 155; *Masing, J.*, Wandel, 2001, p. 20 f.

[535] See *Bauböck, R.*, Expansive citizenship, 2005, p. 764 f.; *Aleinikoff, T. A./Klusmeyer, D.*, Citizenship policies, 2002, p. 45; *Earnest, D. C.*, Voting rights, 2003, pp. 13-15.

[536] See *Chopin, I.*, Administrative practices, 2006, p. 251; *Waldrauch, H.*, Statistics, 2006, p. 298 f.; *Hansen, R./Weil, P.*, Introduction, 2002, p. 10; *Thränhardt, D.*, Einbürgerung, 2008, p. 30; *Reinans, S. A./Hammar, T.*, Changes, 1995, p. 200. For a more critical view see *Koslowski, R.*, Migrants, 2000, p. 189 f. For a description of how the view on dual citizenship changed since the 1960s, see *Hansen, R./Weil, P.*, Dual nationality, 2002 and *Renner, G.*, Doppelstaats-angehörigkeit, 1999.

attributes.[537] Similarly, it has been argued that one of the main functions of citizenship is the clear allocation of individuals to specific states. If naturalization was strongly facilitated by accepting dual citizenship, as suggested in the naturalization model, this function would be undermined.[538] Some commentators have therefore suggested that the link between citizenship and the franchise should be maintained and that dual citizenship should not be tolerated without limits.

Democratic principles and constitutionality: Political scientists and democratic theorists have also discussed whether the voting rights model and the naturalization model are compatible with or even required by core democratic principles. A principle that is frequently referred to in the debate is the principle 'quod omnes tangit ab omnibus approbetur' (whatever touches all must be approved by all). Some democratic theorists argue that in order to comply with this principle, all persons who are permanently affected by the decisions of a democratically elected government or parliament should participate in the election of their members. Members of a population, including foreign residents, should thus be subjects and not only objects of democratic governance. Drawing on the political philosopher Micheal Walzer, Bauböck even argues that the long-term exclusion of foreign residents from political participation constitutes a form of political tyranny of citizens over their foreign compatriots.[539]

This view has so far not been shared by German courts. The Federal Court of Justice has rejected the argument that all resident members of society who are affected by laws or policies should enjoy the right to vote in Bundestag elections or elections on other state levels. In several rulings, it has declared that only Germans as defined in Article 116(1) of the Basic Law are eligible voters. According to these rulings, citizens alone confer democratic legitimacy to the political system. The court has stressed that foreign residents should be included in the electorate, but that this inclusion should be achieved through

---

[537] See *Pechstein, M.*, Stellungnahme, 2008, p. 5; *Brubaker, W. R.*, Introduction, 1989, p. 17; critical: *Davy, U.*, Rechtliche Instrumente, 1999, p. 70 f.

[538] See *Koslowski, R.*, Migrants, 2000, p. 38; *Hansen, R./Weil, P.*, Introduction, 2002, p. 11; *Masing, J.*, Wandel, 2001, p. 59 f.

[539] *Bauböck, R.*, Citizenship, 2006, p. 20. See also *Canefe, N.*, Citizens, 1998, p. 539; *Bryde, B.-O.*, Ausländerwahlrecht, 1989, p. 258; *Schuck, P.*, Plural citizenships, 2002, p. 76.

naturalization. While the voting rights model has thus been rejected by the Federal Court of Justice, the naturalization model has been mentioned as a constitutionally feasible alternative. These rulings have been discussed very controversially in the legal and political science literature; not all scholars agree with the argumentation and conclusions of the court.[540]

National security: A further concern that has more traditionally been raised is that the voting rights model and the naturalization model might be a danger for national security. The concern is based on two hypotheses: First, the assumption that states depend on the loyalty of their citizens and that no individual can be loyal to two countries at the same time. It has been assumed that foreign residents who naturalize in Germany while keeping their previous citizenship or who become entitled to vote without naturalizing may remain loyal to their country of origin. This might make them more prone to being manipulated in their electoral choices. Second, it has been suggested that interstate tensions might arise or aggravate if electors of foreign background engage in protest and organise against political leaders in their country of origin. In order to avoid such developments, commentators used to demand that foreign residents should only acquire the right to vote if they credibly shift their loyalty to Germany and cut all legal ties with their country of origin by naturalizing and revoking their previous citizenship.[541]

In recent years, various researchers have become very critical of these hypotheses. They have challenged the view that individuals own exclusive loyalty to one country and that loyalty can be secured by forcing individuals to hold one citizenship only. Commentators such as Carens or Hammar have stressed that loyalty does not depend on citizenship status or voting rights.[542] Even native citizens may have a special interest in the political developments of particular foreign countries or feel loyal to other states. The official citizenship

---

[540] See *Schreiber, W.*, Handbuch, 2002, p. 41 f.; *Pechstein, M.*, Stellungnahme, 2008, p. 3 f.; for a critical debate on these rulings see *Oeter, S.*, Allgemeines Wahlrecht, 1999. See also Chapter 2.3.1.

[541] These arguments are described for instance in *Bauböck, R.*, Citizenship policies, 2005, p. 8; *Hailbronner, K.*, Citizenship, 1989, p. 78 and *Aleinikoff, T. A./Klusmeyer, D.*, Plural nationality, 2001, p. 81.

[542] *Carens, J. H.*, Citizenship, 2002, p. 113; *Hammar, T.*, Democracy, 1990, p. 209.

status of a person may reveal little about such interests and ties and while conflicts in loyalties may arise, "some such conflict simply comes with living in a rich and complex civil society".[543] These academics therefore argue that foreign residents should not remain disenfranchised or be required to give up their previous citizenship upon naturalization due to loyalty considerations.

In addition, researchers have questioned whether dual citizens or enfranchised foreign residents are indeed more likely to be manipulated and whether their political activities might lead to tensions between countries. Aleinikoff and Klusmeyer as well as Bauböck for instance suppose that while manipulation might occur in few individual cases, overall election results are very unlikely to be influenced by this.[544] Regarding the possibility of interstate tensions, Hailbronner and others have especially focused on the role of dual citizens. They argue that there are remarkably few cases in which dual citizens have created or aggravated tensions between states.[545] Aleinikoff and Klusmeyer as well as Keskin suggest that the spread of dual citizenship may even help to improve intrastate relations, since dual citizens will presumably be interested in preventing or solving conflicts between their different countries of citizenship and might promote peaceful relationships.[546]

Political passivity: Finally, researchers have also discussed whether foreign residents themselves would be interested in acquiring the franchise. Some authors have pointed out that foreign residents enjoy the right to vote in municipal elections in European countries such as Sweden or the Netherlands. Their turnout rates tend to be low in these countries, which is sometimes interpreted as a lack of interest in political debates and developments. Low naturalization rates among foreign residents are also interpreted as a lack of

543 *Martin, D.*, New rules, 2002, p. 39. See also *Spiro, P.*, Dual nationality, 2002, p. 26.

544 *Aleinikoff, T. A./Klusmeyer, D.*, Citizenship policies, 2002, p. 32; *Bauböck, R.*, Citizenship policies, 2005, p. 8.

545 *Hailbronner, K.*, Citizenship law, 2002, p. 129. See also *Gustafson, P.*, Globalisation, 2002, p. 466; *Aleinikoff, T. A./Klusmeyer, D.*, Plural nationality, 2001, p. 63.

546 *Aleinikoff, T. A./Klusmeyer, D.*, Plural nationality, 2001, p. 85; *Keskin, H.*, Bürgerrechte, 1999, p. 34.

interest in citizenship and the franchise.[547] Other researchers caution that low turnout rates and naturalization rates are not necessarily a sign of indifference. In a commentary on Sweden, Bäck and Soininen for instance argue that low turnout rates among foreign residents should be expected, given that immigrants often show characteristics which are associated with low turnout such as low educational attainments, young age and high mobility. They also stress that foreign residents may not use their right to vote for some years after immigration if they have not yet acquired sufficient knowledge of the language of the country as well as about political developments and political parties. Even where foreign residents are aware of political debates and developments, they may not vote if they do not feel adequately represented by any of the parties. Some foreign residents may also come from non-democratic countries of origin and may therefore have no experience in democratic practice.[548] As regards low naturalization rates, authors have similarly stressed that they are not necessarily a sign of disinterest in citizenship and voting rights, but that many different factors may explain this phenomenon.[549]

Overall, most academics who debate the naturalization model and the voting rights model concur that the political integration of foreign residents is an important goal. Nonetheless, they disagree which of these models would be constitutionally feasible, whether they would lead to desired results and how they might be implemented in practice.

Most authors who favour the voting rights model suggest that foreign residents should be granted the right to vote after five years of residence in Germany. There is disagreement, however, about whether this should apply to specific groups of long-term foreign residents only, for instance to EU citizens, or whether all legal foreign residents or even illegal immigrants should be enfranchised. Proponents of the voting rights model also disagree whether

---

[547] For more details on these arguments see *Bauböck, R.*, Boundaries, 1994, p. 204; *Hayduk, R.*, Non-citizen voting, 2002, p. 7 f.; *Martiniello, M.*, Political participation, 2006, p. 85.

[548] *Bäck, H./Soininen, M.*, Immigrants, 1998, p. 36. See also *Aleinikoff, T. A./Klusmeyer, D.*, Citizenship policies, 2002, p. 55; *Martiniello, M.*, Political participation, 2006, p. 86 f.; *Hammar, T.*, Democracy, 1990, pp. 142-168.

[549] See *Hammar, T.*, Democracy, 1990, pp. 85-89.

foreign residents should receive the right to vote on all state levels or whether they should be entitled to vote in municipal elections only.[550]

Academics who prefer the naturalization model have followed Hammar in proposing a large range of options as to how the current naturalization requirements could be lowered and the acquisition of German citizenship at birth be facilitated. Among other proposals, it has been suggested that the minimum residence period required for naturalization could be lowered, that naturalization fees could be reduced, that minimum income criteria could be abolished and that foreign residents could be encouraged to naturalize via public information campaigns. Many academics also recommend that dual citizenship should become generally tolerated upon naturalization or at least allowed in more individual cases.[551]

In addition to naturalization requirements, many scholars have discussed the current ius soli-legislation in Germany. Almost all legal and political scholars who have commented on the topic recommend that the obligation to choose should be abolished and that ius soli-citizens should be entitled to retain both citizenships beyond their 23rd birthday.[552] They substantiate this recommendation from an administrative, a legal and an integration-based perspective. From an administrative perspective, researchers criticise the costs which the obligation to choose entails. If a larger number of ius soli-citizens apply to retain both of their citizenships, each of these cases will need to be assessed individually. This will bind many financial and personal resources among municipal administrations.[553] From a legal perspective, Wallrabenstein,

---

550 As regards the case of illegal immigrants, see *Rubio-Marín, R.*, Immigration, 2000, p. 6. As regards the debate on the state level on which the franchise should be granted: *Thränhardt, D.*, Allgemeines Wahlrecht, 1999, p. 24; *Aleinikoff, T. A./Klusmeyer, D.*, Citizenship policies, 2002, p. 52; *Hammar, T.*, Democracy, 1990, pp. 184-187. As regards the proposal of voting rights for EU citizens see *Koslowski, R.*, Migrants, 2000, p. 135; *Thränhardt, D.*, Allgemeines Wahlrecht, 1999, p. 25.

551 See *Bauböck, R.*, Citizenship policies, 2005, p. 13; *Aleinikoff, T. A./Klusmeyer, D.*, Citizenship policies, 2002, pp. 20 f. and 38; *Sieveking, K.*, Stellungnahme, 2008, p. 10; *Carens, J. H.*, Citizenship, 2002, p. 109 ff.; *Renner, G.*, Mehrstaatigkeit, 1999, p. 92; *Thränhardt, D.*, Einbürgerung, 2008, p. 41.

552 See *Göbel-Zimmermann, R./Eichhorn, A.*, Entwicklungen II, 2010, p. 351.

553 See *Borttscheller, R. H.*, Ausbleibende Integration, 2001, p. 16; *Lämmermann, F.*, Ius soli, 2011, p. 6; *Thränhardt, D.*, Einbürgerung, 2008, p. 42.

Masing and Marx have pointed out that many children who are born in Germany acquire two citizenships at birth on the basis of ius sanguinis principle, i.e. because their parents have different citizenships. In contrast to ius soli-citizens, these dual citizens do not have to choose between their citizenships when they attain full age. The authors argue that this difference in treatment might constitute an act of discrimination and might therefore be constitutionally questionable.[554] Finally, some authors have argued that the obligation to choose may have undesired consequences from an integration-based perspective. If a larger number of ius soli-citizens should choose to keep their foreign citizenship and revoke the German one, this would result in a loss of rights and might lead to their marginalization. It would also endanger the goal to increase the congruence of resident population and demos.[555]

In addition to abolishing the obligation to choose, some commentators have also proposed that the ius soli-principle should be extended to more cases or based on different criteria. Under current law, a child born in Germany to foreign parents only acquires the German citizenship qua ius soli if at least one parent fulfils specific requirements in terms of residence duration and residence permit.[556] Jungnickel suggests that these rules might be simplified, e.g. by granting German citizenship to all children who are born in Germany to parents who have themselves been born in Germany.[557]

Overall, the different strategies proposed under the naturalization model have received more support than the voting rights model.[558] Concerns regarding its constitutionality have led many commentators to advise against any attempts to introduce the latter model in Germany.[559] Nonetheless, the naturalization model has not received acclaim everywhere. Many authors question its effectiveness.

---

554 See *Wallrabenstein, A.*, Stellungnahme, 2007, p. 5 f.; *Masing, J.*, Wandel, 2001, p. 51 ff.; *Marx, R.*, Stellungnahme, 2007, p. 19. For a different opinion see *Berlit, U.*, Stellungnahme, 2007, p. 18.

555 See *Hagedorn, H.*, Einbürgerung, 2001, p. 228; *Masing, J.*, Wandel, 2001, p. 38 f.; *Davy, U.*, Einleitung, 1999, p. 13; *Marx, R.*, Stellungnahme, 2007, p. 27.

556 See Chapter 2.3.3.

557 *Jungnickel, M.*, Anhörung, 2007, p. 3.

558 See *Oeter, S.*, Allgemeines Wahlrecht, 1999, p. 49; *Hammar, T.*, Democracy, 1990, p. 218; *Ziegler, K.*, Diskussionsbericht, 1999, p. 251.

559 See for instance *Davy, U.*, Einleitung, 1999, p. 9.

They stress that a facilitation of naturalization, notably the acceptance of dual citizenship, does not necessarily lead to an increase in naturalization rates. Hagedorn for instance has pointed out that the decision to naturalize depends on many individual and contextual factors, and that naturalization requirements defined in citizenship law are just one of them.[560] If naturalization rates would not increase despite a facilitation of requirements, the goal to raise the congruence between demos and resident population might not be reached with this model.

7.1.2.2. Political debates

The question whether and how foreign migrants should be integrated into the demos did not receive notable attention from parliamentarians in the Bundestag or from members of the Bundesrat until the late 1970s. Foreign residents who had been living in Germany up to that point were mainly workers who had come to Germany through the recruitment programs of the guest worker period. Politicians and employers expected them to remain in Germany for a limited period of time only before they would return to their countries of origin. Their integration into the German demos was not considered necessary.[561]

During the late 1970s and 1980s, the expectation that guest-workers would eventually return to their countries of origin proved to be increasingly incorrect. Many workers remained in Germany even after the stop of guest worker recruitments, started a family or brought family members from their home country to Germany. The ombudsman for foreigners of the Federal Government (*Ausländerbeauftragter*), Heinz Kühn, was the first member of the government to acknowledge this fact and to discuss how long-term foreign residents could be included in the political community. In a report published in 1979, he proposed that they should be granted the right to vote in municipal elections after 8 or 10 years of residence in Germany.[562]

---

560 *Hagedorn, H.*, Einbürgerung, 2001, p. 143 f. See also *Babka von Gostomski, C.*, Repräsentativbefragung, 2008, p. 32; *Koslowski, R.*, Migrants, 2000, p. 189 f.

561 See *Brubaker, W. R.*, Citizenship, 1994, p. 174; *Castles, S.*, Guests, 1985, pp. 517 and 522.

562 See *Castles, S.*, Guests, 1985, p. 525.

The parliamentary groups represented in the Bundestag were divided on this proposal. On the one hand, all parliamentary groups agreed that the foreign population living in Germany should be integrated into the German demos in order to increase the congruence between resident population and electorate.[563] In 1982, the liberal-conservative government under the leadership of Chancellor Helmut Kohl for instance stated that „it cannot be considered appropriate to exclude the permanently resident foreign population of Germany over generations from sharing rights of political participation".[564] The political parties however disagreed as to how the political inclusion of foreign residents should be achieved. Kühn's proposal to grant foreign residents the right to vote was taken up by the Green parliamentary group. In 1984, they tabled a bill which aimed at granting all foreign residents who are in possession of a resident permit the right to vote, first in municipal elections and later also in elections at the state and federal levels. The bill, however, failed due to the opposition of other parliamentary groups: The CDU/CSU, at that time in a coalition government with the liberal FDP, were strictly against the introduction of the franchise for foreigners. The FDP supported the proposal in principle, but did not actively promote that a reform be put into practice. Members of the social-democratic SPD were divided on the question.[565]

While most parliamentary groups were ambivalent or opposed the franchise for foreigners during the 1980s, support was higher in some German Länder. Towards the end of the 1980s, Hamburg and Schleswig-Holstein adopted reforms that would have extended the right to vote in municipal elections to foreign residents who had lived in these Länder for eight and five years, respectively. Both laws met with strong resistance. Members of the Bundestag and the Bavarian State Government questioned the constitutionality of these

---

563 See *Hailbronner, K.*, Citizenship law, 2002, p. 122; *Davy, U.*, Einleitung, 1999, p. 9.

564 Quoted from *Hagedorn, H.*, Einbürgerung, 2001, p. 39. In the German original, the full sentence reads: „Die damalige konservative Bundesregierung erkannte 1982 selbst, daß ‚es nicht als sinnvoll angesehen werden kann, die im Bundesgebiet dauernd wohnhafte ausländische Bevölkerung über Generationen hinweg von der Teilhabe an den politischen Mitwirkungsrechten auszuschließen'."

565 See *Castles, S.*, Guests, 1985, pp. 527 ff. and 532; *Hammar, T.*, Democracy, 1990, p. 170; *Meier-Braun, K.-H.*, Einwanderungsland, 2006, p. 205 f.

reforms and called upon the Federal Court of Justice to settle the question. In 1990, the Court judged that the introduction of the municipal franchise for foreigners is unconstitutional. The Court argued that according to the Basic Law only Germans may be members of the demos in federal, state and municipal elections. In that same ruling, the court however also declared that the municipal franchise for EU citizens might be introduced via a constitutional amendment, thus anticipating later developments. On a general note, the court declared that a higher degree of congruence between the resident population and the demos should be promoted by policy makers. Rather than introducing the right to vote for foreign residents, however, it stated that the naturalization of foreigners would be the appropriate strategy.[566]

Bills and proposals to facilitate naturalization had been discussed in the Bundestag since the early 1980s. Nonetheless, none of these proposals obtained the necessary support and all bills were rejected.[567] This changed after the court ruling. During the early 1990s, the conservative-liberal government, still under the leadership of Chancellor Kohl, adopted and enacted two reforms of the citizenship law. Both reforms facilitated naturalization for long-term foreign residents and young foreign residents who had grown up in Germany.[568]

The opposition parties were not satisfied with these reform steps. During the 1990s, the SPD tabled several bills and motions to introduce the ius soli-principle into German citizenship law and to further facilitate naturalization, e.g. by reducing fees or by allowing dual citizenship in all cases of naturalization. The Green parliamentary group (Bündnis 90/Die Grünen) and the Left parliamentary group (PDS/Linke Liste) tabled bills and motions with similar goals. They admitted that the naturalization of foreign residents would not guarantee their successful integration into the German society. Nonetheless, they argued that political and social tensions might be avoided or at least be limited if a higher number of foreign residents would acquire German citizenship.[569]

---

566 See *Rubio-Marín, R.*, Immigration, 2000, pp. 203-206.

567 See *Davy, U.*, Einleitung, 1999, p. 1.

568 See *Hagedorn, H.*, Einbürgerung, 2001, p. 39 f., see also Chapter 2.3.3.

569 Bills and motions of the parliamentary group SPD: BT-Drs. 12/4533 of 10.03.1993; BT-Drs. 13/259 of 19.01.1995; BT-Drs. 13/2833 of 30.10.1995; BT-Drs. 13/7711 of 16.05.1997; bills

Proposals to introduce the ius soli-principle and to facilitate naturalization, for instance by allowing dual citizenship, were also tabled by several Länder in the Bundesrat during the 1990s.[570] None of these proposals was successful, since especially the CDU/CSU was strongly opposed to tolerating dual citizenship upon naturalization. Members of these parties stressed that citizenship should only be acquired once foreign residents are fully integrated into the German society and once they are willing to cut citizenship ties to their country of origin.
After the Treaty of Maastricht of 1992 introduced the right to vote in municipal elections for EU citizens in Germany, parliamentary groups in the Bundestag and representatives of several Länder in the Bundesrat put the franchise for foreign residents from third countries back on the agenda.[571] Some bills aimed at extending the right to vote in municipal elections to long-term foreign residents, others went further and proposed to grant foreign residents the right to vote in Bundestag elections. The supporters justified these proposals by stating that the enfranchisement of foreigners would create an incentive for parties to take their interests better into consideration and to protect them from discrimination. None of the bills were adopted since the governing parties, especially the CDU/CSU, remained strongly opposed to the municipal franchise for foreigners. They insisted that the franchise should remain a prerogative of citizens.[572]
The political debate concerning the political integration of foreigners culminated in 1999. One year before, the liberal-conservative government had lost the Bundestag election and a red-green coalition under Chancellor Schröder had been sworn in as the new government. It broke with the long-held paradigm that

and motions of the parliamentary group Bündnis 90/Die Grünen: BT-Drs. 12/1714 of 04.12.1991; BT-Drs. 12/5135 of 16.06.1993; BT-Drs. 12/7424 of 27.04.1994; BT-Drs. 13/423 of 08.02.1995; BT-Drs. 13/3657 of 01.02.1996; BT-Drs. 13/3719 of 07.02.1996; BT-Drs. 13/7677 of 15.05.1997; bills and motions of the parliamentary group PDS/Linke Liste: BT-Drs. 12/5125 of 15.06.1993.

570 Bundesrat document (*Bundesratsdrucksache*, BR-Drs.) 140/92 of 27.02.1992; BR-Drs. 402/93 of 09.06.1993; BR-Drs. 403/93 of 09.06.1993; BR-Drs. 745/95 of 03.11.1995; BR-Drs. 180/97 of 11.03.1997; BR-Drs. 186/97 of 12.03.1997.

571 BT-Drs. 12/5125 of 15.06.1993; BT-Drs. 12/5127 of 15.06.1993; BT-Drs. 12/5128 of 15.06.1993; BT-Drs. 12/5135 of 16.06.1993; BT-Drs. 13/3519 of 17.01.1996; BT-Drs. 13/3520 of 17.01.1996; BT-Drs. 13/9301 of 26.11.1997; BR-Drs. 515/97 of 09.07.1997. See also *Davy, U.*, Einleitung, 1999, p. 10.

572 See *Hagedorn, H.*, Einbürgerung, 2001, p. 183; *Davy, U.*, Einleitung, 1999, p. 9.

'Germany is not an immigration country' and stated in its coalition paper that the integration of long-term foreign residents should be strengthened. In 1999, the government tabled a bill to reform the citizenship law. It aimed at introducing the ius soli-principle into German citizenship law. In addition, it aimed at abolishing the requirement that naturalization applicants have to revoke their previous citizenship. The governing parties considered this requirement to hinder many foreign residents from applying for naturalization.[573] Especially the latter part of the reform initiated a heated debate among parliamentary groups in the Bundestag. The PDS supported the government bill, but FDP and CDU/CSU opposed the proposal to accept dual citizenship. CDU/CSU argued that membership in the demos should only be granted at the end of the integration process, once foreign residents are prepared to give up citizenship rights in their country of origin.[574] Based on these views, the CDU/CSU parties even initiated a public signature campaign against dual citizenship. It has been suggested that this campaign led to the electoral defeat of the governing parties in the state elections in Hesse in the same year. Due to the defeat, the governing parties lost their majority in the Bundesrat. This limited the chances for a successful adoption of the reform. In the end, the reform of the citizenship law was passed with the support of the opposition party FDP, but only after the governing parties had made major concessions to the reform opponents. Most notably, the general toleration of dual citizenship was withdrawn. Instead, the law maintained the principle that persons applying for naturalization must reject their previous citizenship but increased the number of exceptions in which it is accepted.[575]

While the political debate centered on the Citizenship Act at the end of the 1990s, the franchise for foreigners largely disappeared from the political agenda. In contrast to earlier legislative periods, only few bills were tabled which –

[573] See *Meier-Braun, K.-H.*, Einwanderungsland, 2006, p. 206; *Hagedorn, H.*, Einbürgerung, 2001, p. 204; *Green, S.*, Beyond ethnoculturalism, 2000, p. 116.

[574] See *Huber, E.*, Doppelte Staatsbürgerschaft, 1999; *Hailbronner, K.*, Germany, 2006, p. 227 f.; *Zeitlmann, W.*, Doppelte Staatsbürgerschaft, 1999, p. 143 f.; *Westerwelle, G.*, Optionsmodell, 1999, p. 137.

[575] See *Hagedorn, H.*, Einbürgerung, 2001, p. 40 f.; *Hansen, R./Weil, P.*, Introduction, 2002, p. 3. See also Chapter 2.3.3.

unsuccessfully – aimed at extending the right to vote to foreign residents.[576] Three years after the reform of the Citizenship Act, however, the Enquete Commission on Demographic Change mentioned the option of enfranchising foreign residents. In their final report, the members of the commission briefly discussed how the societal and political participation of foreign residents in Germany might be furthered while enabling them to maintain their cultural habits and identity. In addition to promoting bilingualism and counteracting racism and discrimination, the members of the commission explicitly recommended the introduction of the franchise for foreigners. They however limited this proposal to the municipal level:

> "As is already provided for in the majority of EU-states, the municipal franchise should also be extended after five years to immigrants from third countries who are permanently living in Germany."[577]

This proposal did not provoke a new debate about the political integration of foreign residents. During the second legislative period of the red-green government (2002-2005), the political debate rather focused on finding a new approach to regulate and channel immigration to Germany.[578] A new Immigration Act was adopted in 2004 after a long and contested legislative process. In addition to regulating immigration, this Act also introduced changes to the citizenship law. It for instance provided that participation in an integration course would reduce the required residence period for naturalization by one year. Other minor changes of the Citizenship Act were adopted and enacted in 2005.[579] During these years, only the FDP tabled a motion which mentioned the enfranchisement for foreign residents from third countries as one measure to

---

576 BT-Drs. 14/1126 of 09.06.1999 and BR-Drs. 45/99 of 26.01.1999.

577 *Enquete-Kommission 'Demographischer Wandel'*, Schlussbericht, 2002, p. 135. In the German original, the quote reads: „Wie in der Mehrzahl der EU-Staaten bereits vorgesehen, sollte die Erweiterung des kommunalen Wahlrechts auch auf Zugewanderte aus Drittstaaten, die sich dauerhaft in Deutschland aufhalten, nach fünf Jahren vorgesehen werden."

578 See *Meier-Braun, K.-H.*, Einwanderungsland, 2006, p. 206.

579 See also Chapter 2.3.3.

improve their integration in Germany. Again, the proposal focused on the franchise for municipal elections.[580]

The debate on the political integration of foreign residents restarted during the mid-2000s. By this time, it had become clear that the naturalization rate had not increased as had been the goal of the citizenship reform in 2000, but had instead declined almost continuously. As a reaction to these trends, especially Bündnis 90/Die Grünen and Die Linke, both opposition parties since 2005, proposed new strategies to increase the convergence between resident population and electorate. Table 10 provides an overview of the various reform proposals which were tabled during the last three electoral terms.[581]

In bills and motions tabled since 2006 (16th and 17th legislative period, see Table 10), both the Green and the Left parliamentary groups stated that the development of naturalization rates since the reform of the Citizenship Act was not satisfactory. They declared that the current naturalization requirements were too restrictive, potentially discriminating and that they had a deterring effect on many foreign residents rather than encouraging naturalization.[582]

In order to achieve a higher degree of democratic inclusiveness and to enable foreign residents to protect their interests, the Green parliamentary group proposed that naturalization should be further facilitated, for instance by reducing the required duration of residence in Germany and by abolishing the requirement that naturalization applicants pass a naturalization test. They also argued in favour of abolishing language requirements for certain groups of foreign residents such as young adults or retirees and suggested that dependence on public welfare should not preclude these groups of individuals from naturalizing. Finally, the Green parliamentary group also argued that the retention of the previous citizenship upon naturalization should generally be accepted or at least tolerated in more cases.[583]

---

580 BT-Drs. 15/4401 of 01.12.2004, p. 3.

581 The table only includes bills and motions that aim at enfranchising foreign residents in national level elections or that aim at facilitating naturalization and the acquisition of citizenship by children, but does not include proposals to extend the franchise at the municipal level.

582 BT-Drs. 16/1770 of 31.05.2006, p. 1 f.; BT-Drs. 16/2650 of 20.09.2006, p. 4.

583 See BT-Drs. 16/2650 of 20.09.2006; BT-Drs. 17/3411 of 26.10.2010.

The proposals of the Left parliamentary group went even further. Its members suggested that all naturalization requirements regarding income or employment should be abolished, that language requirements should be lowered and that naturalization fees should be reduced to a symbolical amount. Similar to the Green parliamentary group, the Left argued in favour of abolishing the renunciation requirement. It also suggested that a country-wide public naturalization campaign should be initiated in order to encourage foreign residents to naturalize.[584]

In addition to the Green and the Left parliamentary groups, the Social-Democratic SPD also tabled two draft bills during the 17th legislative period which aimed at changing the naturalization law. The proposed legal changes resembled those proposed by the Green and the Liberal parliamentary groups: The SPD argued that naturalization in Germany should be further facilitated by reducing requirements, most notably by tolerating dual citizenship in all naturalization cases.[585] None of the different reform proposals which were tabled since the mid-2000s was adopted. All proposals were rejected or were still under discussion when the research for this study had to be closed.

While the bills and motions tabled by parliamentary groups in the Bundestag overall aimed at facilitating naturalization, discussions in the Bundesrat went into a different direction. Nine German Länder tabled a draft bill in 2007 which aimed at specifying and de facto increasing naturalization requirements. Among other measures, the bill proposed that foreign residents should only be entitled to acquire German citizenship if they pass an oral and written language test and if they can prove knowledge of constitutional values and norms. In order to impart this knowledge to foreign residents, the Länder proposed to organize naturalization courses. Further, they argued that rules as to which criminal convictions preclude naturalization should be tightened, but that the required residence period should be lowered for particularly well integrated foreign residents. Under these conditions, the Länder argued, it would be ensured that

---

584 See BT-Drs. 16/1770 of 31.05.2006; BT-Drs. 17/2351 of 30.06.2010.

585 See BT-Drs. 17/773 of 23.02.2010; BT-Drs. 17/7654 of 09.11.2011.

Table 10: Bills and motions to change the citizenship criterion of the franchise or to change access to German citizenship, tabled during electoral terms 15 to 17

Electoral period	Document number	Title	Authors	Proposed change of Citizenship law or Federal election law	Status of motion or bill
15	---	---	---	---	---
16	BT-Drs. 16/1770	Motion: Facilitating naturalization - Eliminating exclusion *("Antrag: Einbürgerung erleichtern - Ausgrenzung ausschließen")*	Die Linke	Facilitation of naturalization, e.g. by accepting dual citizenship, encouraging naturalization. Increase number of cases in which ius soli applies, abolishment of obligation to choose.	Rejected
	BT-Drs. 16/2650	Draft bill: Draft bill to change the Citizenship Act *("Gesetzesentwurf: Entwurf eines Gesetzes zur Änderung des Staatsangehörigkeits-rechtes")*	Bündnis 90/ Die Grünen	Facilitation of naturalization, e.g. by accepting dual citizenship. Increase number of cases in which ius soli applies, abolishment of obligation to choose.	Rejected
	BR-Drs. 137/07	Draft bill: Draft bill to change the Citizenship Act *("Gesetzesentwurf: Entwurf eines Gesetzes zur Änderung des Staatsangehörigkeits-gesetzes")*	Bundesrat	Increase naturalization requirements, e.g. by testing knowledge of German language.	Rejected
	BT-Drs. 16/5904	Motion: Introducing the municipal right to vote for third country citizens *("Antrag: Kommunales Wahlrecht für Drittstaatenangehörige einführen")*	Die Linke	Franchise for long-term third country citizens, first in municipal elections, later in state and federal elections.	Rejected
	BT-Drs. 16/9165	Motion: For the abolishment of the obligation to choose in the Citizenship Act *("Antrag: Für die Abschaffung der Optionspflicht im Staats-angehörigkeitsgesetz")*	Die Linke	Abolishment of obligation to choose.	Rejected

Continuation of Table 10

Electoral period	Document number	Title	Authors	Proposed change of Citizenship law or Federal election law	Status of motion or bill
16	BR-Drs. 647/08	Draft bill: Draft bill to amend the Citizenship Act *("Gesetzesantrag: Entwurf eines Gesetzes zur Änderung des Staatsangehörigkeitsgesetzes")*	Bundesrat	Abolishment of obligation to choose.	Rejected
	BT-Drs. 16/12849	Draft bill: Draft bill to cancel the obligation to choose from citizenship law *("Gesetzesentwurf: Entwurf eines Gesetzes zur Streichung des Optionszwangs aus dem Staatsangehörigkeitsrecht")*	Bündnis 90/ Die Grünen	Abolishment of obligation to choose.	Rejected
17	BT-Drs. 17/542	Draft bill: Draft bill to abolish the obligation to choose from citizenship law *("Gesetzesentwurf: Entwurf eines Gesetzes zur Streichung des Optionszwangs aus dem Staatsangehörigkeitsrecht")*	Bündnis 90/ Die Grünen	Abolishment of obligation to choose.	Rejected
	BT-Drs. 17/773	Draft bill: Draft bill to change the citizenship law *("Gesetzesentwurf: Entwurf eines Gesetzes zur Änderung des Staatsangehörigkeitsrechts")*	SPD	Abolishment of obligation to choose. Facilitation of naturalization, e.g. by accepting dual citizenship	Rejected
	BR-Drs. 142/10	Draft bill: Draft bill to change the Citizenship Act *("Gesetzesantrag: Entwurf eines Gesetzes zur Änderung des Staatsangehörigkeitsgesetzes")*	Bundesrat	Abolishment of obligation to choose.	Rejected

Continuation of Table 10

Electoral period	Document number	Title	Authors	Proposed change of Citizenship law or Federal election law	Status of motion or bill
17	BT-Drs. 17/1146	Motion: Introducing the municipal right to vote for third country citizens *("Antrag: Kommunales Wahlrecht für Drittstaatenangehörige einführen")*	Die Linke	Franchise for all foreign residents, first in municipal elections, later in state and federal elections.	Referred to responsible Committes
	BT-Drs. 17/2351	Motion: Eliminating exclusion - Comprehensively facilitating naturalization *("Antrag: Ausgrenzung beenden - Einbürgerungen umfassend erleichtern")*	Die Linke	Facilitation of naturalization, e.g. by accepting dual citizenship, abolishment of obligation to choose.	Rejected
	BT-Drs. 17/3411	Draft bill: Draft bill to change the citizenship law *("Gesetzesentwurf: Entwurf eines Gesetzes zur Änderung des Staatsangehörigkeitsrechts")*	Bündnis 90/ Die Grünen	Increase number of cases in which ius soli applies, abolishment of obligation to choose, facilitation of naturalization, e.g. by accepting dual citizenship.	Rejected
	BT-Drs. 17/5896	Draft bill: Draft bill to change the Basic Law and to reform the electoral law *("Gesetzesentwurf: Entwurf eines Gesetzes zur Änderung des Grund-gesetzes und zur Reformierung des Wahlrechts")*	Die Linke	Federal franchise for foreign residents after five years of residence in Germany.	Rejected
	BT-Drs. 17/7654	Motion: Modernising the citizenship law - Allowing multiple and dual citizenship *("Antrag: Staatsangehörigkeitsrecht modernisieren - Mehrfache bzw. doppelte Staatsbürgerschaft ermöglichen")*	SPD	Abolishment of obligation to choose, facilitation of naturalization, e.g. by accepting dual citizenship.	Referred to responsible Committees

Source: Legal documents obtained from Parliamentary Material Information System (in German: Dokumentations- und Informationssystem; DIP), accessible at: http://dipbt.bundestag.de/dip21.web/bt. See Annex 3.

only foreign residents who are well-integrated into German society and are in fact able to participate in the political and societal life may join the demos.[586]

In addition to naturalization requirements, the Green and the Left parliamentary groups as well as the SPD also addressed the ius soli-legislation in different motions and bills.[587] In particular, the parties recommended that the obligation to choose should be abolished. They justified this proposal by arguing that the obligation to choose might provoke conflicts between ius soli-citizens and their parents. In addition, they stressed that the congruence between the resident population and the electorate would be reduced if a large number of ius soli-citizens were to decide against the German citizenship. The parties also pointed out that the obligation to choose might be discriminatory and therefore constitutionally questionable, since it only concerns children who are dual citizens qua ius soli but not children who are dual citizens because they were born to parents with different citizenships. Further, they pointed out that the current legal situation binds excessive administrative resources since all ius soli-citizens have to be informed of their obligation to choose and advised about the complicated legal options.

In addition to abolishing the obligation to choose, parliamentary groups in the Bundestag also recommended to apply the ius soli-principle in a larger number of cases: Under currently applicable law, the German citizenship is acquired qua ius soli if at least one foreign parent has lived in Germany for eight years or more and is in possession of a permanent right of residence. The Green parliamentary group suggested that the required residence period should be shortened to six years or abolished for certain groups of foreign residents altogether, such as citizens from other EU member states. The Left

586 See BR-Drs. 137/07 of 23.02.2007, p. 1. The bill was introduced by the following Länder: Baden-Württemberg, Bavaria, Hamburg, Hessen, Lower Saxony, North Rhine-Westphalia, Rhineland-Palatinate, Saarland and Thuringia.

587 See BT-Drs. 16/2650 of 20.09.2006; BT-Drs. 16/9165 of 08.05.2008; BT-Drs. 16/12849 of 05.05.2009; BT-Drs. 17/542 of 27.01.2010; BT-Drs. 17/773 of 23.02.2010; BT-Drs. 17/2351 of 30.06.2010; BT-Drs. 17/3411 of 26.10.2010; BT-Drs. 17/7654 of 09.11.2011.

parliamentary group went even further by proposing that the ius soli-principle should be applied to all births in Germany.[588]

Concerns about the ius soli-regulation were shared by some Länder. Berlin, Bremen and Brandenburg tabled draft bills with the aim of abolishing the obligation to choose on two occasions and justified their bills with similar arguments as the above mentioned parliamentary groups.[589] To date, all proposals to reform the citizenship law which were tabled during the 16th electoral term and most of the proposals discussed during the 17th electoral term have failed to obtain the required majorities and were rejected. Only one of these reform proposals is still pending at the time of writing.

Proposals to integrate foreign residents into the demos by granting them the right to vote in Bundestag elections irrespective of their citizenship have also not been successful. The Left parliamentary group tabled several bills and motions during the 16th and 17th electoral period in order to grant long-term foreign residents the right to vote on all state levels, including in Bundestag elections.[590] It argued that since the reform of the citizenship law had failed to increase naturalization numbers, the political integration of long-term foreign residents should be achieved by means of their enfranchisement. The Left parliamentary group acknowledged that the Federal Constitutional Court had declared the introduction of the municipal franchise for third-country foreign residents unconstitutional under the current legal principles of the Basic Law. Based on this ruling, the members of the group proposed to change the Basic Law to allow for the enfranchisement of foreign residents on the municipal and/or federal

588 See BT-Drs. 16/1770 of 31.05.2006; BT-Drs. 16/2650 of 20.09.2006; BT-Drs. 17/3411 of 26.10.2010.

589 See BR-Drs. 647/08 of 02.09.2008; BR-Drs. 142/10 of 12.03.2010. Brandenburg only supported the second bill.

590 BT-Drs. 16/5904 of 04.07.2007; BT-Drs. 17/1146 of 23.03.2010; BT-Drs. 17/5896 of 25.05.2011. In addition, different parties in the Bundestag as well as Länder in the Bundesrat tabled bills and motions which aim at introducing the right to vote for foreign residents on the municipal level only (BT-Drs. 16/6628 of 10.10.2007; BT-Drs. 16/13165 of 27.05.2009; BT-Drs. 17/1047 of 16.03.2010; BT-Drs. 17/1150 of 23.03.2010; BR-Drs. 623/07 of 05.09.2007). Since this study focuses on federal level elections only, these bills and motions were not included in the table and not considered for the policy scenarios.

level in the future. Two of these bills and motions have been rejected and one is currently being discussed in the responsible committees of the Bundestag.

In order to quantify the impact of the different reform proposals on the development of the electorate, four policy assumptions were defined. These policy assumptions draw from the bills and motions which were tabled and discussed during the last ten years, but were not adopted. They can all be categorized either as falling under Hammar's 'voting rights model' or his 'naturalization model'. Only the bill tabled by the Bundesrat in 2007 (BT-Drs. 137/07), which aimed at increasing naturalization requirements, was not used for the policy assumptions. While the bill itself was rejected in the Bundestag, many of its proposals were in fact implemented when the Citizenship Act was amended in 2007 (see Chapter 2.3.3.).

Assumption Voting Rights Model **(VR)**: Enfranchisement of foreign residents after five years of lawful residence. The first policy assumption is based on the proposal to enfranchise all adult foreign residents after five years of permanent lawful residence in Germany. Estimating the number of individuals who might be affected by such a reform in the next years is a challenging endeavour since it depends on a large number of factors. If mainly short-term migrants come to Germany in the future and if many long-term foreign residents decide to re-migrate to their countries of origin or to third countries, the number of enfranchised individuals will be low. By contrast, if a larger number of immigrants decides to remain in Germany for more than five years and if foreign residents who are already living in Germany decide to stay, the number of persons who will be enfranchised might be very high. Future naturalization trends and the question whether children of foreign residents will acquire the German citizenship from birth will also play a role.

Overall, the multitude of assumptions that are necessary to project the foreign population of Germany by duration of residence would make it very difficult to arrive at reliable conclusions. For this reason, it was decided here to proceed with the following, simpler estimation procedure: In the year 2000, around 77% of all foreign residents had lived in Germany for five years or longer (Figure 71). During the years that followed, this share increased slightly. In 2010, 83%

of all foreign residents in Germany had lived there for at least five years. Following this trend, it was assumed here that the proportion of foreign residents who fulfil the residence requirement of five years will remain at an average level of 80% during the projection period. In other words, it was assumed that four out of five adult foreign residents who are projected to live in Germany in the future would join the electorate if the voting rights model was introduced.

Figure 71: Proportion of foreign residents (all ages) by residence duration in Germany, 2000-2010

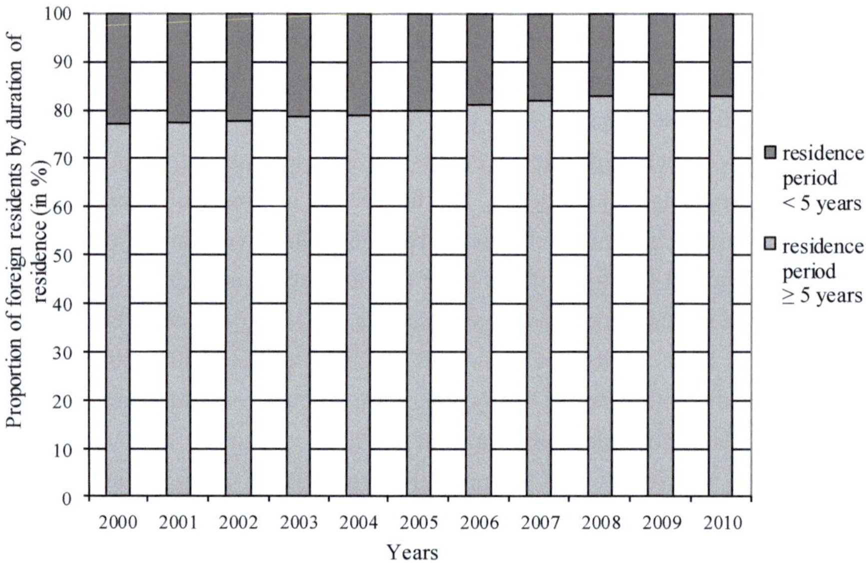

Source: Own illustration. Data taken from Statistics on foreign population, obtained from the Federal Statistical Office.

<u>Assumption Naturalization Model 1 **(N1)**: Facilitation and encouragement of naturalization.</u> The next policy assumption draws on the proposal that foreign residents should be encouraged to naturalize in Germany and that naturalization requirements should be lowered, for instance by reducing fees, by lowering the required duration of residence in Germany or by abolishing the requirement to renounce the previous citizenship. The proposal to accept dual citizenship is one

of the most frequently mentioned proposals. Many academics and policy makers assume that if this requirement was abolished, foreign residents' willingness to naturalize would increase and the naturalization rate in Germany would rise. Nonetheless, it is far from certain whether a reduction of naturalization requirements would indeed have this effect. Many factors may influence foreign residents' willingness to naturalize, among them micro-level characteristics such as age or period of residence, meso-level characteristics such as the support or disapproval of family members or the larger community as well as macro-level factors such as political or economic developments in Germany and countries of origin. The exact influence of each of these factors is not clear.

Due to the difficulty of estimating the influence of legal changes on future naturalization trends, a simplified assumption had to be made: In 2005, the following Western European countries (among the 15 'old' EU-member states) allowed naturalization candidates to retain their previous citizenship: Belgium, Finland, France, Greece, Ireland, Italy, Portugal, Sweden and the United Kingdom.[591] These countries had an average naturalization rate of 3.3% in the same year.[592] It was assumed here that the naturalization rate in Germany would increase and remain at this same average level of 3.3% throughout the projection period if naturalization requirements would be reduced. Nonetheless, it is important to stress that this is a simplified assumption. It is not certain that naturalization rates would indeed rise to such an extent after a change of the citizenship law.

Assumption Naturalization Model 2 **(N2)**: Extension of ius soli-principle. The next assumption focuses on the ius soli-principle. The Green and the Left parliamentary groups have suggested to extend the scope of application of the ius soli-legislation so that more children born in Germany acquire German

591 See *Chopin, I.*, Administrative practices, 2006, p. 251.

592 Own calculation based on the following data: Data for France and Greece taken from the Eurostat statistics on 'Acquisition of citizenship', available at: http://epp.eurostat.ec.europa.eu/portal/page/portal/population/data/main_tables (last retrieved on 16.01.2013); data for other countries taken from: *Organisation for Economic Co-operation and Development (OECD)*, Migration outlook, 2009, Statistical Series A.1.6. Acquisition of nationality in selected OECD countries. More recent data reveal that the naturalization rate was still at an average level of 3.3% in these countries in 2009: *Sartori, F.*, Acquisitions, 2011, p. 3.

citizenship at birth. The Green parliamentary group proposed that all children born to citizens from other EU countries should acquire German citizenship at birth, as well as children who would otherwise be stateless. The Left parliamentary group went further by proposing that all children born in Germany should acquire German citizenship at birth, as it is already practiced for instance in the USA. Here, the effects of the more radical proposal of the Left parliamentary group shall be tested. It will be assumed that all children who are born in Germany to a foreign mother acquire the German citizenship qua ius soli during the projection period.

Assumption Naturalization model 3 **(N3)**: Abolishment of obligation to choose.
The last policy assumption draws on the different bills and motions which propose to abolish the obligation to choose. It will be assumed that these proposals will be adopted and that ius soli-citizens will not be required to opt between their citizenships by age 23 during the entire projection period.

7.2. Overview of scenarios

The six policy assumptions which were defined in Chapter 7.1. are presented as an overview in Table 11. Two assumptions were defined that target the age criterion of the franchise and four assumptions were defined which focus on the political integration of foreign residents and their children.

The effect of these six reform proposals on the development of the electorate will be tested separately, resulting in six 'single assumption' scenarios (see Table 12: scenarios 1 to 6). Additionally, the assumptions were combined to four 'mixed assumption' scenarios (scenarios 7 to 10). Each of these mixed scenarios shows how different combinations of reforms would influence the electorate if they were enacted jointly. Thus, scenario 7 for instance shows how the proportion of electors and the median age of the electorate would develop if the voting age were to be lowered to 16 years and adult foreign residents were entitled to vote after five years of legal residence in Germany. Scenario 10 quantifies the effects of the proxy vote model if it would be combined with the three naturalization model assumptions, i.e. a facilitation of naturalization, an extension of the ius soli-principle and the abolishment of the obligation to choose. The results of the different single and mixed assumption scenarios will be presented in the following.

Table 11: Overview of policy assumptions

Criterion	Model	Abbreviation	Assumptions
Age criterion	Voting age model	**VA**	Minimum voting age is lowered to 16 years
	Proxy vote model	**PV**	Minimum voting age is completely abolished
Citizenship criterion	Voting rights model	**VR**	Enfranchisement of foreign residents after five years of lawful residence
	Naturalization model	**N1**	Facilitation and encouragement of naturalization
		N2	Extension of ius soli principle
		N3	Abolishment of obligation to choose

Source: Own illustration

Table 12: Overview: Combining policy assumptions into scenarios

<table>
<tr><td colspan="3" rowspan="3"></td><td colspan="2">Age criterion</td></tr>
<tr><td>VA</td><td>PV</td></tr>
<tr><td>Sc. 1</td><td>Sc. 2</td></tr>
<tr><td rowspan="4">Citizenship criterion</td><td>VR</td><td>Sc. 3</td><td>Sc. 7</td><td>Sc. 8</td></tr>
<tr><td>N1</td><td>Sc. 4</td><td rowspan="3">Sc. 9</td><td rowspan="3">Sc. 10</td></tr>
<tr><td>N2</td><td>Sc. 5</td></tr>
<tr><td>N3</td><td>Sc. 6</td></tr>
</table>

Source: Own illustration

7.3. Projection results

7.3.1. Single assumption scenarios

In the *first policy scenario* it was assumed that the minimum voting age would be lowered from 18 to 16 years in 2010 and remain at this level throughout the projection period. All 16- to 17- year old German citizens – including ius soli-citizens – would acquire the active right to vote and become members of the electorate. Figure 72 shows the number of adolescents who would profit from this reform in each projection year.

In 2010, around 1.5 million German citizens were 16 or 17 years old and would therefore have been enfranchised. According to the 16 demographic projections presented in the previous chapter, the number of 16- and 17- year old German citizens will decrease during the projection period. In 2030 roughly 1.3 million 16- and 17- year old Germans will live in Germany and would profit from a reduction of the minimum voting age.

Figure 72: Projected number of German citizens aged 16 and 17, 2010-2030

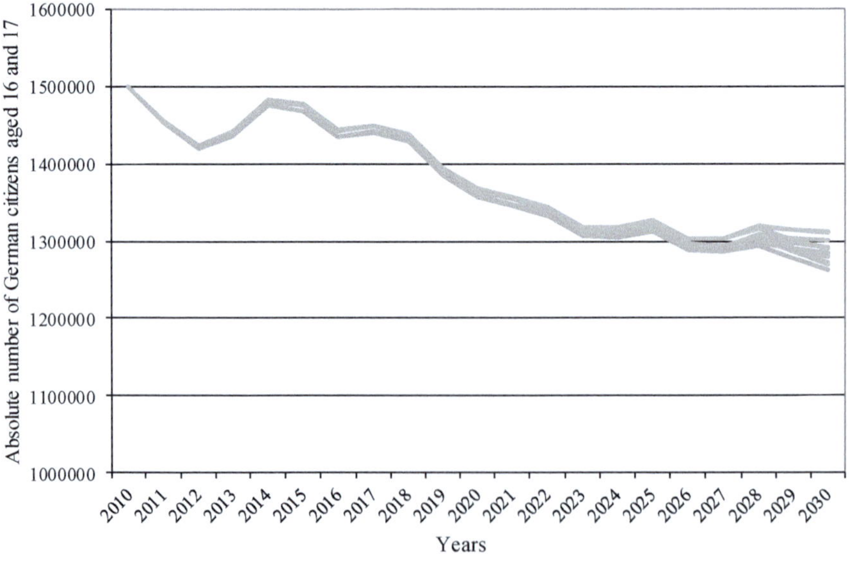

Source: Own calculations based on demographic data provided by the Federal Statistical Office.

Even though more than one million individuals would profit from the first policy scenario in each projection year, the effect on the proportion of eligible voters would be modest. This becomes visible in Figure 73.

Figure 73: Projected proportion of eligible voters among the resident population of Germany, 2010-2030. No legal changes (left) versus policy scenario 1 (right)

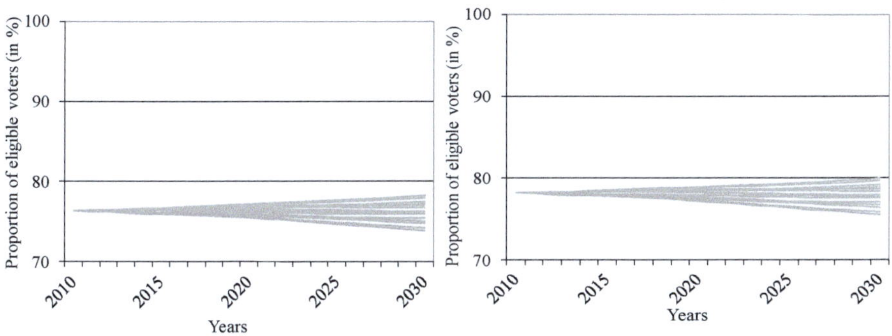

Source: Own calculations based on demographic data provided by the Federal Statistical Office.

The left side of the figure shows how the proportion of eligible voters would develop in each of the 16 demographic scenarios provided that the electoral law and citizenship law would remain unchanged. The right side of the figure shows how this indicator would develop in the same 16 demographic scenarios if the voting age would be defined as 16 years throughout the projection period.

If the minimum voting age had been lowered to 16 years in 2010, 78% rather than 76% of all residents of Germany would have been members of the electorate. In 2030, the proportion of eligible voters would lie between 76% and 80% rather than between 74% and 78%. In other words, irrespective of whether a reduction of the voting age is assumed or not, the general trend stays the same: The proportion of eligible voters may decline or increase in the future and the projected values for 2030 lie within a range of four percentage points both with and without the reform.

The enfranchisement of 16- to 17- year old citizens would also have a minor effect on the development of the median age of the electorate only (Figure 74). In the 16 demographic scenarios presented in the previous chapter, the median age would increase from 49.8 years (2010) to between 56.0 and 57.2 years (2030), provided that the current legal framework would be maintained (left side of the figure). This would amount to an increase of 6.2 to 7.4 years during the projection period.

Figure 74: Projected median age of the electorate, 2010-2030. No legal changes (left) versus policy scenario 1 (right)

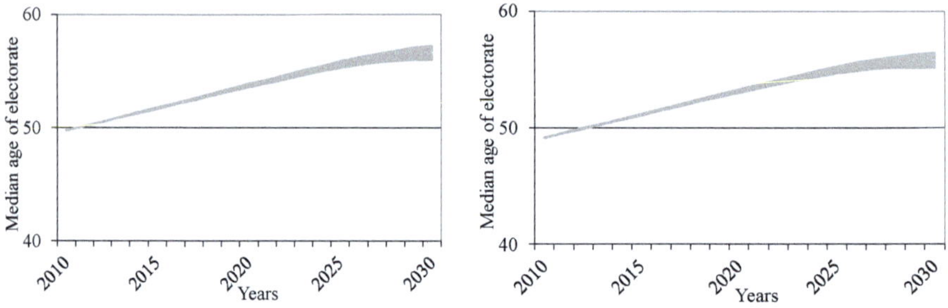

Source: Own calculations based on demographic data provided by the Federal Statistical Office.

By including 16- and 17-year old adolescents into the electorate, the median age would initially be lowered to 49.1 years in 2010. Until 2030, it would rise to between 55.2 and 56.4 years, which would amount to a similar increase of around 6.1 to 7.3 years (right side of the figure). By lowering the voting age, the demographically induced increase of the median age would thus not slow down. The only impact of the first policy scenario would be that the increase of the median age would start from at a slightly lower level.

The *second policy scenario* would have a stronger impact. It was assumed that the voting age requirement would be completely abolished, i.e. that the right to vote would be conferred to all German citizens irrespective of their age. In 2010, 12.5 million German citizens aged 0 to 17 were living in Germany, including ius soli-citizens (see Figure 75).

If the voting age requirement had been abolished in this year, the electorate would thus have increased by more than 12 million members. Until 2030, the population of German children and adolescents will decline. As the demographic scenarios presented in the previous chapter reveal, between 10.0 and 11.7 million German children aged 0 to 17 will live in Germany in that year, depending on which demographic scenario is chosen. In 2030, the electorate would thus count between 10 and 12 million additional members, provided that the voting age criterion would to remain abolished throughout the projection period.

Figure 75: Projected number of underage German citizens, 2010-2030

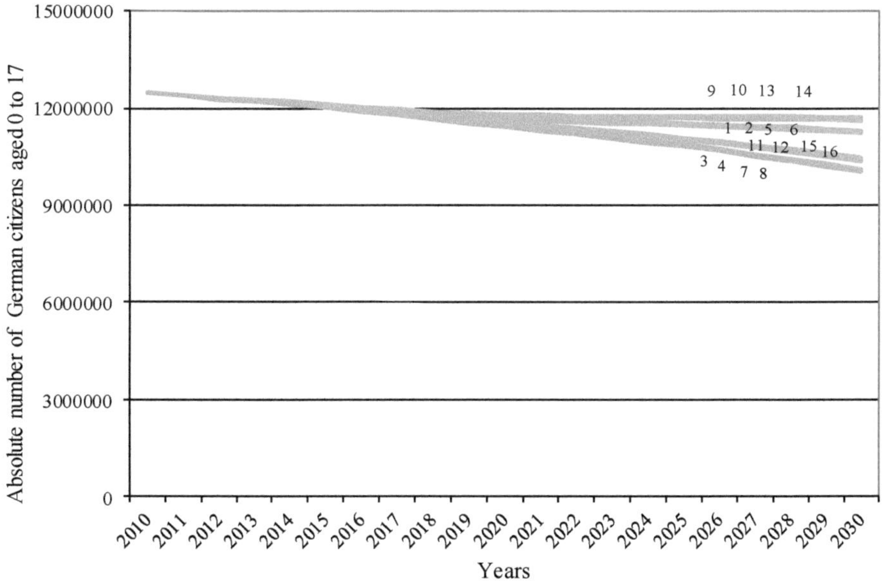

Source: Own calculations based on demographic data provided by the Federal Statistical Office.

The proportion of eligible voters in Germany would increase substantially as a result of this reform (Figure 76). It would have increased by 15 percentage points in 2010 if the minimum voting age had been abolished in that year: Instead of 76%, almost 92% of all residents of Germany would have been entitled to vote. In 2030, the proportion of eligible voters would still be between 13 and 14 percentage points higher than in the absence of the reform, depending on the scenario. Between 88% and 91% of all members of the resident population would enjoy the right to vote, rather than between 74% and 78%.

Figure 76: Projected proportion of eligible voters among the resident population of Germany, 2010-2030. No legal changes (left) versus policy scenario 2 (right)

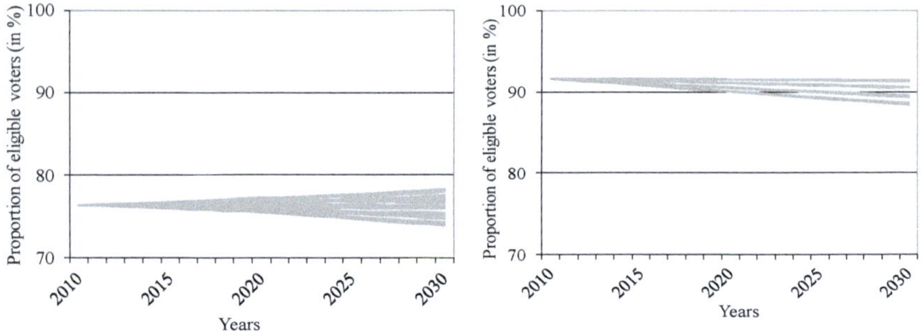

Source: Own calculations based on demographic data provided by the Federal Statistical Office.

The abolishment of the age requirement would also have a strong impact on the median age of the electorate (Figure 77). If the minimum voting age had been abolished in 2010, the median age would have declined immediately by nearly five years from 49.8 years to 44.9 years. If the age criterion would remain abolished during the projection period, the median age would reach between 49 and 51 years in 2030, around 7 years less than in the absence of a reform.

Figure 77: Projected median age of the electorate, 2010-2030. No legal changes (left) versus policy scenario 2 (right)

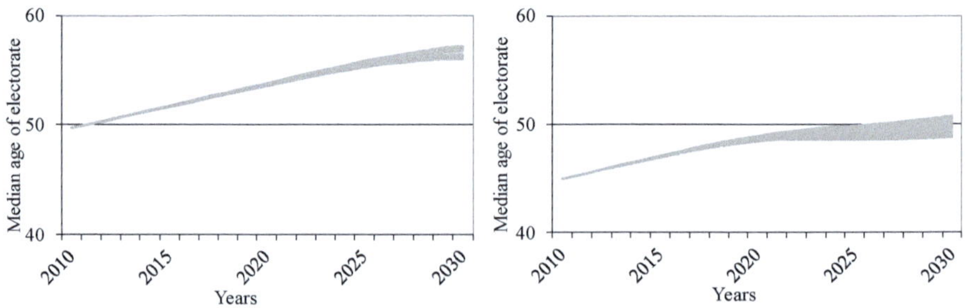

Source: Own calculations based on demographic data provided by the Federal Statistical Office.

The *third policy scenario* tests how many adult foreign residents (aged 18 and older) would profit from an enfranchisement after five years of legal residence in Germany and how this reform would influence the development of the electorate. Due to a lack of data on the future composition of the foreign population by length of residence, a continuation of past trends was assumed: It is expected that 80% of the adult foreign population in Germany would fulfil the residence requirement in each projection year and thus gain the right to vote.[593]

Figure 78: Projected number of adult foreign residents in Germany, 2010-2030

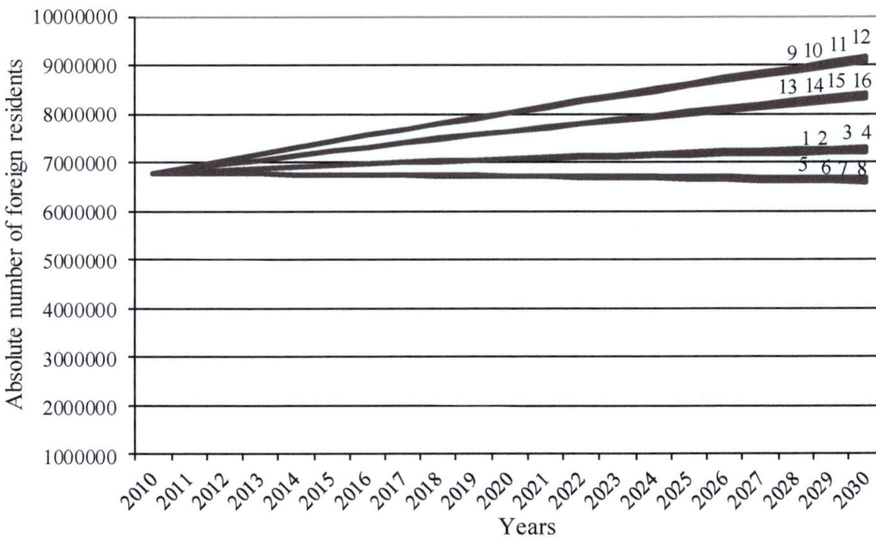

Source: Own calculations based on demographic data provided by the Federal Statistical Office.

Following this assumption, 4.6 million foreign residents would have joined the electorate in 2010 (Figure 78). In the future, the number of adult foreign residents who would profit from the voting rights reform depends on how theforeign population will develop. If the foreign population will grow strongly over the next twenty years (demographic scenarios 9 to 12) a maximum of 6.7 million adult foreign residents would acquire the right to vote in Bundestag elections in 2030. Conversely, if the adult foreign population will increase only slightly in size (scenarios 5 to 8) around 4.9 million foreign residents would profit from the reform in 2030.

593 See Chapter 7.1.2.2.

By including these long-term foreign residents into the electorate, the proportion of eligible voters would increase substantially. If the reform had been introduced in 2010, it would have increased immediately by 5.6 percentage points from 76.4% to 82.0% (see Figure 79). In 2030, the proportion of eligible voters among the total population would even be between 7 and 8 percentage points higher than in the absence of the reform: It would reach between 82% and 85% rather than between 74% and 78%.

Figure 79: Projected proportion of eligible voters among the resident population of Germany, 2010-2030. No legal changes (left) versus policy scenario 3 (right)

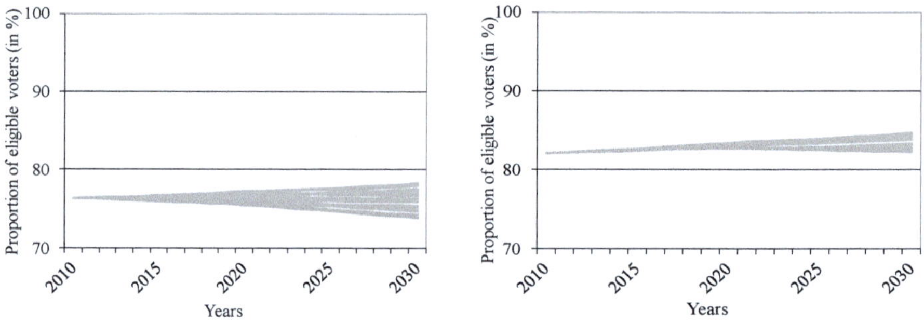

Source: Own calculations based on demographic data provided by the Federal Statistical Office.

It is remarkable that the proportion of eligible voters might increase or decrease during the projection period if the current legal framework was maintained (left side of figure), but that it increases in all scenarios once the majority of foreign residents are enfranchised in policy scenario 3 (right side of figure). This may appear somewhat surprising at first glance. It can however be explained by referring back to the demographic scenarios presented in Chapter 6: Until 2030, the proportion of foreign residents among the population in Germany will grow in all 16 projection scenarios. By enfranchising the majority of them, the degree to which they add to the proportion of eligible voters must also increase over time and put an upward pressure on the proportion of eligible voters.

The adoption of the voting rights model is also likely to affect the median age of the electorate, since the foreign population has a younger age structure than the German population. Figure 80 shows the size of the different age groups among the German and among the foreign population in the base-year of the population projection, 2010. As can be seen, the age groups 40 to 50 are the quantitatively strongest among the German population. Among the foreign population, by contrast, age groups 30 to 40 are quantitatively strong.

Figure 80: Populations of German citizens and of foreign residents by age and sex, 2010

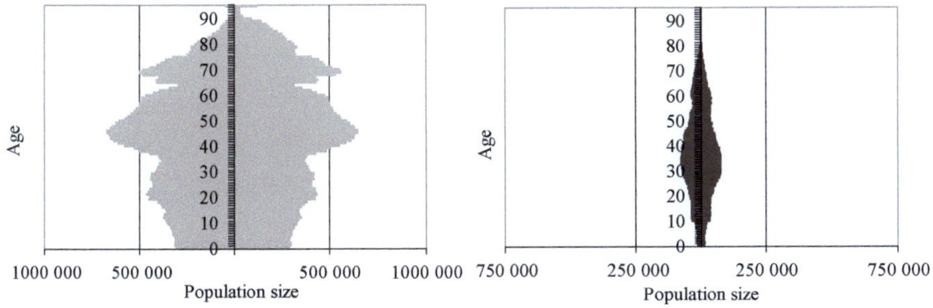

Source: Own illustration based on Population Statistics of 2010, obtained from the Federal Statistical Office.

If 80% of the adult foreign population had been enfranchised in 2010, a relatively large number of younger adults would therefore have joined the electorate. This would have lowered the median age of the electorate. Nonetheless, it is not possible to quantify the effect of the voting rights model on the development of the median age during the entire projection period. This would require detailed information on how many foreign residents would fulfil the residence requirement of five years in each age group and in each projection year. Such detailed information can only be obtained by more complex projections than have been calculated here.[594] Given that foreign residents are on average younger than Germans, it appears at least likely that the enfranchisement of long-term foreign residents would have a depressing effect on the median age, both in 2010 and beyond.

594 Such a projection would have to distinguish by age, sex, citizenship and duration of residence, thus increasing the number of assumptions, raising data requirements and adding more complexity to the model and calculations.

In *the fourth policy scenario*, it was assumed that 3.3% of all foreign residents would acquire German citizenship in each projection year. Figure 81 shows the absolute number of persons who would naturalize in the demographic scenarios over time, given this assumption.

Figure 81: Projected number of naturalization cases in Germany, 2010-2030

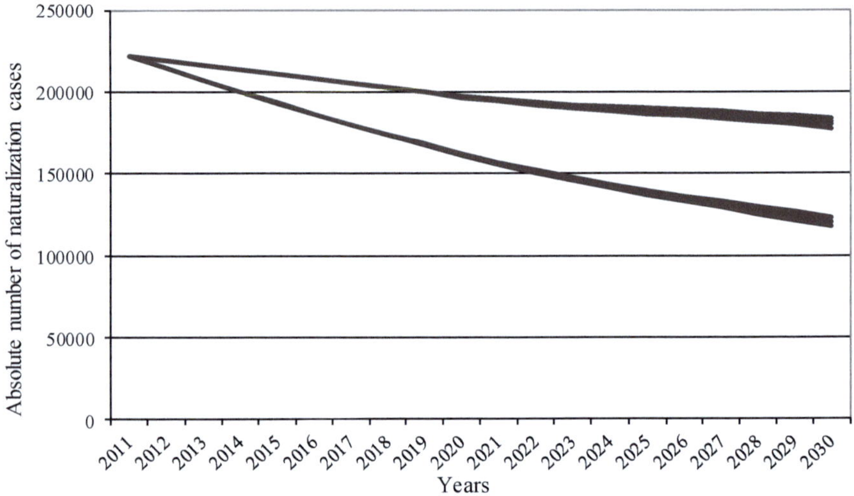

Source: Own calculations based on demographic data provided by the Federal Statistical Office.

In the first projection year around 222.000 foreign residents would acquire German citizenship. During the projection period, the number of naturalization cases would develop along one of two possible trajectories, depending on which migration assumption is chosen in the scenarios. If future net migration levels among foreign residents are high (+200.000 persons), the annual number of naturalization cases would decline modestly to reach around 184.000 persons in 2030. If net migration numbers are lower (+100.000 persons), the decline in naturalization numbers would be stronger. Around 118.000 persons would acquire the German citizenship in 2030. It is important to note that not all naturalized persons would immediately join the German electorate. The numbers displayed in Figure 81 also include children and adolescents of minor age who would only become members of the electorate upon reaching the minimum voting age. Adult foreign residents, by contrast, would gain voting rights immediately after acquiring German citizenship.

Figure 82: Projected proportion of eligible voters among the resident population of Germany, 2010-2030. No legal changes (left) versus policy scenario 4 (right)

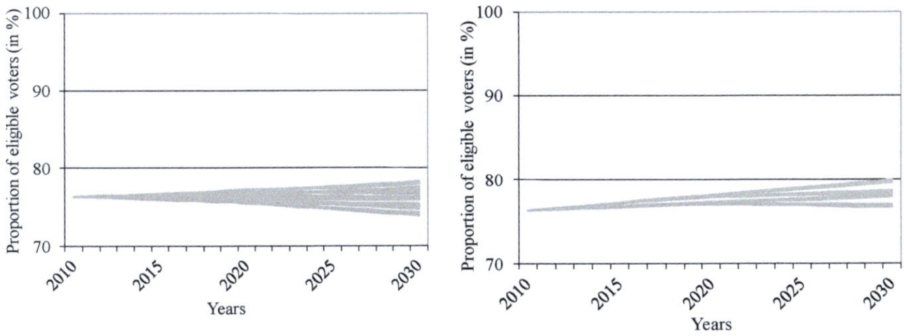

Source: Own calculations based on demographic data provided by the Federal Statistical Office.

The proportion of eligible voters would increase over the projection period once 3.3% of all foreign residents would naturalize each year (see Figure 82). From 76% in 2010 it would increase to between 77% and 80% in 2030. In other words, even in scenarios which assume a high annual net migration level of +200.000 persons per year, a naturalization rate of 3.3% would suffice to increase the congruence between the resident population and the electorate. By contrast, if the naturalization rate would remain at a level of 1.0% or 1.6%, as presumed in the 16 demographic scenarios in the previous chapter, a decline in the proportion of eligible voters would be possible (left graph in Figure 82): At the lower end of the spectrum, the indicator might decrease to 74%.

The median age of the electorate also increases somewhat more slowly during the projection period and would reach between 55.4 and 56.5 years in 2030 if a naturalization rate of 3.3% is assumed. In the 16 demographic scenarios which were calculated in the previous chapter and that presumed naturalization rates of 1.0% and 1.6%, by contrast, the median age of the electorate would reach between 56.0 and 57.2 years in 2030. The median age would thus be around 0.6

year lower in 2030 if a naturalization rate of 3.3% could be maintained during the projection period (Figure 83).

Figure 83: Projected median age of the electorate, 2010-2030. No legal changes (left) versus policy scenario 4 (right)

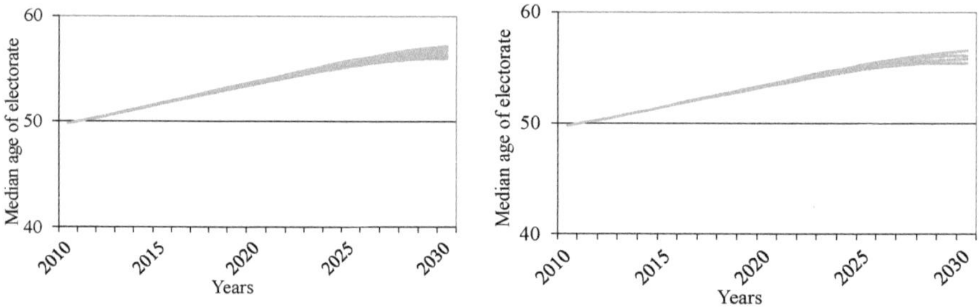

Source: Own calculations based on demographic data provided by the Federal Statistical Office.

By contrast to the preceding policy scenarios, both policy scenarios five and six only have a minor impact on the development of the electorate. In *policy scenario five* it was assumed that the ius soli-principle would be extended and that all children born to foreign parents in Germany would become German citizens at birth. In 2010, around 27.000 newborn children would have profited from this reform (see Figure 84). These children would otherwise not have acquired German citizenship, since their parents currently do not fulfil the ius soli-requirements.

In the later projection years, the number of children who would profit from an extended ius soli-principle would strongly be influenced both by migration developments and the fertility rates of foreign women. The number of children who profit from the reform would be largest if migration numbers and fertility rates are high (scenarios 9 and 10, as well as 13 and 14). Under the assumptions taken in scenario 10, for instance, 27.000 newborn children would acquire German citizenship in 2030. Conversely, if the fertility of foreign women declines during the projection period and if net migration numbers are lower, the additional number of children who acquire German citizenship qua ius soli would decline to around 12.400 children in 2030 (scenarios 7 and 8).

Figure 84: Projected additional number of children who would acquire German citizenship qua ius soli, 2010-2030

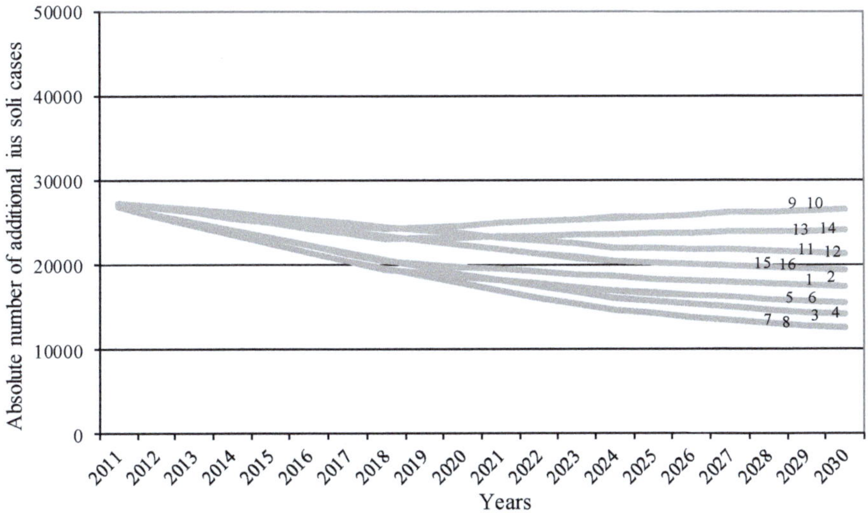

Source: Own calculations based on demographic data provided by the Federal Statistical Office.

The effect of this reform on the electorate would be minimal. While the proportion of eligible voters would lie between 73.90% and 78.25% in 2030 in case the current ius soli legislation is retained, it would reach a marginally higher range of 73.95% and 78.29% under the new regulation (Figure 85). The median age of the electorate would equally decrease only minimally as a consequence of the reform. Instead of reaching between 56.00 and 57.19 years, it would lie between 55.98 and 57.17 years in 2030 (see Figure 86).

The fact that an extension of the ius soli-principle has so little visible effect on how the median age of the electorate develops during the projection period does not mean that its long-term effects will be equally negligible. Children who would profit from the ius soli-reform only join the electorate 18 years after their birth. The first cohort of ius soli-citizens who would profit from the reform in this scenario was born in 2010 and would join the electorate in 2028. Later born cohorts would acquire full voting rights in the years thereafter. During the projection period of twenty years which is considered here, only the first three cohorts born in 2010, 2011 and 2012 would reach the minimum voting age of 18 years and join the electorate. This explains the very low effect of the reform according to the scenario results. If a longer time period would be considered, more ius soli-cohorts would reach the minimum voting age and stronger effects might be detected. Consequently, it should not be followed from the little effects visible here that the extension of the ius soli-principle would not influence the median age of the electorate somewhat more strongly in the longer term.

Figure 85: Projected proportion of eligible voters among the resident population of Germany, 2010-2030. No legal changes (left) versus policy scenario 5 (right)

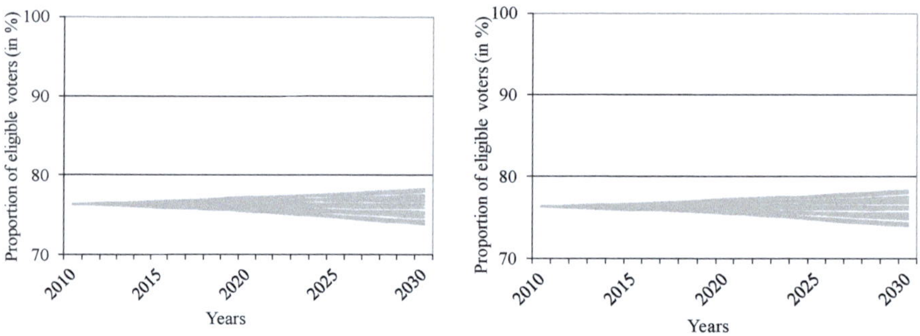

Source: Own calculations based on demographic data provided by the Federal Statistical Office.

Figure 86: Projected median age of the electorate, 2010-2030. No legal changes (left) versus policy scenario 5 (right)

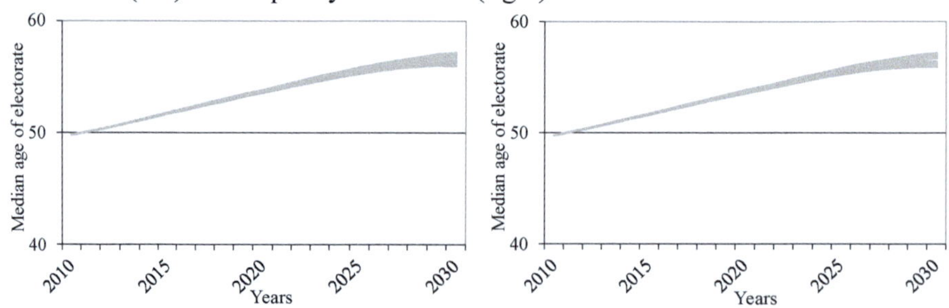

Source: Own calculations based on demographic data provided by the Federal Statistical Office.

The effect of *policy scenario six* on the development of the electorate would also be very small. In this policy scenario it was assumed that the obligation to choose would be abolished. Ius soli-citizens would be entitled to retain both their German citizenship and their foreign citizenship beyond their 23rd birthday. In the demographic scenarios calculated in the preceding chapter, it was assumed that 90% of all ius soli-citizens will retain their German citizenship – either because they opt for it or because they are entitled to keep both citizenships under one of the exception clauses.[595] If the obligation to choose were to be abolished, the number of additional ius soli-citizens who would retain the German citizenship would therefore be small. Only the remaining 10% of ius soli-citizens who were assumed to lose the German citizenship during the projection period would profit. The size of this group of ius soli-citizens can be predicted fairly accurately, since the ius soli-cohorts who will turn 23 during the projection period were already born in 2010, the base-year of the projections (Figure 87).

Figure 87: Projected number of additional ius soli-citizens who would keep their German citizenship, 2010-2030

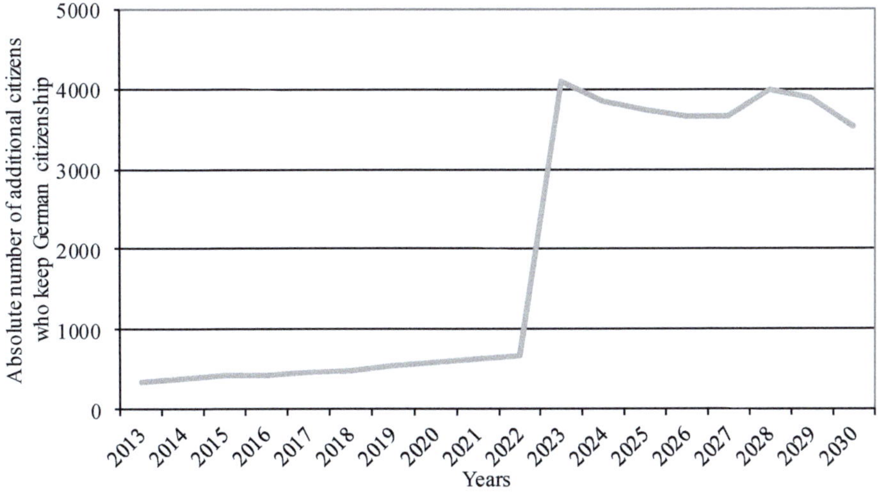

Source: Own calculations based on demographic data provided by the Federal Statistical Office.

595 For more detailed information on the legal rules, see Chapter 2.3.3.

Between 2013 and 2022, around 330 to 670 individuals would profit from the reform. Starting from 2023, the quantitatively larger cohorts of ius soli-citizens who were born after the enactment of the citizenship reform in 2000 will turn 23. From this year onwards, the 10% minority of ius soli-citizens who were presumed to lose their German citizenship due to the current obligation to choose would comprise between 3.500 and 4.100 individuals per year.

Figure 88: Projected proportion of eligible voters among the resident population of Germany, 2010-2030. No legal changes (left) versus policy scenario 6 (right)

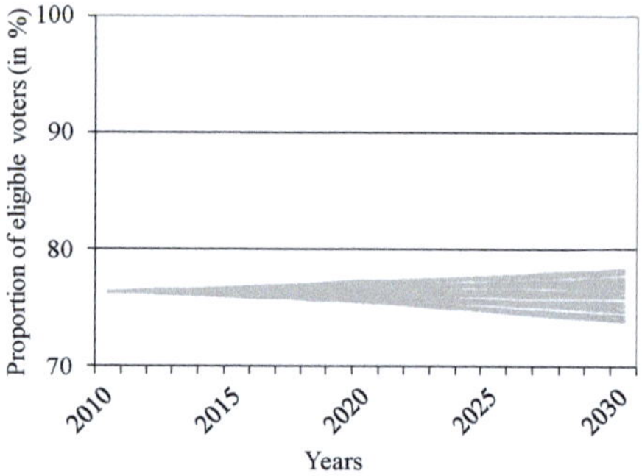

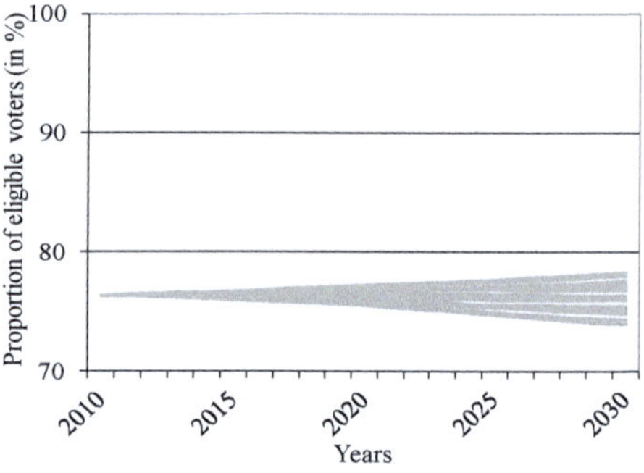

Source: Own calculations based on demographic data provided by the Federal Statistical Office.

Figure 89: Projected median age of the electorate, 2010-2030. No legal changes (left) versus policy scenario 6 (right)

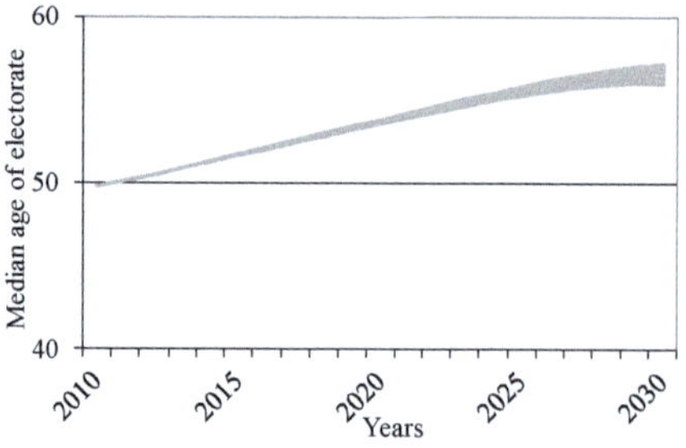

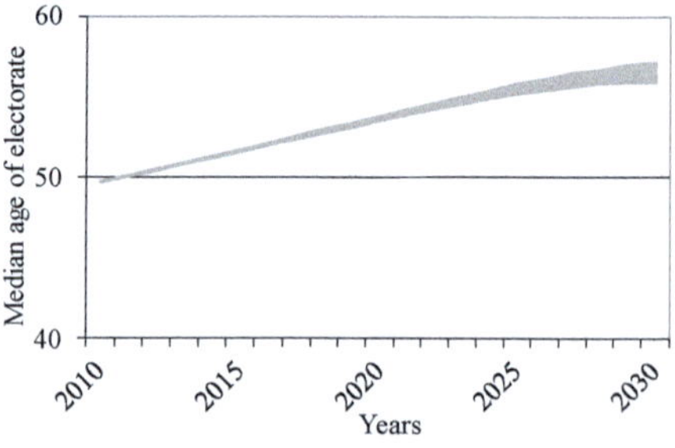

Source: Own calculations based on demographic data provided by the Federal Statistical Office.

These numbers are too small to substantially influence the future size and age structure of the electorate. Under current legal conditions, the proportion of eligible voters would range between 73.90% and 78.25% in 2030. Abolishing the obligation to choose would only raise these proportions minimally to 73.93% and 78.29%, respectively (Figure 88). The reform would also not have a strong effect on the development of the median age. Under current legal conditions, it would reach between 56.00 and 57.19 years in 2030. If the obligation to choose would be abolished, it would lie between 55.98 and 57.17 years in the last projection year (Figure 89).

Table 13 shows the main findings for the single assumption scenarios in a comparative overview. The upper part of the table shows the proportion of eligible voters in 2010 in case the different policy reforms would have been enacted in that year (short term impact of reform) and how this indicator would develop until 2030 (longer-term impact of reform). For 2030, the table shows both the highest and lowest possible value which might be reached according to the projection results. To facilitate comparison, the last row of the upper table shows how the proportion of eligible voters would develop in 2010 and until 2030 (maximum and minimum values) in the 16 demographic scenarios presented in the previous chapter. These scenarios assumed that the current legal framework would not be changed until the end of the projection period. The lower part of the table shows the findings – short- and long-term effects of the reforms as well as the development in the absence of reforms – for the median age of the electorate.

The proxy vote model would have the quantitatively strongest effect on the proportion of eligible voters and the median age of the electorate (values highlighted in bold in the table). The proportion of eligible voters would increase most strongly in this scenario, both in the short (i.e. in 2010) and in the longer term (until 2030). The median age of the electorate would also increase less strongly than in any other scenario.

The voting rights model has the second-strongest impact on the proportion of eligible voters, again both in the short and in the longer term (in italics). The voting age model and the naturalization model come next in terms of quantitative impact. In direct comparison, the impact of the former scenario on the proportion of eligible voters is somewhat stronger in the short term (in 2010), whereas high naturalization rates have a stronger impact in the longer term (until 2030). The voting age model also has the second strongest impact on the development of the median age. Policy scenarios five and six (extension of ius soli-principle and abolishment of obligation to choose) only have a minimum impact on the indicators measured here, at least during a projection period of twenty years.

Table 13: Overview of results, policy scenarios 1 to 6

Single assumption policy scenarios	**Proportion of eligible voters**		
	2010	2030 - minimum	2030 - maximum
1 - Voting age (VA)	78.20	75.53	79.90
2 - Proxy vote (PV)	**91.68**	**88.41**	**91.47**
3 - Voting rights (VR)	*82.03*	*82.29*	*84.72*
4 - Naturalization rate (N1)	76.35	76.75	79.96
5 - Extension ius soli (N2)	76.35	73.95	78.29
6 - Abolishment obligation to choose (N3)	76.35	73.93	78.29
16 Demographic scenarios (no legal changes)	76.35	73.90	78.25
Single assumption policy scenarios	**Median age**		
	2010	2030 - minimum	2030 - maximum
1 - Voting age (VA)	*49.15*	*55.15*	*56.39*
2 - Proxy vote (PV)	**44.95**	**48.78**	**50.74**
3 - Voting rights (VR)	---	---	---
4 - Naturalization rate (N1)	49.76	55.37	56.49
5 - Extension ius soli (N2)	49.76	55.98	57.17
6 - Abolishment obligation to choose (N3)	49.76	55.98	57.17
16 Demographic scenarios (no legal changes)	49.76	56.00	57.19

Source: Own illustration

7.3.2. *Mixed assumption scenarios*

If the six policy reforms would not be adopted individually but in combination, the effect on the electorate would be stronger. The influence of different combinations of reforms can be quantified with the help of the four mixed assumption scenarios calculated here.

In *policy scenario seven*, the voting age reform and the voting rights reform were combined. In other words, it was assumed that the minimum voting age would be lowered to 16 years, and that all adult foreign residents who have lawfully lived in Germany for at least five years – presumably 80% of the foreign population – would acquire the right to vote in 2010. It was further assumed that these rights would not be changed throughout the projection period. The effect of the reforms on the proportion of eligible voters are visualized in Figure 90. Since a projection based on age, sex and citizenship does not provide information on residence duration of foreign residents by age (see explanation on policy scenario 3), the effect on the median age of the electorate could not be calculated for this scenario.

Figure 90: Projected proportion of eligible voters among the resident population of Germany, 2010-2030. No legal changes (left) versus policy scenario 7 (right)

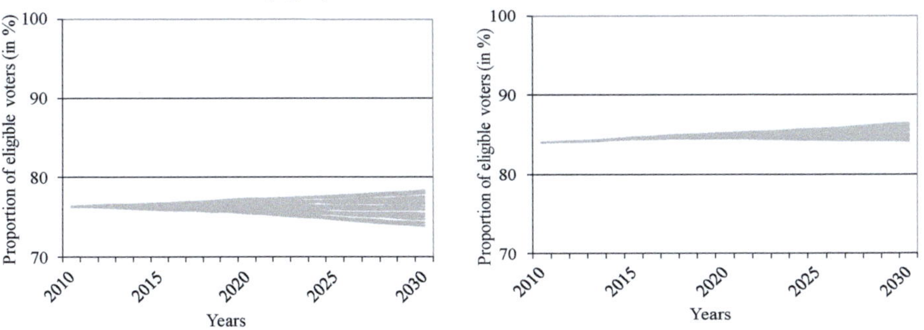

Source: Own calculations based on demographic data provided by the Federal Statistical Office.

By enfranchising both 16- and 17-year old German citizens and long-term adult foreign residents, the proportion of eligible voters would immediately increase from 76.4% to 84.0% in 2010. Only 16% of the resident German population would remain disenfranchised, most of them German children aged 0 to 15.

Until 2030, the combination of the voting rights model and the voting age model would prevent the proportion of eligible voters from declining. It would remain stable at 84.0% or even increase to a level of 86.4%.

An even stronger congruence between resident population and electorate could be reached in *policy scenario eight*. In this scenario, the proxy vote model and the voting rights model were combined, i.e. it was assumed that the minimum voting age would be abolished and that long-term foreign residents would be granted the right to vote. By enfranchising all German children and adolescents and most adult foreign residents, the proportion of eligible voters would immediately increase to 98.3% in 2010 (Figure 91). Throughout the projection period, the proportion of eligible voters would remain high: Between 97.7% and 98.3% of the resident population would be members of the demos in 2030.

Figure 91: Projected proportion of eligible voters among the resident population of Germany, 2010-2030. No legal changes (left) versus policy scenario 8 (right)

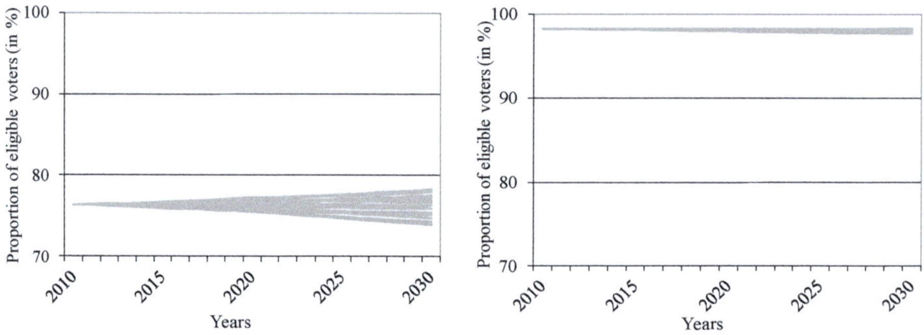

Source: Own calculations based on demographic data provided by the Federal Statistical Office.

The effect of *policy scenario nine* would be somewhat more modest. In this policy scenario, it was assumed that the voting age would be lowered to 16 years and that the German citizenship law would be reformed, resulting in an increase in the naturalization rate, an extension of the ius soli-principle and an abolishment of the obligation to choose. If implemented together, these reforms would initially increase the proportion of eligible voters by two percentage points from 76.4% to 78.2%. Over time, the effect of the reforms would become stronger, mainly because an increasing number of foreign residents would be included in the electorate. By 2030, the proportion of eligible voters would lie between 78.5% and 81.7% (Figure 92).

The effects of the reforms on the median age of the electorate would be modest in the beginning but become stronger over time. In 2010, the implementation of the different reforms would lower the median age by 0.6 years from 49.8 to 49.2 years. Until 2030, it would reach between 54.5 and 55.7 years, rather than between 56.0 and 57.2 years (Figure 93). In other words, if the reforms were combined, the median age of the electorate would be 1.5 years lower in 2030 than in the absence of a reform.

Figure 92: Projected proportion of eligible voters among the resident population of Germany, 2010-2030. No legal changes (left) versus policy scenario 9 (right)

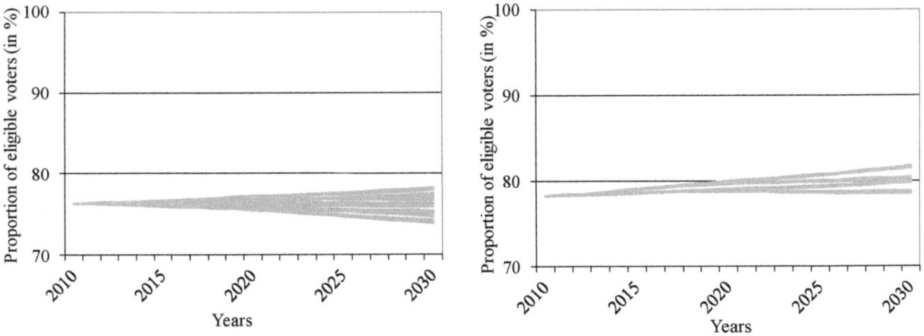

Source: Own calculations based on demographic data provided by the Federal Statistical Office.

Figure 93: Projected median age of the electorate, 2010-2030. No legal changes (left) versus policy scenario 9 (right)

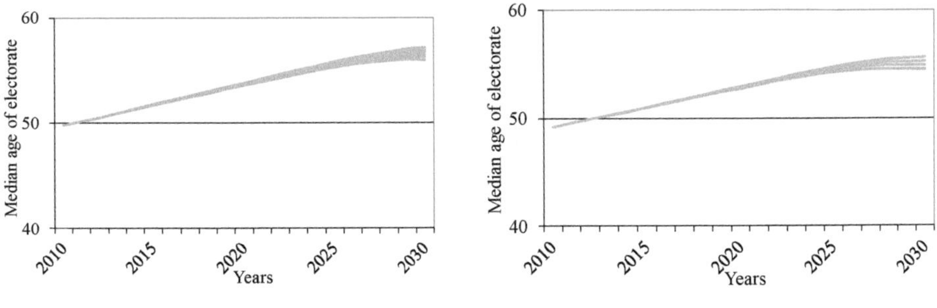

Source: Own calculations based on demographic data provided by the Federal Statistical Office.

The last scenario that was calculated, *policy scenario ten,* would again have a strong influence on the development of the electorate. In this scenario, the proxy vote model and the different naturalization models were combined, i.e. it was assumed that the voting age would be abolished and that changes in the citizenship law would lead to an increase of naturalization rates, an extension of the ius soli-principle and an abolishment of the obligation to choose. Together, these reforms would immediately increase the proportion of eligible voters by 15 percentage points. 91.7% of the resident population of Germany would enjoy the right to vote in 2010. As in the previous scenario, the effect of the citizenship reforms would increase slightly over time. By 2030, between 91.9% and 93.6% of the resident population would be entitled to vote in Bundestag elections (Figure 94).

Figure 94: Projected proportion of eligible voters among the resident population of Germany, 2010-2030. No legal changes (left) versus policy scenario 10 (right)

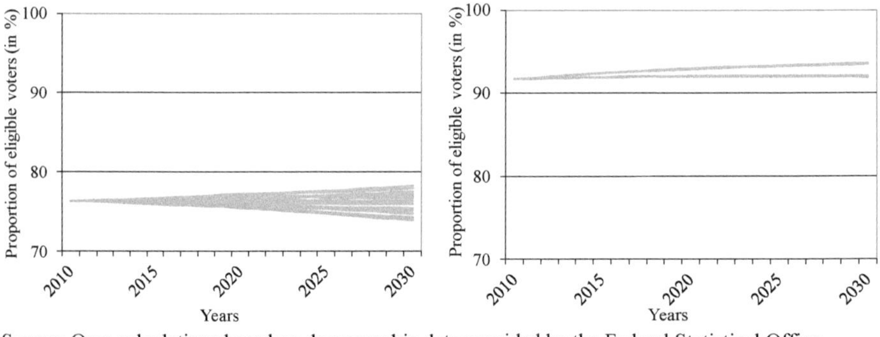

Source: Own calculations based on demographic data provided by the Federal Statistical Office.

The reforms of policy scenario 10 would also strongly influence the median age of the electorate. The introduction of the different reforms would immediately lower the median age by almost five years from 49.8 years to 45.0 years in 2010. It would then increase to about 48 years in 2020. From this year onward, the ageing process of the electorate would slow down and in some scenarios almost come to a halt. In 2030, the median age would lie between 48.3 and 50.2 years, up to eight years lower than in the absence of the reforms (Figure 95).

Figure 95: Projected median age of electorate, 2010-2030. No legal changes (left) versus policy scenario 10 (right)

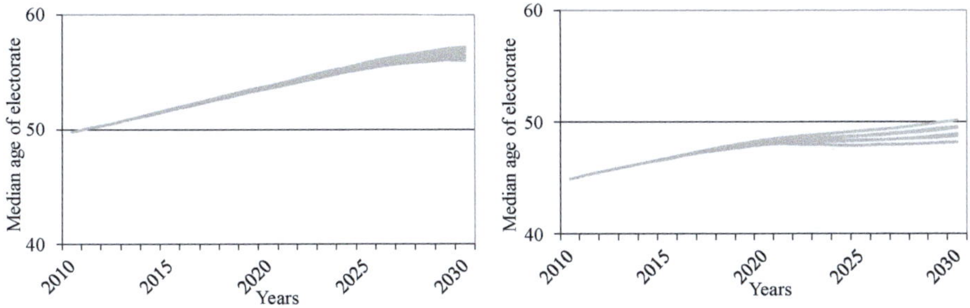

Source: Own calculations based on demographic data provided by the Federal Statistical Office.

The main findings for the mixed assumption scenarios are displayed in Table 14. The direct comparison shows that scenarios which include the proxy vote model would have the biggest impact on the proportion of eligible voters (scenarios 8 and 10; in bold and in italics). Scenarios 7 and 9, in which the voting age model was combined with the voting rights model and the naturalization models, respectively, would have a smaller quantitative influence. For the mixed assumption scenarios 9 and 10, the influence of the different reforms on the development of the median age could also be calculated. Among the two, the combination of the proxy vote model and the three naturalization models would have a stronger effect.

7.3.3. Summary of main findings

Overall, the following insights can be gained from the ten policy scenarios presented here: First, all policy options would raise the proportion of eligible voters and would slow the increase in the median age of the electorate during the projection period. The size of these effects, however, differs strongly. Some reforms, such as the abolishment of the obligation to choose, would only have a very small effect on the proportion of eligible voters and the median age of the electorate. Other reforms, particularly the abolishment of the minimum voting age, would influence the development of these indicators to a stronger degree.

Table 14: Overview of results, policy scenarios 7 to 10

Mixed assumption policy scenarios	Proportion of eligible voters		
	2010	2030 - minimum	2030 - maximum
7 - Voting age and voting rights	84.03	84.04	86.43
8 - Proxy vote and voting rights	**98.34**	**97.68**	**98.29**
9 - Voting age and naturalization models	78.20	78.52	81.72
10 - Proxy vote and naturalization models	*91.68*	*91.93*	*93.60*
16 Demographic scenarios (no legal changes)	76.35	73.90	78.25
Mixed assumption policy scenarios	**Median age**		
	2010	2030 - minimum	2030 - maximum
7 - Voting age and voting rights	---	---	---
8 - Proxy vote and voting rights	---	---	---
9 - Voting age and naturalization models	49.15	54.49	55.65
10 - Proxy vote and naturalization models	44.95	48.25	50.18
16 Demographic scenarios (no legal changes)	49.76	56.00	57.19

Source: Own illustration

The impact of the different policy reforms essentially depends on how many persons would be enfranchised. The larger the number of individuals who would gain the right to vote, the stronger would be the effect on the proportion of eligible voters and the median age of the electorate. The future number of persons who would gain the right to vote in each reform is in turn influenced by demographic trends such as fertility, mortality or migration. The number of children who would be enfranchised under the proxy vote model, for instance, is most strongly influenced by the future development of fertility rates. Due to this dependence on demographic trends, the exact number of persons who would profit from different policy reforms is not certain today. This has to be taken into account when estimating the effect of the various policy options. Nonetheless, the projections reveal at least the rough size of different population groups who would be enfranchised by different reforms in the future and they allow comparisons of these groups. It is for instance certain that the number of ius soli-citizens who lose their citizenship due to the obligation to choose will be smaller than the number of German citizens below voting age in each projection year. Therefore one can state with certainty that the proxy vote model would have a stronger effect on the electorate than the abolishment of the obligation to choose.

Chapter 8. The development of the German electorate: Trends and consequences

8.1. Studying developments of the German electorate from an interdisciplinary perspective

It has been the goal of this study to investigate the link between electoral law, demographic trends and the development of the German electorate. Political debates and dynamics, election results and policy outcomes are ultimately based on the participation of this population group and they receive their democratic legitimacy from it. Any changes in the size and composition of the electorate over time may therefore influence the development of a polity as a whole.
Reforms of electoral law and citizenship law as well as demographic trends are two factors that can account for past changes in the size and age structure of the electorate and that have to be considered when anticipating future changes. So far, researchers have often focused on one of these factors only. For instance, political scientists have analysed how electoral law or citizenship law define membership in electorates, but have not been as interested in the influence of demographic trends.[596] Similarly, demographers and social scientists have analysed past demographic developments or have projected the population of Germany by age, sex and sometimes also by citizenship, but have not used these data to analyse possible developments of the demos.[597] Where researchers combined analyses of electoral law and demographic trends, they have often focused on specific population groups only while ignoring others. Some publications for instance trace the demographic development of the foreign population in Germany and discuss how they may be integrated into the demos by changes in law, but do not comment on other enfranchised or disenfranchised population groups.[598]

---

[596] See for instance *Massicotte, L./Blais, A./Yoshinaka, A.*, Rules of the game, 2004.
[597] See for instance *Münz, R./Seifert, W./Ulrich, R.*, Zuwanderung, 1999.
[598] See for instance *Rubio-Marín, R.*, Immigration, 2000.

This study has been based on the argument that both electoral law and demographic trends have to be taken into consideration to understand past, present and future developments of the electorate and of disenfranchised population groups. If only one of the two factors is considered or if only some population groups are analysed, there is a risk of misestimating trends: Analyses which focus only on legal changes cannot capture to what extent the congruence between population and electorate may change due to demographic trends, even when the law remains the same. Similarly, studies which focus exclusively on demographic trends risk to present these developments as inevitable when in fact policy makers may respond and adjust membership criteria in the demos to new demographic realities. By combining legal and demographic perspectives in an interdisciplinary approach such shortcomings may be avoided.

In order to investigate the influence of both demographic and legal changes on the German electorate, this study was divided into two major parts. Part 1 of the study discussed past developments by focusing first on legal changes and then turning to demographic trends. Both chapters first took a general perspective and described how law and demography may influence electorates in general. Then, both chapters focused on the study country Germany. These analyses revealed that the legal definition of who should be given the right to vote have changed frequently in the past sixty years. Age and citizenship are currently the two criteria by which the largest number of persons is disenfranchised in Germany. The analyses also showed that different demographic factors have shaped membership structures in the German electorate in often contrasting ways. Fertility and mortality trends among German citizens as well as fertility and migration trends among foreign residents had the quantitatively strongest impact during past decades.

These insights were used to project the German population into the future in Part 2 of the study. It was the aim of these projections to test two hypotheses which have received much attention in the academic literature in recent years: First, the hypothesis that the electorate will age in the future and second, the expectation that an increasing proportion of the population will be excluded from the franchise due to lack of citizenship. The key results of the demographic projections and policy scenarios shall be summarized and evaluated in the following. In addition, the projection results shall briefly be linked to previously mentioned debates on future democratic practices and outcomes.

8.2. The influence of demographic trends on the development of the electorate

The results of the demographic projections, presented in Chapter 6, have confirmed that the size and age structure of the electorate are indeed likely to undergo profound changes in the future. The main expectations expressed in the academic literature appear to be correct: According to all 16 demographic projections presented in this study, the median age of the electorate will increase from a current level of 49.8 years to between 56.0 and 57.2 years in 2030, irrespective of which combination of fertility, mortality, migration and naturalization assumptions was chosen. The proportion of foreign residents among the population also increased at least slightly in all 16 demographic scenarios. Interestingly, it even increased in scenarios which assumed low net migration figures and a comparatively high naturalization rate in the future.

Nonetheless, an increase in the proportion of foreign residents will not necessarily translate into a decrease in the proportion of eligible voters. The results of the 16 demographic projections reveal that the proportion of eligible voters may decline from currently 76% to a minimum of 74% in 2030, but that it may also rise to 78% in 2030. The reason why both an increase and a decrease of the proportion of eligible voters are possible is that the development of the population of underage German citizens also matters. The number of German children and adolescents and the proportionate size of this population group will decline in the future. This was the result of all 16 demographic scenarios that were calculated here. While the increase in the number of foreign residents thus pushes the proportion of eligible voters downward, the decrease in the number of children has the opposite effect. In addition, the demographic projections revealed that the number of eligible voters in Germany will decline in all scenarios. This will also put a downward pressure on the proportion of eligible voters. Because of these contrasting developments, the proportion of eligible voters may both increase and decline in the future. It will depend on which of the different trends will be strongest.

Overall, the results of the 16 demographic projections confirm that the future development of the electorate depends on a large range of demographic factors. These factors develop simultaneously and may have contrasting effects on the proportion of eligible voters and on the median age of the electorate. Therefore, the future development of the electorate cannot be estimated by considering one demographic component alone, such as migration, or by considering the development of only one population group, such as foreign residents. Instead, different demographic factors and different population groups have to be studied in order to understand which developments are possible.

How reliable are these projection results? As was pointed out in earlier chapters of this study, demographic projections aim at estimating future demographic trends which are inherently uncertain. Demographic trends depend on the behaviour of individual persons, are therefore influenced by many different factors and may develop in unexpected ways. In addition, environmental catastrophes, wars or epidemics may disrupt demographic trends and lead to unpredictable changes in behaviour.

This study aimed at accounting for different sources of uncertainty with several strategies. On the one hand, the underlying assumptions for the demographic projections were based on as broad a range of information as possible: Time-series data, research findings as well as projections which were published in past years were taken into account. Admittedly, these sources of input may not be free from errors themselves. Time-series data may be inaccurate if they do not capture all demographic events that take place during a particular period of time. Research findings on past demographic trends may not provide a full account of the factors that triggered observed developments and previous projections may have misestimated future trends. Nonetheless, by comparing and combining different types of quantitative and qualitative information, it was attempted to overcome these potential weaknesses and to identify the most plausible demographic trends.

A further measure that was taken to deal with uncertainty was the formulation of alternative assumptions on future trends. Alternative assumptions were particularly defined for those demographic trends which have been most controversially debated in the academic literature, such as the question whether fertility levels will rise again in the future or whether mortality rates will stop declining at some point. Two different assumptions were defined for such demographic components in order to capture contrasting expectations. The different assumptions were then combined to 16 different scenarios, each representing an alternative set of fertility, mortality, migration and naturalization assumptions. Rather than predicting that a particular demographic development will take place, this study thus aimed at illustrating a range of plausible developments.

Two sources of uncertainty could not be avoided in this study: First, the population of ius soli-children was modelled and projected as a separate population group, since their access to the franchise differs from that of the German majority population. This projection would ideally have required separate data on the demographic behaviour of ius soli-citizens. As explained in different chapters of this work, such separate data were not available. Therefore, it had to be assumed that the demographic behaviour of ius soli-citizens does not differ from that of the German majority population and the same demographic assumptions were applied to both population groups. Since the ius soli-population only forms a small group among the total resident population of Germany, it is not likely that this simplified assumption had a strong influence on projection results.

Second, for a few core demographic factors, reliable quantitative data were not available at all. The naturalization behaviour of German citizens is a case in point. Reliable time-series of mortality data for foreign residents in Germany could also not be obtained. These data gaps were filled by comparing research findings, individual data points and anecdotal evidence. Nonetheless, it is possible that somewhat different assumptions would have been defined if reliable time-series of data had been available. Again, however, citizenship changes among Germans and mortality of foreign residents do not appear to have influenced the development of the German electorate as strongly as other demographic factors in the past. It may be assumed that they will also not be among the most important factors influencing the development of the electorate in the future. In this case, the simplified assumptions taken here should not have a strong influence on projection results.

Due to the mentioned sources of uncertainty, the 16 demographic projections should be used and interpreted with caution. Nonetheless, and this is a central finding of the study, the results of the demographic projections appear to be robust, since they all point in the same direction: Irrespective of which future demographic trends were assumed in the projections, the results always suggest that the proportion of foreign residents will increase at least slightly during the next twenty years and that the median age of the electorate will increase. The fact that these results emerged from all 16 scenarios indicates that these two demographic trends can indeed be predicted with a high degree of certainty. This is particularly true for the increase in the median age. The results for this indicator were exceptionally similar in all 16 scenarios. The reason for the relative precision with which the ageing of the electorate can be predicted is that most individuals who will constitute the electorate during the projection period were already born in 2010. The size of these cohorts will somewhat change in the future due to mortality, migration and changes of citizenship, but the rough future size and age structure of the electorate is enshrined in the population pyramid of the base-year already.

8.3. The influence of legal changes on the development of the electorate

Political scientists, democratic theorists and legal scholars have debated a range of potential reforms to adapt electoral criteria to these changing demographic contexts. The results of the policy scenarios, presented in Chapter 7 of this study, for the first time quantify the possible consequences of different legal changes. The scenarios suggest that the development of the electorate may be influenced by changing both electoral law and citizenship law. Some policy options, however, would have markedly stronger effects than others.

The proportion of eligible voters could be increased in a particularly strong way either by abolishing the age limit to the franchise (proxy vote model) or by enfranchising long-term foreign residents (voting rights model). Depending on how demographic trends evolve and which of the two reform options would be implemented, between 82% and 92% of the resident population of Germany would be enfranchised in 2030. The other policy scenarios – lowering the minimum voting age to 16 years, facilitating naturalization procedures, extending the ius soli principle and abolishing the obligation to choose for ius soli-citizens – would have smaller effects on the proportion of eligible voters. In case of the last two reform options, the proportion of eligible voters would in fact only be marginally higher in 2030 than if the current legal framework would be maintained.

The development of the median age of the electorate would also be influenced to varying degrees by the different policy options. Again, the proxy vote model would have the biggest effect. If the minimum voting age would be abolished, as suggested in this scenario, the median age would reach between 49 years and 51 years in 2030. This would roughly be the same median age that was measured in 2010 under currently applicable law. Other policy options would also influence in the future development of the median age, but would overall have a smaller impact. Again, the extension of the ius soli principle and the abolishment of the obligation to choose would have the least notable influence. In both scenarios, the median age values that were projected for 2030 were only marginally lower than those that would be reached if no legal reform were to be enacted.

If different policy options would be adopted and implemented in combination, the effect on the proportion of eligible voters and the median age of the electorate could be increased. This was revealed by the mixed policy scenarios. They show that different combinations of policy options might raise the proportion of eligible voters to more than 90% during the projection period and might also strongly reduce the increase in the median age of the electorate until 2030.

Overall, the results of the policy scenarios thus demonstrate that the future development of the electorate will not depend on demographic trends alone.

Instead, policy makers may react to these trends and shape the electorate by changing criteria that limit access to the franchise. The results of the policy scenarios however also show that the reforms have to be chosen and considered carefully: Not all changes in law have a similarly strong and lasting impact on how the proportion of eligible voters and the median age of the electorate develop.

When comparing the effect of different reform options, doubts about the certainty of the calculated results may arise: How likely is it that the different policy options would indeed influence the development of the demos to the extent that has been projected here?

A certain degree of uncertainty is indeed attached to policy scenario calculations. It was stressed in earlier sections of this study that the effect of different policy reforms depends on how many and which persons would be affected by them. Reforms that would lead to the enfranchisement of large numbers of persons have a stronger impact on the size of the electorate than reforms which would affect fewer individuals. Similarly, the enfranchisement of young persons would have a stronger effect on the median age of the electorate than the enfranchisement of older persons. The number and age of persons who would be affected by any of the mentioned reforms in turn depends on demographic trends. The future number of children who would gain the suffrage through changes of the minimum voting age is for instance strongly dependent on future fertility rates. Similarly, future migration and naturalization trends influence the number of foreign residents who would profit from changes of the citizenship criterion. Depending on how demographic trends will develop in the future, the effect of policy scenarios may differ from the results that were obtained in this study.

Nonetheless, it is important to stress that all policy scenarios were implemented into 16 demographic scenarios. These 16 demographic projections, calculated in Chapter 6, cover a large range of different demographic trends that may occur in the future. By introducing the different policy options in this variety of scenarios, the effect of reforms in different demographic settings could be tested at least to some extent. The effect of the proxy vote model, for instance, was calculated both for future scenarios which assumed an increase in fertility rates and scenarios which were based on an assumption of fertility decline. Similarly, the voting rights model was applied both to scenarios with high and low migration assumptions. The uncertainty attached to the effects of different policy scenarios on the electorate could thereby not be entirely removed, but it could be reduced by outlining a range of plausible developments and outcomes.

In addition to their dependence on demographic trends, a second source of uncertainty applies to some policy scenarios: As was stressed in Chapter 7, two policy scenarios are based on assumptions which may themselves be uncertain. First, the voting rights scenario assumes that the future proportion of long-term foreign residents in Germany will remain at the same level observed in the past and that 80% of the foreign population would therefore enjoy the right to vote in each projection year. De facto, however, the proportion of long-term foreign residents may be higher or lower than this value, depending for instance on future migration and naturalization trends. Second, the naturalization scenario is based on the assumption that 3.3% of all foreign residents in Germany would acquire German citizenship each year if naturalization requirements and procedures would be facilitated. Whether a change in law would indeed lead to such an increase in the naturalization rate, however, is difficult to predict since policy makers cannot influence naturalization behaviour in a direct way. These sources of uncertainty could not be removed in the framework of this study. More complex projections by age, sex, citizenship and residence duration as well as a larger number of scenarios with alternative naturalization assumptions would have been necessary to show a wider range of possible outcomes. This, however, was beyond the scope of this study and must be left for future research.

Due to these sources of uncertainty, the exact results of the policy scenario should be used with due caution. Nevertheless, and this is another core finding of this study, the results of the policy scenarios may be ranked according to the size of their effect: Irrespective of which demographic trends were assumed for the future, the policy scenarios suggest that the proxy vote model and the voting rights model would have a substantially larger influence on the proportion of eligible voters – and, as regards the proxy vote model, also on the median age – than all other policy options that were tested in this study. These two policy options thus appear to be the most powerful ones which policy makers may use to adjust membership in the electorate to changing demographic contexts. The abolishment of the obligation to choose and the extension of the ius soli-principle would have marginal impact only on the proportion of eligible voters and the median age of the electorate. The effect of the naturalization model and the voting age model lie between these two ends of the spectrum. This knowledge about the relative effect of different reform options may add a new and valuable perspective to debates on policy changes which have so far mostly revolved around democratic principles, normative considerations and constitutional concerns.

While the proxy vote model and the voting rights model would have the strongest impact on the future development of the electorate, this does not imply that they are most likely to be adopted and implemented. In fact, these two policy options appear to have raised the most controversial debates during the last years and have been confronted with serious constitutional concerns. As was described in Chapter 7, many legal scholars have argued that only Germans can be members of the electorate according to Article 20(2) of the Basic Law. They therefore consider a potential enfranchisement of foreign residents, as suggested in the voting rights model, as unconstitutional. Similar concerns apply in the case of the proxy vote model: Legal scholars have argued that if parents would be entitled to vote in lieu of their children, this might constitute an act of plural voting and therefore breach core principles enshrined in the Basic Law. These views are not uncontested. As was described in previous chapters, some academics argue that the two models are in line with constitutional principles and that they may therefore be adopted in the future. So far, however, this view has not been universally accepted. It therefore appears highly doubtful whether the required majorities to adopt one of the two models could be obtained and whether the reforms would withstand an examination by the Federal Constitutional Court.

While other policy options have also caused heated disputes, these have more often focused on normative and political arguments rather than on constitutional concerns (see Chapter 7). The proposals to allow dual citizenship upon naturalization and to abolish the obligation to choose, for instance, have met with strong resistance by some political parties. Nonetheless, the debates have mostly revolved around questions of identity and the meaning of citizenship. Opponents of dual citizenship have stressed that newcomers should only be accepted as members of the electorate if they are prepared to demonstrate their allegiance to the German state and society by revoking all previous links to their country of origin. Supporters of dual citizenship consider such demonstrations of allegiance as inappropriate in an increasingly interconnected world. These differences in opinion may certainly lead to the defeat of any future proposals to adopt such reforms. Nonetheless, if support should increase in the future, the adoption of new naturalization rules and the abolishment of the obligation to choose would at least not be hindered by constitutional concerns. The adoption of these policy options may therefore be considered more likely than the adoption of the proxy vote model or the voting rights model.

Can policy makers in Germany influence the future development of the electorate by changing electoral law or citizenship law? This has been one of the central questions of this study. Overall, the following conclusions can be drawn: From a purely quantitatively oriented perspective, the question can be answered in the affirmative. Policy options such as the proxy vote model are theoretically available and have been debated by policy makers already. They would have a strong effect both on the proportion of eligible voters and on the development of the median age of the electorate. By considering the above-mentioned debates about the constitutionality of different policy options, however, this study has to conclude with a more nuanced and sceptical answer. Not all of the policy options that are theoretically available to policy makers may de facto prove to be feasible. The policy options which showed the strongest effect in the scenarios may fail to convince for constitutional considerations. The policy options that remain available – the voting age model, the naturalization model, the extension of the ius soli principle and the abolishment of the obligation to choose – would have smaller effects only. If all of these different reforms would be implemented together, as illustrated in policy scenario 9 in Chapter 7 of this study, policy makers could keep the proportion of eligible voters from declining. They could however not prevent a future increase in the median age of the electorate. While policy makers thus appear to have some leeway in shaping the size of the electorate, it appears certain at this point that the electorate will age in the future. This can at least not be prevented by the policy options which have been considered here and which appear to be constitutionally viable.

8.4. Future changes in the size and age structure of the electorate and their consequences

Irrespective of whether electoral law or citizenship law will be changed in the years to come or whether the current legal framework will remain unmodified, the electorate of Germany will look differently in the future than it does today. It will age and in the absence of reforms, a larger proportion of residents will be excluded from voting in Bundestag elections due to lack of citizenship. If one or several of the policy options mentioned in this study will be implemented, the electorate will gain new members – German children or foreign residents, depending on the reform that is chosen.

These results raise the question whether changes in the membership of the demos may influence political processes and outcomes in Germany. After all, if democracy is the rule of, by and for the members of an electorate, then any changes in the size and composition of this group might alter the issues which receive the largest attention and the values, visions and preferences which gain the strongest support. In recent years, scholars from different disciplines have already started to discuss the interplay between changes in membership of the electorate on the one hand and debates, election results and policy outcomes on the other hand.

Some of the hypotheses and arguments which have been exchanged in the academic and political discussion have been reviewed in Chapter 7 of this work. Researchers and policy makers have for instance controversially discussed 1) whether an increase in the number of older electors might give this group a larger degree of influence on political debates, election results and policy outcomes; 2) whether the long-term exclusion of foreign residents from the franchise may lead to a loss of democratic legitimacy of the entire political system; 3) whether the enfranchisement of foreign residents or of German adolescents and/or children would have consequences for election results or political debates[599] and 4) whether particular parties might profit from an introduction of the proxy vote model.[600] It was beyond the scope of this study to critically discuss these hypotheses and their major premises and assumptions in detail. This will have to be left for future research. Nonetheless, a few perspectives shall be mentioned here which researchers may consider when investigating the link between the demographic size of a particular population group and its influence on political debates, electoral results or policy outcomes. First, future research could analyse the attitudes, values and policy expectations of different population groups as well as their degree of mobilization, for instance in interest groups. After all, the hypothesis that a demographically strong population group might shift the content and style of political debates explicitly or implicitly presupposes that most members of this group share the same attitudes and publicly advocate them. Further, the hypothesis presupposes that these attitudes differ from those of other population groups. Some research in this area has already been conducted, for instance by Wilkoszewski and Muth as well as by Bergmann and colleagues. These scholars have focused on older people in Germany and other industrialized countries and have tried to elucidate whether they share policy preferences which are different from those of other population groups. Overall, these studies have found that older persons are indeed likely to share certain policy preferences, but they stress that other individual-level characteristics apart from age are of importance too. Wilkoszewski and Muth as well as Bergmann and colleagues for instance found that older persons are somewhat less likely to support policies which grant more

---

599 See *Wüst, A.*, Politische Repräsentation, 2006; *Wüst, A.*, Naturalized citizens, 2004. See also *Diehl, C./Blohm, M.*, Apathy, 2001; *Kroh, M./Tucci, I.*, Party identification, 2010; *Claro da Fonseca, S.*, Neue Bürger, 2006, p. 33.

600 *Hoffmann-Lange, U./De Rijke, J.*, Wahlverhalten, 2008. See also *Goerres, A./Tiemann, G.*, Kinder, 2009.

financial assistance to young families and are more likely to support increases in pensions than younger persons. Nonetheless, characteristics such as socio-economic status, employment histories, ethnic background and gender, degree of religiosity, health, educational background, family status and geographic location also influence attitudes and may in fact be more influential than age.[601] These research results suggest that public pressure for increases in pensions and the like will not necessarily grow when the number of older electors increases. Future research could aim at substantiating these findings and extend the focus to other population groups which will increase in size due to demographic trends, such as electors with foreign ethnic background.

Second, researchers who are interested in the link between the size of particular population groups and their influence on election outcomes could investigate the political interest, turnout rates and party preferences of these groups. This might reveal whether the demographically-induced growth of a population group might indeed lead to changes in the electoral success of different parties, as is sometimes suggested. Again, some researchers in Germany have already started to focus on this topic. The political scientist Wüst for instance has analysed the political preferences and party identification of naturalized persons in Germany. His findings suggest that many ethnic German resettlers support the Christian-democratic CDU/CSU while naturalized persons with Turkish background tend to identify more strongly with the social democratic SPD and other left-wing parties. Party preferences thus appear to differ by the former citizenship of naturalized persons.[602] Hoffmann-Lange and de Rijke have similarly analysed whether particular parties might profit from an introduction of the proxy vote model. They have estimated the political preferences of parents with children and conclude that the Green party would be likely to profit and the CDU/CSU would be likely to lose if parents would become entitled to exercise extra votes

---

[601] *Wilkoszewski, H./Muth, E.*, Demographic change, 2009, p. 21; *Wilkoszewski, H.*, Age trajectories, 2009, p. 25 f.; *Bergmann, M./Konzelmann, L./Rattinger, H.*, Rentner-Demokratie, 2012, p. 389. See also *Naegele, G.*, Politics, 1999, p. 98 f.; *Walker, A./Maltby, T.*, Ageing Europe, 1997, p. 110.

[602] See *Wüst, A.*, Politische Repräsentation, 2006; *Wüst, A.*, Naturalized citizens, 2004; see also *Diehl, C./Blohm, M.*, Apathy, 2001; *Kroh, M./Tucci, I.*, Party identification, 2010; *Claro da Fonseca, S.*, Neue Bürger, 2006, p. 33.

on behalf of their children. The total effect of the proxy model on election results however appears to be small.[603] Future research could focus more strongly on the question whether such party preferences are likely to remain stable in the future. During recent years, the strength of party affiliation has declined in Germany and other Western societies, a process referred to as 'dealignment'.[604] It may well be that these processes also weaken the party affiliation of naturalized citizens as well as of parents with young children. If this is the case, then their currently measured preferences may reveal little about future electoral choices.

Third, in order to understand the influence of demographic changes on policy outcomes, researchers might focus more strongly on the constitutional, institutional and societal context in which political debates and policy reforms are taking place. This could shed light on the question whether a particular group of electors may be able to dictate or prevent policy outcomes in the future due to their demographic size. Constitutional law, for instance, sets limits to which reforms may be adopted and enacted in a polity. Any reforms of policies that particular groups of electors may try to push on the political agenda need to remain within these boundaries. Similarly, existing institutions and policies as well as trends in public opinion might be analysed to estimate whether different policy reforms are likely to be adopted in any given demographic context. Major reforms that would entail a radical shift in existing practices or policies or that are perceived as illegitimate or detrimental to the interests of society at large may be much less likely to be adopted than minor reforms that would imply incremental changes only or that would correspond to the interests of the majority population.[605]

Overall, before concluding that changes in the size and age structure of the German electorate will lead to changes in political debates, election results or

603 *Hoffmann-Lange, U./De Rijke, J.*, Wahlverhalten, 2008. See also *Goerres, A./Tiemann, G.*, Kinder, 2009.

604 See for instance *Goerres, A.*, Grey vote, 2008.

605 See *Hall, P. A.*, Policy paradigms, 1993, pp. 279 f. and 290 f.

policy outcomes in the future, more research is necessary on these three and other topics. Without further insights, it appears premature to assume that a causal relationship exists between the size of a particular population group and its influence on democratic practices and outcomes. Simplistic and overly dramatic predictions about a 'rule of the old', a dominance of electors with foreign background in Bundestag elections or the like are not warranted.

Once a wider historical perspective is taken, current and future demographic changes may even be understood as part of a long-term process rather than as a historical exception. As discussed in this study, changes in fertility, mortality, migration and naturalization have continuously reshaped membership structures in democratic electorates. Similarly, many changes in electoral law have been enacted over the course of history which have sometimes radically reshaped the boundaries of democratic demoi. This is also true for the particular case of Germany. This study has shown that during the last sixty years of German history demographic trends and changes in electoral law and citizenship law have changed the size and the age structure of the electorate. Taking such a wider historical perspective may deprive current and future changes from their sometimes seemingly worrisome character. Instead, these changes may be considered as standing in line and continuing past trends, rather than as a radically new phenomenon: "The term 'the people' has only has *one* permanent characteristic: that of change".[606]

[606] Gusy and Ziegler make this statement with reference to Germany. In the German original, the quote reads: "Der Begriff 'Volk' besitzt nur *ein* Kontinuitätsmerkmal: das des Wandels." See *Gusy, C./Ziegler, K.*, Volksbegriff, 1999, p. 222.

Annex 1: Constitutions and electoral laws which regulate the right to vote in European countries (for Table 1)

Austria:	Austrian Federal Act for the Election of the National Council of 1992, BGBl. No. 471/1992
Belgium:	Belgian Electoral Code of 12. April 1894, current version available at: http://www.droitbelge.be/codes.asp#ele (last accessed: 14.04.2014)
Denmark:	Danish Parliamentary Election Act of 13. May 1987, current version available at: http://www.thedanishparliament.dk/Publications/Parliamentary%20Election%20Act%20of%20Denmark.aspx (last accessed: 14.04.2014)
Finland:	Constitution of 1999, No. 731/1999 and Election Act of 1998, No. 714/1998
France:	Electoral Code of 27. October 1964, available at: http://www.legifrance.gouv.fr/ (last accessed: 14.04.2014)
Germany:	Federal Election Act of 07. May 1956, current version available at: http://www.gesetze-im-internet.de/bwahlg/BJNR003830956.html (last accessed: 14.04.2014)
Greece:	Constitution of Greece of 11. June 1975, available at: http://www.hri.org/docs/syntagma/ (last accessed: 14.04.2014)
Iceland:	Constitution of the Republic of Iceland of 17. June 1944, available at: http://www.government.is/constitution/ (last accessed: 14.04.2014) and Act No. 24 Concerning Parliamentary Elections to the Althing of 16. May 2000, available at: http://legislationline.org/topics/country/24/topic/6 (last accessed: 14.04.2014)
Ireland:	Constitution of Ireland of 01. July 1937, available at: http://legislationline.org/topics/country/23/topic/6 (last accessed: 14.04.2014) and Electoral Act of 05. November 1992, available at: http://www.irishstatutebook.ie/1992/en/act/pub/0023/print.html (last accessed: 14.04.2014)

Italy: Constitution of Italy of 22. December 1947, available at: http://www.senato.it/documenti/repository/istituzione/costituzione_inglese.pdf (last accessed: 14.04.2014)

Luxembourg: Electoral law of 18. February 2003, available at: http://www.legilux.public.lu/leg/a/archives/2009/0038/2009A0470A.html (last accessed: 14.04.2014)

Netherlands: Elections Act of 28. September 1989, available at: http://legislationline.org/topics/country/12/topic/6 (last accessed: 14.04.2014)

Norway: Constitution of Norway of 17. May 1814, available at: http://www.stortinget.no/en/In-English/About-the-Storting/The-Constitution/The-Constitution/ (last accessed: 14.04.2014) and Representation of the People Act of 28. June 2002, available at: http://legislationline.org/topics/country/11/topic/6 (last accessed: 14.04.2014)

Portugal: Constitution of Portugal of 2. April 1976, available at: http://www.wipo.int/wipolex/en/details.jsp?id=5452 (last accessed: 14.04.2014)

Spain: Constitution of Spain of 29. December 1978, available at: http://noticias.juridicas.com/base_datos/Admin/constitucion.html (last accessed: 14.04.2014) and Law on Regime of General Elections of 19. June 1985, available at: http://noticias.juridicas.com/base_datos/Admin/lo5-1985.html (last accessed: 14.04.2014)

Sweden: Constitution of Sweden (The Instrument of Government) of 1974, available at:http://www.riksdagen.se/en/Documents-and-laws/Laws/The-Constitution/ (last accessed: 14.04.2014)

Switzerland: Federal Constitution of the Swiss Confederation of 18. April 1999, available at: http://www.admin.ch/ch/d/sr/101/ (last accessed: 14.04.2014)

United Kingdom: Representation of the People Act of 09. March 2000, available at: http://www.legislation.gov.uk/ukpga/2000/2/contents (last accessed: 14.04.2014) and Electoral Administration Act of 11. July 2006, available at:

http://www.legislation.gov.uk/ukpga/2006/22/contents (last accessed: 14.04.2014)

All legal documents were consulted in October 2011 and thus reflect the regulations in force at this time.

Annex 2: The Federal Election Acts and legal reforms that have regulated the right to vote in Germany, 1949–2010 (for Table 2)

- Election Act for the first Bundestag and the first Federal Convention of the Federal Republic of Germany of 15. June 1949, BGBl I 1949:21.
  (in German: *Wahlgesetz zum ersten Bundestag und zur ersten Bundesversammlung der Bundesrepublik Deutschland – Erstes Bundeswahlgesetz; 1. BWahlG)*
- Act to amend the Election Act for the first Bundestag and the first Federal Convention of the Federal Republic of Germany of 20. December 1952, BGBl I 1952:831.
  (in German: *Gesetz zur Änderung des Wahlgesetzes zum ersten Bundestag und zur ersten Bundesversammlung der Bundesrepublik Deutschland*)
- Election Act for the second Bundestag and the Federal Convention of 08. July 1953, BGBl I 1953:470.
  (in German: *Wahlgesetz zum zweiten Bundestag und zur Bundesversammlung – Zweites Bundeswahlgesetz; 2. BWahlG*)
- Federal Election Act of 07. May 1956, BGBl I 1956:383.
  (in German: *Bundeswahlgesetz; (3.) BWahlG*)
- First Act to reform the criminal law of 25. June 1969, BGBl I 1969:645.
  (in German: *Erstes Gesetz zur Reform des Strafrechts – Erstes Strafrechtsreformgesetz;1. StrRG*)
- Act to change the Federal Election Act of 03. July 1972, BGBl I 1972:1061.
  (in German: *Gesetz zur Änderung des Bundeswahlgesetzes*)
- Introductory Act to the Criminal Code of 02. March 1974, BGBl I 1974:469.
  (in German: *Einführungsgesetz zum Strafgesetzbuch; EGStGB)*
- Act to change the Federal Election Act of 24. June 1975, BGBl I 1975:1593.
  (in German: *Gesetz zur Änderung des Bundeswahlgesetzes*)
- Fifth Act to change the Federal Election Act of 20. July 1979, BGBl I 1979:1149.
  (in German: *Fünftes Gesetz zur Änderung des Bundeswahlgesetz*)
- Seventh Act to change the Federal Election Act of 15. March 1985, BGBl I 1085:521.
  (in German: *Siebtes Gesetz zur Änderung des Bundeswahlgesetzes*)

- Act to reform the law of guardianship and tutelage for adults of 12. September 1990, BGBl I 1990:2002.
  (in German: *Gesetz zur Reform des Rechts der Vormundschaft und der Pflege für Volljährige – Betreuungsgesetz; BtG*)
- Eleventh Act to change the Federal Election Act of 27. July 1993, BGBl I 1993:1217.
  (in German: *Elftes Gesetz zur Änderung des Bundeswahlgesetzes*)
- Fourteenth Act to change the Federal Election Act of 23. April 1998, BGBl I 1998:706.
  (in German: *Vierzehntes Gesetz zur Änderung des Bundeswahlgesetzes*)
- Act to change the electoral and parliamentary law of 17. March 2008, BGBl I 2008:394.
  (in German: *Gesetz zur Änderung des Wahl- und Abgeordnetenrechts*)

Annex 3: International treaties, legal acts and parliamentary documents referred to in the dissertation

- Act on the Matters of Expellees and Refugees of 22. May 1953, BGBl. I 1953:201
  („*Gesetz über die Angelegenheiten der Vertriebenen und Flüchtlinge – Bundesvertriebenengesetz; BVFG*“).
- Act to Change Regulations on Asylum Procedures, Aliens Law and Citizenship Law of 30. June 1993, BGBl I 1993:1062
  („*Gesetz zur Änderung asylverfahrens-, ausländer- und staatsangehörigkeitsrechtlicher Vorschriften*“).
- Act to Reform the Citizenship Law of 15. July 1999, BGBl. I 1999:1618, also used in the most recent version: publication in BGBl. III, subsection 102-1, last changed by law of 01. June 2012, BGBl. I 2012:1224
  („*Gesetz zur Reform des Staatsangehörigkeitsrechts – Staatsangehörigkeitsgesetz; StAG*“).
- Act to Revise the Aliens Law of 09. July 1990, BGBl. I 1990:1354
  („*Gesetz zur Neuregelung des Ausländerrechts*”).
- Basic Law for the Federal Republic of Germany of 23. May 1949, BGBl I. 1949:1, also used in the most recent version: publication in BGBl. III, subsection 100-1, last changed by law of 11. July 2012, BGBl. I 2012:1478
  („*Grundgesetz für die Bundesrepublik Deutschland- Grundgesetz; GG*”).
- Bundesrat document BR-Drs. 45/99 of 26. January 1999:
  Draft bill by the Länder Hesse and Rhineland-Palatinate: Draft bill to change the Basic Law
  („*Gesetzesantrag der Länder Hessen und Rheinland-Pfalz: Entwurf eines Gesetzes zur Änderung des Grundgesetzes*“).
- Bundesrat document BR-Drs. 137/07 of 23. February 2007:
  Draft bill by the Länder Bavaria, Hamburg, Hesse, Lower Saxony, Saarland: Draft bill to change the Citizenship Act
  („*Gesetzesentwurf der Länder Bayern, Hamburg, Hessen, Niedersachsen, Saarland: Entwurf eines Gesetzes zur Änderung des Staatsangehörigkeitsgesetzes*“).
- Bundesrat document BR-Drs. 140/92 of 27. February 1992:

Motion by the Länder Brandenburg, Bremen, Hamburg, Hesse, Lower Saxony, North Rhine-Westphalia, Rhineland-Palatinate, Saarland and Schleswig-Holstein: Bundesrat resolution to amend the citizenship law
(„*Antrag der Länder Brandenburg, Bremen, Hamburg, Hessen, Niedersachsen, Nordrhein-Westfalen, Rheinland-Pfalz, Saarland und Schleswig-Holstein: Entschließung des Bundesrates zur Novellierung des Staatsangehörigkeitsrechts*“).

- Bundesrat document BR-Drs. 142/10 of 12. March 2010:
  Draft bill by the Länder Berlin, Bremen: Draft bill to change the Citizenship Act
  („*Gesetzesantrag der Länder Berlin, Bremen: Entwurf eines Gesetzes zur Änderung des Staatsangehörigkeitsgesetzes*“).
- Bundesrat document BR-Drs. 180/97 of 11. March 1997:
  Draft bill by the Land Rhineland-Palatinate: Draft bill to regulate immigration
  („*Gesetzesantrag des Landes Rheinland-Pfalz: Entwurf eines Gesetzes zur Regelung der Zuwanderung*“).
- Bundesrat document BR-Drs. 186/97 of 12. March 1997:
  Draft bill by the Land Hesse: Draft bill to facilitate the acquisition of German citizenship by children of foreign parents
  („*Gesetzesantrag des Landes Hessen: Entwurf eines Gesetzes zur Erleichterung des Erwerbs der deutschen Staatsangehörigkeit durch Kinder ausländischer Eltern*“).
- Bundesrat document BR-Drs. 402/93 of 09. June 1993:
  Draft bill by the Land Lower Saxony: Draft bill to change and supplement the citizenship law
  („*Gesetzesantrag des Landes Niedersachsen: Entwurf eines Gesetzes zur Änderung und Ergänzung des Staatsangehörigkeitsrechts*”).
- Bundesrat document BR-Drs. 403/93 of 09. June 1993:
  Motion by the Land Lower Saxony: Resolution of the Bundesrat to facilitate naturalization and to accept dual citizenship
  („*Antrag des Landes Niedersachsen: Entschließung des Bundesrates zur Erleichterung der Einbürgerung und Zulassung von Doppelstaatsangehörigkeit*“).
- Bundesrat document BR-Drs. 515/97 of 09. July 1997:

Draft bill by the Länder Brandenburg, Hesse, Lower Saxony, North Rhine-Westphalia, Saarland, Saxony-Anhalt and Schleswig-Holstein: Draft bill to change the Basic Law
(*„Gesetzesantrag der Länder Brandenburg, Hessen, Niedersachsen, Nordrhein-Westfalen, Saarland, Sachsen-Anhalt, Schleswig-Holstein: Entwurf eines Gesetzes zur Änderung des Grundgesetzes*").

- Bundesrat document BR-Drs. 623/07 of 05. September 2007:
  Draft bill by the Land Rheinland-Palatinate: Draft bill to amend the Basic Law
  (*„Gesetzesantrag des Landes Rheinland-Pfalz: Entwurf eines Gesetzes zur Änderung des Grundgesetzes*").
- Bundesrat document BR-Drs. 647/08 of 02. September 2008:
  Draft bill by the Land Berlin: Draft bill to amend the Citizenship Act
  (*„Gesetzesantrag des Landes Berlin: Entwurf eines Gesetzes zur Änderung des Staatsangehörigkeitsgesetzes*").
- Bundesrat document BR-Drs. 745/95 of 03. November 1995:
  Motion by the Länder Hamburg, Hesse, Lower Saxony, Saarland, Saxony-Anhalt, Schleswig-Holstein: Resolution of the Bundesrat to reform the citizenship law
  (*„Antrag der Länder Hamburg, Hessen, Niedersachsen, Saarland, Sachsen-Anhalt, Schleswig-Holstein: Entschließung des Bundesrates zur Neuregelung des Staatsangehörigkeitsrechts*").
- Bundestag document BT-Drs. 11/4528 of 11. May 1989:
  Draft bill of the Federal Government: Draft bill to reform the law on guardianship and care for adults (Law on care)
  (*„Gesetzentwurf der Bundesregierung: Entwurf eines Gesetzes zur Reform des Rechts der Vormundschaft und Pflegschaft für Volljährige (Betreuungsgesetz — BtG)*").
- Bundestag document BT-Drs. 12/1714 of 04. December 1991:
  Draft bill by Member of Parliament Konrad Weiß (Berlin) and the parliamentary group Bündnis 90/Die Grünen: Draft bill to regulate the rights of persons entitled to permanent residency and immigrants
  (*„Gesetzentwurf des Abgeordneten Konrad Weiß (Berlin) und der Gruppe BÜNDNIS 90/DIE GRÜNEN: Entwurf eines Gesetzes zur Regelung der Rechte von Niederlassungsberechtigten, Einwanderinnen und Einwanderern*").

- Bundestag document BT-Drs. 12/4533 of 10. March 1993:
  Draft bill by the parliamentary group SPD: Draft bill to facilitate naturalization and to accept dual citizenship
  („*Gesetzentwurf der Fraktion der SPD: Entwurf eines Gesetzes zur Erleichterung der Einbürgerung und Hinnahme der Doppelstaats-angehörigkeit*").
- Bundestag document BT-Drs. 12/5125 of 15. June 1993:
  Resolution proposal by Member of Parliament Ulla Jelpke and the parliamentary group PDS/Linke Liste: Regarding the government declaration 'The current situation of German-Turkish relations, fight against violence and extremism and measures for better integration of foreign residents in Germany'
  („*Entschließungsantrag der Abgeordneten Ulla Jelpke und der Gruppe der PDS/Linke Liste: Zur Regierungserklärung ‚Aktuelle Lage der deutsch-türkischen Beziehungen, Bekämpfung von Gewalt und Extremismus sowie Maßnahmen für eine verbesserte Integration der Ausländer in Deutschland*'").
- Bundestag document BT-Drs. 12/5127 of 15. June 1993:
  Draft bill by the parliamentary group PDS/Linke Liste: Draft bill to change Article 38 of the Basic Law
  („*Gesetzentwurf der Gruppe der PDS/Linke Liste: Entwurf eines Gesetzes zur Änderung des Artikels 38 des Grundgesetzes*").
- Bundestag document BT-Drs. 12/5128 of 15. June 1993:
  Draft bill by the parliamentary group PDS/Linke Liste: Draft for a twelfth law to change the Federal Election Act
  („*Gesetzentwurf der Gruppe der PDS/Linke Liste: Entwurf eines Zwölften Gesetzes zur Änderung des Bundeswahlgesetzes*").
- Bundestag document BT-Drs. 12/5135 of 16. June 1993:
  Resolution proposal by Members of Parliament Ingrid Köppe et. al and the parliamentary group Bündnis 90/Die Grünen to make a Federal Government declaration regarding the current situation of German-Turkish relations, fight against violence and extremism and measures for better integration of foreign residents in Germany
  („*Entschließungsantrag der Abgeordneten Ingrid Köppe [...][et al.] und der Gruppe BÜNDNIS 90/DIE GRÜNEN zur Abgabe einer Erklärung der Bundesregierung zu dem Thema Aktuelle Lage der deutsch-türkischen*

Beziehungen, Bekämpfung von Gewalt und Extremismus sowie Maßnahmen für eine verbesserte Integration der Ausländer in Deutschland").

- Bundestag document BT-Drs. 12/7424 of 27. April 1994:
  Resolution proposal by Members of Parliament Dr. Klaus-Dieter Feige et al. and the parliamentary group Bündnis 90/Die Grünen regarding the draft bill of the parliamentary group SPD – Bundestag documents 12/4533, 12/7318 – draft bill to facilitate naturalization and to accept dual citizenship.
  („*Entschließungsantrag der Abgeordneten Dr. Klaus-Dieter Feige [...][et al.] und der Gruppe BÜNDNIS 90/DIE GRÜNEN zum Gesetzentwurf der Fraktion der SPD — Drucksachen 12/4533,12/7318 — Entwurf eines Gesetzes zur Erleichterung der Einbürgerung und Hinnahme der Doppelstaatsangehörigkeit*").
- Bundestag document BT-Drs. 13/259 of 19. January 1995:
  Motion by Members of Parliament Dr. Cornelie Sonntag-Wolgast et al. and the parliamentary group SPD: Facilitation of naturalization by accepting dual citizenship
  („*Antrag der Abgeordneten Dr. Cornelie Sonntag-Wolgast [...][et al.] und der Fraktion der SPD: Erleichterung der Einbürgerung unter Hinnahme der doppelten Staatsangehörigkeit*").
- Bundestag document BT-Drs. 13/423 of 08. February 1995:
  Draft bill by Members of Parliament Cem Özdemir et al. and the parliamentary group Bündnis 90/Die Grünen: Draft bill to change the citizenship law (StG)
  („*Gesetzentwurf der Abgeordneten Cem Özdemir [...][et al.] und der Fraktion BÜNDNIS 90/DIE GRÜNEN: Entwurf eines Gesetzes zur Änderung des Staatsangehörigkeitsrechts (StG)*").
- Bundestag document BT-Drs. 13/2375 of 20. September 1995:
  Resolution proposal by Member of Parliament Dr. Dagmar Enkelmann and the parliamentary group PDS regarding the recommended resolution by the Committee for the Scrutiny of Elections, Immunity and the Rules of Procedure to change the Rules of Procedure of the German Bundestag – Bundestag document 13/2342
  („*Entschließungsantrag der Abgeordneten Dr. Dagmar Enkelmann und der Gruppe der PDS zur Beschlußempfehlung des Ausschusses für Wahlprüfung, Immunität und Geschäftsordnung zur Änderung der Geschäftsordnung des Deutschen Bundestages - Drucksache 13/2342*").

- Bundestag document BT-Drs. 13/2833 of 30. October 1995:
  Motion by the parliamentary group SPD: New regulation of the citizenship law
  („*Antrag der Fraktion der SPD: Neuregelung des Staatsangehörigkeitsrechts*").
- Bundestag document BT-Drs. 13/3519 of 17. January 1996:
  Draft bill by Members of Parliament Dr. Uwe-Jens Heuer et al. and the parliamentary group PDS: Draft bill to change Article 38 of the Basic Law
  („*Gesetzentwurf der Abgeordneten Dr. Uwe-Jens Heuer [...][et al.] und der Gruppe der PDS: Entwurf eines Gesetzes zur Änderung des Artikels 38 des Grundgesetzes*").
- Bundestag document BT-Drs. 13/3520 of 17. January 1996:
  Draft bill by Members of Parliament Dr. Uwe-Jens Heuer et al. and the parliamentary group PDS: Draft of a thirteenth law to change the Federal Election Act
  („*Gesetzentwurf der Abgeordneten Dr. Uwe-Jens Heuer [...][et al.] und der Gruppe der PDS: Entwurf eines Dreizehnten Gesetzes zur Änderung des Bundeswahlgesetzes*").
- Bundestag document BT-Drs. 13/3657 of 01. February 1996:
  Motion by Members of Parliament Cem Özdemir et al. and the parliamentary group Bündnis 90/Die Grünen – Minimum criteria for a reform of the citizenship law
  („*Antrag der Abgeordneten Cem Özdemir [...][et al.] und der Fraktion BÜNDNIS 90/DIE GRÜNEN - Mindestkriterien für eine Reform des Staatsangehörigkeitsrechts*").
- Bundestag document BT-Drs. 13/3719 of 07. February 1996:
  Resolution proposal by the parliamentary group Bündnis 90/Die Grünen regarding the draft bill by Members of Parliament Cem Özdemir et al. and the parliamentary group Bündnis 90/Die Grünen – Bundestag documents 13/432, 13/3472 – Draft bill to change the citizenship law (StG)
  („*Entschließungsantrag der Fraktion BÜNDNIS 90/DIE GRÜNEN zu dem Gesetzentwurf der Abgeordneten Cem Özdemir [...][et al.] und der Fraktion BÜNDNIS 90/DIE GRÜNEN — Drucksachen 13/423, 13/3472 — Entwurf eines Gesetzes zur Änderung des Staatsangehörigkeitsrechts (StG)*").
- Bundestag document BT-Drs. 13/7597 of 06. May 1997:

Answer by the Federal Government to the brief enquiry of Members of Parliament Johannes Singhammer et al. and the parliamentary group CDU/CSU – Bundestag document 13/7466 – "Children are our future" – Young persons' opportunities for participation in our society
(„*Antwort der Bundesregierung auf die Kleine Anfrage der Abgeordneten Johannes Singhammer [...][et al.] und der Fraktion der CDU/CSU — Drucksache 13/7466 — „Kinder sind unsere Zukunft" — Beteiligungsmöglichkeiten junger Menschen in unserer Gesellschaft*").

- Bundestag document BT-Drs. 13/7677 of 15. May 1997:
  Motion by Members of Parliament Cem Özdemir et al. and the parliamentary group Bündnis 90/Die Grünen: Set clear signals for integration: For an immediate reform of the citizenship law
  („*Antrag der Abgeordneten Cem Özdemir [...][et al.] und der Fraktion BÜNDNIS 90/DIE GRÜNEN: Klare Integrationssignale setzen: Für eine sofortige Reform des Staatsangehörigkeitsrechts*").
- Bundestag document BT-Drs. 13/7711 of 16. May 1997:
  Motion of Members of Parliament Siegfried Vergin et al. and the parliamentary group SPD: European Year against Racism 1997
  („*Antrag der Abgeordneten Siegfried Vergin [et al.] und der Fraktion der SPD: Europäisches Jahr gegen Rassismus 1997*").
- Bundestag document BT-Drs. 13/9301 of 26. November 1997:
  Draft bill by Members of Parliament Cem Özdemir et al. and the parliamentary group Bündnis 90/Die Grünen: Draft bill to change the Basic Law (Introduction of the municipal right to vote for foreigners)
  („*Gesetzentwurf der Abgeordneten Cem Özdemir [...][et al.] und der Fraktion BÜNDNIS 90/DIE GRÜNEN: Entwurf eines Gesetzes zur Änderung des Grundgesetzes (Einführung des kommunalen Wahlrechts für Ausländerinnen und Ausländer)*").
- Bundestag document BT-Drs. 14/1126 of 09. June 1999:
  Draft bill by Members of Parliament Dr. Evelyn Kenzler et al. and the parliamentary group PDS: Draft bill to democratize the electoral law
  („*Gesetzentwurf der Abgeordneten Dr. Evelyn Kenzler [...][et al.] und der Fraktion der PDS: Entwurf eines Gesetzes zur Demokratisierung des Wahlrechts*").
- Bundestag document BT-Drs. 14/8800 of 28. March 2002:

Final report of the Enquete Commission 'Demographic change – Challenges of our ageing society for the individual and politics'
(„*Schlussbericht der Enquête-Kommission ‚Demographischer Wandel – Herausforderungen unserer älter werdenden Gesellschaft an den Einzelnen und die Politik'*").

- Bundestag document BT-Drs. 15/1544 of 11. September 2003:
  Motion by Members of Parliament Ingrid Arndt-Brauer et al: Daring more democracy by introducing a right to vote from birth
  („*Antrag der Abgeordneten Ingrid Arndt-Brauer [...][et al.]: Mehr Demokratie wagen durch ein Wahlrecht von Geburt an*").
- Bundestag document BT-Drs. 15/4401 of 01. December 2004:
  Motion by Members of Parliament Dr. Max Stadler et al. and the parliamentary group FDP: Cultural diversity – universal values – new ways to a rational integration policy
  („*Antrag der Abgeordneten Dr. Max Stadler [...][et al.] und der Fraktion der FDP: Kulturelle Vielfalt – Universelle Werte – Neue Wege zu einer rationalen Integrationspolitik*").
- Bundestag document BT-Drs. 15/4788 of 28. January 2005:
  Recommended resolution and report of the Committee on Internal Affairs (4th Committee) regarding the motion by Members of Parliament Ingrid Arndt-Brauer et al. – Bundestag document 15/1544 –: Daring more democracy by introducing the right to vote from birth
  („*Beschlussempfehlung und Bericht des Innenausschusses (4. Ausschuss) zu dem Antrag der Abgeordneten Ingrid Arndt-Brauer [...][et al.] – Drucksache 15/1544 –: Mehr Demokratie wagen durch ein Wahlrecht von Geburt an*").
- Bundestag document BT-Drs. 16/1770 of 31. May 2006:
  Motion by the Members of Parliament Sevim Dagdelen et al. and the parliamentary group Die Linke: Facilitating naturalization – Eliminating exclusion
  („*Antrag der Abgeordneten Sevim Dagdelen [...][et al.] und der Fraktion DIE LINKE: Einbürgerungen erleichtern – Ausgrenzungen ausschließen*").
- Bundestag document BT-Drs. 16/2650 of 20. September 2006:
  Draft bill by Members of Parliament Josef Philip Winkler et al. and the parliamentary group Bündnis 90/Die Grünen: Draft bill to change the citizenship law

(*„Gesetzentwurf der Abgeordneten Josef Philip Winkler [...][et al.] und der Fraktion BÜNDNIS 90/DIE GRÜNEN: Entwurf eines Gesetzes zur Änderung des Staatsangehörigkeitsrechtes*“).

- Bundestag document BT-Drs. 16/3543 of 22. November 2006:
  Motion by Members of Parliament Kai Gehring et al. and the parliamentary group Bündnis 90/Die Grünen: Strengthening the participation of children and adolescents – increasing orientation towards children and adolescents through a new participatory culture
  (*„Antrag der Abgeordneten Kai Gehring [...][et al.]und der Fraktion BÜNDNIS 90/DIE GRÜNEN: Partizipation von Kindern und Jugendlichen stärken – mehr Kinder- und Jugendfreundlichkeit durch eine neue Beteiligungskultur*“).
- Bundestag document BT-Drs. 16/5780 of 20.06.2007:
  Resolution proposal by Members of Parliament Kai Gehring et al. and the parliamentary group Bündnis 90/Die Grünen regarding the Federal Government's reply to the major interpellation by Members of Parliament Kai Boris Gehring et al. and the parliamentary group Bündnis 90/Die Grünen – Bundestag documents 16/1554, 16/4818 – Adolescents in Germany: Perspectives through access, participation and intergenerational justice
  (*„Entschließungsantrag der Abgeordneten Kai Gehring [...][et al.] und der Fraktion BÜNDNIS 90/DIE GRÜNEN zu der Antwort der Bundesregierung auf die Große Anfrage der Abgeordneten Kai Boris Gehring [...][et al.] und der Fraktion BÜNDNIS 90/DIE GRÜNEN – Drucksachen 16/1554, 16/4818 – Jugendliche in Deutschland: Perspektiven durch Zugänge, Teilhabe und Generationengerechtigkeit*“).
- Bundestag document BT-Drs. 16/5904 of 04. July 2007:
  Motion by Members of Parliament Sevim Dagdelen et al. and the parliamentary group Die Linke: Introducing the municipal right to vote for third country citizens
  (*„Antrag der Abgeordneten Sevim Dagdelen [...][et al.] und der Fraktion DIE LINKE: Kommunales Wahlrecht für Drittstaatenangehörige einführen*“).
- Bundestag document BT-Drs. 16/6628 of 10. October 2007:
  Draft bill of Members of Parliament Josef Philip Winkler et al. and the parliamentary group Bündnis 90/Die Grünen: Draft bill to change the Basic Law (Municipal right to vote for foreign residents)

(*„Gesetzentwurf der Abgeordneten Josef Philip Winkler [...][et al.] und der Fraktion BÜNDNIS 90/DIE GRÜNEN: Entwurf eines Gesetzes zur Änderung des Grundgesetzes (Kommunales Ausländerwahlrecht*)“).

- Bundestag document BT-Drs. 16/6647 of 10. October 2007:
  Motion of Members of Parliament Kai Gehring et al. and the parliamentary group Bündnis 90/Die Grünen: Lower the active voting age for federal elections to 16 years
  (*„Antrag der Abgeordneten Kai Gehring [...][et al.] und der Fraktion BÜNDNIS 90/DIE GRÜNEN: Aktives Wahlalter bei Bundestagswahlen auf 16 Jahre absenken*“).
- Bundestag document BT-Drs. 16/9165 of 08. May 2008:
  Motion by Members of Parliament Sevim Dagdelen et al. and the parliamentary group Die Linke: For the abolishment of the obligation to choose in the Citizenship Act
  (*„Antrag der Abgeordneten Sevim Dagdelen [...][et al.] und der Fraktion DIE LINKE: Für die Abschaffung der Optionspflicht im Staatsangehörigkeitsgesetz*“).
- Bundestag document BT-Drs. 16/9265 of 26. May 2008:
  Answer by the Federal Government to the brief enquiry by Members of Parliament Sevim Dagdelen et al. and the parliamentary group Die Linke – Bundestag document 16/9064 – Development of naturalization numbers in the year 2007 and the need to amend the Citizenship Act
  (*„Antwort der Bundesregierung auf die Kleine Anfrage der Abgeordneten Sevim Dagdelen [...][et al.] und der Fraktion DIE LINKE – Drucksache 16/9064 – Entwicklung der Einbürgerungszahlen im Jahr 2007 und Änderungsbedürftigkeit des Staatsangehörigkeitsgesetzes*“).
- Bundestag document BT-Drs. 16/9868 of 27. June 2008:
  Motion by Members of Parliament Katharina Landgraf et al.: Giving a voice to the future – For the right to vote from birth
  (*„Antrag der Abgeordneten Katharina Landgraf [...][et al.]: Der Zukunft eine Stimme geben – Für ein Wahlrecht von Geburt an*“).
- Bundestag document BT-Drs. 16/12344 of 18. March 2009:
  Draft bill by Members of Parliament Kai Gehring et al. and the parliamentary group Bündnis 90/Die Grünen: Draft bill to amend the Basic Law (Article 38)

(“*Gesetzentwurf der Abgeordneten Kai Gehring [...][et al.] und der Fraktion BÜNDNIS 90/DIE GRÜNEN: Entwurf eines ... Gesetzes zur Änderung des Grundgesetzes (Artikel 38)*“).

- Bundestag document BT-Drs. 16/12345 of 18. March 2009:
  Draft bill of Members of Parliament Kai Gehring et al. and the parliamentary group Bündnis 90/Die Grünen: Draft bill to lower the voting age in the Federal Election Act and in the European Election Act
  („*Gesetzentwurf der Abgeordneten Kai Gehring [...][et al.] und der Fraktion BÜNDNIS 90/DIE GRÜNEN: Entwurf eines Gesetzes zur Herabsetzung des Wahlalters im Bundeswahlgesetz und im Europawahlgesetz*“).
- Bundestag document BT-Drs. 16/12849 of 05. May 2009:
  Draft bill by Members of Parliament Josef Philip Winkler et al. and the parliamentary group Bündnis 90/Die Grünen: Draft bill to cancel the obligation to choose from citizenship law
  („*Gesetzentwurf der Abgeordneten Josef Philip Winkler [...][et al.] und der Fraktion BÜNDNIS 90/DIE GRÜNEN: Entwurf eines Gesetzes zur Streichung des Optionszwangs aus dem Staatsangehörigkeitsrecht*“).
- Bundestag document BT-Drs. 16/13165 of 27. May 2009:
  Motion by Members of Parliament Sevim Dagdelen et al. and the parliamentary group Die Linke: Allowing for participation – Introducing the municipal right to vote
  („*Antrag der Abgeordneten Sevim Dagdelen [...][et al.] und der Fraktion DIE LINKE: Teilhabe ermöglichen – Kommunales Wahlrecht einführen*“).
- Bundestag document BT-Drs. 17/542 of 27. January 2010:
  Draft bill by Members of Parliament Memet Kilic et al. and the parliamentary group Bündnis 90/Die Grünen: Draft bill to abolish the obligation to choose from citizenship law
  („*Gesetzentwurf der Abgeordneten Memet Kilic [...][et al.] und der Fraktion BÜNDNIS 90/DIE GRÜNEN: Entwurf eines Gesetzes zur Streichung des Optionszwangs aus dem Staatsangehörigkeitsrecht*“).
- Bundestag document BT-Drs. 17/773 of 23. February 2010:
  Draft bill by Members of Parliament Rüdiger Veit et al. and the parliamentary group SPD: Draft bill to change the citizenship law

(„*Gesetzentwurf der Abgeordneten Rüdiger Veit [...][et al.] und der Fraktion der SPD: Entwurf eines Gesetzes zur Änderung des Staatsangehörigkeitsrechts*“).

- Bundestag document BT-Drs. 17/1047 of 16. March 2010:
  Draft bill by the parliamentary group SPD: Draft bill to change the Basic Law (Article 28 Paragraph 1)
  („*Gesetzentwurf der Fraktion der SPD: Entwurf eines...Gesetzes zur Änderung des Grundgesetzes (Artikel 28 Absatz 1)*“).
- Bundestag document BT-Drs. 17/1146 of 23. March 2010:
  Motion by Members of Parliament Sevim Dagdelen et al. and the parliamentary group Die Linke: Introducing the municipal right to vote for third-country nationals
  („*Antrag der Abgeordneten Sevim Dagdelen [...][et al.] und der Fraktion DIE LINKE: Kommunales Wahlrecht für Drittstaatenangehörige einführen*“).
- Bundestag document BT-Drs. 17/1150 of 23. March 2010:
  Draft bill by Members of Parliament Memet Kilic et al. and the parliamentary group Bündnis 90/Die Grünen: Draft bill to change the Basic Law (Article 28 Paragraph 1 – Municipal right to vote)
  („*Gesetzentwurf der Abgeordneten Memet Kilic [...][et al.] und der Fraktion BÜNDNIS 90/DIE GRÜNEN: Entwurf eines Gesetzes zur Änderung des Grundgesetzes (Artikel 28 Absatz 1 – Kommunales Ausländerwahlrecht)*“).
- Bundestag document BT-Drs. 17/2351 of 30. June 2010:
  Motion by Members of Parliament Sevim Dagdelen et al. and the parliamentary group Die Linke: Eliminating exclusion – Comprehensively facilitating naturalization
  („*Antrag der Abgeordneten Sevim Dagdelen [...][et al.] und der Fraktion DIE LINKE: Ausgrenzung beenden – Einbürgerungen umfassend erleichtern*“).
- Bundestag document BT-Drs. 17/3411 of 26. October 2010:
  Draft bill by Members of Parliament Memet Kilic et al. and the parliamentary group Bündnis 90/Die Grünen: Draft bill to change the citizenship law
  („*Gesetzentwurf der Abgeordneten Memet Kilic [...][et al.] und der Fraktion BÜNDNIS 90/DIE GRÜNEN: Entwurf eines Gesetzes zur Änderung des Staatsangehörigkeitsrechts*“).

- Bundestag document BT-Drs. 17/5896 of 25. May 2011:
  Draft bill by Members of Parliament Halina Wawzyniak et al. and the parliamentary group Die Linke: Draft bill to change the Basic Law and to reform the election law
  („*Gesetzentwurf der Abgeordneten Halina Wawzyniak [...][et al.] und der Fraktion DIE LINKE: Entwurf eines Gesetzes zur Änderung des Grundgesetzes und zur Reformierung des Wahlrechts*“).
- Bundestag document BT-Drs. 17/7654 of 09. November 2011:
  Motion by Members of Parliament Rüdiger Veit et al. and the parliamentary group SPD: Modernising the citizenship law – Allowing multiple and dual citizenship
  („*Antrag der Abgeordneten Rüdiger Veit [...][et al.] und der Fraktion der SPD: Staatsangehörigkeitsrecht modernisieren – Mehrfache bzw. doppelte Staatsbürgerschaft ermöglichen*“).
- Convention on the Rights of Persons with Disabilities (CRPD) of 13. December 2006, available at:
  http://www.un.org/disabilities/convention/conventionfull.shtml (accessed on 14.04.2014).
- Election Act for the first Bundestag and the first Federal Convention of the Federal Republic of Germany of 15. June 1949, BGBl. I 1949:21
  („*Wahlgesetz zum ersten Bundestag und zur ersten Bundesversammlung der Bundesrepublik Deutschland – Erstes Bundeswahlgesetz; 1. BWahlG*“).
- Election Act for the second Bundestag and the Federal Convention of 08. July 1953, BGBl. I 1953:470
  („*Wahlgesetz zum zweiten Bundestag und zur Bundesversammlung – Zweites Bundeswahlgesetz; 2. BWahlG*”).
- European Convention for the Protection of Human Rights and Fundamental Freedoms (ECHR) of 04. November 1950, available at:
  http://www.conventions.coe.int/Treaty/Commun/QueVoulezVous.asp?NT=005&CL=ENG (accessed on 14.04.2014).
- European Convention on the Participation of Foreigners in Public Life at Local Level of 05. February 1992, available at:
  http://conventions.coe.int/Treaty/EN/Treaties/Html/144.htm (accessed on 14.04.2014).

- Federal Election Act of 07. May 1956, BGBl. I 1956:383. Also used in the most recent version: publication from 23. July 1993, BGBl. I 1993:1288, last changed by law of 12. July 2012, BGBl. I 2012:1501 („*Bundeswahlgesetz; BWahlG*").
- Guidelines on Naturalization of 15. December 1977, GMBl. 1978:16 („*Einbürgerungsrichtlinien*").
- International Convention on the Protection of the Rights of All Migrant Workers and Members of their Families of 18. December 1990, available at: http://www2.ohchr.org/english/bodies/cmw/cmw.htm (accessed on 14.04.2014).
- International Covenant on Civil and Political Rights (ICCPR) of 16. December 1966, available at: http://www.ohchr.org/en/professionalinterest/pages/ccpr.aspx (accessed on 14.04 2014).
- Nationality Act of the German Empire and States of 22. July 1913, RGBl. 1913:583 („*Reichs- und Staatsangehörigkeitsgesetz; RuStAG*").
- Universal Declaration of Human Rights (UDHR) of 10. December 1948, available at: http://www.un.org/en/documents/udhr/ (accessed on 14.04.2014).

Bibliography

Ahlburg, Dennis A./Lutz, Wolfgang [Introduction, 1998]: Introduction: The need to rethink approaches to population forecasts, in: Population and Development Review, vol. 24 (1998), Supplement, pp. 1-14

Alcamo, Joseph [SAS approach, 2009]: The SAS Approach: Combining qualitative and quantitative knowledge in environmental scenarios, in: *Joseph Alcamo (ed.)*, Environmental Futures: The practice of environmental scenario analysis, Amsterdam et al.: Elsevier, 2009, pp. 123-150

Alders, Maarten/Keilman, Nico/Cruijsen, Harri [Assumptions, 2007]: Assumptions for Long-Term Stochastic Population Forecasts in 18 European Countries, in: European Journal of Population, vol. 23 (2007), no. 1, pp. 33-69

Aleinikoff, T. Alexander/Klusmeyer, Douglas [Plural nationality, 2001]: Plural Nationality: Facing the future in a migratory world, in: *T. Alexander Aleinikoff/Douglas Klusmeyer (ed.)*, Citizenship Today. Global perspectives and practies, Washington D.C.: Carnegie Endowment for International Peace, 2001, pp. 63-88

Aleinikoff, T. Alexander/Klusmeyer, Douglas [Citizenship policies, 2002]: Citizenship Policies for an Age of Migration, Washington D.C.: Carnegie Endowment for International Peace, 2002

Alho, Juha [Probabilistic forecasts, 1984]: Probabilistic Forecasts. The case of population projections, in: Scandinavian Housing and Planning Research, vol. 1 (1984), no. 2, pp. 99-105

Altenhofen, Lutz/Weber, Ingberg [Mortalität, 1993]: Mortalität der ausländischen und der einheimischen Bevölkerung in der Bundesrepublik Deutschland, in: Sozial- und Präventivmedizin, vol. 38 (1993), no. 4, pp. 222-230

Amt für Statistik Berlin-Brandenburg [Bevölkerung, 1971-1990]: Fortgeschriebene Bevölkerung in Berlin-West nach Geburts-, Altersjahren und Geschlecht (1971-1990), Potsdam: Statistical Office of Berlin-Brandenburg, 1971-1990

Anil, Merih [Citizenship law, 2006]: The New German Citizenship Law and its Impact on German Demographics: Research notes, in: Population Research and Policy Review, vol. 25 (2006), no. 5-6, pp. 443-463

Anil, Merih [Naturalisation practices, 2007]: Explaining the Naturalisation Practices of Turks in Germany in the Wake of the Citizenship Reform of 1999, in: Journal of Ethnic and Migration Studies, vol. 33 (2007), no. 8, pp. 1363-1376

Author not named [Wahlrecht, 2011]: Forderung nach Wahlrecht für alle Behinderten, Institut für Menschenrechte, 2011, available at: http://www.focus.de/politik/weitere-meldungen/institut-fuer-menschenrechte-forderung-nach-wahlrecht-fuer-alle-behinderten_aid_673638.html (last accessed: 14.04.2014)

Avramov, Dragana/Cliquet, Robert [Economy of time, 2003]: Economy of Time and Population Policy. Rethinking the 20th century life course paradigm, in: Zeitschrift für Bevölkerungswissenschaft, vol. 28 (2003), no. 2-4, pp. 369-402

Aylsworth, Leon E. [Alien suffrage, 1931]: The Passing of Alien Suffrage, in: The American Political Science Review, vol. 25 (1931), no. 1, pp. 114-116

Babel, Bernhard [Bevölkerungsvorausberechnungen, 2007]: Bevölkerungsvorausberechnungen unter besonderer Berücksichtigung von Unsicherheiten. Deterministische und stochastische Modelle für Fertilität, Migration und Mortalität sowie Modellrechnungen zur Bevölkerungsentwicklung in Deutschland, Lohmar/Köln: Josef Eul Verlag, 2007

Babka von Gostomski, Christian [Repräsentativbefragung, 2008]: Türkische, griechische, italienische und polnische Personen sowie Personen aus den Nachfolgestaaten des ehemaligen Jugoslawien in Deutschland. Erste Ergebnisse der Repräsentativbefragung "Ausgewählte Migrantengruppen in Deutschland 2006/2007" (RAM), Nürnberg: Bundesamt für Migration und Flüchtlinge, 2008, available at: http://www.migration-online.de/data/wp11ramersteergebnisse.pdf (last accessed: 14.04.2014)

Bäck, Henry/Soininen, Maritta [Immigrants, 1998]: Immigrants in the Political Process, in: Scandinavian Political Studies, vol. 21 (1998), no. 1, pp. 29-50

Bade, Klaus J./Oltmer, Jochen [Einwanderungsland, 2003]: Zwischen Aus- und Einwanderungsland: Deutschland und die Migration seit der Mitte des 17. Jahrhunderts, in: Zeitschrift für Bevölkerungswissenschaft, vol. 28 (2003), no. 3/4, pp. 263-306

Bader-Zaar, Birgitta [Überblick, 2004]: Historischer Überblick zur Wahlrechtsentwicklung, in: *Forum Politische Bildung (ed.)*, Von Wahl zu Wahl, Innsbruck et al.: Studien Verlag, 2004, pp. 22-27

Bauböck, Rainer [Boundaries, 1994]: Changing the Boundaries of Citizenship. The inclusion of immigrants in democratic polities, in: *Rainer Bauböck (ed.)*, From Aliens to Citizens. Redefining the status of immigrants in Europe, Aldershot et al.: Avebury, 1994, pp. 199-232

Bauböck, Rainer [Preface, 1994]: Preface, in: *Rainer Bauböck (ed.)*, From Aliens to Citizens. Redefining the status of immigrants in Europe, Aldershot et al.: Avebury, 1994, pp. vii-xiii

Bauböck, Rainer [History, 1998]: Sharing History and Future? Time horizons of democratic membership in an age of migration, in: Constellations, vol. 4 (1998), no. 3, pp. 320-345

Bauböck, Rainer [Public culture, 2001]: Public Culture in Societies of Immigration, Malmö: IMER, 2001, available at: https://www.mah.se/upload/Forskningscentrum/MIM/Publications/WB%201.01.pdf (last accessed: 14.04.2014)

Bauböck, Rainer [Demokratische Beteiligung, 2003]: Wessen Stimme zählt? Thesen über demokratische Beteiligung in der Einwanderungsgesellschaft, in: Wiener Hefte - Migration und Integration in Theorie und Praxis, vol. 1 (2003), no. 1, pp. 26-44

Bauböck, Rainer [Citizenship policies, 2005]: Citizenship Policies: International, state, migrant and democratic perspectives, Geneva: Global Commission on International Migration, 2005, available at: http://www.unitar.org/ny/sites/unitar.org.ny/files/GMP_citizenship%20policies.pdf (last accessed: 14.04.2014)

Bauböck, Rainer [Expansive citizenship, 2005]: Expansive Citizenship - Voting beyond territory and membership, in: Political Science and Politics, vol. 38 (2005), no. 4, pp. 763-767

Bauböck, Rainer [Citizenship, 2006]: Citizenship and Migration - Concepts and controversies, in: *Rainer Bauböck (ed.)*, Migration and Citizenship. Legal status, rights and political participation, Amsterdam: Amsterdam University Press, 2006, pp. 15-31

Bauböck, Rainer [Introduction, 2006]: Introduction, in: *Rainer Bauböck (ed.)*, Migration and Integration. Legal status, rights and political participation, Amsterdam: Amsterdam University Press, 2006, pp. 9-13

Bauböck, Rainer [Stakeholder citizenship, 2007]: Stakeholder Citizenship and Transnational Political Participation: A normative evaluation of external voting, in: Fordham Law Review, vol. 75 (2007), no. 5, pp. 2393-2447

Bauböck, Rainer, et al. [Acquisition and Loss]: Acquisition and Loss of Nationality. Policies and trends in 15 European states. Volume 1: Comparative analyses, Amsterdam: Amsterdam University Press, 2006

Beauftragte der Bundesregierung für Migration, Flüchtlinge und Integration [Migrationsbericht, 2010]: 8. Bericht der Beauftragten der Bundesregierung für Migration, Flüchtlinge und Integration über die Lage der Ausländerinnen und Ausländer in Deutschland, Berlin: Die Bundesregierung, 2010, available at: http://www.bke.de/content/application/explorer/public/newsletter/ news letter-38/2010-07-07-langfassung-lagebericht-ibpropertypublicationfile. pdf (last accessed: 14.04.2014)

Beckman, Ludvig [Citizenship, 2006]: Citizenship and Voting Rights: Should resident aliens vote?, in: Citizenship Studies, vol. 10 (2006), no. 2, pp. 153-165

Beckman, Ludvig [Who should vote?, 2008]: Who Should Vote? Conceptualizing universal suffrage in studies on democracy, in: Democratization, vol. 15 (2008), no. 1, pp. 29-48

Beckman, Ludvig [Frontiers, 2009]: The Frontiers of Democracy. The right to vote and its limits, Basingstoke/New York: Palgrave Macmillan, 2009

Beier, Henning M., et al. [Fertilität, 2012]: Medizinische und biologische Aspekte der Fertilität, in: *Günter Stock, et al. (ed.)*, Zukunft mit Kindern. Fertilität und gesellschaftliche Entwicklung in Deutschland, Österreich und der Schweiz, Frankfurt/New York: Campus Verlag, 2012, pp. 294-390

Benhabib, Seyla [Political theory, 2002]: Political Theory and Political Membership in a Changing World, in: *Ira Katznelson/Helen V. Milner (ed.)*, Political Science: The state of the discipline, New York/London/Washington D.C.: W.W. Norton & Company, 2002, pp. 404-432

Berger, Wolfgang [Partizipationsformen, 1998]: Verwaltungsorientierte Partizipationsformen für Kinder und Jugendliche, in: *Christian Palentien/Klaus Hurrelmann (ed.)*, Jugend und Politik. Ein Handbuch für Forschung, Lehre und Praxis, 2nd edition, Neuwied/Kriftel/Berlin: Hermann Luchterhand Verlag GmbH, 1998, pp. 398-413

Bergmann, Michael/Konzelmann, Laura/Rattinger, Hans [Rentner-Demokratie, 2012]: Deutschland auf dem Weg in die "Rentner-Demokratie"? - Eine empirische Untersuchung alterspezifischer Einstellungsunterschiede und ihrer Bedeutung für das Wahlverhalten auf Basis einer aktuellen

Bevölkerungsumfrage, in: Politische Vierteljahresschrift, vol. 53 (2012), no. 3, pp. 371-393

Berlit, Uwe [Stellungnahme, 2007]: Stellungnahme aus Anlass der öffentlichen Anhörung "Einbürgerung/Staatsangehörigkeit" des Innenausschusses des Deutschen Bundestages am 10. Dezember 2007, Deutscher Bundestag: A-Drs. 16(4)311 E, 2007, available at: http://webarchiv.bundestag.de/cgi/show.php?fileToLoad=1270&id=1134 (last accessed: 14.04.2014)

Bernhardt, Brian [Self-determination, 2010]: A Theory of Democratic Self-Determination: Affectedness, sovereignty, and non-territorial political borders, Broomfield (Colorado): One Earth Future Foundation, 2010, available at: https://oneearthfuture.org/research/publications/theory-democratic-self-determination-affectedness-sovereignty-and (last accessed: 14.04.2014)

Bertram, Hans, et al. [Familienpolitik, 2012]: Familienpolitik für Kinder und Eltern, in: *Günter Stock, et al. (ed.)*, Zukunft mit Kindern. Fertilität und gesellschaftliche Entwicklung in Deutschland, Österreich und der Schweiz, Frankfurt/New York: Campus Verlag, 2012, pp. 198-293

Betts, Katharine [Democracy, 2002]: Democracy and Dual Citizenship, in: People and Place, vol. 10 (2002), no. 1, pp. 57-70

Bijak, Jakub [Forecasting, 2006]: Forecasting International Migration: Selected theories, models, and methods, Warsaw: Central European Forum for Migration Research, 2006, available at: http://www.cefmr.pan.pl/docs/cefmr_wp_2006-04.pdf (last accessed: 14.04.2014)

Bijak, Jakub/Kupiszewski, Marek/Kicinger, Anna [Migration scenarios, 2004]: International Migration Scenarios for 27 European Countries, 2002-2052, Warsaw: Central European Forum for Migration Research, 2004, available at: http://www.cefmr.pan.pl/docs/cefmr_wp_2004-04.pdf (last accessed: 14.04.2014)

Binstock, Robert H. [Older people, 2000]: Older People and Voting Participation: Past and future, in: The Gerontologist, vol. 40 (2000), no. 1, pp. 18-31

Birg, Herwig [Life expectancy, 2000]: An Approach for Forecasting Life Expectancy and its Application in Germany, in: Zeitschrift für Bevölkerungswissenschaft, vol. 25 (2000), no. 1, pp. 175-198

Birg, Herwig [Bevölkerungsentwicklung, 2000]: Trends in der Bevölkerungsentwicklung. Auswirkungen der Bevölkerungsschrumpfung, der Migration und der Alterung der Gesellschaft in Deutschland und Europa bis 2050, insbesondere im Hinblick auf den Bedarf an Wohnraum. Ein Gutachten im Auftrag des Verbandes deutscher Hypothekenbanken, Frankfurt am Main: Fritz Knapp Verlag, 2000

Birg, Herwig/Flöthmann, E.-Jürgen [Bevölkerungsprojektionen, 1993]: Bevölkerungsprojektionen für das vereinigte Deutschland bis zum Jahr 2100 - unter besonderer Berücksichtigung von Wanderungen. Studienbericht im Auftrag der Enquete-Kommission des Deutschen Bundestages "Schutz der Erdatmosphäre", Bielefeld: Universität Bielefeld, Institut für Bevölkerungsforschung und Sozialpolitik, 1993

Birg, Herwig/Flöthmann, E.-Jürgen [Projektionsrechnungen, 2001]: Demographische Projektionsrechnungen für die Rentenreform 2000, Bielefeld: Universität Bielefeld, Institut für Bevölkerungsforschung und Sozialpolitik, 2001

Blais, André/Massicotte, Louis/Yoshinaka, Antoine [Right to vote, 2001]: Deciding Who Has the Right to Vote: A comparative analysis of election laws, in: Electoral Studies, vol. 20 (2001), no. 1, pp. 41-62

Blockmans, Willem P. [Typology, 1978]: A Typology of Representative Institutions in Late Medieval Europe, in: Journal of Medieval History, vol. 4 (1978), no. 2, pp. 189-215

Böcker, Anita/Thränhardt, Dietrich [Multiple citizenship, 2006]: Multiple Citizenship and Naturalization: An evaluation of German and Dutch policies, in: Journal of International Migration and Integration, vol. 7 (2006), no. 1, pp. 71-94

Bongaarts, John [Fertility, 2001]: Fertility and Reproductive Preferences in Post-Transitional Societies, in: Population and Development Review, vol. 27 (2001), Supplement: Global Fertility Transition, pp. 260-281

Bongaarts, John [Fertility transition, 2002]: The End of the Fertility Transition in the Developed World, in: Population and Development Review, vol. 28 (2002), no. 3, pp. 419-443

Bongaarts, John [Long-range trends, 2005]: Long-Range Trends in Adult Mortality: Models and projection methods, in: Demography, vol. 42 (2005), no. 1, pp. 23-49

Bongaarts, John [How long, 2006]: How Long Will We Live?, in: Population and Development Review, vol. 32 (2006), no. 4, pp. 605-628

Bongaarts, John/Feeney, Griffith [Quantum, 1998]: On the Quantum and Tempo of Fertility, in: Population and Development Review, vol. 24 (1998), no. 2, pp. 271-291

Booth, Heather [Demographic forecasting, 2006]: Demographic Forecasting: 1980 to 2005 in review, in: International Journal of Forecasting, vol. 22 (2006), no. 3, pp. 547-581

Borchers, Kevin [Datenlage, 2008]: Die Datenlage im Bereich der internationalen Migration. Europa und seine Nachbarregionen, Nürnberg: Bundesamt für Migration und Flüchtlinge, 2008, available at: http://www.bamf.de/SharedDocs/Anlagen/DE/Publikationen/WorkingPapers /wp18-internationale-migration.pdf?__blob=publicationFile (last accessed: 14.04.2014)

Börjeson, Lena, et al. [Scenario types, 2006]: Scenario Types and Techniques: Towards a user's guide, in: Futures, vol. 38 (2006), no. 7, pp. 723-739

Borttscheller, Ralf H. [Ausbleibende Integration, 2001]: Die ausbleibende Integration: Politische und gesellschaftliche Folgen von doppelten Staatsbürgerschaften als Regelfall, in: *Hartmut Koschyk/Rolf Stolz (ed.)*, Alte und neue Deutsche? Staatsangehörigkeits- und Integrationspolitik auf dem Prüfstand, München: Akademie für Politik und Zeitgeschehen der Hans-Seidel-Stiftung, 2001, pp. 15-17

Breit, Gotthard [Lincoln, 2003]: Abraham Lincoln, in: *Peter Massing/Gotthard Breit (ed.)*, Demokratie-Theorien. Von der Antike bis zur Gegenwart, 2nd edition (licensed edition for Bundeszentrale für politische Bildung), Bonn/Schwalbach: Wochenschau Verlag, 2003, pp. 165-169

Brennan, Jason [Competent electorate, 2011]: The Right to a Competent Electorate, in: The Philosophical Quarterly, vol. 61 (2011), no. 245, pp. 700-724

Bretz, Manfred [Bevölkerungsvorausberechnungen, 2001]: Zur Treffsicherheit von Bevölkerungsvorausberechnungen, in: Wirtschaft und Statistik (2001), no. 11, pp. 906-921

Brodie, Janine [Introduction, 2004]: Introduction: Globalization and citizenship beyond the national state, in: Citizenship Studies, vol. 8 (2004), no. 4, pp. 323-332

Brubaker, William R. [Introduction, 1989]: Introduction, in: *William R. Brubaker (ed.)*, Immigration and the Politics of Citizenship in Europe and

North America, Lanham/New York/London: University Press of America/ German Marshall Fund of the United States, 1989, pp. 1-27

Brubaker, William R. [Citizenship, 1994]: Citizenship and Nationhood in France and Germany, 2nd edition, Cambridge/London: Harvard University Press, 1994

Bryde, Brun-Otto [Ausländerwahlrecht, 1989]: Ausländerwahlrecht und grundgesetzliche Demokratie, in: Juristenzeitung, vol. 44 (1989), no. 6, pp. 257-304

Bujard, Martin, et al. [Kinder, 2012]: (Keine) Lust auf Kinder?, Wiesbaden: Bundesinstitut für Bevölkerungsforschung, 2012, available at: http://www.bib-demografie.de/SharedDocs/Publikationen/DE/Broschueren/keine_lust_auf_kinder_2012.pdf?__blob=publicationFile&v=17 (last accessed: 14.04.2014)

Bundesamt für Migration und Flüchtlinge [Migrationsbericht 2008, 2010]: Migrationsbericht des Bundesamtes für Migration und Flüchtlinge im Auftrag der Bundesregierung 2008, Nürnberg: Bundesamt für Migration und Flüchtlinge, 2010, available at: http://www.bamf.de/SharedDocs/Anlagen/DE/Publikationen/Migrationsberichte/migrationsbericht-2008.html;jsessionid=734592E319E7A002D9208C6797E0A788.1_cid286 (last accessed: 14.04.2014)

Bundesamt für Migration und Flüchtlinge [Migrationsbericht 2010, 2011]: Migrationsbericht des Bundesamtes für Migration und Flüchtlinge im Auftrag der Bundesregierung 2010, Nürnberg: Bundesamt für Migration und Flüchtlinge, 2011, available at: http://www.bamf.de/SharedDocs/Anlagen/DE/Publikationen/Migrationsberichte/migrationsbericht-2010.pdf?__blob=publicationFile (last accessed: 14.04.2014)

Bundesamt für Migration und Flüchtlinge [Aktuelle Zahlen, 2012]: Aktuelle Zahlen zu Asyl, Nürnberg: Bundesamt für Migration und Flüchtlinge, 2012, available at: http://www.bamf.de/SharedDocs/Anlagen/DE/Downloads/Infothek/Statistik/statistik-anlage-teil-4-aktuelle-zahlen-zu-asyl.pdf?__blob=publicationFile (last accessed: 14.04.2014)

Bundesministerium des Innern [Modellrechnungen, 2000]: Modellrechnungen zur Bevölkerungsentwicklung in der Bundesrepublik Deutschland bis zum Jahr 2050, Berlin, 2000

Bundeswahlleiter [Wahl, 2010]: Wahl zum 17. Deutschen Bundestag am 27. September 2009. Heft 5: Textliche Auswertung der Wahlergebnisse, Wiesbaden: Bundeswahlleiter, 2010, available at: http://www.bundeswahlleiter.de/de/bundestagswahlen/BTW_BUND_09/veroeffentlichungen/Heft5_komplett.pdf (last accessed: 14.04.2014)

Buttler, Günter [Steigende Lebenserwartung, 2002]: Steigende Lebenserwartung - was verspricht die Demographie?, in: Zeitschrift für Gerontologie und Geriatrie, vol. 36 (2002), no. 2, pp. 90-94

Canefe, Nergis [Citizens, 1998]: Citizens versus Permanent Guests: Cultural memory and citizenship laws in a reunified Germany, in: Citizenship Studies, vol. 2 (1998), no. 3, pp. 519-544

Carens, Joseph H. [Citizenship, 2002]: Citizenship and Civil Society: What rights for residents?, in: *Randall Hansen/Patrick Weil (ed.)*, Dual Nationality, Social Rights and Federal Citizenship in the U.S. and Europe. The reinvention of citizenship, New York/Oxford: Berghahn Books, 2002, pp. 100-118

Caselli, Graziella/Vallin, Jacques [Population dynamics, 2006]: Population Dynamics: Movement and structure, in: *Graziella Caselli/Jacques Vallin/Guillaume Wunsch (ed.)*, Demography. Analysis and synthesis. A treatise in population studies, Burlington/San Diego/London: Elsevier, 2006, pp. 23-48

Castles, Stephen [Guests, 1985]: The Guests who Stayed - The debate on 'foreigners policy' in the German Federal Republic, in: International Migration Review, vol. 19 (1985), no. 3, pp. 517-534

Castles, Stephen [Guest worker, 1986]: The Guest-Worker in Western Europe - An obituary, in: International Migration Review, vol. 20 (1986), no. 4, Special Issue: Temporary Worker, pp. 761-778

Castles, Stephen [Democracy, 1994]: Democracy and Multicultural Citizenship. Australian debates and their relevance for Western Europe, in: *Rainer Bauböck (ed.)*, From Aliens to Citizens. Redefining the status of immigrants in Europe, Aldershot et al.: Avebury, 1994, pp. 3-27

Castles, Stephen [Migration policies, 2004]: Why Migration Policies Fail, in: Ethnic and Racial Studies, vol. 27 (2004), no. 2, pp. 205-227

Castles, Stephen [Factors, 2007]: The Factors that Make and Unmake Migration Policies, in: *Alejandro Portes/Josh DeWind (ed.)*, Rethinking Migration.

New theoretical and emperical perspectives, New York/Oxford: Berghahn Books, 2007, pp. 29-61

Chopin, Isabelle [Administrative practices, 2006]: Administrative Practices in the Acquisition of Nationality, in: *Rainer Bauböck, et al. (ed.)*, Acquisition and Loss of Nationality. Policies and trends in 15 European states. Volume 1: Comparative analyses, Amsterdam: Amsterdam University Press, 2006, pp. 221-268

Cicekli, Bulent [Turkish migrants, 1999]: The Rights of Turkish Migrants in Europe under International Law and EU Law, in: International Migration Review, vol. 33 (1999), no. 2, pp. 300-353

Cinar, Dilek [Aliens, 1994]: From Aliens to Citizens. A comparative analysis of rules of transition, in: *Rainer Bauböck (ed.)*, From Aliens to Citizens. Redefining the status of immigrants in Europe, Aldershot et al.: Avebury, 1994, pp. 49-72

Clarke, James/van Dam, Elsbeth/Gooster, Liz [New Europeans, 1998]: New Europeans: Naturalization and citizenship in Europe, in: Citizenship Studies, vol. 2 (1998), no. 1, pp. 43-67

Claro da Fonseca, Sara [Neue Bürger, 2006]: Neue Bürger - neue Kandidaten? Die Parteien im Wettstreit um Migrantenstimmen, Berlin: Wissenschafts-zentrum Berlin für Sozialfragen, 2006, available at: http://bibliothek.wzb.eu/artikel/2006/f-13185.pdf (last accessed: 14.04.2014)

Cohen, Jean L. [Changing paradigms, 1999]: Changing Paradigms of Citizenship and the Exclusiveness of the Demos, in: International Sociology, vol. 14 (1999), no. 3, pp. 245-268

Coleman, David [Immigration, 2006]: Immigration and Ethnic Change in Low-Fertility Countries: A third demographic transition, in: Population and Development Review, vol. 32 (2006), no. 3, pp. 401-446

Conrad, Christoph/Lechner, Michael/Werner, Welf [East German fertility, 1996]: East German Fertility after Unification: Crisis or adaptation?, in: Population and Development Review, vol. 22 (1996), no. 2, pp. 331-358

Costa, Dora L. [Improving health, 2005]: Causes of Improving Health and Longevity at Older Ages: A review of the explanations, in: Genus, vol. 61 (2005), no. 1, pp. 21-38

Cyrus, Norbert/Vogel, Dita [Förderung, 2008]: Förderung politischer Integration von Migrantinnen und Migranten. Begründungszusammenhänge und Handlungsmöglichkeiten, Oldenburg: Interdisciplinary Center for Education and Communication in Migration Processes, 2008, available at: http://www.politis-europe.uni-oldenburg.de/download/WP13_CyrusVogel PartizipationDeutsch2008.pdf (last accessed: 14.04.2014)

Dahl, Robert A. [Democracy, 1989]: Democracy and its Critics, New Haven/ London: Yale University Press, 1989

Davy, Ulrike [Einleitung, 1999]: Einleitung: Von Reformansätzen zur praktischen Neugestaltung des Staatsangehörigkeitsrechts, in: *Ulrike Davy (ed.)*, Politische Integration der ausländischen Wohnbevölkerung, Baden-Baden: Nomos Verlagsgesellschaft, 1999, pp. 7-14

Davy, Ulrike (ed.) [Integration, 1999]: Politische Integration der ausländischen Wohnbevölkerung, Baden-Baden: Nomos Verlagsgesellschaft, 1999

Davy, Ulrike [Rechtliche Instrumente, 1999]: Rechtliche Instrumente der Integration: In welchem Kontext steht die Verleihung der Staatsangehörigkeit?, in: *Ulrike Davy (ed.)*, Politische Integration der ausländischen Wohnbevölkerung, Baden-Baden: Nomos Verlagsgesellschaft, 1999, pp. 58-81

Day, Stephen/Shaw, Jo [European Union, 2002]: European Union Electoral Rights and the Political Participation of Migrants in Host Polities, in: International Journal of Population Geography, vol. 8 (2002), no. 2, pp. 183-199

de Beer, Joop [Conceptual framework, 1995]: A Conceptual Framework for Projecting International Migration, in: *Saskia Voets/Jeanette Schoorl/Bart De Bruijn (ed.)*, The Demographic Consequences of International Migration, The Hague: Netherlands Interdisciplinary Demographic Institute, 1995, pp. 325-343

de Beer, Joop [Uncertainty, 1995]: Experiences from Including Uncertainty of Migration in National Population Forecasts in the Netherlands, presented at Conference: Analysis of errors in demographic forecasts with implications on policy, Koli (Finland), 30.03.-02.04.1995

Deinert, Horst [Handbuch, 1994]: Handbuch der Betreuungsbehörde. Leitfaden für behördliche Aufgaben im neuen Betreuungsrecht, second completely revised and extended edition, Köln et al.: Carl Heymanns Verlag KG, 1994

Deutscher Bundestag [Bericht, 2002]: Stenografischer Bericht, Plenarprotokoll 14/233, 2002, available at: http://dipbt.bundestag.de/doc/btp/14/14233.pdf #P.23196 (last accessed: 14.04.2014)

Diehl, Claudia/Blohm, Michael [Apathy, 2001]: Apathy, Adaptation or Ethnic Mobilisation? On the attitudes of a politically excluded group, in: Journal of Ethnic and Migration Studies, vol. 27 (2001), no. 3, pp. 401-420

Diehl, Claudia/Blohm, Michael [Rights, 2003]: Rights or Identity? Naturalization processes among "labour migrants" in Germany, in: International Migration Review, vol. 37 (2003), no. 1, pp. 133-162

Diehl, Claudia/Blohm, Michael [Entscheidung, 2008]: Die Entscheidung zur Einbürgerung. Optionen, Anreize und identifikative Aspekte, in: Kölner Zeitschrift für Soziologie und Sozialpsychologie, vol. 60 (2008), special edition 48: Migration und Integration, pp. 437-464

Dippolt, Martina/Goujon, Anne/Wils, Annababette [User's manual, 1998]: Software for Population - Development - Environment (PDE) Analysis. A population projection model with interacting states: User's manual, Laxenburg: International Institute for Applied Systems Analysis, 1998, available at: http://webarchive.iiasa.ac.at/Research/POP/pub/software/pde/manual.pdf (last accessed: 14.04.2014)

Dorbritz, Jürgen [Demographisches Wissen, 2004]: Demographisches Wissen, Einstellungen zum demographischen Wandel und Ursachen des Geburtenrückgangs, in: Zeitschrift für Bevölkerungswissenschaft, vol. 29 (2004), no. 3-4, pp. 329-361

Dorbritz, Jürgen [Kinderlosigkeit, 2005]: Kinderlosigkeit in Deutschland und in Europa - Daten, Trends und Einstellungen, in: Zeitschrift für Bevölkerungswissenschaft, vol. 30 (2005), no. 4, pp. 359-408

Dorbritz, Jürgen [Germany, 2008]: Germany: Family diversity with low actual and desired fertility, in: Demographic Research, vol. 19 (2008), no. 17, pp. 557-598

Earnest, David C. [Resident aliens, 2003]: Voting Rights for Resident Aliens: A comparison of 25 democracies, presented at Conference: Annual meeting of the Northeast Political Science Association and the International Studies Association-Northeast, Philadelphia, 2003

Earnest, David C. [Voting rights, 2003]: Noncitizen Voting Rights: A survey of an emerging democratic norm, presented at Conference: Annual convention of the American Political Science Association, Philadelphia, 28.-31.08.2003

Eckhard, Jan [Kinderlosigkeit, 2006]: Kinderlosigkeit durch Partnerschafts-losigkeit. Der Wandel der Partnerschaftsbiographien und Zusammenhänge mit der Geburtenentwicklung, in: Zeitschrift für Bevölkerungswissenschaft, vol. 31 (2006), no. 1, pp. 105-126

Efler, Michael [Stellungnahme, 2008]: Stellungnahme zum Entwurf eines Gesetzes zur Änderung des Grundgesetzes (Kommunales Ausländerwahlrecht) BT-Drs. 16/6628 und zum Antrag BT-Drs. 16/5904, Deutscher Bundestag: A-Drs. 16(4)459 G, 2008, available at: http://webarchiv.bundestag.de/cgi/show.php?fileToLoad=1270&id=1134 (last accessed: 14.04.2014)

Ehrhardt, Jens, et al. [Theorien, 2012]: Theorien der Fertilität, in: *Günter Stock, et al. (ed.)*, Zukunft mit Kindern. Fertilität und gesellschaftliche Entwicklung in Deutschland, Österreich und der Schweiz, Frankfurt/New York: Campus Verlag, 2012, pp. 72-115

Ellis, Andrew [History, 2007]: The History and Politics of External Voting, in: *Andrew Ellis, et al. (ed.)*, Voting from Abroad. The international IDEA handbook, Stockholm/Mexico City: International Institute for Democracy and Electoral Assistance/The Federal Electoral Institute of Mexico, 2007, pp. 41-48

Ellis, Andrew, et al. [Voting, 2007]: Voting from Abroad. The international IDEA handbook, Stockholm/Mexico City: International Institute for Democracy and Electoral Assistance/The Federal Electoral Institute of Mexico, 2007

Enquete-Kommission 'Demographischer Wandel' [Zwischenbericht, 1998]: Zweiter Zwischenbericht der Enquete-Kommission 'Demographischer Wandel'. Herausforderungen unserer älter werdenden Gesellschaft an den Einzelnen und die Politik, Bonn: Deutscher Bundestag/Bonner Universitäts-Buchdruckerei, 1998

Enquete-Kommission 'Demographischer Wandel' [Schlussbericht, 2002]: Schlussbericht der Enquete-Kommission "Demographischer Wandel - Herausforderungen unserer älter werdenden Gesellschaft an den Einzelnen und die Politik", 2002, available at: http://dipbt.bundestag.de/dip21/btd/14/088/1408800.pdf (last accessed: 14.04.2014)

Ersanilli, Evelyn/Koopmans, Ruud [Rewarding integration, 2010]: Rewarding Integration? Citizenship regulations and the socio-cultural integration of immigrants in the Netherlands, France and Germany, in: Journal of Ethnic and Migration Studies, vol. 36 (2010), no. 5, pp. 773-791

Ette, Andreas/Sauer, Leonore [Auswanderung, 2010]: Auswanderung aus Deutschland. Daten und Analysen zur internationalen Migration deutscher Staatsangehöriger, Wiesbaden: Verlag für Sozialwissenschaften, 2010

European Commission [Demographic future, 2007]: Europe's Demographic Future. Facts and figures on challenges and opportunities, Luxembourg: Office for Official Publications of the European Communities, 2007, available at: www.ec.europa.eu/social/BlobServlet?docId=1540&langId=en (last accessed: 14.04.2014)

European Commission [Demography report, 2011]: Demography Report 2010. Older, more numerous and diverse Europeans, Luxembourg: Office for Official Publications of the European Communities, 2011, available at: http://ec.europa.eu/social/main.jsp?langId=en&catId=502&newsId=1007&furtherNews=yes (last accessed: 14.04.2014)

Eurostat [Online database, 2012]: Online Database: Population projections, available at: http://epp.eurostat.ec.europa.eu/portal/page/portal/population/data/main_tables (last accessed: 14.04.2014)

Faist, Thomas/Gerdes, Jürgen/Rieple, Beate [Dual citizenship, 2007]: Dual Citizenship as a Path-Dependent Process, in: *Alejandro Portes/Josh De Wind (ed.)*, Rethinking Migration. New theoretical and empirical perspectives, New York/Oxford: Berghahn Books, 2007, pp. 90-121

Foster, Caroline [Limits, 2000]: The Limits to Low Fertility: A biosocial approach, in: Population and Development Review, vol. 26 (2000), no. 2, pp. 209-234

Fox, Gregory H. [Political participation, 2000]: The Right to Political Participation in International Law, in: *Gregory H. Fox/Brad R. Roth (ed.)*, Democratic Governance and International Law, Cambridge et al.: Cambridge University Press, 2000, pp. 48-90

Frankenberg, Günter [Stellungnahme, 2004]: Stellungnahme zum öffentlichen Fachexpertengespräch im Innenausschuss des Deutschen Bundestages zum Antrag "Mehr Demokratie wagen durch ein Wahlrecht von Geburt an", Deutscher Bundestag: A-Drs. 15(4)172, 2004, available at: http://webarchiv.bundestag.de/archive/2007/0206/ausschuesse/archiv15/a04/Oeffentliche_Anhoerungen/Anhoerungen_6/Stellungnahme_1.pdf (last accessed: 14.04.2014)

Frejka, Tomas/Sobotka, Tomás [Fertility, 2008]: Overview Chapter 1: Fertility in Europe. Diverse, delayed and below replacement, in: Demographic Research, vol. 19 (2008), no. 3, pp. 15-46

Frejka, Tomas, et al. [Summary, 2008]: Summary and General Conclusions: Childbearing trends and policies in Europe, in: Demographic Research, vol. 19 (2008), no. 2, pp. 5-14

Gauthier, Anne H. [Impact, 2007]: The Impact of Family Policies on Fertility in Industrialized Countries: A review of the literature, in: Population Research and Policy Review, vol. 26 (2007), no. 3, pp. 323-346

Gianni, Matteo [Multiculturalism, 1998]: Taking Multiculturalism Seriously: Political claims for a differentiated citizenship, in: *Karen Slawner/Mark E. Denham (ed.)*, Citizenship after Liberalism, New York et al.: Peter Lang, 1998, pp. 33-55

Gisart, Brigitte [Grundlagen, 2009]: Grundlagen und Daten der Wahl zum 17. Deutschen Bundestag am 27. September 2009, in: Wirtschaft und Statistik (2009), no. 8, pp. 743-763

Glenn, Norval D./Grimes, Michael [Aging, 1968]: Aging, Voting, and Political Interest, in: Americal Sociological Review, vol. 33 (1968), no. 4, pp. 563-575

Göbel-Zimmermann, Ralph/Eichhorn, Alexander [Entwicklungen I, 2010]: Entwicklungen des Staatsangehörigkeitsrechts seit 2000 - eine kritische Bilanz (Teil 1), in: Zeitschrift für Ausländerrecht und Ausländerpolitik, vol. 30 (2010), no. 9, pp. 293-302

Göbel-Zimmermann, Ralph/Eichhorn, Alexander [Entwicklungen II, 2010]: Entwicklungen des Staatsangehörigkeitsrechts seit 2000 - eine kritische Bilanz (Teil 2), in: Zeitschrift für Ausländerrecht und Ausländerpolitik, vol. 30 (2010), no. 10, pp. 348-351

Goerres, Achim [Grey vote, 2008]: The Grey Vote: Determinants of older voters' party choice in Britain and West Germany, in: Electoral Studies, vol. 27 (2008), no. 2, pp. 285-304

Goerres, Achim/Tiemann, Guido [Kinder, 2009]: Kinder an die Macht? Die politischen Konsequenzen des stellvertretenden Elternwahlrechts, in: Politische Vierteljahresschrift, vol. 50 (2009), no. 1, pp. 50-64

Goldstein, Joshua R./Kreyenfeld, Michaela [Der Osten, 2011]: Der Osten liegt vorn: 20 Jahre nach der Wende liegt die ostdeutsche über der westdeutschen Geburtenrate, in: ifo Dresden berichtet, vol. 18 (2011), no. 5, pp. 6-10

Goldstein, Joshua R./Sobotka, Tomás/Jasilioniene, Aiva ['Lowest-low' fertility, 2009]: The End of 'Lowest-Low' Fertility?, Rostock: MPIDR, 2009, available at: http://www.demogr.mpg.de/papers/working/wp-2009-029.pdf (last accessed: 14.04.2014)

Goujon, Anne [Education, 2003]: Education as a Dimension in Forecasting: Multi-state population projections by education and future literate life expectancy - Methodology, applications, and results, Dissertation, Vienna: University of Vienna, Department of Economic and Computer Science, 2003

Goujon, Anne, et al. [New times, 2007]: New Times, Old Beliefs: Projecting the future size of religions in Austria, in: Vienna Yearbook of Population Research (2007), pp. 237-270

Green, Simon [Beyond ethnoculturalism, 2000]: Beyond Ethnoculturalism? German citizenship in the new millenium, in: German Politics, vol. 9 (2000), no. 3, pp. 105-124

Green, Simon [Ideology, 2005]: Between Ideology and Pragmatism: The politics of dual nationality in Germany, in: International Migration Review, vol. 39 (2005), no. 4, pp. 921-952

Groenendijk, Kees/Guild, Elspeth/Barzilay, Robin [Legal status, 2000]: The Legal Status of Third Country Nationals who Are Long-Term Residents in a Member State of the European Union, Strasbourg: Council of Europe, 2000, available at: http://cmr.jur.ru.nl/cmr/docs/status.pdf
(last accessed: 14.04.2014)

Gründinger, Wolfgang [Wer wählt, 2008]: Wer wählt, der zählt, in: *Stiftung für die Rechte zukünftiger Generationen (ed.)*, Wahlrecht ohne Altersgrenze? Verfassungsrechtliche, demokratietheoretische und entwicklungspsychologische Aspekte, München: Oekom Verlag, 2008, pp. 21-52

Guiraudon, Virginie [Citizenship rights, 1998]: Citizenship Rights for Non-Citizens: France, Germany, and the Netherlands, in: *Christian Joppke (ed.)*, Challenge to the Nation-State. Immigration in Western Europe, Oxford/New York: Oxford University Press, 1998, pp. 272-318

Gustafson, Per [Globalisation, 2002]: Globalisation, Multiculturalism and Individualism: The Swedish debate on dual citizenship, in: Journal of Ethnic and Migration Studies, vol. 28 (2002), no. 3, pp. 463-481

Gusy, Christoph [Integration, 1999]: Integration durch Staatsangehörigkeit, in: *Ulrike Davy (ed.)*, Politische Integration der ausländischen Wohnbevölkerung, Baden-Baden: Nomos Verlagsgesellschaft, 1999, pp. 262-271

Gusy, Christoph/Ziegler, Katja [Volksbegriff, 1999]: Der Volksbegriff des Grundgesetzes: Ist die Position des Bundesverfassungsgerichts alternativenlos?, in: *Ulrike Davy (ed.)*, Politische Integration der ausländischen Wohnbevölkerung, Baden-Baden: Nomos Verlagsgesellschaft, 1999, pp. 222-247

Hagedorn, Heike [Liberale Trends, 1999]: Wer soll Deutscher werden? Liberale Trends in der deutschen Einbürgerungspolitik, in: *Ulrike Davy (ed.)*, Politische Integration der ausländischen Wohnbevölkerung, Baden-Baden: Nomos Verlagsgesellschaft, 1999, pp. 152-172

Hagedorn, Heike [Einbürgerung, 2001]: Wer darf Mitglied werden? Einbürgerung in Deutschland und Frankreich im Vergleich, Opladen: Leske + Buderich, 2001

Hailbronner, Kay [Citizenship, 1989]: Citizenship and Nationhood in Germany, in: *William Rogers Brubaker (ed.)*, Immigration and the Politics of Citizenship in Europe and North America, Lanham/New York/London: University Press of America/German Marshall Fund of the United States, 1989, pp. 67-79

Hailbronner, Kay [Citizenship law, 2002]: Germany's Citizenship Law under Immigration Pressure, in: *Randall Hansen/Patrick Weil (ed.)*, Dual Nationality, Social Rights and Federal Citizenship in the U.S. and Europe. The reinvention of citizenship, New York/Oxford: Berghahn Books, 2002, pp. 121-135

Hailbronner, Kay [Germany, 2006]: Germany, in: *Rainer Bauböck, et al. (ed.)*, Acquisition and Loss of Nationality. Volume 2: Country analyses. Policies and trends in 15 European countries, Amsterdam: Amsterdam University Press, 2006, pp. 213-251

Hailbronner, Kay [Country report, 2010]: Country Report: Germany, San Domenico di Fiesole: European University Institute/Robert Schuman Centre for Advanced Studies/EUDO Citizenship Observatory, 2010, available at: http://eudo-citizenship.eu/docs/CountryReports/Germany.pdf (last accessed: 14.04.2014)

Hall, Peter A. [Policy paradigms, 1993]: Policy Paradigms, Social Learning, and the State: The case of economic policymaking in Britain, in: Comparative Politics, vol. 25 (1993), no. 3, pp. 275-296

Hammar, Tomas [Dual citizenship, 1985]: Dual Citizenship and Political Integration, in: International Migration Review, vol. 19 (1985), no. 3, pp. 438-450

Hammar, Tomas [State, 1989]: State, Nation, and Dual Citizenship, in: *William Rogers Brubaker (ed.)*, Immigration and the Politics of Citizenship in Europe and America, Lanham/New York/London: University Press of America/German Marshall Fund of the United States, 1989, pp. 81-95

Hammar, Tomas [Democracy, 1990]: Democracy and the Nation State. Aliens, denizens and citizens in a world of international migration, Aldershot et al.: Avebury, 1990

Hannemann, Anke/Scholz, Rembrandt [Mortality, 2009]: The Mortality of Non-Germans in Germany - A comparison of results estimated from the official statistics and the Central Register of Foreigners, in: Rostocker Center - Discussion Paper (2009), no. 26, pp. 1-28

Hanschmann, Felix [Stellungnahme, 2008]: Rechtliche Stellungnahme zum Entwurf eines Gesetzes zur Änderung des Grundgesetzes (kommunales Ausländerwahlrecht), Deutscher Bundestag: A-Drs 16(4)459 F, 2008, available at: http://webarchiv.bundestag.de/cgi/show.php?fileToLoad=1270 &id=1134 (last accessed: 14.04.2014)

Hansen, Mogens H. [Athenian democracy, 1992]: The Tradition of the Athenian Democracy A.D. 1750-1990, in: Greece & Rome, vol. 39 (1992), no. 1, pp. 14-30

Hansen, Randall/Weil, Patrick (ed.) [Dual nationality, 2002]: Dual Nationality, Social Rights and Federal Citizenship in the U.S. and Europe. The reinvention of citizenship, New York/Oxford: Berghahn Books, 2002

Hansen, Randall/Weil, Patrick [Introduction, 2002]: Introduction. Dual citizenship in a changed world: Immigration, gender and social rights, in: *Randall Hansen/Patrick Weil (ed.)*, Dual Nationality, Social Rights and Federal Citizenship in the U.S. and Europe. The reinvention of citizenship, New York/Oxford: Berghahn Books, 2002, pp. 1-15

Harring, Marius/Palentien, Christian/Rohlfs, Carsten [Politische Orientierung, 2008]: Politische Orientierung und soziales Engagement Jugendlicher im Kontext veränderter Lebensbedingungen, in: *Stiftung für die Rechte zukünftiger Generationen (ed.)*, Wahlrecht ohne Altersgrenze? Verfassungsrechtliche, demokratietheoretische und entwicklungs-psychologische Aspekte, München: Oekom Verlag, 2008, pp. 169-185

Hattenhauer, Hans [Minderjährigenwahlrecht, 1998]: Über das Minderjährigenwahlrecht, in: *Christian Palentien/Klaus Hurrelmann (ed.)*, Jugend und Politik. Ein Handbuch für Forschung, Lehre und Praxis, Second edition, Neuwied/Kriftel/Berlin: Hermann Luchterhand Verlag GmbH, 1998, pp. 238-259

Haug, Sonja [Interethnische Kontakte, 2010]: Interethnische Kontakte, Freundschaften, Partnerschaften und Ehen von Migranten in Deutschland, Nürnberg: Bundesamt für Migration und Flüchtlinge, 2010, available at: http://www.bamf.de/SharedDocs/Anlagen/DE/Publikationen/WorkingPapers/wp33-interethnische-kontakte.pdf?__blob=publicationFile (last accessed: 14.04.2014)

Haupt, Arthur/Kane, Thomas T. [Handbook, 2004]: Population Reference Bureau's Population Handbook, Fifth edition, Washington D.C.: Population Reference Bureau, 2004

Hayduk, Ronald [Non-citizen voting, 2002]: Non-Citizen Voting: Pipe dream or reality, 2002, available at: http://ias7.berkeley.edu/Events/conferences/Morelia/briefing/noncitizenvoting.pdf (last accessed: 14.04.2014)

Heinz, Wolfgang [Sanktionensystem, 2012]: Das strafrechtliche Sanktionensystem und die Sanktionierungspraxis in Deutschland 1882-2010, Konstanzer Inventar Sanktionsforschung, 2012, available at: http://www.uni-konstanz.de/rtf/kis/Sanktionierungspraxis-in-Deutschland-Stand-2010.pdf (last accessed: 14.04.2014)

Held, David [Globalization, 1997]: Globalization and Cosmopolitan Democracy, in: Peace Review, vol. 9 (1997), no. 3, pp. 309-314

Heußner, Hermann K. [Stellvertreterwahlrecht, 2008]: Dürfen Eltern für ihre Kinder wählen? Die verfassungsrechtliche Zulässigkeit eines elterlichen Stellvertreterwahlrechts, in: *Stiftung für die Rechte zukünftiger Generationen (ed.)*, Wahlrecht ohne Altersgrenze? Verfassungsrechtliche, demokratie-theoretische und entwicklungspsychologische Aspekte, München: Oekom Verlag, 2008, pp. 227-254

Hinrichs, Karl [Enfranchising children, 2002]: Do the Old Exploit the Young? Is enfranchising children a good idea?, in: Archives européennes de sociologie, vol. 43 (2002), no. 1, pp. 35-58

Hobe, Stephan [Staatsvolk, 1994]: Das Staatsvolk nach dem Grundgesetz, in: Juristenzeitung, vol. 49 (1994), no. 4, pp. 191-195

Hoffmann-Lange, Ursula/De Rijke, Johann [Wahlverhalten, 2008]: Das Wahlverhalten junger Menschen und Wahlrecht, in: *Stiftung für die Rechte zukünftiger Generationen (ed.)*, Wahlrecht ohne Altersgrenze? Verfassungsrechtliche, demokratietheoretische und entwicklungspsychologische Aspekte, München: Oekom Verlag, 2008, pp. 95-117

Huber, Erwin [Doppelte Staatsbürgerschaft, 1999]: Die Diskussion um die doppelte Staatsbürgerschaft aus der Sicht der Bayerischen Staatsregierung, in: *Andreas Goldberg/Faruk Sen (ed.)*, Deutsche Türken - Türkische Deutsche? Die Diskussion um die doppelte Staatsbürgerschaft, Münster/Hamburg/London: LIT Verlag, 1999, pp. 11-17

Hurrelmann, Klaus [Wahlalter, 1998]: Für eine Herabsetzung des Wahlalters, in: *Christian Palentien/Klaus Hurrelmann (ed.)*, Jugend und Politik. Ein Handbuch für Forschung, Lehre und Praxis, Second edition, Neuwied/ Kriftel/Berlin: Hermann Luchterhand Verlag GmbH, 1998, pp. 280-289

Im Hof, Ulrich [Schweiz, 2007]: Geschichte der Schweiz, Eighth edition, Stuttgart: Verlag W. Kohlhammer, 2007

Jesse, Eckhard [Wahlrecht, 1985]: Wahlrecht zwischen Kontinuität und Reform. Eine Analyse der Wahlsystemdiskussion und der Wahlrechtsänderungen in der Bundesrepublik Deutschland 1949-1983, Düsseldorf: Droste Verlag, 1985

Jesse, Eckhard [Reformvorschläge, 2003]: Reformvorschläge zur Änderung des Wahlrechts, in: Aus Politik und Zeitgeschichte (2003), no. B 52, pp. 3-11

Jesse, Eckhard [Stellungnahme, 2004]: Stellungnahme zum Antrag "Mehr Demokratie wagen durch ein Wahlrecht von Geburt an", Deutscher Bundestag: A-Drs. 15(4)172 B, 2004, available at: http://webarchiv.bundestag.de/archive/2007/0206/ausschuesse/archiv15/a04/Oeffentliche_Anhoerungen/Anhoerungen_6/Stellungnahme_3.pdf (last accessed: 14.04.2014)

Jones, Philip J. [Communes, 1964]: Communes and Despots: The city state in late-medieval Italy, in: Transactions of the Royal Historical Society, fifth series, vol. 15 (1964), pp. 71-96

Joppke, Christian [Immigration challenges, 1998]: Immigration Challenges the Nation-State, in: *Christian Joppke (ed.)*, Challenge to the Nation-State. Immigration in Western Europe and the United States, Oxford: Oxford University Press, 1998, pp. 5-46

Jungnickel, Martin [Anhörung, 2007]: Anhörung des Innenausschusses des Deutschen Bundestages vom 10. Dezember 2007 "Einbürgerung/Staatsangehörigkeit", Deutscher Bundestag: A-Drs. 16(4)311 D, 2007, available at: http://webarchiv.bundestag.de/cgi/show.php?fileTo Load=1270&id=1134 (last accessed: 14.04.2014)

Kannisto, Vaino, et al. [Mortality, 1994]: Reductions in Mortality at Advanced Ages: Several decades of evidence from 27 countries, in: Population and Development Review, vol. 20 (1994), no. 4, pp. 793-810

Kaufmann, Eric/Goujon, Anne/Skirbekk, Vegard [Political affiliation, 2012]: American Political Affiliation, 2003-2043: A cohort component projection, in: Population Studies: A Journal of Demography, vol. 66 (2012), no. 1, pp. 53-67

Keilman, Nico/Pham, Dinh Q./Hetland, Arve [Population forecasts, 2002]: Why Population Forecasts Should Be Probabilistic - Illustrated by the case of Norway, in: Demographic Research, vol. 6 (2002), pp. 409-454

Kemper, Franz-Josef [Wanderungen, 2006]: Internationale Wanderungen und ausländische Bevölkerung in Deutschland, in: Zeitschrift für Bevölkerungswissenschaft, vol. 3/4 (2006), no. 31, pp. 389-412

Keskin, Hakki [Bürgerrechte, 1999]: Der Kampf für Bürgerrechte muß fortgesetzt werden, in: *Andreas Goldberg/Faruk Sen (ed.)*, Deutsche Türken - Türkische Deutsche? Die Diskussion um die doppelte Staatsbürgerschaft, Münster/Hamburg/London: LIT Verlag, 1999, pp. 29-37

Keyfitz, Nathan [Limits, 1981]: The Limits of Population Forecasting, in: Population and Development Review, vol. 7 (1981), no. 4, pp. 579-593

Keyfitz, Nathan [Knowledge, 1982]: Can Knowledge Improve Forecasts?, in: Population and Development Review, vol. 8 (1982), no. 4, pp. 729-751

Keyssar, Alexander [Right to vote, 2009]: The Right to Vote. The contested history of democracy in the United States, Second revised edition, New York: Basic Books, 2009

Kibele, Eva/Scholz, Rembrandt/Shkolnikov, Vladimir M. [Migrant mortality, 2008]: Low Migrant Mortality in Germany for Men Aged 65 and Older: Fact or artifact?, in: European Journal of Epidemiology, vol. 23 (2008), no. 6, pp. 389-393

Kirshner, Alexander [International status, 2003]: The International Status of the Right to Vote, 2003, available at: http://archive.fairvote.org/media/rtv /kirshner.pdf (last accessed: 14.04.2014)

Kohler, Hans-Peter/Billari, Francesco C./Ortega, José A. [Lowest-low fertility, 2002]: The Emergence of Lowest-Low Fertility in Europe during the 1990s, in: Population and Development Review, vol. 28 (2002), no. 4, pp. 641-680

Kohls, Martin [Healthy-migrant-effect, 2008]: Healthy-Migrant-Effect, Erfassungsfehler und andere Schwierigkeiten bei der Analyse der Mortalität von Migranten, Nürnberg: Bundesamt für Migration und Flüchtlinge, 2008, available at: http://www.bamf.de/SharedDocs/Anlagen/DE/Publikationen/WorkingPapers/wp15-healthy-migrant-effekt.html (last accessed: 14.04.2014)

Kohls, Martin [Mortalität, 2008]: Leben Migranten wirklich länger? Eine empirische Analyse der Mortalität von Migranten in Deutschland, 2008, available at: http://www.bamf.de/SharedDocs/Anlagen/DE/Publikationen/WorkingPapers/wp16-leben-Migranten-laenger.html (last accessed: 14.04.2014)

Kohls, Martin [Morbidität, 2011]: Morbidität und Mortalität von Migranten in Deutschland, Nürnberg: Bundesamt für Migration und Flüchtlinge, 2011, available at: http://www.bamf.de/SharedDocs/Anlagen/DE/Publikationen/Forschungsberichte/fb09-mortalitaet.html (last accessed: 14.04.2014)

Koslowski, Rey [Migrants, 2000]: Migrants and Citizens. Demographic change in the European state system, Ithaca/London: Cornell University Press, 2000

Kosow, Hannah/Gaßner, Robert [Scenario analysis, 2008]: Methods in Future and Scenario Analysis. Overview, assessment, and selection criteria, Bonn: German Development Institute, 2008, available at: http://mercury.ethz.ch/serviceengine/Files/ISN/95979/ipublicationdocument_singledocument/34fa9cb0-ef42-4b7a-9fdb-b668ce5219b8/en/Study+39e.pdf (last accessed: 14.04.2014)

Kostakopoulou, Theodora [Third-country nationals, 2002]: Long-Term Resident Third-Country Nationals in the European Union: Normative expectations and institutional openings, in: Journal of Ethnic and Migration Studies, vol. 28 (2002), no. 3, pp. 443-462

Krebs, David [Amputierte Wahl, 2008]: Wider die amputierte Wahl oder: Physiker und Philosophen als Hebammen einer echten Demokratie, in: *Stiftung für die Rechte zukünftiger Generationen (ed.)*, Wahlrecht ohne Altersgrenze? Verfassungsrechtliche, demokratietheoretische und entwicklungspsychologische Aspekte, München: Oekom Verlag, 2008, pp. 267-300

Kreyenfeld, Michaela/Konietzka, Dirk [Wandel, 2008]: Wandel der Geburten- und Familienentwicklung in West- und Ostdeutschland, in: *Norbert F. Schneider (ed.)*, Lehrbuch Moderne Familiensoziologie. Theorien, Methoden, empirische Befunde, Opladen/Farmington Hills: Verlag Barbara Budrich, 2008, pp. 121-137

Krieger, Tim [Generationengerechtigkeit, 2008]: Generationengerechtigkeit und das "Wahlrecht von Geburt an" - Kritische Anmerkungen aus Sicht der Public-Choice-Theorie, in: *Stiftung für die Rechte zukünftiger Generationen (ed.)*, Wahlrecht ohne Altersgrenze? Verfassungsrechtliche, demokratietheoretische und entwicklungspsychologische Aspekte, München: Oekom Verlag, 2008, pp. 301-329

Kroh, Martin/Tucci, Ingrid [Party identification, 2010]: The Party Identification of Germany's Immigrant Population: Parties should not fear eased naturalization requirements, in: Weekly Report, vol. 6 (2010), no. 4, pp. 20-26

Lämmermann, Falk [Ius soli, 2011]: Ein Jahrzehnt ius soli - Bilanz und Ausblick, in: Zeitschrift für Ausländerrecht und Ausländerpolitik, vol. 31 (2011), no. 1, pp. 1-8

Lanzieri, Giampaolo [Europop, 2009]: Europop 2008: A set of population projections for the European Union, presented at Conference: XXVI IUSSP International Population Conference, Marrakech, 27.09.-02.10.2009

Lanzieri, Giampaolo [Projections, 2011]: Fewer, Older and Multicultural? Projections of the EU populations by foreign/national background, Luxembourg: Publications Office of the European Union, 2011, available at: http://epp.eurostat.ec.europa.eu/cache/ITY_OFFPUB/KS-RA-11-019/EN/KS-RA-11-019-EN.PDF (last accessed: 14.04.2014)

Lee, Ronald D. [Probabilistic approaches, 1998]: Probabilistic Approaches to Population Forecasting, in: Population and Development Review, vol. 24 (1998), Supplement, pp. 156-190

Lesthaeghe, Ron [Second demographic transition, 2010]: The Unfolding Story of the Second Demographic Transition, in: Population and Development Review, vol. 36 (2010), no. 2, pp. 211-251

Lesthaeghe, Ron/Willems, Paul [Low fertility, 1999]: Is Low Fertility a Temporary Phenomenon in the European Union?, in: Population and Development Review, vol. 25 (1999), no. 2, pp. 211-228

Lijphart, Arend [Unequal participation, 1997]: Unequal Participation: Democracy`s unresolved dilemma. Presidential address, American Political Science Association, 1996, in: The American Political Science Review, vol. 91 (1997), no. 1, pp. 1-14

Linden, Markus [Interessensymmetrie, 2007]: Interessensymmetrie trotz Vielfalt? Modi gleichwertiger Inklusion in pluralistischen Demokratietheorien, in: *Winfried Thaa (ed.)*, Inklusion durch Repräsentation, Baden-Baden: Nomos Verlagsgesellschaft, 2007, pp. 61-81

Linke, Wilfried [Mortality trends, 1995]: Mortality Trends of Immigrant Populations, in: *Saskia Voets/Jeanette Schoorl/Bart De Bruijn (ed.)*, The Demographic Consequences of International Migration, The Hague: Netherlands Interdisciplinary Demographic Institute (NIDI), 1995, pp. 123-161

Lippke, Richard L. [Disenfranchisement, 2001]: The Disenfranchisement of Felons, in: Law and Philosophy, vol. 20 (2001), no. 6, pp. 553-580

López-Guerra, Claudio [Expatriates, 2005]: Should Expatriates Vote?, in: The Journal of Political Philosophy, vol. 13 (2005), no. 2, pp. 216-234

Lutz, Wolfgang/Goldstein, Joshua R. [Introduction, 2004]: Introduction: How to deal with uncertainty in population forecasting?, in: International Statistical Review, vol. 72 (2004), no. 1, pp. 1-4

Lutz, Wolfgang/Scherbov, Sergei [Bevölkerungsprognosen, 1998]: Probabilistische Bevölkerungsprognosen für Deutschland, in: Zeitschrift für Bevölkerungswissenschaft, vol. 23 (1998), no. 2, pp. 83-109

Lutz, Wolfgang/Scherbov, Sergei [Future changes, 1999]: What Do We Know about Future Changes in the Proportions of Children and Elderly in Europe?, Laxenburg: International Institute for Applied Systems Analysis, 1999, available at: http://www.iiasa.ac.at/Admin/PUB/Documents/IR-99-012.pdf (last accessed: 14.04.2014)

Lutz, Wolfgang/Skirbekk, Vegard [Policies, 2005]: Policies Addressing the Tempo Effect in Low-Fertility Countries, in: Population and Development Review, vol. 31 (2005), no. 4, pp. 699-720

Lutz, Wolfgang/Goldstein, Joshua R./Prinz, Christopher [Alternative approaches, 1996]: Alternative Approaches to Population Projection, in: *Wolfgang Lutz (ed.)*, The Future Population of the World. What can we assume today?, London: Earthscan, 1996, pp. 17-50

Lutz, Wolfgang/Goujon, Anne/Doblhammer-Reiter, Gabriele [Demographic dimensions, 1998]: Demographic Dimensions in Forecasting: Adding education to age and sex, in: Population and Development Review, vol. 24 (1998), Supplement, pp. 42-58

Lutz, Wolfgang/Sanderson, Warren C./Scherbov, Sergei [Expert opinion, 1996]: Probabilistic Population Projections Based on Expert Opinion, in: *Wolfgang*

Lutz (ed.), The Future Population of the World. What can we assume today?, Second edition, London: Earthscan, 1996, pp. 397-428

Lutz, Wolfgang/Sanderson, Warren C./Scherbov, Sergei [Population projections, 1998]: Expert-based Population Projections, in: Population and Development Review, vol. 24 (1998), Supplement, pp. 139-155

Luy, Marc [Sterblichkeitsentwicklung, 2004]: Verschiedene Aspekte der Sterblichkeitsentwicklung in Deutschland von 1950 bis 2000, in: Zeitschrift für Bevölkerungswissenschaft, vol. 29 (2004), no. 1, pp. 3-62

Malacic, Janez [Migration trends, 2002]: International Migration Trends in Central and Eastern Europe during the 1990's and at the Beginning of the 21st Century, in: *Vladimir Iontsev (ed.)*, World in the Mirror of International Migration, Moscow: MAX Press, 2002, pp. 114-128

Manton, Kenneth G./Stallard, Eric/Tolley, H. Dennis [Limits, 1991]: Limits to Human Life Expectancy: Evidence, prospects, and implications, in: Population and Development Review, vol. 17 (1991), no. 4, pp. 603-637

Martin, David [New rules, 2002]: New Rules for Dual Nationality, in: *Randall Hansen/Patrick Weil (ed.)*, Dual Nationality, Social Rights and Federal Citizenship in the U.S. and Europe. The reinvention of citizenship, New York/Oxford: Berghahn Books, 2002, pp. 34-60

Martiniello, Marco [Political participation, 2006]: Political Participation, Mobilisation and Representation of Immigrants and their Offspring in Europe, in: *Rainer Bauböck (ed.)*, Migration and Citizenship. Legal status, rights and political participation, Amsterdam: Amsterdam University Press, 2006, pp. 83-112

Marx, Reinhard [Stellungnahme, 2007]: Stellungnahme zu den Gesetzesentwürfen des Bundesrates - BT-Drs. 16/5107 - und der Fraktion Bündnis 90/Die Grünen - BT-Drs. 16/2650 - sowie dem Antrag der Fraktion Die Linke - BT-Drs. 16/1779 zum Staatsangehörigkeitsrecht, Deutscher Bundestag: A-Drs. 16(4)311 A, 2007, available at: http://webarchiv.bundestag.de/cgi/show.php?fileToLoad=1270&id=1134 (last accessed: 14.04.2014)

Masing, Johannes [Wandel, 2001]: Wandel im Staatsangehörigkeitsrecht vor den Herausforderungen moderner Migration, Tübingen: Mohr Siebeck, 2001

Massey, Douglas S. [Synthenic theory 2002]: A Synthetic Theory of International Migration, in: *Vladimir Iontsev (ed.)*, World in the Mirror of International Migration, Moscow: MAX Press, 2002, pp. 142-152

Massey, Douglas S., et al. [Theories, 1993]: Theories of International Migration: A review and appraisal, in: Population and Development Review, vol. 19 (1993), no. 3, pp. 431-466

Massicotte, Louis/Blais, André/Yoshinaka, Antoine [Rules of the game, 2004]: Establishing the Rules of the Game: Election laws in democracies, Toronto/Buffalo/London: University of Toronto Press, 2004

Massing, Peter/Breit, Gotthard (ed.) [Demokratie-Theorien, 2003]: Demokratie-Theorien. Von der Antike bis zur Gegenwart, Second edition, Bonn/ Schwalbach: Wochenschau Verlag; licensed edition for Bundes-zentrale für Politische Bildung, 2003

Maurer, Andreas [Europawahlen, 2009]: Europawahlen, in: *Werner Weidenfeld/Wolfgang Wessels (ed.)*, Europa von A bis Z. Taschenbuch der europäischen Integration, Eleventh edition, Baden-Baden: Nomos Verlagsgesellschaft; licensed edition for Bundeszentrale für Politische Bildung, 2009, pp. 231-238

McDonald, Peter [Low fertility, 2006]: Low Fertility and the State: The efficacy of policy, in: Population and Development Review, vol. 32 (2006), no. 3, pp. 485-510

Meier-Braun, Karl-Heinz [Einwanderungsland, 2006]: Der lange Weg ins Einwanderungsland Deutschland. Zuwanderung und Ausländerpolitik in Deutschland, in: Der Bürger im Staat, vol. 56 (2006), no. 4, pp. 204-209

Menning, Sonja [Wahlverhalten, 2009]: Wahlverhalten und politische Partizipation älterer Menschen, Berlin: Deutsches Zentrum für Altersfragen, 2009, available at: http://www.dza.de/fileadmin/dza/pdf/GeroStat_Report_Altersdaten_Heft_3_2009.pdf (last accessed: 14.04.2014)

Merk, Peter [Wahlrecht, 1998]: Wahlrecht ohne Altersgrenze?, in: *Christian Palentien/Klaus Hurrelmann (ed.)*, Jugend und Politik. Ein Handbuch für Forschung, Lehre und Praxis, Second edition, Neuwied/Kriftel/Berlin: Hermann Luchterhand Verlag GmbH, 1998, pp. 260-279

Milewski, Nadja [First child, 2007]: First Child of Immigrant Workers and their Descendants in Germany: Interrelation of events, disruption, or adaptation?, in: Demographic Research, vol. 17 (2007), no. 29, pp. 859-896

Miller, Mark J. [Participation, 1989]: Political Participation and Representation of Noncitizens, in: *William Rogers Brubaker (ed.)*, Immigration and the Politics of Citizenship in Europe and North America, Lanham/New

York/London: University Press of America/German Marshall Fund of the United States, 1989, pp. 129-143

Monz, Leo [Reform, 1999]: Die Reform des Staatsangehörigkeitsrechts. Chancen für eine gleichberechtigte Zukunft aller Kinder verbessert, in: *Andreas Goldberg/Faruk Sen (ed.)*, Deutsche Türken - Türkische Deutsche? Die Diskussion um die doppelte Staatsbürgerschaft, Münster/Hamburg/ London: LIT Verlag, 1999, pp. 43-50

Müller-Graff, Peter-Christian/Kainer, Friedemann [Visapolitik, 2009]: Asyl-, Einwanderungs- und Visapolitik, in: *Werner Weidenfeld/Wolfgang Wessels (ed.)*, Europa von A bis Z, Eleventh edition, Bonn: Nomos Verlags-gesellschaft; licensed edition for Bundeszentrale für Politische Bildung, 2009, pp. 78-83

Münch, Ursula [Asylpolitik, 1993]: Asylpolitik in der Bundesrepublik Deutschland. Entwicklung und Alternativen, Second edition, Opladen: Leske + Budrich, 1993

Münz, Rainer/Ulrich, Ralf [Wachstum, 1997]: Das zukünftige Wachstum der ausländischen Bevölkerung in Deutschland. Demographische Prognosen bis 2030, Berlin: Humboldt-Universität Berlin, 1997

Münz, Rainer/Ulrich, Ralf [Immigration, 1999]: Immigration and Citizenship in Germany, in: German Politics and Society, vol. 17 (1999), no. 4, pp. 1-33

Münz, Rainer/Seifert, Wolfgang/Ulrich, Ralf [Zuwanderung, 1999]: Zuwanderung nach Deutschland. Strukturen, Wirkungen, Perspektiven, Second edition, Frankfurt/New York: Campus Verlag, 1999

Münz, Rainer, et al. [Migrationsmuster, 1997]: Migrationsmuster, Integration und Exklusion von Ausländern. Deutschland und Österreich im Vergleich, Berlin: Humboldt-Universität Berlin, 1997

Myrberg, Nanouschka [Room for all, 2008]: Room for All? Spaces and places for thing assemblies: The case of the all-thing on Gotland, Sweden, in: Viking and Medieval Scandinavia, vol. 4 (2008), pp. 133-157

Naegele, Gerhard [Politics, 1999]: The Politics of Old Age in Germany, in: *Alan Walker/Gerhard Naegele (ed.)*, The Politics of Old Age in Europe, Buckingham/Philadelphia: Open University Press, 1999, pp. 91-109

Nash, Michael [Voting, 2002]: Voting as a Means of Social Inclusion for People with a Mental Illness, in: Journal of Psychiatric and Mental Health Nursing, vol. 9 (2002), no. 6, pp. 697-703

Neale, Thomas H. [Eighteen year old vote, 1983]: The Eighteen Year Old Vote: The twenty-sixth amendment and subsequent voting rates of newly enfranchised age groups, Washington D.C.: Congressional Research Service, 1983, available at: http://digital.library.unt.edu/ark:/67531/metacrs8805/m1/1/high_res_d/83-103GOV_1983May20.pdf (last accessed: 14.04.2014)

Nees, Albin [Stellungnahme, 2004]: Stellungnahme des Deutschen Familienverbandes zum Antrag "Mehr Demokratie wagen durch ein Wahlrecht von Geburt an", Deutscher Bundestag: A-Drs. 15(4)172 C, 2004, available at: http://webarchiv.bundestag.de/archive/2007/0206/ausschuesse/archiv15/a04/Oeffentliche_Anhoerungen/Anhoerungen_6/Stellungnahme_4.pdf (last accessed: 14.04.2014)

Nie, Norman H./Verba, Sidney/Kim, Jae-on [Political participation, 1974]: Political Participation and the Life Cycle, in: Comparative Politics, vol. 6 (1974), no. 3, pp. 319-340

Nohlen, Dieter [Wahlrecht, 2007]: Wahlrecht und Parteiensystem, Fifth edition, Opladen/Farmington Hills: Barbara Budrich Verlag, 2007

Nolte, Ellen/Shkolnikov, Vladimir M./McKee, Martin [Mortality patterns, 2000]: Changing Mortality Patterns in East and West Germany and Poland. II: Short-term trends during transition and in the 1990s, in: Journal of Epidemiology and Community Health, vol. 54 (2000), no. 12, pp. 899-906

Oeppen, Jim/Vaupel, James [Broken limits, 2002]: Broken Limits to Life Expectancy, in: Science, vol. 296 (2002), no. 5570, pp. 1029-1031

Oerter, Rolf [Wahlrecht, 2008]: Wahlrecht und Entwicklung: Die wachsenden Kompetenzen zur politischen Partizipation, in: *Stiftung für die Rechte zukünftiger Generationen (ed.)*, Wahlrecht ohne Altersgrenze? Verfassungsrechtliche, demokratietheoretische und entwicklungspsychologische Aspekte, München: Oekom Verlag, 2008, pp. 187-209

Oeter, Stefan [Allgemeines Wahlrecht, 1999]: Allgemeines Wahlrecht und Ausschluß von der Wahlberechtigung: Welche Vorgaben enthält das Grundgesetz?, in: *Ulrike Davy (ed.)*, Politische Integration der ausländischen Wohnbevölkerung, Baden-Baden: Nomos Verlagsgesellschaft, 1999, pp. 30-57

Olshansky, S. Jay/Carnes, Bruce A. [Future, 2009]: The Future of Human Longevity, in: *Peter Uhlberg (ed.)*, International Handbook of Population Ageing, Heidelberg: Springer, 2009, pp. 731-745

Olshansky, S. Jay/Carnes, Bruce A./Brody, Jacob [Life span, 2002]: A Biodemographic Interpretation of the Life Span, in: Population and Development Review, vol. 28 (2002), no. 3, pp. 501-513

Olshansky, S. Jay/Carnes, Bruce A./Cassel, Christine [Methuselah, 1990]: In Search of Methuselah: Estimating the upper limits to human longevity, in: Science, vol. 250 (1990), no. 4981, pp. 634-640

Olshansky, S. Jay/Carnes, Bruce A./Désesquelles, Aline [Prospects, 2001]: Prospects for Human Longevity, in: Science, vol. 291 (2001), no. 5508, pp. 1491-1492

Opfermann, Heike/Grobecker, Claire/Krack-Roberg, Elle [Bereinigung, 2006]: Auswirkung der Bereiningung des Ausländerzentralregisters auf die amtliche Ausländerstatistik, Wiesbaden: Statistisches Bundesamt, 2006, available at: https://www.destatis.de/DE/Publikationen/WirtschaftStatistik/ Bevoelkerung/Bevoelkauslaenderzentralregister.pdf?__blob=publicationFile (last accessed: 14.04.2014)

Organisation for Economic Co-operation and Development (OECD) [Migration outlook, 2009]: International Migration Outlook 2009, available at: http://www.oecd.org/els/internationalmigrationpoliciesanddata/international migrationoutlook2009.htm#STATISTICS (last accessed: 14.04.2014)

Ortega y Gasset, José [Revolt, 1932]: The Revolt of the Masses, reissued in 1993, New York/London: W.W. Norton & Company, Inc., 1932

Özcan, Veysel [Deutschland, 2005]: Deutschland: Rückläufige Einbürgerungszahlen, Berlin: Netzwerk Migration in Europa, 2005, available at: http://www.migration-info.de/sites/wp11146219.server-he.de/files/attach ments/ausgabe0507.pdf (last accessed: 14.04.2014)

Palentien, Christian [Diskussion, 1998]: Pro- und Contra-Diskussion zu einer Veränderung des Wahlrechts, in: *Christian Palentien/Klaus Hurrelmann (ed.)*, Jugend und Politik. Ein Handbuch für Forschung, Lehre und Praxis, Second edition, Neuwied/Kriftel/Berlin: Hermann Luchterhand Verlag GmbH, 1998, pp. 290-299

Palentien, Christian/Hurrelmann, Klaus (ed.) [Jugend, 1998]: Jugend und Politik. Ein Handbuch für Forschung, Lehre und Praxis, Second edition, Neuwied/Kriftel/Berlin: Hermann Luchterhand Verlag GmbH, 1998

Palentien, Christian/Hurrelmann, Klaus [Veränderte Jugend, 1998]: Veränderte Jugend - Veränderte Formen der Beteiligung Jugendlicher?, in: *Christian Palentien/Klaus Hurrelmann (ed.)*, Jugend und Politik. Ein Handbuch für

Forschung, Lehre und Praxis, Second edition, Neuwied/Kriftel/Berlin: Hermann Luchterhand Verlag GmbH, 1998, pp. 11-31

Palleit, Leander [Wahlrecht, 2011]: Gleiches Wahlrecht für alle? Menschen mit Behinderungen und das Wahlrecht in Deutschland, Berlin: Deutsches Institut für Menschenrechte, 2011, available at: http://www.institut-fuer-menschen rechte.de/publikationen/detailansicht.html?tx_commerce_pi1[showUid]=346 &cHash=2b8f2240ddc546354bb53f0b0823009c (last accessed: 14.04.2014)

Pammett, Jon H. [Elections, 1988]: A Framework for the Comparative Analysis of Elections across Time and Space, in: Electoral Studies, vol. 7 (1988), no. 2, pp. 125-142

Payling, Simon Y. [Elections, 1999]: County Parliamentary Elections in Fifteenth-Century England, in: Parliamentary History, vol. 18 (1999), no. 3, pp. 237-259

Pechstein, Matthias [Stellungnahme, 2008]: Stellungnahme zum Entwurf eines Gesetzes zur Änderung des Grundgesetzes (Kommunales Ausländerwahlrecht), Deutscher Bundestag: A-Drs 16(4)459 B, 2008, available at: http://webarchiv.bundestag.de/cgi/show.php?fileToLoad=1270&id=1134 (last accessed: 14.04.2014)

Pesch, Volker [Mill, 2003]: John Stuart Mill, in: *Peter Massing/Gotthard Breit (ed.)*, Demokratie-Theorien. Von der Antike bis zur Gegenwart, Second edition, Bonn/Schwalbach: Wochenschau Verlag; licensed edition for Bundeszentrale für politische Bildung, 2003, pp. 158-164

Peschel-Gutzeit, Lore Maria [Wahlrecht, 2004]: Wahlrecht von Geburt an, Deutscher Bundestag: A-Drs. 15(4)172 A, 2004, available at: http://webarchiv.bundestag.de/archive/2007/0206/ausschuesse/archiv15/a04/Oeffentliche_Anhoerungen/Anhoerungen_6/Stellungnahme_2.pdf (last accessed: 14.04.2014)

Petersen, Thieß/Lübcke, Britta [Elternschaft, 2006]: Elternschaft als ökonomisches Entscheidungsproblem: Modell-theoretische Grundlagen und familienpolitische Konsequenzen, in: Zeitschrift für Bevölkerungswissenschaft, vol. 31 (2006), no. 2, pp. 187-230

Peterson, Peter G. [Gray dawn, 1999]: Gray Dawn: The global aging crisis, in: Foreign Affairs, vol. 78 (1999), no. 1, pp. 42-55

Phillips, John A./Wetherell, Charles [Reform act, 1995]: The Great Reform Act of 1832 and the Political Modernization of England, in: The American Historical Review, vol. 100 (1995), no. 2, pp. 411-436

Population Reference Bureau [World population, 2010]: World Population Data Sheet, Washington, D.C.: Population Reference Bureau, 2010, available at: http://www.prb.org/pdf10/10wpds_eng.pdf (last accessed: 14.04.2014)

Portes, Alejandro/DeWind, Josh [Dialogue, 2007]: A Cross-Atlantic Dialogue, in: *Alejandro Portes/Josh DeWind (ed.)*, Rethinking Migration. New theoretical and empirical perspectives, New York/Oxford: Berghahn Books, 2007, pp. 3-26

Pötzsch, Olga [Geburtenentwicklung, 2010]: Annahmen zur Geburtenentwicklung in der 12. koordinierten Bevölkerungsvorausberechnung, in: Wirtschaft und Statistik, vol. 1 (2010), pp. 29-40

Presser, Harriet B. [Gender perspective, 2001]: A Gender Perspective for Understanding Low Fertility in Post-Transitional Societies, in: Population and Development Review, vol. 27 (2001), Supplement: Global Fertility Transition, pp. 177-183

Preston, Samuel H. [Values, 1986]: Changing Values and Falling Birth Rates, in: Population and Development Review, vol. 12 (1986), Supplement: Below-Replacement Fertility in Industrial Societies: Causes, Consequences, Policies, pp. 176-195

Preston, Samuel H./Heuveline, Patrick/Guillot, Michel [Demography, 2001]: Demography. Measuring and modeling population processes, Malden/Oxford/Carlton: Blackwell Publishing, 2001

Priddat, Birger P. [Demokratie, 2008]: Demokratie und demographischer Wandel, in: *André Brodocz/Marcus Llanque/Gary S. Schaal (ed.)*, Bedrohungen der Demokratie, Wiesbaden: Verlag für Sozialwissenschaften, 2008, pp. 203-215

Raskin, Jamin B. [Legal aliens, 1993]: Legal Aliens, Local Citizens: The historical, constitutional and theoretical meanings of alien suffrage, in: University of Pennsylvania Law Review, vol. 141 (1993), no. 4, pp. 1391-1470

Rattinger, Hans [Demography, 1992]: Demography and Federal Elections in Germany, 1953-1990 - and Beyond, in: Electoral Studies, vol. 11 (1992), no. 3, pp. 223-247

Razum, Oliver [Commentary, 2006]: Commentary: Of salmon and time travellers - Musing on the mystery of migrant mortality, in: International Journal of Epidemiology, vol. 35 (2006), pp. 919-921

Razum, Oliver/Twardella, Dorothee [Time travel, 2002]: Time Travel with Oliver Twist - Towards an explanation for a paradoxically low mortality among recent immigrants, in: Tropical Medicine and International Health, vol. 7 (2002), no. 1, pp. 4-10

Razum, Oliver/Sahin-Hodoglugil, Nuriye N./Polit, Karin [Health, 2005]: Health, Wealth or Family Ties? Why Turkish work migrants return from Germany, in: Journal of Ethnic and Migration Studies, vol. 31 (2005), no. 4, pp. 719-739

Razum, Oliver/Zeeb, Hajo/Rohrmann, Sabine [Healthy migrant effect, 2000]: The 'Healthy Migrant Effect' - Not merely a fallacy of inaccurate denominator figures, in: International Journal of Epidemiology, vol. 29 (2000), no. 1, pp. 191-192

Razum, Oliver, et al. [Mortality, 1998]: Low Overall Mortality of Turkish Residents in Germany Persists and Extends into a Second Generation: Merely a healthy migrant effect?, in: Tropical Medicine and International Health, vol. 3 (1998), no. 4, pp. 297-303

Reinans, Sven A./Hammar, Tomas [Changes, 1995]: Changes of Citizenship among Immigrant Populations, in: *Saskia Voets/Jeanette Schoorl/Bart De Bruijn (ed.)*, The Demographic Consequences of International Migration, The Hague: Netherlands Interdisciplinary Demographic Institute (NIDI), 1995, pp. 177-204

Renner, Günter [Doppelstaatsangehörigkeit, 1999]: Doppelstaatsangehörigkeit: Gibt es völkerrechtliche Hindernisse?, in: *Ulrike Davy (ed.)*, Politische Integration der ausländischen Wohnbevölkerung, Baden-Baden: Nomos Verlagsgesellschaft, 1999, pp. 173-187

Renner, Günter [Mehrstaatigkeit, 1999]: Mehrstaatigkeit in Deutschland - Ein dauerndes Übel?, in: *Andreas Goldberg/Faruk Sen (ed.)*, Deutsche Türken - Türkische Deutsche? Die Diskussion um die doppelte Staatsbürgerschaft, Münster/Hamburg/London: LIT Verlag, 1999, pp. 77-96

Rennert, Klaus [Stellungnahme, 2008]: Gutachtliche Stellungnahme, betr.: Kommunales Ausländerwahlrecht, Deutscher Bundestag: A-Drs 16(4)459 C, 2008, available at: http://webarchiv.bundestag.de/cgi/show.php?fileToLoad =1270&id=1134 (last accessed: 14.04.2014)

Rittstieg, Helmut [Dual citizenship, 1994]: Dual Citizenship: Legal and political aspects in the German context, in: *Rainer Bauböck (ed.)*, From Aliens to

Citizens. Redefining the status of immigrants in Europe, Aldershot et al.: Avebury, 1994, pp. 111-120

Rogers, Andrei [Population dynamics, 1986]: Parametrized Multistate Population Dynamics and Projections, in: Journal of the American Statistical Association, vol. 81 (1986), no. 393, pp. 48-61

Roth, Klaus [Cicero, 2003]: Cicero, in: *Peter Massing/Gotthard Breit (ed.)*, Demokratie-Theorien. Von der Antike bis zur Gegenwart, Second edition, Bonn/Schwalbach: Wochenschau Verlag; licensed edition for Bundeszentrale für Politische Bildung, 2003, pp. 45-51

Roth, Klaus [Marsilius, 2003]: Marsilius von Padua, in: *Peter Massing/Gotthard Breit (ed.)*, Demokratie-Theorien. Von der Antike bis zur Gegenwart, Second edition, Bonn/Schwalbach: Wochenschau Verlag; licensed edition for Bundeszentrale für politische Bildung, 2003, pp. 75-82

Rottinghaus, Brandon/Baldwin, Gina [Voting, 2007]: Voting Behind Bars: Explaining variation in international enfranchisement practices, in: Electoral Studies, vol. 26 (2007), no. 3, pp. 688-698

Rubio-Marín, Ruth [Immigration, 2000]: Immigration as a Democratic Challenge. Citizenship and inclusion in Germany and the United States, Cambridge: Cambridge University Press, 2000

Saage, Richard [Demokratietheorien, 2005]: Demokratietheorien. Historischer Prozess - Theoretische Entwicklung - Soziotechnische Bedingungen. Eine Einführung, Wiesbaden: Verlag für Sozialwissenschaften, 2005

Salkever, Stephen G. [Women, 1986]: Women, Soldiers, Citizens: Plato & Aristotle on the politics of virility, in: Polity, vol. 19 (1986), no. 2, pp. 232-253

Sanderson, Warren C./Scherbov, Sergei [Electoral majority, 2007]: A Near Electoral Majority of Pensioners: Prospects and policies, in: Population and Development Review, vol. 33 (2007), no. 3, pp. 543-554

Sartori, Fabio [Citizenship, 2010]: Acquisitions of Citizenship Slightly Declining in the EU, in: Eurostat. Statistics in Focus. Population and social conditions (2010), no. 36, pp. 1-8

Sartori, Fabio [Acquisitions, 2011]: Acquisitions of Citizenship on the Rise in 2009, in: Eurostat. Statistics in Focus. Population and social conditions (2011), no. 24, pp. 1-12

Sartori, Giovanni [Democracy, 1987]: The Theory of Democracy Revisited, Chatham: Chatham House Publishers, Inc., 1987

Sassen, Saskia [Transnationalizing, 1998]: The *de facto* Transnationalizing of Immigration Policy, in: *Christian Joppke (ed.)*, Challenge to the Nation-State, Oxford: Oxford University Press, 1998, pp. 49-85

Sauer, Leonore/Ette, Andreas [Auswanderung, 2007]: Auswanderung aus Deutschland. Stand der Forschung und erste Ergebnisse zur internationalen Migration deutscher Staatsbürger, Wiesbaden: Bundesinstitut für Bevölkerungsforschung, 2007, available at: http://www.bib-demografie.de/DE/Veroeffentlichungen/Materialien/Hefte/123.html?nn=3075052 (last accessed: 14.04.2014)

Schmid, Susanne/Borchers, Kevin [Migration, 2010]: Vor den Toren Europas? Das Potenzial der Migration aus Afrika, Nürnberg: Bundesamt für Migration und Flüchtlinge, 2010, available at: http://www.bamf.de/SharedDocs/Anlagen/DE/Publikationen/Forschungsberichte/fb07-vor-den-toren-europas.pdf?__blob=publicationFile (last accessed: 14.04.2014)

Schmid, Susanne/Kohls, Martin [Generatives Verhalten, 2011]: Generatives Verhalten und Migration - Eine Bestandsaufnahme des generativen Verhaltens von Migrantinnen in Deutschland, Nürnberg: Bundesamt für Migration und Flüchtlinge, 2011, available at: http://www.bamf.de/SharedDocs/Anlagen/DE/Publikationen/Forschungsberichte/fb10-generativ esverhaltenundmigration.pdf?__blob=publicationFile (last accessed: 14.04.2014)

Schmidt, Manfred G. [Demokratietheorien, 2006]: Demokratietheorien. Eine Einführung, Third revised and extended edition, Wiesbaden: Verlag für Sozialwissenschaften, 2006

Schmilowski, Frank [Demokratisierung, 2008]: Die Demokratisierung des Wahlrechts in Deutschland. Vom Dreiklassenwahlrecht zum Wahlrecht ohne Altersgrenzen, in: *Stiftung für die Rechte zukünftiger Generationen (ed.)*, Wahlrecht ohne Altersgrenze? Verfassungsrechtliche, demokratie-theoretische und entwicklungspsychologische Aspekte, München: Oekom Verlag, 2008, pp. 73-94

Schnapper, Dominique [European debate, 1997]: The European Debate on Citizenship, in: Daedalus, vol. 126 (1997), no. 3, pp. 199-222

Schoorl, Jeanette [Fertility trends, 1995]: Fertility Trends of Immigrant Populations, in: *Saskia Voets/Jeanette Schoorl/Bart De Bruijn (ed.)*, The Demographic Consequences of International Migration, The Hague:

Netherlands Interdisciplinary Demographic Institute (NIDI), 1995, pp. 97-121

Schorn, Karina/von Schwartzenberg, Margitta [Grundlagen, 2005]: Grundlagen und Daten der Wahl zum 16. Deutschen Bundestag am 18. September 2005, in: Wirtschaft und Statistik (2005), no. 8, pp. 865-884

Schreiber, Wolfgang [Handbuch, 2002]: Handbuch des Wahlrechts zum Deutschen Bundestag. Kommentar zum Bundeswahlgesetz, Seventh edition, Köln et al.: Carl Heymanns Verlag KG, 2002

Schriner, Kay/Ochs, Lisa A./Shields, Todd G. [Suffrage, 1997]: The Last Suffrage Movement: Voting rights for persons with cognitive and emotional disabilities, in: Publius, vol. 27 (1997), no. 3, pp. 75-96

Schuck, Peter [Plural citizenships, 2002]: Plural Citizenships, in: *Randall Hansen/Patrick Weil (ed.)*, Dual Nationality, Social Rights and Federal Citizenship in the U.S. and Europe. The reinvention of citizenship, New York/Oxford: Berghahn Books, 2002, pp. 61-99

Schulze, Alexander [Konsequenzen, 2009]: Sozioökonomische Konsequenzen der Fertilität: Folgen der Geburt von Kindern für den Wohlstand von Paarhaushalten, Wiesbaden: Verlag für Sozialwissenschaften, 2009

Schumpeter, Joseph A. [Capitalism, 1976]: Capitalism, Socialism and Democracy, Fifth edition, London: Allen & Unwin, 1976

Schupp, Jürgen/Söhn, Janina/Schmiade, Nicole [Internationale Mobilität, 2005]: Internationale Mobilität von deutschen Staatsbürgern. Chance für Arbeitslose oder Abwanderung der Leistungsträger?, in: Zeitschrift für Bevölkerungswissenschaft, vol. 30 (2005), no. 2-3, pp. 279-292

Shryock, Henry S. /Siegel, Jacob S. [Demography 1, 1971]: The Methods and Materials of Demography 1, Washington, D.C.: U.S. Government Printing Office, 1971

Shryock, Henry S. /Siegel, Jacob S. [Demography 2, 1971]: The Methods and Materials of Demography 2, Washington, D.C.: U.S. Government Printing Office, 1971

Siegert, Manuel [Integrationsmonitoring, 2006]: Integrationsmonitoring - State of the Art in internationaler Perspektive, Nürnberg: Studie im Auftrag des Bundesamtes für Migration und Flüchtlinge/Europäisches Forum für Migrationsstudien, 2006, available at: http://www.bamf.de/SharedDocs/Anlagen/DE/Publikationen/Expertisen/integrationsmonitoring-expertise.html (last accessed: 14.04.2014)

Sieveking, Klaus [Stellungnahme, 2008]: Stellungnahme zur Anhörung des Innenausschuss des Deutschen Bundestages am 22.9.2008 zum "Entwurf eines Gesetzes zur Änderung des Grundgesetzes (Kommunales Ausländerwahlrecht)" (BT-Drucksache 16/6628) und dem Antrag "Kommunales Wahlrecht für Drittstaatenangehörige einführen" (BT-Drucksache 16/5904), Deutscher Bundestag: A-Drs. 16(4)459 E, 2008, available at: http://www.kommunales-wahlrecht.de/files/sieveking.pdf (last accessed: 14.04.2014)

Sobotka, Tomás [Lowest-low fertility, 2004]: Is Lowest-Low Fertility in Europe Explained by the Postponing of Childbearing?, in: Population and Development Review, vol. 30 (2004), no. 2, pp. 195-220

Sobotka, Tomás [Rising importance, 2008]: The Rising Importance of Migrants for Childbearing in Europe, in: Demographic Research, vol. 19 (2008), no. 9, pp. 225-248

Sohr, Sven/Boehnke, Klaus/Stromberg, Claudia [Politische Persönlichkeiten, 1998]: "Politische Persönlichkeiten" - Eine aussterbende Spezies ?, in: *Christian Palentien/Klaus Hurrelmann (ed.)*, Jugend und Politik. Ein Handbuch für Forschung, Lehre und Praxis, Second edition, Neuwied/Kriftel/Berlin: Hermann Luchterhand Verlag GmbH, 1998, pp. 206-235

Spiro, Peter [Dual nationality, 2002]: Embracing Dual Nationality, in: *Randall Hansen/Patrick Weil (ed.)*, Dual Nationality, Social Rights and Federal Citizenship in the U.S. and Europe. The reinvention of citizenship, New York/Oxford: Berghahn Books, 2002, pp. 19-33

Statistisches Bundesamt [Bevölkerung, 1951-2011]: Bevölkerung nach Alters- und Geburtsjahren, 1950-2010, Wiesbaden: obtained via e-mail from Federal Statistical Office of Germany, 1951-2011

Statistisches Bundesamt [Rechtspflege, 2003-2011]: Rechtspflege. Strafverfolgung, 2002-2010, Wiesbaden: Statistisches Bundesamt, 2003-2011

Statistisches Bundesamt [Fortschreibung, 2008]: Fortschreibung des Bevölkerungsstandes, Wiesbaden: Statistisches Bundesamt, 2008, available at: https://www.destatis.de/DE/Publikationen/Qualitaetsberichte/Bevoelkerung/Bevoelkerungsfortschreibung.pdf?__blob=publicationFile (last accessed: 14.04.2014)

Statistisches Bundesamt [Wanderungsstatistik, 2008]: Wanderungsstatistik, Wiesbaden: Statistisches Bundesamt, 2008, available at: https://www.destatis.de/DE/Publikationen/Qualitaetsberichte/Bevoelkerung/Wanderungsstatistik.pdf?__blob=publicationFile (last accessed: 14.04.2014)

Statistisches Bundesamt [Ausländerstatistik, 2009]: Ausländerstatistik. Ergebnisse des Ausländerzentralregisters, Wiesbaden: Statistisches Bundesamt, 2009

Statistisches Bundesamt [Bevölkerung Deutschlands, 2009]: Bevölkerung Deutschlands bis 2060. 12. koordinierte Bevölkerungsvorausberechnung, Wiesbaden: Statistisches Bundesamt, 2009, available at: https://www.destatis.de/DE/Publikationen/Thematisch/Bevoelkerung/VorausberechnungBevoelkerung/BevoelkerungDeutschland2060Presse5124204099004.pdf?__blob=publicationFile (last accessed: 14.04.2014)

Statistisches Bundesamt [Geburten, 2010]: Statistik der Geburten, Wiesbaden: Statistisches Bundesamt, 2010, available at: https://www.destatis.de/DE/Publikationen/Qualitaetsberichte/Bevoelkerung/Geburten.pdf?__blob=publicationFile (last accessed: 14.04.2014)

Statistisches Bundesamt [Sterbefälle, 2010]: Statistik der Sterbefälle, Wiesbaden: Statistisches Bundesamt, 2010, available at: https://www.destatis.de/DE/Publikationen/Qualitaetsberichte/Bevoelkerung/Sterbefaelle.pdf?__blob=publicationFile (last accessed: 14.04.2014)

Statistisches Bundesamt [Wahlberechtigte, 2010]: Wahlberechtigte und Wähler nach Geschlecht und Altersgruppen seit 1953, Wiesbaden: obtained via e-mail from the office of the Federal Returning Officer of Germany, 2010

Statistisches Bundesamt [Strafverfolgungsstatistik, 2011]: Strafverfolgungsstatistik, Wiesbaden: Statistisches Bundesamt, 2011, available at: https://www.destatis.de/DE/Publikationen/Qualitaetsberichte/Rechtspflege/Strafverfolgung.pdf?__blob=publicationFile (last accessed: 14.04.2014)

Statistisches Bundesamt [Maßregelvollzug, 2011]: Strafvollzugsstatistik. Im psychiatrischen Krankenhaus und in der Entziehungsanstalt aufgrund strafrichterlicher Anordnung Untergebrachte (Maßregelvollzug) 2010/2011, Wiesbaden: Statistisches Bundesamt, 2011

Statistisches Bundesamt [Einbürgerungsstatistik, 2012]: Einbürgerungsstatistik. Qualitätsbericht, Wiesbaden: Statistisches Bundesamt, 2012, available at: https://www.destatis.de/DE/Publikationen/Qualitaetsberichte/Bevoelkerung/Einbuergerungsstatistik.pdf?__blob=publicationFile

(last accessed: 14.04.2014)

Steinhardt, Max Friedrich [Aktuelle Trends, 2007]: Aktuelle Trends der Einbürgerungen in Deutschland, in: Wirtschaftsdienst, vol. 87 (2007), no. 8, pp. 544-549

Stiftung für die Rechte zukünftiger Generationen [Positionspapier, 2008]: Positionspapier der Stiftung für die Rechte zukünftiger Generationen: Rechte von Kindern und Jugendlichen und das Wahlrecht ohne Altersgrenze, in: *Stiftung für die Rechte zukünftiger Generationen (ed.)*, Wahlrecht ohne Altersgrenze? Verfassungsrechtliche, demokratietheoretische und entwicklungspsychologische Aspekte, München: Oekom Verlag, 2008, pp. 357-372

Stiftung für die Rechte zukünftiger Generationen (ed.) [Wahlrecht, 2008]: Wahlrecht ohne Altersgrenze? Verfassungsrechtliche, demokratietheoretische und entwicklungspsychologische Aspekte, München: Oekom Verlag, 2008

Streeck, Wolfgang [Rentnerdemokratie, 2009]: Droht Deutschland eine Rentnerdemokratie?, in: *Max-Planck-Institut für Gesellschaftsforschung (ed.)*, MPIfG Jahrbuch 2009-2010, Köln: Max-Planck-Institut für Gesellschaftsforschung, 2009, pp. 47-52

Sundhaussen, Ulf [Peasants, 2003]: Peasants and the Process of Building Democratic Polities: Lessons from San Marino, in: Australian Journal of Politics and History, vol. 49 (2003), no. 2, pp. 211-221

Swanson, David A./Tayman, Jeff [Demographic forecasts, 1995]: Between a Rock and a Hard Place: The evaluation of demographic forecasts, in: Population Research and Policy Review, vol. 14 (1995), no. 2, pp. 233-249

Taylor, Charles [Democratic exclusion, 1998]: The Dynamics of Democratic Exclusion, in: Journal of Democracy, vol. 9 (1998), no. 4, pp. 143-156

Thaa, Winfried [Einleitung, 2007]: Einleitung, in: *Winfried Thaa (ed.)*, Inklusion durch Repräsentation, Baden-Baden: Nomos Verlagsgesellschaft, 2007, pp. 9-16

Therond, Olivier, et al. [Methodology, 2009]: Methodology to Translate Policy Assessment Problems into Scenarios: The example of the SEAMLESS integrated framework, in: Environmental Science & Policy, vol. 12 (2009), no. 5, pp. 619-630

Thränhardt, Dietrich [Allgemeines Wahlrecht, 1999]: Allgemeines Wahlrecht und Ausschluß von der Wahlberechtigung: Welche Vorgaben enthält das

Demokratieprinzip?, in: *Ulrike Davy (ed.)*, Politische Integration der ausländischen Wohnbevölkerung, Baden-Baden: Nomos Verlagsgesellschaft, 1999, pp. 15-29

Thränhardt, Dietrich [Einbürgerung, 2008]: Einbürgerung. Rahmenbedingungen, Motive und Perspektiven des Erwerbs der deutschen Staatsangehörigkeit, Bonn: Friedrich-Ebert-Stiftung, 2008, available at: http://library.fes.de/pdf-files/wiso/05236.pdf (last accessed: 14.04.2014)

Thränhardt, Dietrich [Kommunales Wahlrecht, 2008]: Kommunales Wahlrecht für Ausländer. Anhörung des Innenausschusses des Deutschen Bundestages, 22. September 2008, Deutscher Bundestag: A-Drs 16(4)459 D, 2008, available at: http://webarchiv.bundestag.de/cgi/show.php?fileToLoad=1270 &id=1134 (last accessed: 14.04.2014)

Tienda, Marta [Demography, 2002]: Demography and the Social Contract, in: Demography, vol. 39 (2002), no. 4, pp. 587-616

Tillmann, Frank [Wähler, 2008]: Was wir heute über die Wähler von morgen wissen - Empirische Befunde der Wählerforschung unter Minderjährigen, in: *Stiftung für die Rechte zukünftiger Generationen (ed.)*, Wahlrecht ohne Altersgrenze? Verfassungsrechtliche, demokratietheoretische und entwicklungspsychologische Aspekte, München: Oekom Verlag, 2008, pp. 119-135

Tremmel, Jörg [Ausprägung, 2008]: Die Ausprägung des Wahlwillens und der Wahlfähigkeit aus entwicklungspsychologischer Sicht, in: *Stiftung für die Rechte zukünftiger Generationen (ed.)*, Wahlrecht ohne Altersgrenze? Verfassungsrechtliche, demokratietheoretische und entwicklungspsychologische Aspekte, München: Oekom Verlag, 2008, pp. 211-225

Tuljapurkar, Shripad/Li, Nan/Boe, Carl [Mortality decline, 2000]: A Universal Pattern of Mortality Decline in the G7 Countries, in: Nature, vol. 405 (2000), no. 6788, pp. 789-792

Turner, Bryan S. [Erosion, 2001]: The Erosion of Citizenship, in: British Journal of Sociology, vol. 52 (2001), no. 2, pp. 189-209

Ulrich, Ralf [Bevölkerungsstruktur, 2001]: Die zukünftige Bevölkerungsstruktur Deutschlands nach Staatsangehörigkeit, Geburtsort und ethnischer Herkunft: Modellrechnung bis 2050. Erstellt im Auftrag der Unabhängigen Kommission "Zuwanderung", Berlin/Windhoek: 2001

Vallin, Jacques [Population, 2006]: Population: Replacement and change, in: *Graziella Caselli/Jacques Vallin/Guillaume Wunsch (ed.)*, Demography.

Analysis and synthesis. A treatise in population studies, Amsterdam et al.: Elsevier, 2006, pp. 9-13

van de Kaa, Dirk J. [Fertility preferences, 2001]: Postmodern Fertility Preferences: From changing value orientation to new behaviour, in: Population and Development Review, vol. 27 (2001), Supplement: Global Fertility Transition, pp. 290-331

van der Eijk, Cees/van Egmond, Marcel [Political effects, 2007]: Political Effects of Low Turnout in National and European Elections, in: Electoral Studies, vol. 26 (2007), no. 3, pp. 561-573

van Notten, Philip [Scenario development, 2006]: Scenario Development: A typology of approaches, in: *OECD (ed.)*, Think Scenarios, Rethink Education, Paris: OECD Publishing, 2006, pp. 69-92

van Parijs, Philippe [Disenfranchisement, 1999]: The Disenfranchisement of the Elderly, and Other Attempts to Secure Intergenerational Justice, in: Philosophy & Public Affairs, vol. 27 (1999), no. 4, pp. 292-333

Vaupel, James [Biodemography, 2004]: The Biodemography of Aging, in: Population and Development Review, vol. 30 (2004), Supplement: Aging, Health, and Public Policy, pp. 48-62

Verwiebe, Roland [Wanderungsgründe, 2005]: Die Wanderungsgründe von innereuropäischen Migranten, in: Zeitschrift für Bevölkerungswissenschaft, vol. 30 (2005), no. 1, pp. 129-152

Vogt, Tobias/Klüsener, Sebastian [Mortality decline, 2011]: The Remarkable Pace of Mortality Decline in Eastern Germany after the German Unification - The role of regional availability of health care, presented at Conference: Population Association of America 2011 Annual Meeting, Washington D.C., 31.03.-02.04.2011

Vogt, Tobias/Vaupel, James [Health care, 2012]: The Importance of Regional Availability of Health Care. Evidence from German reunification, unpublished article, Rostock: Max-Planck-Institute for Demographic Research, 2012

Wagner, Corina/Konzelmann, Laura/Rattinger, Hans [Germany, 2010]: Is Germany Going Bananas? Life-cycle and cohort effects on party performance in Germany from 1953 to 2049, presented at Conference: EPOP Annual Conference 2010, Essex, September 2010

Wahl, Stefanie [Deutschland, 2004]: Deutschland - Ein Auswanderungsland?, Bonn: Institut für Wirtschaft und Gesellschaft Bonn e.V., 2004, available at:

http://www.iwg-bonn.de/uploads/tx_smartextendedcontent/Deutschland_-_ein_Auswanderungsland_-__April_2004-2.pdf (last accessed: 14.04.2014)

Waldrauch, Harald [Wahlrechte, 2003]: Wahlrechte ausländischer Staatsangehöriger in europäischen und klassischen Einwanderungsstaaten: Ein Überblick, in: Wiener Hefte zu Migration und Integration in Theorie und Praxis (2003), no. 1, pp. 55-75

Waldrauch, Harald [Statistics, 2006]: Statistics on Acquisition and Loss of Nationality, in: *Rainer Bauböck, et al. (ed.)*, Acquisition and Loss of Nationality. Volume 1: Comparative analyses. Policies and trends in 15 European countries, Amsterdam: Amsterdam University Press, 2006, pp. 269-315

Walker, Alan [Political participation, 1999]: Political Participation and Representation of Older People in Europe, in: *Alan Walker/Gerhard Naegele (ed.)*, The Politics of Old Age in Europe, Buckingham/Philadelphia: Open University Press, 1999, pp. 7-24

Walker, Alan [Aging, 2006]: Aging and Politics. An international perspective, in: *Robert H. Binstock/Linda K. George (ed.)*, Handbook of Aging and the Social Sciences, Sixth edition, Amsterdam et al.: Elsevier, 2006, pp. 339-359

Walker, Alan/Maltby, Tony [Ageing Europe, 1997]: Ageing Europe, Buckingham/Philadelphia: Open University Press, 1997

Wallrabenstein, Astrid [Stellungnahme, 2007]: Stellungnahme im Rahmen der Anhörung des Innenausschusses des Deutschen Bundestages zu "Einbürgerung/Staatsangehörigkeit" Deutscher Bundestag: A-Ders. 16(4)311 B, 2007, available at: http://webarchiv.bundestag.de/cgi/show.php?fileToLoad=1270&id=1134 (last accessed: 14.04.2014)

Weimann, Mike [Wahlrecht, 2008]: Wahlrecht für Kinder, in: *Stiftung für die Rechte zukünftiger Generationen (ed.)*, Wahlrecht ohne Altersgrenze? Verfassungsrechtliche, demokratietheoretische und entwicklungspsychologische Aspekte, München: Oekom Verlag, 2008, pp. 53-72

Weinmann, Martin/Becher, Inna/Babka von Gostomski, Christian [Einbürgerungsverhalten, 2012]: Einbürgerungsverhalten von Ausländerinnen und Ausländern in Deutschland sowie Erkenntnisse zu Optionspflichtigen. Ergebnisse der BAMF-Einbürgerungsstudie 2011, Nürnberg: Bundesamt für Migration und Flüchtlinge, 2012, available at: http://www.bamf.de/SharedDocs/Anlagen/DE/Publikationen/Forschungsberichte/fb15-einbuergerungsverhalten.pdf?__blob=publicationFile

(last accessed: 14.04.2014)

Weitbrecht, Katrin [Bevölkerung Deutschlands, no year given]: Alter und Struktur der Bevölkerung Deutschlands im Jahr 2050. Ein Vergleich aktueller Prognosen zur Bevölkerungsentwicklung, Frankfurt a.M.: Bildungswerk der Hessischen Wirtschaft, no year given, available at: http://www.11d.de/mit-offenen-augen/pdf/bwhwprognosen.pdf (last accessed: 14.04.2014)

Westerwelle, Guido [Optionsmodell, 1999]: Die Rot-Grüne Koalition hat das Optionsmodell der F.D.P. übernommen, in: *Andreas Goldberg/Faruk Sen (ed.)*, Deutsche Türken - Türkische Deutsche? Die Diskussion um die doppelte Staatsbürgerschaft, Münster/Hamburg/London: LIT Verlag, 1999, pp. 133-139

Westle, Bettina [Teilhabe, 2005]: Generationengerechte politische Teilhabe, Bonn: Friedrich-Ebert-Stiftung, 2005, available at: http://library.fes.de/cgi-bin/populo/digbib.pl?f_ABC=APB-OL-generation&t_listen=x&sortierung=jab (last accessed: 14.04.2014)

Westoff, Charles F. [Fertility decline, 1983]: Fertility Decline in the West: Causes and prospects, in: Population and Development Review, vol. 9 (1983), no. 1, pp. 99-104

Wildte, F. [Thing-steads, 1928]: Scandinavian Thing-Steads, in: Antiquity, vol. 2 (1928), no. 7, pp. 328-336

Wilkoszewski, Harald [Age trajectories, 2009]: Age Trajectories of Social Policy Preferences. Support for intergenerational transfers from a demographic perspective, in: MPIDR Working Paper (2009), WP 2009-034, pp. 1-45

Wilkoszewski, Harald/Muth, Elena [Demographic change, 2009]: Demographic Change and the Acceptance of Population-Related Policies. A comparison of 13 European countries, in: MPIDR Working Paper (2009), WP 2009-035, pp. 1-50

Willutzki, Siegfried [Wahlrecht, 2004]: Wahlrecht von Geburt an, Deutscher Bundestag: A-Drs 15(4)172 D - neu, 2004, available at: http://webarchiv.bundestag.de/archive/2007/0206/ausschuesse/archiv15/a04/Oeffentliche_Anhoerungen/Anhoerungen_6/Stellungnahme_5.pdf (last accessed: 14.04.2014)

Wilmoth, John R. [How long can we live, 2001]: How Long Can We Live? A review essay, in: Population and Development Review, vol. 27 (2001), no. 4, pp. 791-800

Wilson, Gail [Ageing electorate, 1993]: The Challenge of an Ageing Electorate: Changes in the formation of social policy in Europe?, in: Journal of European Social Policy, vol. 3 (1993), no. 2, pp. 91-105

Wilson, Tom/Rees, Phil [Recent developments, 2005]: Recent Developments in Population Projection Methodology: A review, in: Population, Space and Place, vol. 11 (2005), no. 5, pp. 337-360

Wingen, Max [Plädoyer, 2002]: Ein erneutes Plädoyer für eine bevölkerungsbewusste Familienpolitik, in: Zeitschrift für Bevölkerungswissenschaft, vol. 27 (2002), no. 1, pp. 69-85

Wirth, Heike/Dümmler, Kerstin [Childlessness, 2005]: The Influence of Qualification on Women's Childlessness between 1970 and 2001 in Western Germany, in: Zeitschrift für Bevölkerungswissenschaft, vol. 30 (2005), no. 2-3, pp. 313-336

Witte, James C./Wagner, Gert G. [Fertility, 1995]: Declining Fertility in East Germany after Unification: A demographic response to socioeconomic change, in: Population and Development Review, vol. 21 (1995), no. 2, pp. 387-397

Wölk, Monika [Wahlbewußtsein, 1984]: Wahlbewußtsein und Wahlerfahrungen zwischen Tradition und Moderne, in: Historische Zeitschrift, vol. 238 (1984), no. 2, pp. 311-352

Worbs, Susanne [Einbürgerung, 2008]: Die Einbürgerung von Ausländern in Deutschland, Nürnberg: Bundesamt für Migration und Flüchtlinge, 2008, available at: http://www.bamf.de/SharedDocs/Anlagen/DE/Publikationen/WorkingPapers/wp17-einbuergerung.pdf?__blob=publicationFile (last accessed: 14.04.2014)

Wüst, Andreas [New citizens, 2000]: New Citizens - New Voters? Political preferences and voting intentions of naturalized Germans: A case study in progress, in: International Migration Review, vol. 34 (2000), no. 2, pp. 560-567

Wüst, Andreas [Naturalized citizens, 2004]: Naturalized Citizens as Voters: Behaviour and impact, in: German Politics, vol. 13 (2004), no. 2, pp. 341-359

Wüst, Andreas [Politische Repräsentation, 2006]: Wahlverhalten und politische Repräsentation von Migranten, in: Der Bürger im Staat, vol. 56 (2006), no. 4, pp. 228-234

Zeitlmann, Wolfgang [Doppelte Staatsbürgerschaft, 1999]: Doppelte Staatsbürgerschaft - Ein ideologischer Schnellschuß, in: *Andreas Goldberg/Faruk Sen (ed.)*, Deutsche Türken - Türkische Deutsche? Die Diskussion um die doppelte Staatsbürgerschaft, Münster/Hamburg/London: LIT Verlag, 1999, pp. 141-152

Ziegler, Katja [Diskussionsbericht, 1999]: Diskussionsbericht, in: *Ulrike Davy (ed.)*, Politische Integration der ausländischen Wohnbevölkerung, Baden-Baden: Nomos Verlagsgesellschaft, 1999, pp. 248-261

Ziegler, Uta [Dementia, 2010]: Dementia in Germany - Past trends and future developments, Dissertation, Rostock: University of Rostock, 2010

Zinterer, Tanja [Interessenrepräsentation, 2007]: Interessenrepräsentation von Migranten: Von der Süssmuth-Kommission zum Integrationsgipfel, in: *Winfried Thaa (ed.)*, Inklusion durch Repräsentation, Baden-Baden: Nomos Verlagsgesellschaft, 2007, pp. 149-166

Zlotnik, Hania [Migration, 1998]: International Migration 1965-96: An overview, in: Population and Development Review, vol. 24 (1998), no. 3, pp. 429-468

MIX
Papier aus verantwortungsvollen Quellen
Paper from responsible sources
FSC® C105338

FSC
www.fsc.org

If you have any concerns about our products,
you can contact us on
ProductSafety@springernature.com

In case Publisher is established outside the EU,
the EU authorized representative is:
Springer Nature Customer Service Center GmbH
Europaplatz 3, 69115 Heidelberg, Germany

Printed by Libri Plureos GmbH
in Hamburg, Germany